THE TEMPLE
AND
THE LODGE

by the same authors (with Henry Lincoln)
THE HOLY BLOOD AND THE HOLY GRAIL
THE MESSIANIC LEGACY

THE TEMPLE AND THE LODGE

*Michael Baigent
and
Richard Leigh*

ARCADE PUBLISHING • NEW YORK
LITTLE, BROWN AND COMPANY

Dedication

Viens au jardin
Où le lapin
Promène sa bouteille
Que l'on sache à
Sourire dans les neiges
D'antan toujours
Sans besoin de gêne;
Car les yeux d'ors
Des woïvres rouges
Là revelera
La place où cachent
Le mot oublié
Et la pierre perdue
Et le rejêton
De l'acacia
Qui rend temoignage
Par son racines
Déracinés et crus.

Jehan l'Ascuiz

Copyright © 1989 by Michael Baigent and Richard Leigh

First U.S. edition
Library of Congress CIP information is available

ISBN: 1-55970-021-1

Published in the United States by Arcade Publishing, Inc., New York,
a Little, Brown company.

HC

PRINTED IN THE UNITED STATES OF AMERICA

Contents

Acknowledgments

Introduction   xi

Prelude   1

PART ONE   ROBERT BRUCE: HEIR TO CELTIC SCOTLAND

1   Bruce and his Struggle for Power   17

2   Military Monks: the Knights Templar   41

3   Arrests and Torture   51

4   The Disappearance of the Templar Fleet   63

5   Celtic Scotland and the Grail Legends   77

PART TWO   SCOTLAND AND A HIDDEN TRADITION

6   The Templar Legacy in Scotland   87

7   The Scots Guard   103

8   Rosslyn   111

9   Freemasonry: Geometry of the Sacred   123

PART THREE   THE ORIGINS OF FREEMASONRY

10   The Earliest Freemasons   149

11   Viscount Dundee   162

CONTENTS

12 The Development of Grand Lodge 171

13 The Masonic Jacobite Cause 183

14 Freemasons and Knights Templar 193

PART FOUR FREEMASONRY AND AMERICAN
INDEPENDENCE

15 The First American Freemasons 201

16 The Emergence of Masonic Leaders 212

17 The Resistance to Britain 221

18 The War for Independence 230

Interlude 252

19 The Republic 256

Postscript 263

Appendices 268

Notes and References 271

Bibliography 291

Index 300

Illustrations

The author and publishers would like to thank the following for providing photographs: Bodleian Library, Oxford (23); British Library, London (24, 36); Grand Lodge of Free and Accepted Masons of Pennsylvania (34, 35); Jack MacDonald, of Visual Impact Portobello (29, 30, 31); Museum of the United Grand Lodge of England (32, 33); Temple Local History Group (13). All other photographs are by Michael Baigent.

Plates

between pages 2 and 3
1   Kilneuair Church, Loch Awe, Argyll.
2   Kilmartin Church, Argyll.
3   Kilmartin graves.
4   Gravestone, Kilmartin.
5   Chapel of Kilmory, Loch Sween, Argyll.
6   Stone cross, Chapel of Kilmory.

between pages 66 and 67
7   Undated gravestone, Kilmory.
8   Tower, church and preceptory buildings, Garway, Herefordshire.
9   Templar cross, Garway.
10   Templar gravestones, Garway.
11   Celtic figure, Garway.
12   Foundations of original Templar church, Garway.
13   Temple Church, Bristol.

between pages 114 and 115
14   Rosslyn Castle, near Edinburgh.

15   Rosslyn Chapel.
16   Head of the murdered apprentice, Rosslyn Chapel.
17   The Apprentice Pillar, Rosslyn Chapel.
18–19 Examples of 'The Green Man', Rosslyn Chapel.

between pages 146 and 147
20–22 Figures, Rosslyn Chapel.
23   Christ as the Divine Architect, *Bible moralisée*.
24   The Creator as Divine Architect, *Holkham Bible*.
25   Gravestone, Athlit, Israel.

between pages 194 and 195
26   Temple Church, near Edinburgh.
27–8 Seventeenth-century graves, Temple Church, near
      Edinburgh.
29–30 Swords possibly used at the initiation of Baron von Hund.
31   Sword of Alexander Deuchar.
32   English Masonic Knights Templar star jewels.

between pages 258 and 259
33   English Masonic Knights Templar apron.
34   Masonic sash worn by Benjamin Franklin.
35   Masonic apron worn by George Washington.
36   Map of the city of Washington, 1792.

Maps and charts

		page
1	Scotland and Ireland at the time of Robert Bruce.	22–3
2	Genealogy showing the relationship of Robert Bruce to earlier kings of Scotland.	25
3	Probable Templar route into Scotland, 1307–8.	72
4	The French and Indian War, 1754–60.	206
5	The American War for Independence.	231

Acknowledgments

As ever, we should like to thank Ann Evans, for performing, in a fashion that more transcendent agencies might envy, the functions of Providence.

For their help and courtesy in procuring us access to not readily accessible material, we should like particularly to thank Robert and Lindsay Brydon, Neville Barker Cryer, Jenny Hall, John Hamill, Roberta Hankamer and Steven Patrick. We should also like to thank Colin Bloy, Brie Burkeman, Marion Campbell, Tony Colwell, Judith and Andrew Fisken, Denis Graham, Joy Hancox, Chris Horspool, Julian Lea-Jones, Ben Lewis, Pat Lewis, Alison Mansbridge, Tom Maschler, Joy Muir, George Onslow, John Saul, Lucas Siorvanes, James Watts, Pamela Willis, Anthony Wolseley, Lilianne Ziegel, the staff of the British Library Reading Room and, needless to say, our ladies.

Introduction

In Britain, during the last few years, Freemasonry has become both a favourite topic of conversation and a cherished issue of debate. Indeed, Mason-baiting bids fair to become something of a full-fledged blood sport here, rather like priest-baiting in Ireland. With scarcely disguised exuberance and a virtually audible 'Tally-ho!', the newspapers swoop on each new 'Masonic scandal', each new allegation of 'Masonic corruption'. Church synods ponder the compatibility of Freemasonry with Christianity. In order to goad political opponents, local councils propose motions that would compel Freemasons to declare themselves. At parties, Freemasonry crops up with a frequency exceeded, probably, only by Britain's intelligence services and the CIA. Television, too, has made its contribution, conducting at least one late-night symposium on the subject and actually managing to poke its cameras into the beast's ultimate lair, Grand Lodge. On failing to find a dragon, the commentators seemed to feel less relief than an aggrieved sulkiness at having somehow been cheated. In the mean time, of course, people have remained fascinated. One need only pronounce the word 'Freemasonry' in a pub, restaurant, hotel lobby or other public place to see heads twitch, faces swivel attentively, ears fine-tune themselves to eavesdrop. Each new 'exposé' is devoured with an eagerness, even a glee, usually reserved for royal gossip, or for the salacious.

This book is not an exposé. It does not address itself to the role or the activities, real or imagined, of Freemasonry in contemporary society; it does not attempt to investigate allegations of conspiracy or corruption. Neither, of course, is it an apology for Freemasonry. We are not Freemasons ourselves, and we have no vested interest in exculpating the institution from the charges levelled against it. Our orientation has been wholly historical. We have endeavoured to track down the antecedents of Freemasonry, to establish its true origins, to chart its evolution and development, to assess its influence on British and American culture during its own formative years, culminating with the late eighteenth century. We have also tried to address the question of why Freemasonry, nowadays so instinctively regarded with suspicion, with derision, with irony and condescension, should ever have come to enjoy the currency it did – and, for that matter, still does, despite its detractors.

In the process, however, we have inevitably been obliged to confront the kind of questions that loom in the public mind today, and are so often posed by the media. Is Freemasonry corrupt? Is it – even more sinisterly – a vast international conspiracy dedicated to some obscure and (if secrecy is a barometer of villainy) nefarious end? Is it a conduit for 'perks', favours, influence and power-broking in the heart of such institutions as the City and the police? Most important of all, perhaps, is it truly inimical to Christianity? Such questions are not directly pertinent to the pages that follow, but they are of understandable general concern. It will not be inappropriate, therefore, if we offer here the answers to them that emerged in the course of our enquiries.

One has attained a measure of wisdom when, instead of exclaiming 'Et tu, Brute!', one nods ruefully and says, 'Yes, it figures.' Given human nature, it would be surprising if there were not at least some degree of corruption in public and private institutions, and if some of this corruption did not involve Freemasonry. We would argue, however, that such corruption says less about Freemasonry itself than about the ways in which Freemasonry, like any other such structure, can be abused. Greed, self-aggrandisement, favouritism and other such ills have been endemic to human society since the emergence of civilisation. They have availed themselves of, and operated through, every available channel – blood kinship, a shared past, bonds formed in school or in the armed forces, mutual interest, simple friendship, as well, of course, as race, religion and political affiliation. Freemasonry is accused, for example, of making special dispensations for its own. In the Christianised West, until very recently, a man could expect from his fellows precisely the same special dispensation simply by virtue of his membership in the 'freemasonry' of Christianity – by virtue, in other words, of not being a Hindu, a Muslim, a Buddhist or a Jew. Freemasonry is only one of many channels whereby corruption and favouritism can flourish; but if Freemasonry did not exist, corruption and favouritism would flourish all the same. Corruption and favouritism can be found in schools, in regiments, in corporations, in governmental bodies, in political parties, in sects and churches, in innumerable other organisations. None of these is in itself intrinsically reprehensible. No one would think of condemning an entire political party, or an entire church, because certain of its members were corrupt – or more sympathetically disposed towards other members than towards outsiders. No one would condemn the family as an institution because it tends to foster nepotism.

In any moral consideration of the matter, it is necessary to exercise an understanding of elementary psychology, and a modicum of common sense. Institutions are only as virtuous, or as culpable, as the individuals who compose them. If an institution can be considered corrupt in any intrinsic sense at all, it can be considered so only if it profits from the corruption of its members. This might apply to, say, a military dictatorship, to certain totalitarian or single-party states, but it is hardly applicable to Freemasonry. No one has ever suggested that Freemasonry ever gained anything through the transgressions of its brethren. On the contrary, the transgressions of individual Freemasons are entirely selfish and self-serving. Freemasonry as a whole suffers from such transgressions, as does Christianity from the transgressions of its adherents. In the question of corruption, then, Freemasonry is not in itself a culprit, but, on the contrary, another victim of unscrupulous men who are prepared to exploit it, along with anything else, for their own ends.

A more valid question is the compatibility, or lack thereof, between Freemasonry and Christianity. By its very nature, this question, at least, implies an attempt to confront what Freemasonry actually *is*, rather than the ways in which it can be exploited or abused. Ultimately, however, this question, too, is spurious. As is well known, Freemasonry does not purport to be a religion, only to address itself to certain principles or 'truths', which might in some sense be construed as 'religious' – or perhaps 'spiritual'. It may offer a species of methodology, but it does not pretend to offer a theology. This distinction will become clearer in the pages that follow. For the moment, it will be sufficient to make two points in connection with the current antipathy towards Freemasonry on the part of the Anglican Church. Amidst the Church's present preoccupation with Freemasonry in her ranks, these points are generally overlooked. Both are crucial.

In the first place, Freemasonry and the Anglican Church have cohabited congenially since the beginning of the seventeenth century. Indeed, they have done more than cohabited. They have worked in tandem. Some of the most important Anglican

xiii

ecclesiastics of the last four centuries have issued from the lodge; some of the most eloquent and influential Freemasons have issued from the ministry. At no time, prior to the last ten or fifteen years, has the Church ever inveighed against Freemasonry, ever perceived any incompatibility between Freemasonry and its own theological principles. Freemasonry has not changed. The Church would argue that it has not changed either, at least in its fundamental tenets. Why, then, if there has never been any conflict in the past, should there be conflict now? The answer to that question, we would suggest, lies less with Freemasonry than with the attitudes and mentalities of certain contemporary churchmen.

The second point worth considering is, if anything, even more decisive. The official head of the Anglican Church is the British monarch. Since James II was deposed in 1688, the monarch's theological status or 'credentials' have never been subject to question. And yet, since the beginning of the seventeenth century, the British monarchy has also been closely involved in Freemasonry. At least six kings, as well as numerous princes of the blood and prince consorts, have been Freemasons. Would this be possible if there were indeed some theological incompatibility between Freemasonry and the Church? To argue such incompatibility is tantamount, in effect, to impugning the religious integrity of the monarchy.

Ultimately, we would maintain, the current controversy surrounding Freemasonry is a storm in a teacup, a number of non-issues or spurious issues inflated far beyond the status they actually deserve. It is tempting to be flip and suggest that people have nothing better to do than manufacture such tenuous grounds for controversy. Unfortunately, they *do* have better things to do. Certainly the Anglican Church, with incipient schism in its ranks and a disastrously shrinking congregation, could deploy its energy and resources more constructively than in orchestrating crusades against a supposed enemy, which, in fact, is not an enemy at all. And while it is perfectly appropriate, even desirable, for the media to ferret out corruption, we would all be better served if the corrupt individuals themselves were called to account, rather than the institution of which they happen to be members.

At the same time, it must be acknowledged that Freemasonry itself has done little to improve its own image in the public eye. Indeed, by its obsessive secrecy and its stubborn defensiveness, it has only reinforced the conviction that it has something to hide. How little it does in fact have to hide will become apparent in the course of this book. If anything, it has more to be proud of than it does to conceal.

Prelude

Ten years ago, in the spring of 1978, while researching the Knights Templar for a projected television documentary, we became intrigued by the Order's history in Scotland. The surviving documentation was meagre, but Scotland possessed an even greater wealth of legend and tradition about the Templars than did most other places. There were also some very real mysteries – unexplained enigmas which, in the absence of reliable records, orthodox historians had scarcely attempted to account for. If we could penetrate these mysteries, if we could find even a kernel of truth behind the legends and traditions, the implications would be enormous, not only for the history of the Templars, but extending far beyond as well.

A woman we knew had recently moved with her husband to live in Aberdeen. On a visit back to London, they recounted to us a story they had heard from another man, who had worked for a time in an hotel in a small tourist community, formerly a Victorian watering spot, on the western shore of Loch Awe in the Highlands of Argyll. Loch Awe is a large inland lake some twenty-five miles from Oban. The lake itself is twenty-eight miles long and varies in width for the most part from half a mile to a mile. It is dotted with just under two dozen islands of various sizes, some natural, others man-made and formerly connected to the shore by causeways of now submerged stones and timber. Like Loch Ness, Loch Awe is supposed to contain a monster, the 'Beathach Mór', described as a large serpent-like creature with a horse's head and twelve legs sheathed in scales.

On one of the islands, according to the story our informant had heard, there were a number of Templar graves – more than would make sense in the context of accepted history, for the Templars were not known to have been active around Argyll or the Western

Highlands. On the same island, moreover, there were, supposedly, the ruins of a Templar preceptory, which did not figure in any of our lists of Templar holdings. As we received it, at third hand, the name of the island sounded something like 'Innis Shield', but we could not be sure of that, still less of the spelling.

These fragments of information, even though unconfirmed and frustratingly vague, were tantalising. Like many researchers before us, we were familiar with nebulous accounts of bands of Templars surviving the official persecution and dissolution of their Order between 1307 and 1314. We were familiar with stories that one such enclave of knights, fleeing their tormentors on the Continent and in England, had found a refuge in Scotland and, at least for a time, had perpetuated something of their original institutions. But we were also aware that most such traditions had originated with the Freemasons of the eighteenth century, who sought to establish for themselves a pedigree extending directly back to the Templars of four centuries before. In consequence, we were extremely sceptical. We knew that no accepted evidence for any Templar survival in Scotland existed, and that even modern Freemasonry tended, in general, to dismiss all claims to the contrary as sheer invention and wishful thinking.

And yet the tale of the island in the lake continued to haunt us. We had planned a research trip to Scotland for that summer anyway, albeit far to the east. Should we not perhaps make a leisurely westward detour, if only to disprove the story we had heard and exorcise it once and for all from our minds? Accordingly, we decided to extend our trip by a few days and return via Argyll.

As we descended on Loch Awe from the north, we immediately saw, at the head of it, masked by serried firs, the large fifteenth-century Campbell castle of Kilchurn. We proceeded down the eastern side of the lake. After some fifteen miles, an island appeared to our right, perhaps fifty yards from the shore. On it stood the ruins of the thirteenth-century castle of Innis Chonnell, which was occupied, around 1308, by Robert the Bruce's close friend, ally and brother-in-law, Sir Neil Campbell, and which for the next century and a half had been Clan Campbell's primary seat. Then, when a new castle was built at Inverary, at the upper reaches of Loch Fyne, Innis Chonnell was turned into a prison for the enemies of the Campbells – or, as they had by then become, the Earls of Argyll.

A mile south of Innis Chonnell there was a smaller island, just visible from the road through the trees and shrubs fringing the shore. When we stopped, we could see the remains on it of a structure of some sort, and stones which appeared to be graves. On

1 Kilneuair Church, Loch Awe, Argyll. The ruins date from the thirteenth century. In the foreground is a gravestone with a graffiti Templar-style cross.

2 *left* Kilmartin Church, Argyll. In the foreground is an example of the anonymous warriors' graves marked only with a sword. There are some eighty at this site alone.

3 *above* Kilmartin. Further examples of the fourteenth- and fifteenth-century graves of a style unknown except in the Order of the Temple.

4 *right* Detail of gravestone, Kilmartin. This sword has been dated tentatively to the fourteenth century.

5 *above* Ruined thirteenth-century chapel of Kilmory, Loch Sween, Argyll, with the Isle of Jura in the background. This marks the end of the only safe sea route to Scotland during the early years of Robert Bruce.

6 *left* Stone cross of typical Templar style, now housed inside the chapel of Kilmory. Its date has not yet been satisfactorily established.

the opposite side of the road was the hamlet of Portinnisherrich. The island itself, according to the maps we consulted, was variously called Innis Searraiche or Innis Sea-ramhach. We promptly pole-vaulted to the conclusion that this was the 'Innis Shield' we had been seeking.

The island lay some forty yards from the shore, along which there were a number of boats, most of them obviously functional and in regular use. Hoping to rent one and row out to the island, we enquired at the general store in Portinnisherrich. There, however, we encountered a curious evasiveness. Although the area was postcard-scenic, and must have relied to at least some degree on the tourist trade, we were not made to feel in any way welcome. Why, we were asked guardedly, did we want to rent a boat? To explore the island, we replied. No boat was available for rental, we were told; people did not rent boats. Could we hire someone, boat and all, to row us out to the island? No, we were told without any explanation or elaboration, that was not possible either.

Frustrated, and all the more convinced that Innis Searraiche must contain something of relevance, we wandered on foot along the shore. From across the intervening strip of water, the island beckoned tauntingly, almost within stone-throwing distance, yet inaccessible. We discussed the possibility of swimming out to it, and were debating the likely coldness of the water when, just north of the hamlet, we encountered an elderly couple with a tent erected beside a caravan. After an exchange of casual courtesies, they invited us to share a cup of tea with them. They, too, it transpired, came from London. For the last fifteen years or so, however, they had been coming to this spot every summer, setting up their caravan and fishing along Loch Awe.

Inside their caravan, we had to squeeze past the end of a table on to a long bench. To one side, there was a smaller table, or flat surface of some kind, used probably for preparing food. On this, an old book lay open at a page with what appeared to be an engraving of a Masonic tomb – we noted certain Masonic symbols and a skull-and-crossbones. Subsequently, we realised that what we had seen might have been a Masonic 'tracing board' of the kind used in the eighteenth century. In any case, we enquired, quite casually, about the prevalence of Freemasonry in the area – whereupon the book was quickly but discreetly closed and our query was deflected with a shrug.

We asked our hosts if they could tell us anything about the island. Not much, they replied. Yes, there were ruins of some sort out there. And yes, there were some graves, though not many. And not that old. In fact, the couple told us, most of the graves were fairly recent. But the island, they said, did seem to enjoy some sort of special significance. They did not venture to suggest what it might be. Bodies, they reported, were sometimes brought there for burial from considerable distances – sometimes even flown across the Atlantic from the United States.

Quite clearly this had nothing to do with thirteenth- or fourteenth-century Templars. Nevertheless, it was intriguing. It might, of course, involve nothing more than a tradition of local families, whose descendants, in accordance with some established ritual or custom, were buried in native soil. On the other hand, there might, just possibly, be something more to the matter, something pertaining perhaps to Freemasonry, which our hosts were patently loath to discuss. They had a boat of their own, which they used for fishing. We asked if we could hire it, or if they would row us out to the island. At first, they were a little reluctant, repeating their assertion that we would find nothing of interest, but at last, perhaps infected by our curiosity, the man offered to row us out while his wife prepared another pot of tea.

The island proved disappointing. It was extremely small, no more than thirty yards across. It did contain the ruins of a diminutive chapel, but these consisted of nothing more than some sections of wall jutting a few feet up from the soil. There was no way of ascertaining whether the delapidated mossy remains were indeed once a Templar chapel. They were certainly too small to have been a preceptory.

As for the graves, most of them were, as we'd been told, of comparatively recent date. The earliest dated from 1732, the latest from the 1960s. Certain family names occurred – Jameson, McAllum, Sinclair. On one stone, of First World War vintage, there was a Masonic square and compasses. The island obviously had something to do with local families, some of whom, probably incidentally, were involved in Freemasonry. But there was nothing that could be construed as Templar, certainly nothing to support the account we had heard of a Templar graveyard. If there was any mystery about the place at all, it appeared to be both local and minor.

Thwarted and frustrated, we decided to find a bed-and-breakfast for the night, collect our thoughts and, if possible, work out how the information we'd received could have been so flagrantly askew. We proceeded down the eastern shore of Loch Awe, towards the road that led to Loch Fyne and thence to Glasgow. By this time, dusk was approaching. We stopped at a village named Kilmartin past the southern end of the loch and asked where we might find a place to stay. We were directed to a large converted house a few miles beyond the town, near some ancient Celtic cairns. Having checked in there, we returned to Kilmartin for a drink at the pub.

Although larger than Portinnisherrich, Kilmartin was still little more than a hamlet, with a petrol station, a pub, a recommendable restaurant and some two dozen houses all concentrated on one side of the road. On the other side was a large parish church with a tower. The whole structure had either been built, or extensively restored, during the last century.

We did not expect to discover anything of consequence at Kilmartin. It was only idle curiosity that led us to enter the churchyard. But there, not on an island in a lake, but in the grounds of a parish church, were rank after strictly regimented rank of badly weathered flatstones. There were upwards of eighty of them. Some had sunk so deeply into the ground that the grass was already growing over them. Others were still intact and clearly defined among the more modern raised tombs and family burial plots. Many of the stones, particularly those of later date and better condition, were adorned with elaborate carvings – decorative motifs, family or clan devices, a welter of Masonic symbols. Others had been worn completely smooth. But what interested us were those that bore no decoration save a single simple and austere straight sword.

These swords varied in size and sometimes, even if only slightly, in design. According to the practice of the time, the dead man's sword would be laid on the stone. Its outline would be incised and then chiselled. The carving would thus reflect precisely the dimensions, shape and style of the original weapon. It was this stark anonymous sword that marked the earliest of the stones, those most badly worn, weathered and eroded. On the later stones, names and dates were added to the sword, then decorative motifs, family and clan devices, Masonic symbols. There were even some women's graves. It seemed we had found the Templar graveyard we were seeking.

The sheer existence of the ranked graves in Kilmartin must surely have elicited questions from visitors other than ourselves. Who *were* the fighting men buried there? Why were there so many of them in such an out-of-the-way place? What explanations were offered by local authorities and antiquarians? The plaque at the church shed only meagre light on the matter. All it said was that the earliest of the slabs dated from around 1300, the latest from the early eighteenth century. 'Most', the plaque concluded, 'are the work of a group of sculptors working around Loch Awe in the late 14th–15th Centuries.' *What* group of sculptors? If they were known to have constituted a 'group' in any formal or organised sense, as clearly seemed to be the case, surely something more must be known about them. And was it not rather unusual for sculptors to congregate in 'groups', unless for some specific purpose or under some specific aegis – that of a royal or aristocratic court, for example, or of a religious order? In any case, if the plaque was vague about who had carved the stones, it was worse than vague about who had been buried under them. It said nothing.

Whatever the impressions conveyed by books, films and romanticised history, swords were a rare and expensive commodity in the early fourteenth century. Every fighting man did not, as a matter of course, own one. Many were too poor and had to use axes or spears. Nor, for that matter, was there much of an arms industry in Scotland at the time – and particularly in this part of Scotland. Most of the blades then in use in the country had to be imported, which made them all the more costly. Given these facts, the graves at Kilmartin could not have been those of 'ordinary rank-and-file' soldiery, the fourteenth-century equivalent of 'cannon-fodder'. On the contrary, the men commemorated by the stones had to be of some social consequence – well-to-do individuals, affluent gentry, if not full-fledged knights.

But was it plausible that men of wealth and social status would be buried *anonymously*? Far more than today, prominent individuals of the fourteenth century plumed themselves on their family, their ancestry, their lineage, their pedigree; and this was particularly true in Scotland, where clan affiliations and relationships enjoyed especial significance and where identity and blood descent were given a sometimes obsessive emphasis. Such things were insistently stressed in life, and duly memorialised in death.

Finally, why were the earliest of the graves at Kilmartin – the anonymous graves, marked only by the straight sword – so lacking in all Christian symbolism, lacking even in anything as basic as a cross? In an age when the Church's hegemony over Western Europe was virtually unchallenged, only tombs with effigies on them were left unadorned by Christian iconography; and such tombs were invariably placed in chapels or churches. The tombs at Kilmartin, however, were situated outdoors, were devoid of effigies, yet still lacked religious adornment. Was the hilt of the sword itself intended to denote the cross? Or were the graves those of men perceived, in one sense or another, not to have been properly Christian?

6

From 1296 on, Sir Neil Campbell – Bruce's friend, ally and eventual brother-in-law – had been 'Bailie' of Kilmartin and Loch Awe, and since Kilmartin itself had been one of his seats, it would have been reasonable to suppose that the earliest of the graves there were those of Sir Neil's men. But that would not serve to explain their anonymity, nor the absence of Christian symbolism. Unless, of course, the men who served under Sir Neil were not native to the area, not conventionally Christian and had some reason to keep their identities concealed, even in death.

During the course of our research, we had explored most of the ruins of Templar preceptories still surviving in England, and many of those in France, Spain and the Middle East. We were familiar, almost to the point of satiation, with the varieties of Templar sculpture, Templar devices, Templar embellishment – and, in the few instances where they could still be found, Templar graves. Those graves displayed the same characteristics as the graves in Kilmartin. They were invariably simple, austere, devoid of decoration. Frequently, though not always, they were marked by the simple straight sword. They were always anonymous. Indeed, it was the very anonymity of Templar graves that distinguished them from the elaborate inscriptions, decorations, monuments and sarcophagi of other nobles. The Templars were, after all, a monastic order, a society of warrior monks, soldier mystics. Even if only in theory, they had supposedly renounced, as individuals at least, the trappings and pretensions of the material world. When one entered the Temple, one effectively relinquished one's identity, becoming subsumed by the Order. The stark unadorned image of the straight sword was supposed to bear testimony to the ascetic, self-abnegating piety which obtained within the Order's ranks.

Historians – especially Masonic historians – had long sought either to prove or disprove, definitively, the alleged survival of the Templars in Scotland after the Order had been officially suppressed elsewhere. But these historians had looked for (and in) documentation, not 'on the ground'. Not surprisingly, they had found no conclusive evidence one way or the other, because most of the relevant documentation had been lost, destroyed, suppressed, falsified or deliberately discredited. On the other hand, historians of Argyll, who were aware of the graves at Kilmartin, had had no reason to think of the Templars, since the Templars were not known to have been active, or even present, in the region. So far as their European bases were concerned, the Templars were strongest in France, Spain, Germany, Italy and England. Such holdings as they officially possessed in Scotland were, at least according to readily accessible records, far to the east, in the vicinity of Edinburgh and Aberdeen. There would have been no grounds for supposing an enclave of the Order to have existed in Argyll unless one were specifically looking for it. Thus, it appeared to us, the graves at Kilmartin had preserved their secret from historical researchers of both camps – chroniclers of the Templars and of Freemasonry on the one hand and, on the other, chroniclers of the immediate region, who had no reason even to think of Templars.

Needless to say, we were excited by our discovery. And we felt it to be all the more significant because it seemed to pertain not only to the Templars. There appeared to be a coherent pattern linking the earliest graves at Kilmartin (those we supposed were Templar) and the later ones, adorned with family blazons, clan devices and Masonic symbolism. The earlier graves seemed to grade gradually into the later ones – or, rather, the later ones seemed, by a process of assimilation and accretion, to have *evolved* out of the earlier. The motifs were essentially the same, only becoming more elaborately embellished with the years; the later decorations did not simply replace the straight sword, but were added to it. The graves at Kilmartin seemed to offer their own mute but eloquent testimony to an ongoing development – to bear witness to a story spanning four centuries, from the beginning of the fourteenth to the beginning of the eighteenth. In the pub that evening, we attempted to decipher the chronicle in the stones.

Could we really have stumbled upon an enclave of refugee Templars who, on the dissolution of their Order, had found a haven in what was then the wilderness of Argyll? Might they have taken in yet more refugees from abroad? Argyll, though difficult to reach by land in the early fourteenth century, was readily accessible by sea, and the Templars possessed a substantial fleet which was never found by their persecutors in Europe. Had the green, forest-shagged hills and glens around us once housed an entire community of white-mantled knights, like a 'lost tribe' or 'lost city' in an adventure story; and had the Order here perpetuated itself, its rituals and observances? But if it were to perpetuate itself beyond a single generation, the knights would have had to secularise – or, at least, would have had to abrogate their vow of chastity, and marry. Was this perhaps part of the process to which the stones bore witness – the gradual intermarriage of refugee Templars and members of the clan system? And out of that alliance between the Templars and the clans of Argyll, might there have originated one of the skeins that were to lead to later Freemasonry? In the stones of Kilmartin, might we not perhaps be confronted by a concrete answer to one of the most perplexing questions in European history – the origins and development of Freemasonry itself?

We did not include any of what we had discovered in our film, which had, by that time, already been partially scripted. Its orientation, moreover, was primarily towards the Templars in the Holy Land and France. And if our findings in Scotland proved valid, they would, we felt, warrant a film of their own. For the moment, however, all we had was a plausible theory, with, in the absence of immediately accessible documentation, no way of confirming it.

In the mean time, other projects, other commitments, had begun to intervene, and our discoveries in Scotland were shunted ever further into the background. We did not lose sight of them, however. They continued to haunt us, and to exercise a hold on our imaginations. During the ensuing nine years, we proceeded, if only in a desultory manner, to gather additional information.

We consulted the work of Marion Campbell, probably the region's most prominent local historian, and established a personal correspondence with her. She advised us to be wary of any premature conclusions, but she was intrigued by our theory. If there were no records of the Templars holding land in Argyll, she said, this was more likely to indicate an absence of records than an absence of Templars. And she found it indeed possible that the arrival of Templars in the region might explain the sudden appearance of the anonymous straight sword amid the more traditional, more familiar Celtic embellishments and motifs.[1]

We also consulted such additional published work as existed on the stones at Kilmartin, from the researches of nineteenth-century antiquarians to a more recent opus, published in 1977 under the auspices of the Royal Commission on the Ancient and Historical Monuments of Scotland.[2] To our disappointment, most such material concentrated primarily on the later, more elaborately embellished stones. The earlier stones, marked by the single anonymous straight sword, were largely ignored, if only because nothing was known about them and no one had anything much to say. Nevertheless, certain important facts did emerge. We learned from Marion Campbell, for example, that the stones in the churchyard at Kilmartin had not originally been situated there. Some had been inside the church – or, rather, inside a much earlier church. Others had been scattered throughout the surrounding countryside and only later relocated. We also learned that Kilmartin was not the only such graveyard in the region. In fact, there were no fewer than sixteen. But Kilmartin did seem to have the greatest concentration of older stones, marked by the anonymous straight sword.

Only three firm conclusions could be drawn. The first was that the background of the carvings, and especially the older carvings, remained a mystery. The second, on which virtually everyone agreed, was that these earlier carvings dated from the beginning of the fourteenth century – the time of Robert the Bruce in Scotland and the suppression of the Knights Templar elsewhere in Europe. The third conclusion was that the graves with the anonymous straight sword represented a *new* style, a new development, in the region, which had appeared suddenly and inexplicably, although Templar holdings elsewhere had been using the design prior to its sudden appearance in Argyll. We had already seen it, in a context pre-dating the earliest stones at Kilmartin, as close to home as Temple Garway, in Herefordshire, which *was* indisputably Templar.[3]

In *Incised Effigial Slabs in Latin Christendom* (1976), the late F. A. Greenhill published the results of a lifetime spent tabulating medieval graves all over Europe, from the Baltic to the Mediterranean, from Riga to Cyprus. Among the 4460 graves he lists and describes, he found some without inscriptions, but they were extremely rare. Military gravestones were even rarer. In England, for example, he had found only four, not counting the one at Garway, of which he was unaware. In Ireland, he had found only one. In all of Scotland *except* Argyll, he had again found only one. In Argyll, he had found sixty anonymous military gravestones. It was thus clear that the concentration of stones at Kilmartin and adjacent sites was genuinely unique. Almost equally unique was the extraordinary concentration of Masonic graves.

Another important source of evidence for us was the Israeli Archaeological Survey Association, which had excavated the old Templar castle of Athlit in the Holy Land.[4] Athlit had been built in 1218 and finally abandoned, along with all the other remnants of the crusaders' Kingdom of Jerusalem, in 1291. When the castle was excavated, it proved to contain a graveyard with upwards of a hundred stones. Most, of course, had been very badly weathered, and shallow incisions, such as the straight swords we had found in Scotland, had not survived. But a few more deeply chiselled designs had, and these were particularly interesting. One was on the stone of a Templar maritime commander – perhaps an admiral – and consisted of a large anchor. One, though very severely worn, still showed a mason's square and plumb stone. One – believed to be that of the 'Master of the Templar Masons' – bore a cross with decorations, a mason's square and maul. With only two exceptions, these are the earliest known incidence of gravestones bearing Masonic devices. One of the exceptions is Reims and dates from 1263. The other, of comparable age, is also in France – at the former Templar preceptory of Bure-les-Templiers in the Côte d'Or. Here, then, was persuasive evidence to support the 'chronicle in stone' we had tried to decipher at Kilmartin – a chronicle which, if we had deciphered it correctly, attested to an important early connection between the Templars and what was later to evolve into Freemasonry.

In our enthusiasm at our discovery, we had forgotten our original purpose in coming to Argyll – the account of a Templar graveyard on an island in Loch Awe. We had assumed the account had become garbled, and actually referred to Kilmartin. What we did not know at the time was that we had visited the wrong island.

In the autumn of 1987, we returned to Argyll and Loch Awe. By this time, we had learned that the island which prompted our previous visit was not Innis Searraiche, but Inishail, some miles to the north. (In fact, we had passed it the first time without even noticing it.)

But if Inishail was the 'right' island, it proved no more fruitful than the 'wrong' island we had visited nine years before – although we had no difficulty on this occasion in hiring a boat. We did find the ruins of a church dating from the relevant period, the early fourteenth century, but the structure was clearly not Templar. The last regular service conducted in the place, we learned, had been in 1736, and by the end of the century it was already derelict. When we saw it, the interior was a matted tangle of grass, weeds and nettles which covered a number of hopelessly worn and cracked graveslabs lining the floor. Outside, there were more slabs, the older ones so sunken and overgrown as to be scarcely visible – although others, of later date, were still upright. Among the most recent graves were those of the Eleventh Duke of Argyll, who had died in 1973, and Brigadier Reginald Fellowes, CBE, MC and Bar, Légion d'Honneur, who had died in 1982. The man from whom we had hired our boat reported that he often crossed to Inishail and explored the island. He told us of a slab he had only just discovered, not yet recorded by the Royal Commission. Suspecting there might be others, we probed with our pocketknives and indeed found some, but there was nothing to be gleaned from them. If the site is ever properly cleared, these slabs may yet have much of consequence to reveal. Our own amateurish and probably sloppy reconnaissance, however, revealed no suggestion of anything Templar. This was disappointing; but at least we now knew the truth about the hitherto elusive island.

Elsewhere around Loch Awe, we found nothing any more conclusive than what existed at Kilmartin – vestiges which were very possibly Templar, which we could argue plausibly to be Templar, but which were not provably so. On a hill to the south-east of the loch, however, at the ruined thirteenth-century church of Kilneuair, we found something curious. In the grass were slabs similar to the later, ornately embellished slabs at Kilmartin. On one of these, the design was surmounted by an unmistakable Templar cross. But the cross was not part of the original, meticulously chiselled adornment. It had been clumsily carved into the stone like graffiti at some later date, perhaps as late as the seventeenth or eighteenth century. This could hardly be taken as evidence of Templars in the area. It did indicate, however, that someone thereabouts, at some subsequent time, had had some sort of interest in the Templars.

We proceeded south-west, past the imposing fortress of Castle Sween on the loch of the same name. In the early fourteenth century, Loch Sween had been a strategically crucial port on the sea-route running from Ulster through the Isles of Islay and Jura, and its castle, besieged and captured by Bruce around 1308–9, had been the major strongpoint of the region. The castle itself, reputedly the oldest stone castle on the Scottish mainland, was obviously a maritime citadel, with its own harbour for galleys. Fallen stones, some of them dressed, indicated where a breakwater, an inner harbour and a jetty had been situated. If, at the time of the suppression of their Order, Templars from Europe had fled by sea to Scotland, this would have been perhaps their most likely disembarkation.

Beyond the castle lay the sea, with the Isle of Jura across the sound to the west, its hills cloaked in cloud. Here, on the coast, stood the small ruined thirteenth-century chapel of Kilmory, which had ministered to the once-thriving maritime parish. Inside and around the chapel, there were some forty graveslabs of the same period and kind we had learned to recognise from Kilmartin. But there were two other items of greater significance, providing evidence which was perhaps less copious than we would have liked, but which was of sufficient calibre to confirm our theory.

Templar churches invariably had a cross either carved above the entrance or standing freely outside. The cross, whether simple or embellished, was always of distinctive design – equal-armed, with the end of each arm wider than its base. Inside the chapel of Kilmory stood just such a cross, dating from before the fourteenth century. Had this cross been found anywhere else in Europe, no one would have had any hesitation in recognising it as Templar and ascribing the chapel to the Order. Furthermore, inside the church lay a fourteenth-century graveslab incised with a sailing galley, an armed figure and another Templar cross, this one worked into a Floreate design.

But there was more. On that same fourteenth-century graveslab was something that reassured us that our decipherment of the 'chronicle in stone' had not only been tenable, but was, in its general outline, accurate. Above the head of the armed figure with its Templar cross was carved a Masonic set-square.

It was now safe to say that there were Templars on Loch Sween, and that Kilmory had almost certainly been a Templar chapel – not purpose-built for the Order, but, at any rate, taken over by them. Given this evidence, it was not just possible, but probable, that the graves at Kilmartin and elsewhere in the region were indeed Templar.

ONE
Robert Bruce: Heir to Celtic Scotland

I

Bruce and his Struggle for Power

On 18 May 1291, Acre, the last bastion of the Western crusaders in the Holy Land, fell to the Saracens, and the Latin Kingdom of Jerusalem, born of the First Crusade nearly two centuries before, finally and irrevocably collapsed. Thus ended the great European dream of a Christian Middle East. The resonant and sacred sites of scripture – from Egypt, through Palestine, to Lebanon and Syria – were to remain in Islamic hands, effectively off-limits to Christians until Napoleon's time some five centuries later.

With the loss of the Holy Land, the Knights Templar lost not only their primary sphere of military operations, but also their primary *raison d'être*. In military terms at least, they could no longer justify their existence. Their kindred military-religious orders had bases elsewhere, and other crusades to fight. The Knights Hospitaller of St John were to establish themselves first on Rhodes, then on Malta, and to spend the next three centuries wresting control of the Mediterranean for an ever more mercantile Christendom. The Teutonic Knights had already found their new vocation on the Baltic, exterminating the pagan tribes there and creating a Christian principality which extended from Prussia, through Latvia, Lithuania and Estonia, to the Gulf of Finland. The Spanish orders of Santiago, Calatrava and Alcantera had yet to expel the Moors from the Iberian peninsula, while the Portuguese Knights of Christ were to devote themselves increasingly to maritime exploration. Only the Templars – most wealthy, most powerful and most prestigious of the orders – were left without a purpose and without a home. Their own ambition to establish a principality for themselves in the Languedoc was thwarted and remained stillborn.

The decade and a half that followed the fall of Acre was to be a period of decline for the Temple. Then, at dawn on Friday, 13 October 1307, Philippe IV of France ordered the arrest of all Templars in his domains. During the next seven years, the Inquisition moved on to the centre of the stage to finish what the French king had started. Templars throughout Europe were imprisoned, tried, interrogated, tortured and executed. In 1312, the Order of the Temple was officially dissolved by the Pope. In 1314, the last Grand Master of the Order, Jacques de Molay, was burned at the stake, and the Temple effectively ceased to exist.

Robert Bruce's career spans this crucial period precisely. He first appeared in a position of prominence in 1292, a year after the fall of Acre, when he became Earl of Carrick. His life attained its climax with the Battle of Bannockburn in 1314, some three months after Jacques de Molay's death. In 1306, a year before the persecution of the Temple began, Bruce himself had been excommunicated, and was to remain at odds with the Papacy for another twelve years. Because he had ceased to be recognised by the Pope, it was impossible for Rome to treat with him or impose her will in his domains. In effect, the papal writ no longer ran in Scotland – or, at least, those parts of Scotland which Bruce controlled, and which lay, therefore, 'beyond the pale'. And thus, in those parts of Scotland, the decree which abolished the Temple elsewhere in Europe was not, in accordance with the strict letter of the law, applicable. If knights of the Order, fleeing persecution on the Continent, hoped to find a refuge anywhere, it would have been under Bruce's protection.

A spate of archaic legends and traditions has for centuries linked Bruce with the Templars, even if the association between them has not been satisfactorily defined. The graves in Argyll provided persuasive evidence for these legends and traditions: they dated from the relevant period, and were located in a region where it would have been natural for refugee Templars to seek safety. The closer one looks at Bruce, moreover, the clearer it becomes that he and the Templars had much in common.

The Celtic Kingdom of Scotland

Bruce is usually perceived as the central figure in medieval Scotland's struggle for independence. But Bruce was intent on something more – something much more radical and much more ambitious – than just thwarting English domination. What he sought was nothing less than the restoration of a uniquely Celtic kingdom, with specifically Celtic institutions. These may even have included ritual human sacrifice.

In medieval Ireland and Wales, even where England's Norman sovereigns had not established their sway, there was no centralised authority. Both countries were torn by internecine squabbles between a multitude of local princelings or chieftains and their clans. Scotland was the 'only Celtic realm with well-formed and independent political institutions at the beginning of the "high middle ages"'.[1]

In Roman times, of course, Scotland had been dominated by the Picts, who continued to play a prominent role in Scottish history until the mid-ninth century. But in the late fifth century, Celtic settlers from Ireland, particularly from Ulster, had begun to settle in the west of the country and to establish what is now called the Kingdom of the Dalriada – one of whose ancient strongholds was Dunadd, just three miles from Kilmartin. For 350 years, the Dalriada in the west and the Picts elsewhere struggled for supremacy, each at intervals gaining a temporary ascendancy, then losing it again. Though often violent, the struggle was not always so. It was also cultural and dynastic, and there were periodic high-level intermarriages between the two peoples. By c.843, however, the Dalriada had effectively triumphed. The Picts were not so much defeated militarily as subsumed. Pictish language and culture entirely, albeit gradually, disappeared, and Scotland, under the aegis of the Dalriada king, Kenneth MacAlpin, became a unified Celtic kingdom. Around 850, Kenneth was installed at Scone as monarch of all Scotland. There were still to be internal vicissitudes, intrigues and strife of the kind immortalised by Shakespeare in *Macbeth*, but under Kenneth MacAlpin's descendant, David I, the feudal Kingdom of Scotland finally emerged in 1124 – a quarter of a century after Western crusaders had established the Latin Kingdom of Jerusalem.

Although the Normans had first ventured into Scotland under William Rufus, son of William the Conqueror, there was no large-scale or successful Norman penetration until David's time. David himself was thoroughly Celtic, the son of the Celtic king, Malcolm III. During his reign, however, large numbers of Norman – and also Flemish – knights were allowed into the country. So, too, was monasticism, chiefly under the auspices of the Cistercians. Nevertheless, Scotland remained a wholly Celtic kingdom, and there is evidence that much Celtic thought – both pagan and Christian – persisted there long after it had vanished from Ireland. Among the unique institutions created by David was the office, subsequently hereditary, of the 'Royal Steward' of the realm, later called the 'Stewart', the office from which the Stuart dynasty was to derive. The Steward was a kind of hereditary manager of the royal household, or hereditary court chancellor, very similar to the so-called 'Mayor of the Palace' in Merovingian France three centuries before. Just as the Mayors of the Palace eventually supplanted the Merovingians and formed the Carolingian dynasty, so, in Scotland, the Stewards (though more peacefully) were to supplant the dynasty of David. The first Steward, Walter fitz Alan, was of Celtic Breton descent, the son of one Alan fitz Flaald. Alan may also have been descended from a Scottish thane, Banquo of Lochaber, whose legend finds its way into Shakespeare's play.

Among King David's entourage was a Norman knight, Robert de Brus. David conferred upon him the Vale of Annan, which guarded the approaches to Scotland through Carlisle. He was also a close friend of the English king, Henry I, and held extensive lands in Yorkshire. Robert's family is generally believed to have come from Brus or Bruis, now Brix, just south of Cherbourg. More recently, however, it has been suggested that he was in fact of Flemish origin, descended from Robert de Bruges, the wealthy castellan of that city three-quarters of a century before.[2] Robert disappeared from Bruges in 1053, the year in which Matilde of Flanders married William, Duke of Normandy. He may well have accompanied her into France and then, thirteen years later, accompanied her husband on the invasion of England.

Although the Robert de Brus of King David's time was of Norman (and possibly Flemish) descent, his great-grandson married David's great-granddaughter, the niece of the Celtic kings Malcolm IV and William I. The Robert Bruce who was later to figure so prominently in Scottish history could thus claim blood descent from the ancient Celtic royal house, and eventually back to Kenneth MacAlpin of the Dalriada. And when Robert Bruce's daughter married Walter the Steward, or Stewart, the dynasty later known as the Stuarts was born.

The Celtic element remained prevalent in Scottish society until the end of the thirteenth century. Thus, for example, the most influential noblemen in the realm were the thirteen earls, or thanes, who derived their lineage and authority directly from the older kingdom of the Dalriada. Among these earls, the most important was the Earl of Fife, who exercised the hereditary right to place the new king on the throne during the coronation ceremony. The coronation itself was traditionally held at Scone, two miles up the

Tay River from Perth, and the throne of the kingdom was built around the famous Stone of Scone, supposedly brought to the site by Kenneth MacAlpin in 850. Scone itself had been a sacred or semi-sacred place since pre-Celtic, Pictish times. Its central point was the 'Hill of Belief', now called Moot Hill. Here, in a ritual dating back beyond recorded history, a new monarch would be seated on a stone and invested with the regalia of his office, including probably a rod and a mantle. Thus would the king be wedded to the land, to the people he ruled and to the earth goddess herself, often portrayed in animal guise. In the Irish version of the rite, a mare would be sacrificed and boiled in water in which the newly installed king bathed, while drinking the broth and eating the beast's flesh. In this way, it was believed, the fertility of the land and the people would be ensured. By the twelfth century, in the wake of the Crusades, this archaic principle – the monarch's responsibility for the land's fertility – would be amalgamated with skeins of esoteric Judaeo-Christian tradition to produce the corpus of poems now known as the Grail romances. These, as we shall see, were to have a very specific pertinence to Scotland.

The coronation of Alexander III in 1249 was typical of the Celtic rites that prevailed in Scotland long after they had vanished elsewhere. When Alexander was seated on the throne at Scone, an aged Highland bard formally recited, in Gaelic, the new monarch's genealogy back through the Dalriada to 'the first Scotsman'. As might be expected of a Celtic ruler, Alexander was always accompanied by a harpist. When he travelled, he would be preceded, as tradition decreed for a Celtic chieftain, by seven women singing his glory and his pedigree – a flattering practice at first, no doubt, which must quickly have become both noisy and boring.

Not surprisingly in such a milieu, the Church exercised only the most tenuous of holds. During the ninth century, Scotland seems briefly to have provided a refuge for surviving splinter groups of the Celtic Church in Ireland. Under one of these splinter groups, the 'celi De' or 'Culdees', a monastic system was established, but never came to wield the influence it did across the Irish Sea. Despite an influx of Cistercians in the twelfth century, the Roman Church had all but disappeared. In Lothian, for example, no bishopric was to be founded after c.950. Nor was any religious community to be founded in Strathclyde after that date.

But the Celtic kingdom of Scotland, which had attained its apotheosis with Alexander III, was to die with him. In March 1286, returning one stormy night from a council at Edinburgh, the king

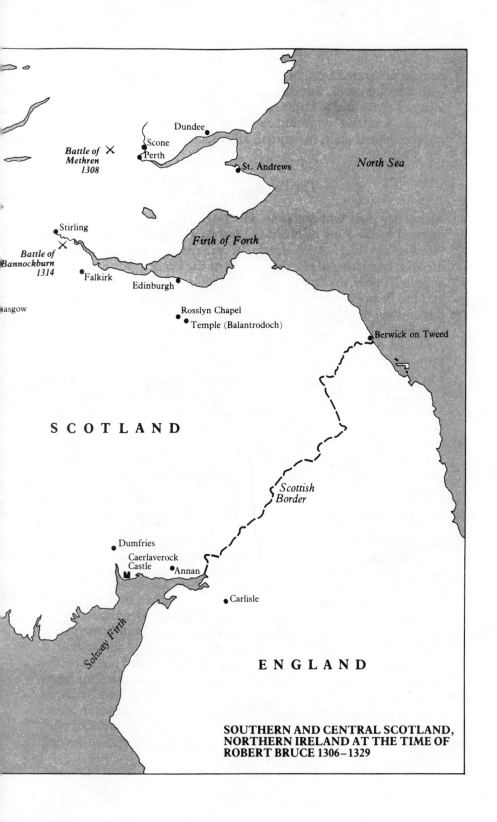

Dundee

Scone

Battle of
Methren
1308

Perth

St. Andrews

North Sea

*Battle of
Bannockburn
1314*

Stirling

Firth of Forth

Falkirk

Edinburgh

asgow

Rosslyn Chapel

Temple (Balantrodoch)

Berwick on Tweed

S C O T L A N D

*Scottish
Border*

Dumfries

Caerlaverock
Castle

Annan

Carlisle

Solway Firth

E N G L A N D

**SOUTHERN AND CENTRAL SCOTLAND,
NORTHERN IRELAND AT THE TIME OF
ROBERT BRUCE 1306–1329**

became separated from his escort and was found the next morning with a broken neck. His demise was not only to precipitate a major internal crisis and a bitter struggle for the throne. It was also to provide England with an excuse for meddling, on a hitherto unprecedented scale, in Scottish affairs.

The Emergence of Bruce

Alexander died without sons. His only daughter, Margaret, was married to the King of Norway, and Scotland had no desire for a Norwegian ruler. Accordingly, a provisional government was formed, consisting of six 'Guardians of the Peace' – the Earl of Fife as premier peer, the Earl of Buchan, James the Stewart, John Comyn and the Bishops of Glasgow and St Andrews. Acting as a regency, this council decided to confer the crown on Margaret of Norway's daughter, also named Margaret, who was then an infant. It was arranged that the child, on attaining her maturity, would marry Prince Edward, subsequently Edward II of England. But in 1290, *en route* home from Norway, the young Margaret died, and the question of the Scottish succession was plunged into turmoil.

More than a dozen candidates presented themselves as claimants to the throne, including John Baliol and the grandfather of Robert Bruce, known as 'the Competitor'. So great was the danger of civil war that the Bishop of St Andrews invited Edward I of England to arbitrate. Thus the Norman monarchy of England received a mandate to intervene in the affairs of the Celtic Kingdom of Scotland.

Edward wasted no time in turning this mandate to his own advantage. When he met with the Scottish claimants in 1291, he proceeded to claim suzerainty over Scotland for himself. Despite protests, the Scottish lords were bullied and intimidated into at least a partial acknowledgment of the English king's self-arrogated status. Having extorted this acknowledgment, he judged the succession to devolve upon John Baliol, who had a legitimate claim, and was duly crowned at Scone. Edward immediately reneged on his promises to respect Scottish independence, demanding a humiliating obedience and fealty from the man he had placed on the throne. By 1294, the English king's demands had goaded the Scots into rebellion. An alliance was formed with France, and Baliol, in 1296, repudiated his allegiance to Edward. By then, however, it was too late – Edward had already sacked Berwick and advanced with his army into Scotland. The Scots were defeated; Baliol, having

GENEALOGY SHOWING RELATIONSHIP OF ROBERT BRUCE
TO EARLIER KINGS OF SCOTLAND

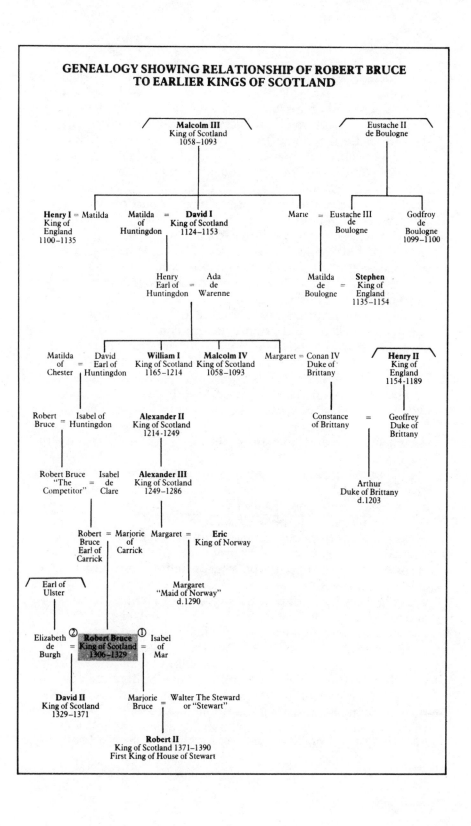

Malcolm III
King of Scotland
1058–1093

Eustache II
de Boulogne

Henry I = Matilda
King of
England
1100–1135

Matilda = **David I**
of   King of Scotland
Huntingdon   1124–1153

Marie = Eustache III
de
Boulogne

Godfroy
de
Boulogne
1099–1100

Henry = Ada
Earl of de
Huntingdon Warenne

Matilda = **Stephen**
de   King of
Boulogne   England
1135–1154

Matilda = David   **William I**   **Malcolm IV**   Margaret = Conan IV   **Henry II**
of   Earl of   King of Scotland King of Scotland   Duke of   King of
Chester Huntingdon 1165–1214   1058–1093   Brittany   England
                                                                      1154–1189

Robert = Isabel of   **Alexander II**
Bruce   Huntingdon   King of Scotland
                      1214-1249

Constance = Geoffrey
of Brittany   Duke of
              Brittany

Robert Bruce Isabel   **Alexander III**
"The   = de   King of Scotland
Competitor" Clare   1249–1286

Arthur
Duke of Brittany
d.1203

Robert = Marjorie   Margaret = **Eric**
Bruce   of   King of Norway
Earl of Carrick
Carrick

Earl of
Ulster

Margaret
"Maid of Norway"
d.1290

Elizabeth ② **Robert Bruce** ① Isabel
de   = **King of Scotland** = of
Burgh   **1306–1329**   Mar

David II
King of Scotland
1329–1371

Marjorie = Walter The Steward
Bruce   or "Stewart"

Robert II
King of Scotland 1371–1390
First King of House of Stewart

surrendered, was publicly humiliated and eventually went into exile.

With Scotland at his feet, Edward embarked on a systematic campaign to eradicate all vestiges, both political and religious, of the old Celtic kingdom. The Stone of Scone, most archaic and sacred of Celtic talismans, was accorded special attention. At Edward's behest, the inscription on it was erased and the stone itself removed from Scone and brought to London.[3] The great seal of Scotland was smashed and coffers of royal records were confiscated. Edward appointed himself, in effect, an *ad hoc* defender of the faith – the archetypal Christian king, promulgating the rule of Rome. To bolster this image, it was profitable to emphasise the pagan aspects of the old Celtic kingdom, which were portrayed as heretical, if not pagan and satanic. By disseminating rumours of sorcery and necromancy, Edward was able to show moral and theological justification for his crusade to annex Scotland.[4]

Having quelled all resistance in the country, Edward left its government in the hands of his own appointee, the Earl of Warenne. Warenne remained arrogantly disdainful of his role, and a year later, in 1297, William Wallace gave the signal for a general rising by assassinating the sheriff of Lanark; he then proceeded, with William Douglas, to attack the pro-English judiciary at Scone. Wallace's insurrection was co-ordinated with similar activity elsewhere under the leadership of the Bishop of Glasgow and James the Stewart.

It was against this turbulent background that the figure of Robert Bruce suddenly emerged, fomenting rebellion in the south. Bruce had already been made Earl of Carrick, one of the largest, most powerful and most deeply Celtic fiefdoms in the country, encompassing most of the western region known as Galloway. His followers and vassals controlled vast tracts of land in Ulster, including all of North Antrim, parts of what is now County Londonderry and Rathlin Island off the coast. Bruce's own holdings, apart from Carrick, included a third of the fiefdoms of Huntingdon, Garioch and Dundee. As we have seen, Bruce was of royal blood, his great-grandfather having married into the line descended from David I.

Towards the end of 1297, Wallace contrived to secure the election of William Lamberton, chancellor of Glasgow Cathedral, as Bishop of St Andrews, Scotland's premier bishopric. Lamberton being a fierce patriot, his investiture, it was hoped, would strengthen the Scottish cause. He promptly embarked for Rome to have his election confirmed by the Pope and to appeal to the Papacy on behalf of his comrades-in-arms. Meanwhile, Wallace was knighted by a prominent Scottish earl – possibly Bruce himself – and in 1298 was elected sole Guardian of the country.

By the spring of that year, however, the revolt had provoked another full-scale English invasion. On 19–20 July 1298, the English army of 2000 horse and 12,000 foot pitched camp near Falkirk, on the Templar estates of Temple Liston (now covered by Edinburgh Airport). Edward's forces were supported by a contingent of Templars and included, significantly enough, two of the Order's high dignitaries, the Master of England and the Preceptor of Scotland. At this time, the Temple had not yet come under persecution and had no particular reason to feel threatened. Even so, its alignment with the English king was highly irregular, an anomaly for which historians have offered no satisfactory explanation. The Templars had always been strictly forbidden to participate in secular warfare, especially against a Christian monarch. Their sole *raison d'être* was to engage in a very specific kind of conflict, the crusade, which was scrupulously defined as hostilities conducted against the infidel. The Scots were hardly infidels, and Scotland was under papal protection. Indeed, Bishop Lamberton had just been personally confirmed in his appointment by Pope Boniface VIII. The only explanation for the Templar involvement is that the pagan and/or old Celtic practices among the rebel Scots were sufficiently prominent to warrant a species of 'mini-crusade'.

In any case, at the Battle of Falkirk, on 22 July 1298, the Scots were badly savaged. English losses were negligible. Only two major figures, in fact, were killed on the English side. These were the two high dignitaries of the Temple.

Following his defeat at Falkirk, Wallace was forced to resign as Guardian, but this did not terminate the revolt. In the autumn of 1298, the rebels appointed John Comyn and Robert Bruce to preside as joint Guardians and continue the struggle. They, however, soon fell to squabbling among themselves, and the friction between them not only deflected them from concerted action against the English, but also nearly got Bruce killed. In 1299, therefore, when Bishop Lamberton returned from Rome, he was appointed third Guardian, to arbitrate between his compatriots. In fact, Lamberton was strongly sympathetic towards Bruce and was soon embroiled in his own quarrel with Comyn. Disgusted by all this discord, Bruce resigned, leaving Scotland temporarily in the hands of Comyn and Lamberton, and proceeded to consolidate his position by other means. These entailed two important dynastic alliances.

Early in the 1290s, Bruce had married Isabel, daughter of the Earl of Mar, while his sister, Christina, married Isabel's brother, who succeeded to the earldom. By his marriage to Isabel of Mar, Bruce had had a daughter, Marjorie, who in 1315 was to marry Walter, son of James the Stewart. But in 1302, Isabel of Mar having died, Bruce undertook, with impressive expediency, the forging of a temporary alliance with the English. He married Elizabeth de Burgh, daughter of the Earl of Ulster, a loyal supporter of the English king. Since the days of the Dalriada, there had been a close connection, both cultural and political, between Ulster and Bruce's own earldom of Carrick. This is discernible even today in the frequency with which 'Carrick' figures as a prefix for place-names in Northern Ireland. By marrying the daughter of the Earl of Ulster, Bruce was able to reactivate the old allegiances between his own fiefdom in Scotland and the Irish lands owned by the former lords of Carrick. He was now in a position to muster considerable support and manpower from across the Irish Sea. And with allies in Ulster, a crucial maritime route could be kept open for supplies and matériel.

In the mean time, the revolt continued without him. At the Battle of Roslin in 1303, Comyn defeated a small English contingent. This, however, proved a short-lived success, for in 1304 Edward invaded Scotland again, forcing Comyn to submit and swear allegiance to the English crown. In 1305, the cause of Scottish independence deteriorated further with the capture of Wallace. With a barbarity extreme even in the Middle Ages, Wallace was, quite literally, 'overkilled'. He was dragged behind a horse for four miles from Westminster to Smithfield, castrated, hanged, cut down while still alive, disembowelled and decapitated. His body was dismembered into four pieces which were placed on display in different locations.

The Murder of John Comyn

Wallace was dead, and Comyn firmly under the English thumb. But in March 1304, a year before Wallace's capture, Bruce's father had died, leaving Bruce with a direct claim to the throne. Three months later, in June, he had concluded a secret agreement with Bishop Lamberton. The tenets of this agreement were never stated publicly, or explicitly, but, in the words of one of Bruce's biographers, G. W. S. Barrow, 'it spoke darkly of "rivals" and "dangers"'.[5] It is now generally accepted that the agreement involved plans for an independent Celtic Scotland, over which Bruce, supported by Lamberton, would preside as monarch. Before any such project could be implemented, however, something had to be done about John Comyn.

The Comyn family, which included the earldoms of Buchan and Monteith, was an old one, and could match the Bruces in power and prestige. John Comyn himself, the head of the house's senior line, was, among his other titles, lord of Lochaber, Badenoch and Tynedale. Although he had quarrelled with Bruce and Lamberton, his integrity as a Scottish patriot had never previously been impugned. With his submission in 1304 to Edward of England, however, he became fair game, and vulnerable.

Subsequent events have proved perplexing: much was unexplained even at the time; much appears to have been deliberately suppressed. What is certain is that on 10 February 1306, at the church of the Grey Friars in Dumfries, Bruce, with his own hand, murdered his adversary. Comyn was stabbed with a dagger before the high altar and left to bleed to death on the church's stone floor. According to several accounts, he did not die immediately and was carried to safety by the monks, who sought to minister to his wounds. Bruce, hearing of this, returned to the church, *dragged him back to the altar* and there slaughtered him.[6] When Comyn's uncle attempted to intervene, he was in turn cut down by Bruce's brother-in-law, Christopher Seton.

Writing sixty-nine years after the event, John Barbour, the only major chronicler of the time and Bruce's first biographer, was curiously vague about this matter – curiously, because Barbour is generally exhaustive in his detail, precisely noting names, dates and statistics. Barbour describes the murder itself at some length, but says virtually nothing about what led to it. He suggests, tentatively, that Bruce and Comyn had jointly formed a pact against the English on which Comyn sought to renege; he suggests that the two men happened, more or less accidentally, to meet in the church, and that the murder occurred on the spur of the moment, in a sudden fit of temper following accusations of treachery. But he himself then admits that other explanations exist, while studiously contriving not to recount them.[7] Later historians acknowledge that there must have been more to the matter than meets the eye, but such explanations as they have ventured are scarcely adequate. There are aspects of Comyn's murder that cannot be explained entirely by the betrayal of a pact, or by the long-standing antipathy between Bruce and himself.

In the first place, there is persuasive evidence that Comyn's murder was not a spontaneous act of anger. On the contrary, it appears to have been carefully premeditated, perhaps even

rehearsed. Comyn seems to have been lured to the church deliberately. Moreover, he was bound to have been attended by an
entourage of his own soldiery – who, with the exception of his
uncle, stood by and did nothing.

Nor is it possible to ignore the setting of the murder. Churches,
after all, were deemed to be sacred ground, providing right of
sanctuary. It was strictly forbidden to shed blood in a church, and
this taboo was held in awed respect by the most powerful men
of the age. Even on those rare occasions when murders were
committed in churches – Thomas à Becket's, for example – they
were generally committed in a fashion calculated not to shed blood.
For Bruce to have used so messy an expedient as a dagger, to have
dragged Comyn back to the altar after he had been rescued by the
monks and to have displayed no remorse or penitence afterwards
suggest more than a loss of temper. It also suggests explicit, even
flamboyant, defiance – not only of the English authority to which
Comyn had sworn allegiance, but also of Rome. More even than a
repudiation of Edward, Comyn's murder seems to have signalled a
repudiation of the Papacy. What is more, it bears the unmistakable
stamp of a ritual killing – an almost ceremonial killing of one
candidate for a throne by another, on consecrated ground, in
accordance with archaic pagan tradition. Nobody at the time
could have been unaware of the powerful symbolism inherent in
Bruce's act – a symbolism so powerful, indeed, as to transcend the
act itself.

The Pope reacted as he could only have been expected to react:
Bruce was summarily excommunicated and was to remain so for
more than a decade. And yet, significantly enough, this made no
impression whatever on the Scottish clergy. Lamberton issued not a
word of criticism of his friend and ally. Neither did Bishop Wishart of
Glasgow, the second most important ecclesiastic in the country at the
time, in whose diocese the murder had taken place. If anything, both
prelates seem to have endorsed Bruce's behaviour – and to have
expected it beforehand. To return to G. W. S. Barrow: 'It does not
seem rash to guess that Wishart knew in advance approximately
when the *coup* was to be carried out.'[8]

With Comyn dead, Bruce immediately laid claim to the throne.
Lamberton supported him. So, too, did Wishart. Indeed, Bruce,
having dispatched his rival, promptly set out for Glasgow, where
Wishart received him for high-level discussions. And when Bruce
embarked on a fresh campaign against the English, both Lamberton
and Wishart, flagrantly indifferent to Rome, extolled it as a
veritable crusade.

With this ecclesiastical blessing, Bruce proceeded to seize the castles commanding the Firth of Clyde, thus protecting supply routes to Ulster and the Western Isles. As if on cue, Bishop Wishart conjured out of hiding the old royal robes and vestments, as well as a banner bearing the arms of the ancient Celtic royal house. Lamberton, meanwhile, supposedly presiding at Berwick over the English council delegated to rule Scotland, slipped away. He surfaced at Scone, where, six weeks after Comyn's death, he formally crowned Bruce king, performed a Mass for the new monarch, did homage and pledged fealty. Historians are agreed that, whatever the circumstances involved in Comyn's murder, these events had to have been prearranged.

There were, in fact, two quite separate coronations. The first, of which few details survive, seems to have been more or less conventional and to have taken place on 25 March 1306, in the Abbey Church at Scone. Lamberton presided, attended by Wishart, Bishop Murray of Moray, the Abbots of Scone and Inchaffray, the Earls of Lennox, Monteith, Athol and probably of Mar.

The second coronation took place two days later, and involved Bruce being placed upon the throne of Scone in accordance with ancient Celtic custom. Traditionally, he should have been ushered on to the royal seat by the country's premier peer, the Earl of Fife, who had for centuries played this role in the crowning of Scottish kings. At the time, however, the Earl of Fife had only just come of age, and was wholly in the power of Edward of England. In consequence, the boy's function was discharged by his sister, Isabel, wife of the Earl of Buchan, one of Comyn's cousins, who rode north from her estates in England especially to perform the ceremony.

In the past, historians have tended to regard Bruce's career, and his campaign for Scottish independence, as essentially political, rather than cultural. In consequence, the Celtic element has been largely ignored and Bruce has been portrayed as a typical Norman potentate of the era: 'It is only in comparatively recent times that the contribution of "Celtic" Scotland to the struggle has been appreciated.'[9] Now, in fact, it becomes apparent that the contribution of Celtic Scotland was crucial. As a specifically Celtic leader, intent on restoring an ancient Celtic kingdom, Bruce's campaign was not just political, but cultural and ethnic as well. Thus, for example, in 1307, when Edward lay on his deathbed, Bruce's propagandists disseminated tales of an alleged prophecy of Merlin. According to this prophecy, the Celtic peoples, on Edward's death, would unite, attain independence, create their own kingdom (extending presumably across the Irish Sea) and live together in peace.[10]

Such prophecies, however, were decidedly premature. Both England and Rome reacted swiftly to Bruce's coronation, for if England saw a restored Celtic monarchy as a political threat, Rome saw it as something even more ominous – a possible resurrection in Scotland of the old, potentially heretical Celtic Church or, worse still, a return to pre-Christian paganism. The general indifference in Scotland to Bruce's excommunication was alarming. So, too, was the insouciance with which further papal fulminations were received.

More difficult to dismiss was the English reaction. By this time, Bruce's support was considerable. It included, in addition to Scotland's most prominent earls, such important families as the Frasers, the Hays, the Campbells, the Montgomeries, the Lindsays and the Setons, some of whom will figure later in this story. But such support was still not sufficient to stem the advance of the English army when it again took the field. On 19 June 1306, at the Battle of Methven, Edward caught the Scots before dawn and inflicted a crushing defeat upon them. The Earl of Athol was captured and executed, as were Simon Fraser, Neil Bruce, Christopher Seton and his brother John. Nor did the ladies associated with Bruce's cause escape the English wrath. Isabel, Countess of Buchan, who had participated in Bruce's Celtic coronation, was placed in a cage hung on a wall outside Berwick Castle and kept there for four years, until 1310. Bruce's sister, Mary, was imprisoned in a similar cage in a tower of Roxburgh Castle and not released until 1314. Marjorie, Bruce's twelve-year-old daughter, was initially sentenced to incarceration in a third cage, this one at the Tower of London, but sense or influence prevailed and she was consigned to a convent instead. For a number of historians, the 'maniacal quality of King Edward's vengeance has always seemed most startling in his treatment of the women prisoners'.[11] But one must remember the unique status enjoyed by women in Celtic societies, as priestesses, prophetesses, receptacles and conduits for royal bloodlines. In Edward's mind, the women of Bruce's entourage must have seemed akin less to Norman chatelaines than to the witches in *Macbeth*.

His army shattered, Bruce himself was forced to flee, seeking refuge first in the mountains of Perthshire, then in Argyll. From Argyll he escaped to Kintyre and thence by sea to the island of Rathlin off the coast of Ulster. Here he is known to have passed part of the winter of 1306–7, but his other movements and activities before February 1307 are uncertain. It is reasonable to suppose, however, that he spent at least some of his time in Ulster proper, capitalising on the old Ulster-Carrick alliance and mustering Irish support. Certainly such support was forthcoming, for when he reappeared he was accompanied by a number of Irish nobles and their followers.

Bruce returned to Carrick in February 1307 with a sizeable force, and resumed operations against the English. Contrary to the prophecies, Edward's death in July did not interrupt hostilities for very long. For the next seven years – precisely the period during which the Templars were being harried on the Continent and in England – the war in Scotland was to continue, with only sporadic pauses. At a meeting of the St Andrews parliament in 1309, Bruce was officially designated 'King of the Scots'. From this point on, he was effectively sovereign of all Scotland and recognised as such – by his own people, by other heads of state, by everyone save the Pope who had excommunicated him and the new king of England, Edward II. The latter was as determined as his father had been to bring the Scots to heel and annex their kingdom to his own domains.

In the winter of 1310–11, Edward launched a fresh offensive. From his experience at Methven, Bruce had learned not to confront his adversary in a set-piece pitched battle. He was invariably outnumbered. In particular, he lacked knights, the heavily armed and armoured mounted soldiery who, with a massed charge at the critical moment, could bludgeon their way through the most tenacious opposition. In consequence, he resorted to hit-and-run raids, conducted by men in light armour, riding light but fast and manoeuvrable horses – in fact, to the kind of tactics employed by the Saracens in the Holy Land. He also relied extensively on skilled archers.

At the same time, the Scots were beginning to display much stiffer resistance, much more rigorous discipline and much more sophisticated martial expertise. By January 1310, moreover, they were receiving considerable shipments of weapons, equipment and matériel from Ireland. So extensive had this traffic become that Edward was provoked into issuing an irate proclamation:

The king commands the Chancellor and Treasurer of Ireland to proclaim in all towns, ports . . . prohibiting under the highest penalties all the exportation of provisions, horses, armour and other supplies . . . to the insurgent Scots, which he hears is carried on by merchants in Ireland.[12]

And yet, as perplexed historians have justifiably pointed out, Ireland was no more capable of large-scale military industry than

Scotland. Whatever weapons and armour there were in Ireland could only have got there from the Continent.

It is possible, of course, that the improved competence of the Scottish army was a natural consequence of prolonged conflict, with men becoming progressively more seasoned and experienced. But it is also possible that contingents of the Scottish forces were already being trained and drilled by refugee Templars – who were, after all, the most disciplined and professional soldiery in Europe at the time, and who could have brought with them from the Holy Land the kind of Saracen tactics that Bruce had now adopted. As for arms from the Continent finding their way to Ireland and thence to Scotland, it is hard to imagine a more likely conduit for such traffic than the Temple – whose installations in Ireland, when raided by royal authorities, proved, as we shall see, to be virtually denuded of weaponry.

Bannockburn and the Templars

The Battle of Bannockburn, which was finally to decide the issue of Scottish independence, resulted not from any skilful strategic manœuvres, but from an almost quaint medieval point of honour. Towards the end of 1313, a small English garrison found itself besieged by Bruce's brother, Edward, at Stirling Castle, the gateway to the Highlands and Argyll. The siege dragged on. Unwilling to waste his resources on its indefinite prolongation, Edward Bruce accepted the terms proposed by the defenders: if, by midsummer of the following year, no English army had appeared within three miles of the castle, the garrison would surrender. It was the kind of challenge that King Edward of England could not honourably decline. And Robert Bruce was thus committed by his brother to precisely the kind of set-piece battle he had shunned since Methven in 1306.

The English monarch's ostensible objective was to relieve Stirling. The sheer size of his army, however, indicates that his real objectives were considerably more ambitious – to annihilate the Scots, defeat Bruce once and for all and impose a military occupation on Scotland. Contemporary chroniclers speak of the English army as numbering 100,000 men. This is obviously an exaggeration of the kind typical during the Middle Ages. Nevertheless, the muster rolls of the time show that Edward called up 21,640 foot soldiers.[13] Not all of these, of course, would actually have arrived in Scotland, after the inevitable attrition resulting from desertion and disease. But those that did would have been complemented by some 3000 mounted knights, each of whom brought his own trained entourage. Modern historians concur that the English forces must have numbered at least 20,000. Such a figure would have given them a numerical superiority of three to one – a ratio echoed in the chronicles of the time. The Scots are believed to have numbered between 7000 and 10,000, with perhaps 500 mounted nobles or 'knights' – far less heavily armed and armoured than their English equivalents.

There is still dispute over the precise site of the Battle of Bannockburn, but it is known to be some two and a half miles from Stirling Castle. The main engagement occurred on 24 June 1314. The date is interesting, for 24 June is St John's Day, a day of particular significance for the Templars.

The precise details of what happened at Bannockburn are vague. No eye-witness account has survived, and such second- or third-hand testimony as exists is distorted and confused. It is generally accepted that skirmishes occurred the day before. It is generally accepted that Bruce, in a classic single combat, killed the English knight Henry de Bohun. Most historians concur that the Scottish army was made up almost entirely of foot soldiers armed with pikes, spears and axes. They also concur that only mounted men in the Scottish ranks carried swords, and that Bruce had few such men – certainly not enough in numbers, in weight of equipment and horses, to match the English knights. And yet, paradoxically, the fourteenth-century chronicler John Barbour states of Bruce that '. . . from the Lowlands he could boast, of armoured men, a full great host'.[14] From such information of the battle as survives, there does indeed seem, at one point, to have been a charge against the English archers by mounted soldiery, who, until then, had been kept in reserve as part of Bruce's personal division. But what is most striking in the chronicles is the decisive intervention – when all the Scottish units were *already engaged* and the entire battle hung in the balance – of what the English regarded as a 'fresh force', which suddenly erupted with banners flying from the Scottish rear.

According to some accounts, this fresh contingent consisted of yeomen, youngsters, camp-followers and other non-combatant personnel whom the English mistook for fighting men. They had supposedly elected a captain from their own ranks, made banners out of sheets, armed themselves with homemade weapons and, as a volunteer column, hurled themselves into the fray. It is a stirring, romantic story which does much credit to Scottish patriotism, but it does not ring true. If the intervention was indeed so spontaneous, so improvised and so unexpected, it would have caught the Scots as much by surprise as it did the English. That no confusion spread through the Scottish ranks suggests the intervention was anticipated. Nor is it easy to imagine the heavily armoured English knights – even if they did improbably mistake a horde of peasants and camp-followers for professional soldiery – fleeing before an attack launched on foot. All the evidence suggests that the decisive intervention came from some reserve of mounted men. Who might these unknown horsemen have been?

The sudden advent of a fresh force, whatever their identity, after a day of combat which had left both English and Scottish armies exhausted, determined the outcome of the battle. Panic swept the English ranks. King Edward, together with 500 of his knights, abruptly fled the field. Demoralised, the English foot-soldiers promptly followed suit, and the withdrawal deteriorated quickly into a full-scale rout, the entire English army abandoning their supplies, their baggage, their money, their gold and silver plate, their arms, armour and equipment. But while some chronicles speak of dreadful slaughter, the recorded English losses do not in fact appear to have been very great. Only one earl is reported to have been killed, only thirty-eight barons and knights. The English collapse appears to have been caused not by the ferocity of the Scottish assault, which they were managing to withstand, but simply by fear.

It is hardly credible that peasants and camp-followers could have inspired such fear. On the other hand, it would certainly have been inspired by a contingent of Templars, even a small one. Whoever the mysterious intruders were, they seem to have been instantly recognisable – which Templars would have been, by their beards, their white mantles and/or their black-and-white banner known as the 'Beauséant'. If they were indeed recognised as such, and if word of their identity spread through the English ranks, the result would have been panic of precisely the sort that occurred.

But why, if the Templars did play so crucial a role at Bannockburn, is there no mention of them in the chronicles? In fact, there would have been a number of reasons for such reticence. From the English point of view, what had happened was too ignominious to be discussed at all, and English accounts are predictably quiet about the battle. As for the Scots, they were intent on depicting Bannockburn as a triumph of their people, their culture, their nationalism; and this triumph would have been in some measure tarnished by suggestions of outside intervention. Then, too, Bruce had very specific political reasons for concealing the presence of refugee Templars in his domains. Although he was still excommunicate, he was also, by 1314, eager for the Church's support, and could not risk alienating the Papacy further. Still less could he risk prompting the Pope to preach a full-scale crusade against Scotland. Something of this sort had occurred in the Languedoc precisely a century before, and the ensuing depredations, which lasted for some forty years, were still fresh in people's memories. Moreover, his chief European supporter was Philippe IV of France, the very man who had first instigated the persecution of the Templars.

After the battle, special recognition was conferred on one in particular of Bruce's vassals, Angus Óg MacDonald:

> The traditional claim of the MacDonalds to fight on the right wing of the royal army – a place of honour – is said to have been granted by Bruce to Angus Óg in recognition of the part played by him and his men in the success of Bannockburn.[15]

Of the territory around Kilmartin, Loch Awe and Loch Sween, some was royal domain under the administration of the royal bailiff, Sir Neil Campbell, Bruce's brother-in-law. All the rest belonged to the MacDonalds. Any Templars settled in the region would, as a matter of course, have fought under the nominal command of Angus Óg.

Bannockburn was one of the half dozen or so most decisive battles of the Middle Ages, and the largest, probably, ever to be fought on British soil. It effectively put an end to English designs on Scotland, which for the next 289 years was to remain an independent kingdom. When, at the beginning of the seventeenth century, the two countries were united under a single monarch, it was not through conquest, but inheritance.

Bannockburn notwithstanding, however, the remaining fifteen years of Bruce's reign were still to be stormy. As he lacked male heirs, there were particular difficulties about whom to designate as his successor. In 1315, some ten months after Bannockburn, the succession was finally settled upon his brother, Edward. A month later, Edward Bruce embarked for Ireland, where at Dundalk in May of the following year, he was crowned king of that country. He would thus, in accordance with the old Celtic dream, have been in a position to unite Ireland and Scotland. In October 1318, however, he died, and the succession to both thrones again fell vacant. In December, it was agreed that on Bruce's death the Scottish throne would pass to his grandson, Robert, the son of Marjorie Bruce and Walter the Stewart.

On 6 April 1320, an extraordinary document – the so-called Declaration of Arbroath – was issued. It took the form of a letter commissioned and signed by eight earls and thirty-one other nobles, including representatives of the Seton, Sinclair and Graham families. This letter adumbrated the legendary history of the Scots from their alleged origins in Scythia and their conversion there by St Andrew. It described Robert Bruce as their deliverer and hailed him (with biblical comparisons traditionally dear to the Templars) as 'a second Maccabaeus or Joshua'. More important, however, is its proclamation of the independence of Scotland and the remarkably modern sophistication of its definition of the relationship of the king to his people:

> The divine providence, the right of succession by the laws and customs of the kingdom . . . and the due and lawful consent and assent of all the people, made him our king and prince. To him we are obliged and resolved to adhere in all things, both upon account of his right and his own merit, as being the person who hath restored the people's safety in defence of their liberties. But, after all, if this prince shall leave these principles he hath so nobly pursued, and consent that we or our kingdom be subjected to the king or people of England, we will immediately endeavour to expel him as our enemy, and as the subverter both of his own and our rights, and will make another king who will defend our liberties.[16]

Bruce, in other words, was not king by 'divine right'. He was king only insofar as he discharged the duties incumbent upon his office. In the context of the age, this was an unusually advanced definition of kingship.

In 1322, Edward II launched his last, rather half-hearted, expedition against Scotland. It came to nothing, and Bruce retaliated with incursions into Yorkshire. In 1323, the two countries concluded what was supposed to be a thirteen-year truce, which lasted only for four. In the mean time, Bruce had become embroiled in a new squabble with the Papacy, then in the throes of its own schism, the so-called 'Avignon Captivity'. For some time, Edward of England had longed to rid the Scottish Church of its powerful nationalist bishops – prelates such as Lamberton of St Andrews, Wishart of Glasgow and William Sinclair of Dunkeld (brother of Sir Henry Sinclair of Rosslin, signatory of the Arbroath Declaration). To this end, the English king had badgered successive popes not to consecrate any new native-born bishops into the Scottish Church. In the Avignon-based Pope John XXII he found a sympathetic ear. Bruce, however, aligned himself with his own bishops in defying the Pontiff's wishes and in 1318 he was again excommunicated, along with James Douglas and the Earl of Moray. A year later, the Pope demanded that the bishops of St Andrews, Dunkeld, Aberdeen and Moray appear before him to explain themselves. They ignored him and, in June 1320, were also excommunicated. Throughout the course of this row, the Pope had persisted in refusing to recognise Bruce as king, pointedly referring to him only as 'ruler of the Kingdom of Scotland'. It was not until 1324 that Pope John XXII relented and Bruce was finally acknowledged monarch in the Church's eyes.

In 1329, Bruce died, to be succeeded, as he had arranged, by his grandson, Robert II, the first of the Stuart dynasty. Before his death, he had expressed the wish that his heart be removed, placed in a casket, taken to Jerusalem and buried in the Church of the Holy Sepulchre. In 1330, therefore, Sir James Douglas, Sir William Sinclair, Sir William Keith and at least two other knights embarked for the Holy Land, Douglas carrying Bruce's heart in a silver casket hung around his neck. Their itinerary took them through Spain, where they made the acquaintance of King Alfonso XI of Castile and León, and accompanied him on his campaign against the Moors of Granada. On 25 March 1330, at the Battle of Tebas de Ardales, the Scots, riding in the vanguard, were surrounded. According to the fourteenth-century chronicle, Douglas removed from his neck the casket containing Bruce's heart and hurled it into the attacking host, crying:

> Brave heart, that ever foremost led,
> Forward! as thou wast wont. And I
> Shall follow thee, or else shall die![17]

Whether Douglas, in the heat of battle, had either time or inclination to compose his thoughts into verse is, one suspects, questionable. Having hurled Bruce's heart at the foe, however, he and his fellow Scots did proceed to follow it, charging headlong into their adversaries. All of them died, with the exception of Sir William Keith, who had broken his arm prior to the battle and so did not participate in it. He is said to have retrieved the heart from the field, miraculously intact in its casket, and to have brought it back with him to Scotland. It was buried in Melrose Abbey, under the east window of the chancel.

Early in the nineteenth century, Bruce's grave at Dunfermline Abbey was opened. According to popular traditions prevalent in the age of Sir Walter Scott, he was found with his leg-bones carefully crossed immediately under his skull. In fact, this was not so; there was, apparently, nothing unusual about the corpse.[18] But the traditions are indicative. It is clear that someone had a vested interest in linking Bruce with the Masonic skull-and-crossbones.

2

Military Monks: the Knights Templar

Even before their dissolution, the Knights Templar had been shrouded in extravagant myth and legend, dark rumours, suspicions and superstitions. In the centuries following their suppression, the mystique surrounding them intensified, and genuine mystery became ever more swathed in spurious mystification. During the eighteenth and nineteenth centuries, as we shall see, certain rites of Freemasonry assiduously sought to establish a pedigree dating back to the Templars. At the same time, other, neo-Templar, organisations began to appear, similarly claiming a pedigree derived from the original Order. Today, there are no fewer than five organisations in existence alleging one or another species of direct descent from the white-mantled warrior-monks of the Middle Ages. And despite the cynicism and scepticism of our age, there is, even for outsiders, something fascinating, even romantic, about the soldier-mystics of 700 years ago, with their black-and-white banner and distinctively splayed red cross. They have passed into the heritage of our folklore and tradition; they appeal to the imagination not just as crusaders, but as something far more enigmatic and evocative – as high-level intriguers and power-brokers, as guardians of fabulous treasure, as sorcerers and arcane initiates, as custodians of a secret knowledge. Time has served them better than they, in the throes of their last ordeals, could ever have anticipated.

Time, however, has also obscured the identity and character of the human beings behind the exotic veil of romance – the human beings and the true nature of the institution they created. Questions still remain, for example, about how orthodox, or heretical, the Templars' beliefs really were. Questions remain about how guilty they were of the charges levelled against them. Questions remain about the internal high-level activities of the Order, their secret grand designs, their project for the creation of a Templar state, their policy of reconciling Christianity, Judaism and Islam. Questions remain about the influences that shaped the Order, the 'infection' of the Cathar heresy and the impact of older, non-Pauline forms of Christian thought encountered by the knights in the Holy Land. Questions remain about what happened to the wealth accumulated by these supposedly poor 'soldiers of Christ' – a wealth which kings sought to plunder and which vanished without trace. Questions remain about the Templars' rituals and the mysterious 'idol' they allegedly worshipped under the cryptic name of 'Baphomet'. And questions remain about the supposed secret knowledge to which the upper echelons of the Order, at least, were reputedly privy. What was the nature of this knowledge? Was it truly 'occult' in the sense charged by the Inquisition, involving forbidden magical practices, obscene and blasphemous rites? Was it political and cultural – pertaining, for example, to the origins of Christianity? Was it scientific and technological, encompassing such things as drugs, poisons, medicine, architecture, cartography, navigation and trade routes? The more closely one examines the Templars, the more such questions as these tend not to resolve themselves, but to proliferate.

As we have noted, the history of the Templars is almost precisely contemporary with that of the feudal Celtic Kingdom of Scotland, from the reign of David I to that of Bruce. On the surface, there would appear to be little else in common between the Scottish monarchy and the military-religious Order created in the Holy Land. And yet a number of connections obtained between them, some dictated by the geopolitics of the medieval world, some by more elusive factors which have never been properly chronicled. By 1314, these connections would have rendered quite possible a Templar presence at Bannockburn.

The Rise of the Templars

According to most sources, the Knights Templar – the Poor Knights of the Temple of Solomon – were created in 1118, although there is significant evidence to suggest they were already in existence at least four years earlier.[1] Their ostensible *raison d'être* was to protect pilgrims in the Holy Land. The evidence suggests, however, that this avowed purpose was a façade, and that the knights were engaged in a much more ambitious, more grandiose geopolitical design which involved the Cistercian Order, Saint Bernard, and Hugues, Count of Champagne and one of the first sponsors and patrons of both the Cistercians and the Templars. The count became a Templar himself in 1124, and the Order's first Grand Master was one of his own vassals, Hugues de Payens. Among the other founding members was Saint Bernard's uncle, André de Montbard.

Until 1128 – four years after David I became king of Scotland – the Templars were said to have consisted of only nine knights, although the actual records show several additional recruits. Besides Hugues de Champagne, these included Fulk, Comte d'Anjou, father of Geoffroy Plantagenet and grandfather of Henry II of England. Nevertheless, the Order's initial enrolment seems to have been relatively small. Then, at the Council of Troyes, conducted under the auspices of Saint Bernard, the Templars were given a monastic rule, the equivalent, so to speak, of a constitution, and were thereby formally established. They represented a new phenomenon: 'For the first time in Christian history, soldiers would live as monks.'[2]

From 1128 on, the Order expanded at an extraordinary pace, receiving not just a massive influx of recruits, but also immense donations of both money and property. Within a year, they owned lands in France, England, Scotland, Spain and Portugal. Within a decade, their possessions would extend to Italy, Austria, Germany, Hungary and Constantinople. In 1131, the king of Aragon bequeathed to them a third of his domains. By the mid-twelfth century, the Temple had already begun to establish itself as the single most wealthy and powerful institution in Christendom, with the sole exception of the Papacy.

In the years immediately following the Council of Troyes, Hugues de Payens and other founding members of the Order travelled extensively in Europe, promoting everything from themselves to the virtues of time-share fiefdoms in Palestine. Hugues and at least one of his comrades are known to have been in both England and Scotland. According to *The Anglo-Saxon Chronicle*, when Hugues visited Henry I:

> ... the king received him with much honour, and gave him rich presents in gold and in silver. And afterwards he sent him into England; and there he was received by all good men, who all gave him presents, and in Scotland also; ... And he invited the folk out to Jerusalem; and there went with him and after him more people than ever did before.[3]

On this first visit, Philip de Harcourt conferred on the Order their preceptory at Shipley in Essex. The Dover preceptory (the remains of its church are still visible today) is believed to date from the same time.

As Grand Master, Hugues de Payens proceeded to appoint regional masters for each of the Temple's 'provinces', as its enclaves of property in each country were called. The first Master of England, of whom little is known, was one Hugh d'Argentein. He was succeeded by a young Norman knight, Osto de St Omer, who presided until 1153–4, then by Richard de Hastings. Under these two masters, the Templars in England embarked on one of their most innovative ventures, a translation of part of the Old Testament into the vernacular. This version of the Book of Judges took the form of a chivalric romance – Joshua and his Fierce Knights.[4]

The relations between the Templars and the rulers of those realms where they possessed lands were mixed. In France, for example, the relationship was always, even at its best, uneasy. In Spain, on the other hand, the relationship was consistently good. In England, too, for the most part, the Order enjoyed a cordial rapport with the monarchy. As we have seen, Henry I received the first knights with open arms, while Stephen, who seized power in 1135, was the son of the Count of Blois, one of the leaders of the First Crusade, and was thus particularly sympathetic to the Templars' activities in the Holy Land. Under his auspices, the network of preceptories began to spread across England. The Earl of Derby donated Bisham; the Earl of Warwick donated land for a preceptory at Warwick itself; Roger de Builli offered the site of Willoughton in Lincolnshire. Stephen's own wife, Mathilda, bestowed tracts of territory in Essex and Oxford which became Temple Cressing and Temple Cowley respectively, two of the most important early preceptories.

During Stephen's reign, too, the Templars built their first central installation in England. This – the 'old Temple' – was located at Holborn. It consisted of the preceptory buildings, a church, a garden, an orchard and a cemetery, all surrounded by a boundary ditch and, it is believed, a wall. Its foundations existed on the site of what is now the Underground station at High Holborn. This did not, however, remain the Order's seat in London for long. By 1161, the knights had already established themselves in the 'new Temple', the site of which even today bears their name and contains not only their original round church, but also a number of graves. 'Barram Novi Templi', or Temple Bar, where Fleet Street meets the Strand, was the gate opening into the Order's precincts. In its heyday, the 'new Temple' extended from Aldwych up the Strand and half-way along Fleet Street, then down to the Thames, where it had its own wharf. Once a year, a general chapter was convened on these premises, attended by the Master of England and all other officers of the Order in Britain, including the Priors of Scotland and Ireland.

Henry II continued the close association of the English monarchy with the Temple, who were especially active in trying to reconcile him with Thomas à Becket. But it was under Henry's son, Richard Cœur de Lion, that that association became closest. Indeed, Richard was on such good terms with the Order that he is often regarded as a kind of honorary Templar. He consorted regularly with the knights; he travelled in their ships, resided in their preceptories. When, having antagonised his fellow potentates, he was obliged to flee the Holy Land, he did so disguised as a Templar, and an entourage of authentic Templars attended him. He was closely embroiled in the transactions between the Templars and their Islamic equivalents, the Hashishim or 'Assassins'. He also sold Cyprus to the Order, and the island later became, for a time, their official seat.

At the same time, the Temple had by then become influential and powerful enough to command respect and allegiance from Richard's brother and arch-rival, King John. Like Richard, John stayed regularly at the London preceptory, making it his part-time residence during the last four years of his reign (1212–16). The Master of England, Aymeric de St Maur, was John's closest advisor, and it was primarily as a result of Aymeric's persuasion that the king signed the Magna Carta in 1215. When John appended his signature to the document, Aymeric was at his side and signed as well. Subsequently, Aymeric was named one of the executors of John's will.

Officially, the Temple's primary sphere of activity was supposed to be the Latin Kingdom of Jerusalem. Europe was supposed to be but a support base, both a source for men and matériel and a channel for their transport to the Holy Land. Certainly the Templars never let 'Outremer' – the 'land across the sea', as they called the Middle East – slip out of their focus. Their activities extended at least from Egypt, if not from points west, all the way to Constantinople. Few decisions were made in the crusader principalities, and little happened there, in which the Templars were not involved. At the same time, however, as their role in the signing of the Magna Carta indicates, the knights were soon deeply embroiled in the internal affairs of most European kingdoms. In England, they enjoyed particular privileges and prerogatives. Thus, for example, the Master of the Temple sat in Parliament as the premier baron of the realm. The Order was also, of course, exempt from taxes, and metal Templar crosses marked its houses and holdings in larger English towns and cities, warding off tax-collectors. Specimens of these crosses, from the Street of the Templars in Leeds, can be seen today in the museum of the Order of St John, Clerkenwell. Within such enclaves, the knights were a law unto themselves. They offered right of sanctuary, like any church. They convened their own courts to try cases of local crime. They ran their own markets and fairs. They were exempt from tolls on roads, bridges and rivers.

Templar possessions in England were extensive and spanned the length and breadth of the country. Some – though by no means all – of the Order's former lands are recognisable today by the prefix 'Temple', as in the London district of Temple Fortune just north of Golders Green. It is generally accepted that wherever this prefix occurs in the British Isles there was once some species of Templar installation. To compile a definitive list of the Order's holdings is today impossible, but even the most conservative estimates show a minimum of seventy-four major properties, including thirty full-scale preceptories[5] and literally hundreds of smaller belongings – villages, hamlets, churches and farms. On occasion, the Order's commercial activities even led them to establish towns of their own. Baldock, for example, near Letchworth in Hertfordshire, was founded by the Templars around 1148. Its name derives from Baghdad.

A substantial section of modern Bristol was once Templar property. Indeed, Bristol was one of the major ports for the Order, and ships trafficked regularly between the city and the Templars' primary Atlantic base of La Rochelle in France. The Close Rolls of Henry III cite the names of two Templar ships – *La Templere* and *Le Buscard*.[6] One of the knights' most lucrative privileges was that of exporting their own wool. This, like the transport of pilgrims, brought in very considerable revenues, as too, did the Order's lands. In Yorkshire alone, during 1308, Temple properties produced an income of £1130.[7] (At that time, a modest castle could be built for £500. A knight and a squire could be employed for a year for £55, a crossbowman for £7. A horse cost £9, making it cheaper to ride a crossbowman.)

In Ireland, the Templars' network of holdings was equally widespread, though less well documented.[8] There were at least six preceptories, one in Dublin, at least three on the south coast in Counties Waterford and Wexford. As in England, there were numerous manors, farms, churches and castles. The preceptory of Kilsaren in County Louth, for example, owned twelve churches and collected tithes from eight others. There was at least one manor,

Temple House, at Sligo, on the west coast. As we shall see, the question of other Templar installations in the west of Ireland is of crucial importance.

For Scotland, records are particularly patchy and unreliable, partly because of the turmoil in the kingdom at the end of the thirteenth century, partly because much appears to have been deliberately concealed. There were at least two major preceptor-ies.[9] One, Maryculter, was near Aberdeen. The other, Balantrod-och –Gaelic for 'Stead of the Warriors' – was larger and consti-tuted the Order's primary Scottish base. Situated near Edinburgh, it is now called Temple. The compilation of Templar properties in Scotland, however, is based on the testimony of one knight, William de Middleton, interrogated by the Inquisition. He mentio-ned Maryculter and Balantrodoch as the two places in which he had personally served. This, of course, does not exclude the possibility, indeed the likelihood, of others at which he did *not* serve; and he had, in any case, every reason to be 'economical with the truth'. In fact, chronicles refer to Templar holdings at Berwick (then part of Scotland) and at Liston, near Falkirk. Quite apart from Argyll, there is evidence of Templar possessions in, at the very least, another ten locations in Scotland; but there is no way of knowing if these were large or small – if they were preceptories, manors or merely farms.

The Financial Influence of the Templars

By virtue of its possessions, its manpower, its diplomatic skills and its martial expertise, the Temple wielded enormous political and military influence. But it was no less influential financially, and wrought profound changes in the economic foundations of the age. Historians generally ascribe the evolution and development of Western Europe's economic institutions to Jewish money-lenders and to the great Italian merchant houses and consortiums. In fact, however, the role of Jewish money-lenders was minor compared to that of the Temple; and the Temple not only pre-dated the Italian houses, but established the machinery and procedures which those houses were later to emulate and adopt. In effect, the origins of modern banking can be attributed to the Order of the Temple. At the peak of their power, the Templars handled much, if not most, of the available capital in Western Europe. They pioneered the concept of credit facilities, as well as the allocation of credit for commercial development and expansion. They performed, in fact, virtually all the functions of a twentieth-century merchant bank.

In theory, canon law forbade Christians to engage in usury, the collecting of interest on loans. One might expect this interdict to have been applied even more stringently to an institution as ostensibly pious as the Temple. Nevertheless, the Temple lent money, and collected interest, on a massive scale. In one proven case, the agreed rate of interest on late payment of debt was 60 per cent per year – 17 per cent more than Jewish money-lenders were allowed to claim. The strictures of canon law against usury were evaded by nothing more elaborate than semantics, euphemism and circumlocution.[10] One can only speculate on the terms used by the Templars themselves in order to avoid speaking explicitly of 'interest', since few of their documents survive; but the recipients of Templar loans, in their repayment instructions, are not bound by any such reserve. In his repayment to the Temple, Edward I, to cite but one of many possible examples, speaks of the capital component and, quite specifically, the 'interest'.[11]

In fact, the English crown was chronically in debt to the Temple. King John borrowed incessantly from the Order. So, too, did Henry III, who between 1260 and 1266, his treasury depleted by military expeditions, even pawned the English crown jewels to the Templars, Queen Eleanor personally taking them to the Order's Paris preceptory. In the years before Henry ascended the throne, the Templars also lent money to the future Edward I. During the first year of his reign, Edward repaid 2000 marks on a total debt to the Order of 28,189 pounds.[12]

One of the most important of the Temple's financial activities was arranging payments at a distance without the actual transfer of funds. In an age when travel was uncertain, when roads were unprotected and plunder a constant risk, men were understandably reluctant to travel with valuables on their persons. The Robin Hood legends bear eloquent testimony to the threat constantly looming over wealthy merchants, tradesmen, even nobles. In consequence, the Temple devised letters of credit. One would deposit a particular sum in, say, the London Temple and receive a species of chit. One could then travel freely to other parts of Britain, to most of the Continent, even to the Holy Land. At one's destination, one had only to present the chit and one would receive cash, in whatever the currency desired. Theft of such letters of credit, as well as fraud, was precluded by an elaborate system of codes to which the Templars alone were privy.

In addition to lending money and providing letters of credit, the

Templars provided, through their network of preceptories, places of safe deposit. In France, the Paris Temple was also the most important royal treasury, housing the state's wealth as well as the Order's, and the knights' treasurer was also the king's. All the finances of the French crown were thus yoked to, and dependent upon, the Temple. In England, the Order's influence was not quite so great. As we have noted, however, the crown jewels, during the reign of King John, were kept at the London Temple – which, under Henry II, John, Henry III and Edward I, served as one of the four royal treasuries. In England, the Templars also acted as tax collectors. Not only did they collect papal taxes, tithes and donations; they collected taxes and revenues for the crown as well – and seem to have been even more fearsome in that capacity than today's Inland Revenue. In 1294, they organised the conversion from old to new money. They frequently acted as trustees of funds or property placed in their custody, as brokers and as debt collectors. They mediated in disputes involving ransom payments, dowries, pensions and a multitude of other transactions.

At the apex of their power, the Templars were accused of pride, arrogance, ruthlessness, and intemperate and dissolute behaviour. 'To drink like a Templar' was a frequent simile in medieval England; and despite their vow of chastity, the knights seem to have wenched as zealously as they drank. But whatever their conduct in such respects as these, their reputation for accuracy, honesty and integrity in financial affairs remained untarnished. One might not like them, but one knew one could rely on them. And they were particularly harsh to any member of their own Order who proved unworthy. In one instance, the Prior of the Temple in Ireland was found guilty of embezzlement. He was imprisoned in the penitential cell of the Templar church in London – a room too small even to lie down in, which can still be seen today – and starved to death. He is said to have taken eight weeks to die.

Like the Swiss banks of today, the Temple maintained a number of long-term trust funds from the dead and/or dispossessed. Not surprisingly, monarchs or other potentates would occasionally try to lay hands on such resources. Thus, for example, Henry II, in one instance, demanded from the Templars the money deposited with them by a disgraced lord. He was told that 'money confided to them in trust they would deliver to no man without the permission of him who had intrusted it to be kept in the Temple'.[13]

'The Poor Knights' most lasting achievement . . . was economic.

No medieval institution did more for the rise of capitalism.'[14] But the very wealth they managed so effectively was to render them an irresistible lure to a monarch whose temerity was equal to his greed.

3

Arrests and Torture

By 1306, the Temple had become a focus of particular attention for King Philippe IV of France, known as Philippe le Bel. Philippe was enormously ambitious. He had grandiose designs for his country, and little compunction about crushing whomever or whatever stood in his way. He had already engineered the kidnapping and murder of one Pope, Boniface VIII, and is widely believed to have orchestrated the death, probably by poison, of another, Benedict XI, who followed. By 1305, he had installed his own puppet on the papal throne – Bertrand de Goth, formerly Archbishop of Bordeaux, who became Pope Clement V. In 1309, Philippe hijacked the Papacy itself, uprooting it from Rome and re-locating it on French soil, at Avignon, where it became, in effect, a mere appendage of the French crown. This inaugurated the so-called Avignon Captivity, a schism which was to produce rival popes and divide the Catholic Church for the next sixty-eight years, until 1377. With the Papacy thus in his pocket, Philippe had the latitude he needed to move against the Temple.

He had a number of motives for doing so, and a personal grudge against the knights as well. He had asked to be received into the Order as an honorary Templar – the kind of status previously conferred on Richard I – and had been insultingly refused. Then, in June 1306, a rioting mob had forced him to seek refuge in the Paris Temple, where he witnessed at first-hand the staggering extent of the Order's wealth and resources. Philippe desperately needed money, and the Templar treasure must have made him salivate. In the king's attitude towards the knights, greed was thus dangerously compounded with humiliation and vindictiveness. Finally, the Templars posed – or would have seemed in Philippe's eyes to have posed – a very real threat to the stability of his kingdom. In 1291, as we have seen, Acre, the last bastion of the Western crusaders in the

Holy Land, had fallen to the Saracens, and the Latin Kingdom of Jerusalem had been irretrievably lost. This had left the Templars – the best-trained, best-equipped, most professional military force in the Western world – without a *raison d'être* and, more ominously for Philippe, without a home.

They had already established a provisional base on Cyprus, but harboured more ambitious designs. Not surprisingly, they dreamed of a state or principality of their own, similar to the Ordenstadt created by their kindred Order, the Teutonic Knights, in Prussia and on the Baltic. But the Ordenstadt was on the extreme fringe of Christian Europe, far beyond the reach of the Papacy and the power of any secular potentate. Moreover, the Ordenstadt could be rationalised and justified as another form of crusade – a crusade against the heathen tribes of north-eastern Europe, against the pagan Prussians and Balts and Lithuanians, against the Orthodox (and therefore heretical) city-states of north-western Russia such as Pskov and Novgorod. The Templars, on the other hand, who already wielded immense influence in France, contemplated creating their own Ordenstadt in the very heart of European Christendom – in the Languedoc, which, during the previous century, had effectively been annexed by the French crown.[1] For Philippe, the prospect of a Templar principality on his southern doorstep – a principality encompassing territory to which he laid claim – could only foster resentment and alarm.

Philippe planned his stratagem meticulously. A catalogue of charges was compiled, partly from the king's spies who had infiltrated the Order, partly from the voluntary confession of an alleged renegade knight. Armed with these accusations, Philippe was free to act; and when he administered his blow, it was sudden, swift and lethal. In an operation worthy of a modern secret police raid, the king issued sealed orders to his seneschals and bailiffs throughout the country. These orders were to be opened everywhere simultaneously and implemented at once. At dawn on Friday, 13 October 1307, all Templars in France were to be seized and placed under arrest by the king's men, their preceptories placed under royal sequestration, their goods confiscated. But although Philippe's objective of surprise seemed to have been attained, the most alluring prize of all – the Order's legendary wealth – eluded him. It was never found, and what became of the fabulous 'treasure of the Templars' has remained a mystery.

In fact, it is questionable whether Philippe's surprise coup was as unexpected as he, or subsequent historians, believed. There is considerable evidence to suggest the Templars received some kind of advance warning. Shortly before the swoop, for example, the Grand Master, Jacques de Molay, called in many of the Order's books and extant rules, and had them burnt. A knight who withdrew from the Temple around this time was told by the Treasurer that he was extremely 'wise', as some sort of crisis was imminent. An official edict was circulated to all French preceptories, stressing that no information about the Order's rites or rituals was to be released.

In any case, whether the Templars were warned in advance or whether they simply sensed what was in the wind, certain precautions were definitely taken. In the first place, many knights fled, and those who were captured seem to have submitted passively, as if under instructions to do so – at no point is there any record of French Templars actively resisting the king's seneschals. In the second place, there are indications of an organised flight by a particular group of knights, virtually all of whom were in some way associated with the Order's Treasurer.[2]

Given these manifestations of preparedness, it is not surprising that the treasure of the Temple, together with almost all its documents and records, should have disappeared. Under interrogation by the Inquisition, one knight spoke of the treasure being smuggled from the Paris preceptory shortly before the arrests. The same witness declared that the Preceptor of France also left the capital with fifty horses, and put to sea – there is no indication from where – with eighteen galleys, none of which was ever seen again.[3] Whether this was true or not, the whole of the Templar fleet does seem to have escaped the king's clutches. There is no report of any of the Order's ships being taken – not only then, but ever. On the contrary, the ships appear to have vanished utterly, along with whatever they might have been carrying.

In France, the arrested Templars were tried and many were subjected to hideous torture. Accusations grew ever wilder, and strange confessions were extracted. Grim rumours began to circulate about the country. The Templars, it was said, worshipped a demonic power called 'Baphomet'. At their secret ceremonies, they supposedly prostrated themselves before a bearded male head, which spoke to them and invested them with magical virtues. Unauthorised witnesses of these ceremonies were reported to have disappeared. And there were other charges as well, even more vague. The Templars were accused of infanticide, of teaching women how to abort, of obscene kisses at the induction of postulants, of homosexuality. But one charge levelled against them stands out as most bizarre and seemingly improbable. These soldiers of Christ, who had fought and laid down their lives for Christendom by the hundreds, were accused of ritually denying Christ, of repudiating, trampling and spitting on the Cross.

This is not the place to explore the validity or otherwise of these charges. We ourselves have considered them in detail elsewhere.[4] So have numerous other commentators. Indeed, entire books have been written on the trials of the Templars and the question of the Order's guilt or innocence. In the present context, it is sufficient simply to acknowledge that the Templars were almost certainly 'tainted' with religious heterodoxy, if not full-fledged heresy. Most of the other accusations against them, however, were in all likelihood trumped up, fabricated or exaggerated out of all proportion. Of all the knights interrogated and subjected to torture, for example, only two, according to the Inquisition records, ever confessed to homosexuality. If homosexuality did exist within the Order, it is unlikely to have done so on a scale greater than in any other closed male community, military or monastic.

The trials commenced within six days of the initial arrests. At first, the prosecution of the Temple was undertaken by the king's legal officers. But Philippe also had a pope in his pocket, and quickly bullied his puppet into supporting him with all the august weight of papal authority. The persecution inaugurated by the French crown rapidly spread far beyond France, and was taken over by the Inquisition. It was to continue for seven years. What seems to us today a minor, generally obscure fragment of medieval history was to become the single most dominant issue of its time, dramatically eclipsing events in far-away Scotland, galvanising opinions and reactions across the Christian world, sending tremors throughout Western culture. The Temple, it must be remembered, was, with the sole exception of the Papacy, the most important, most powerful, most prestigious, most apparently unshakable institution of its age. At the time of Philippe's attack, it was nearly two centuries old and was regarded as one of the central pillars of Western Christendom. For most of its contemporaries, it seemed as immutable, as durable, as permanent as the Church herself. That such an edifice should be so summarily demolished rocked the foundation upon which rested the assumptions and beliefs of an epoch. Thus, for example, Dante, in *The Divine Comedy*, expresses his shock and his sympathy for the persecuted 'White Mantles'. Indeed, the superstition which holds Friday the 13th to be a day of misfortune is believed to stem from Philippe's initial raids on Friday, 13 October 1307.

The Order of the Temple was officially dissolved by Papal decree on 22 March 1312, without a definitive verdict of guilt or innocence ever being pronounced. In France, however, the knights were to be harried for another two years. Finally, in March 1314, Jacques de Molay, the Grand Master, and Geoffroi de Charnay, the Preceptor of Normandy, were roasted to death over a slow fire on the Île de la Cité in the Seine. A plaque on the site commemorates the event.

The Inquisition

The zeal with which Philippe harried the Templars is more than a little suspicious. One can understand his seeking to extirpate the Order within his own domains, but to go so far as to seek out every Templar in Christendom is surely a little obsessive. Did he fear the Order's vengeance? He can hardly have been motivated by moral fervour. Nor is it likely that a monarch who had contrived the death of at least one pope, and probably a second, would be fastidious about purity of faith. As for loyalty to the Church, the Church had effectively become his. He did not have to be loyal to it. He could define his own loyalty.

In any case, Philippe badgered his fellow monarchs to join him in his persecution of the Temple. In this endeavour, he met with only qualified success. In Lorraine, for example, which was part of Germany at the time, the Templars were supported by the reigning duke. A few were tried and quickly exonerated. Most appear to have obeyed their Preceptor, who reputedly instructed them to shave their beards, don secular garb and melt into the local populace – who, significantly enough, did not betray them.

In Germany proper, the Templars openly defied their would-be judges, appearing in court fully armed and manifestly prepared to defend themselves. Intimidated, the judges promptly pronounced them innocent, and when the Order was officially dissolved, many German Templars found a welcome in the Order of St John or in the Teutonic Order. In Spain, too, the Templars resisted their persecutors and found a haven in other Orders, especially Calatrava. And a new Order was created, Montesa, primarily as a refuge for fugitive Templars.

In Portugal, the Templars were cleared by an inquiry and simply modified their name, becoming the Knights of Christ. They survived under this title well into the sixteenth century, their maritime explorations leaving an indelible mark on history. (Vasco da Gama was a Knight of Christ; Prince Henry the Navigator was a Grand Master of the Order. Ships of the Knights of Christ sailed

55

under the Templars' familiar red *patté* cross. And it was under the same cross that Columbus's three caravels crossed the Atlantic to the New World. Columbus himself was married to the daughter of a former Grand Master of the Order, and had access to his father-in-law's charts and diaries.)

If Philippe found little support for harrying the Templars elsewhere on the Continent, he had reason to expect greater co-operation from England. Edward II, after all, was his son-in-law. But Edward was initially reluctant. Indeed, the English monarch makes it clear in his letters that he not only found the charges against the Templars incredible, but also doubted the integrity of those making them. Thus, on 4 December 1307, less than a month and a half after the first arrests, he wrote to the kings of Portugal, Castile, Aragon and Sicily:

> He [Philippe's envoy] dared to publish before us . . . certain horrible and detestable enormities repugnant to the Catholic faith, to the prejudice of the aforesaid brothers, endeavouring to persuade us [that we] ought to imprison all the brethren . . .[5]

And he concluded by requesting that the recipient:

> . . . turn a deaf ear to the slanders of ill-natured men, who are animated, as we believe, not with the zeal of rectitude, but with a spirit of cupidity and envy . . .[6]

Ten days later, however, Edward received from the Pope an official bull sanctioning and provisionally justifying the arrests. This obliged him to act, but still he did so with marked reluctance and a signal lack of fervour. On 20 December, he wrote to all sheriffs in England, instructing them three weeks later to take 'ten or twelve men they trusted' and arrest all members of the Temple in their domains. In the presence of at least one reliable witness, an inventory was to be made of all possessions found on Templar premises. And the Templars themselves were to be placed in custody, but not 'in hard and vile prison'.[7]

English Templars were held at the Tower of London, as well as at the castles of York, Lincoln and Canterbury. The action against them proceeded in a decidedly dilatory fashion. Thus, for example, the English Master, William de la More, was arrested on 9 January 1308, and lodged in Canterbury Castle, along with two other brethren and sufficient possessions to ensure him considerable comfort, if not luxury. On 27 May, he was released and, two months later, granted the income from six Templar estates for his support. Only in November, as a result of renewed pressure, was he

re-arrested and subjected to a harsher discipline. By then, however, most English Templars had had ample opportunity to escape,
by going to ground amid the civilian populace, by finding a refuge
in other orders or by fleeing the country.

In September 1309, the papal inquisitors arrived in England,
and such Templars as had been arrested were lodged for interrogation in London, York or Lincoln. During the course of the next
month, Edward, as if prompted by an afterthought, wrote to his
representatives in Ireland and Scotland, ordering that all Templars
not yet arrested were to be apprehended and placed in the castles
at Dublin and Edinburgh.[8] It is thus clear that a great many
Templars were still at large, and with the king's knowledge.

Between 20 October and 18 November 1309, some forty-seven
Templars were interrogated in London on the basis of a list of
eighty-seven charges. No confessions were elicited apart from the
acknowledgement that officers of the Order, like priests, claimed
the right to grant absolution from sin. Frustrated, the Inquisitors
decided to resort to torture. As travelling emissaries of the Pope,
they had, of course, no machinery or manpower of their own with
which to administer torture, and had to make formal application
to the secular authorities. They did this in the second week of
December. Edward granted them permission only for 'limited
torture', and this, too, failed to elicit confessions.

On 14 December 1309 — more than two years after the first
arrests in France and a year after the demand for more stringent
measures in England — Edward again wrote to his sheriffs. He had
heard, he said, that Templars were still 'wandering about in
secular habit, committing apostasy'.[9] Once again, however,
neither he nor his officers pursued the matter with any inordinate
vigour. On 12 March 1310, he wrote to the Sheriff of York: 'As
the king understands that he [the sheriff] permits the Templars . . .
to wander about in contempt of the king's order,'[10] they are to be
kept inside the castle. And yet on 4 January 1311, Edward once
more wrote to the Sheriff of York, noting that, despite all previous
orders, Templars were *still* allowed to wander about.[11] In the
mean time, while this desultory fuss was developing over Templars
already in captivity, nothing was done about the numerous
knights in England who had escaped arrest. More zealous efforts
on the part of the Inquisition led to the discovery and apprehen-
sion of only nine such fugitives. The Pope complained to the
Archbishop of Canterbury, and to other prominent prelates elsewhere, that a number of Templars had so completely integrated
themselves with the civilian populace as to marry — which they

could not have done without at least some co-operation from English authorities.

By this time, torture was already being applied to members of the Order in custody. In June, 1310, however, the Inquisition produced a document detailing their lack of success. They protested that they had had difficulty in getting torture applied correctly and effectively. It did not, they complained, appear native to English justice; and even though the king had reluctantly consented to it, the jailors had offered only tepid co-operation. A number of suggestions were made to render the trials more effective. Among these was a recommendation that the arrested Templars be transferred to France, where they could be 'properly' tortured by men with both the taste and the expertise for such pastimes.

On 6 August 1310, the Pope wrote a letter of protest castigating the English king for his refusal to allow sensible torture. At last, Edward capitulated and instructed that Templars in the Tower be taken to the Inquisitors for what was euphemistically called 'the application of ecclesiastical law'. Even this, however, seems to have been less than successful, for twice in October the king had to repeat his decree.

At last, in June 1311, the Inquisition in England made the breakthrough it had been seeking for so long. This breakthrough did not, significantly enough, result from further torture of Templars already in captivity, but from a fugitive Templar only recently apprehended in Salisbury, one Stephen de Stapelbrugge. Stephen became the first Templar in England to confess to heretical practices within the Order. During his induction, he reported, he was shown a crucifix and instructed to deny that 'Jesus was God and man and that Mary was his mother'.[12] He was then, he said, ordered to spit on the cross. Stephen also confessed to many of the other charges levelled against the Templars. The Order's 'errors', he declared, had originated around the Agen region in France.

This last assertion adds a measure of plausibility to Stephen's testimony. During the twelfth and thirteenth centuries, Agen had been one of the hotbeds of the Albigensian or Cathare heresy, and Cathares had survived in the vicinity at least as late as 1250. There is overwhelming evidence that the Templars had become 'infected', to use the clerical term, with Cathare thought, and even provided a haven for Cathares fleeing the Inquisition.[13] Indeed, one of the Order's most important and influential Grand Masters, Bertrand de Blanchefort, came from a long-established Cathare family. Moreover, Agen lay in the Templar province of Provence. Between 1248 and 1250, the Master of Provence was one Roncelin de Fos. Then, between 1251 and 1253, Roncelin was Master of England. By 1260, he was again Master of Provence, and presided in that capacity until 1278. It is thus quite possible that Roncelin brought aspects of heretical Cathare thought from their native soil in France to England. This suggestion is supported by the testimony before the Inquisition of Geoffroy de Gonneville, Preceptor of Aquitaine and Poitou. According to Geoffroy, unnamed individuals alleged that all evil and perverse rules and innovations in the Temple had been introduced by a certain Brother Roncelin, formerly a Master of the Order.[14] The Brother Roncelin in question is bound to have been Roncelin de Fos.

Perhaps a bit too conveniently, Stephen de Stapelbrugge's confession was quickly followed by two others which substantiated it, from Thomas Tocci de Thoroldeby and John de Stoke. According to Thomas, a former Master of England, Brian de Jay, had said that 'Christ was not the true God, but a mere man'. John de Stoke's testimony was particularly important, for he had previously been Treasurer of the Temple in London. As Treasurer, he would have been the highest ranking non-military officer of the Order in England; and as the London Temple was also a royal depository, he would have been personally known to both Edward I and Edward II. He was to be the most importantly placed Templar in England to confess to anything.

In his previous testimonies, John de Stoke had denied all accusations. Now, however, he declared that on a visit to Temple Garway in Herefordshire, the Grand Master Jacques de Molay had claimed Jesus to be 'the son of a certain woman, and since he said that he was the Son of God, he was crucified'.[15] According to John de Stoke, the Grand Master had instructed him, on that basis, to deny Jesus. The inquisitors asked him in whom or what he was supposed to believe. The Grand Master had enjoined him, John said, to believe in 'the great omnipotent God, who created heaven and earth, and not in the Crucifixion'.[16] This is not even Cathare: for the Cathares God the creator was evil. It could be construed as more or less orthodox Judaism or Islam; and certainly, during years of activity in the Holy Land, the Temple had absorbed a good deal of both Judaic and Islamic thought.

The Inquisition was quick to exploit the confessions of Stephen de Stapelbrugge, Thomas de Thoroldeby and John de Stoke. Within a few months, most of the Templars in captivity in England had made essentially similar admissions. On 3 July 1311, most of them reconciled themselves to the Church, either by confessing to certain specific crimes and abjuring them, or by admitting to a general formula of guilt and agreeing to do penance. The proceedings at this point amounted, in effect, to a kind of 'plea-bargaining', or even to an 'out-of-court settlement'. In return for their co-operation, English Templars were treated lightly. There were no wholesale burnings such as there were in France. Instead, the 'penitents' were consigned to monasteries to rehabilitate their souls. Reasonable funds were provided for their upkeep.

It is worth noting, however, that of the confessions obtained in England, most were from elderly and infirm knights. England, after all, was neither a front line for military activity nor, so far as the Order was concerned, a major political or commercial centre such as France. It therefore provided a kind of 'rest home'. Ageing or ill veterans of the Holy Land would be, so to speak, 'pensioned off' to preceptories in England as sinecures.[17] At the time of their trial, a number of them were too feeble to move very far from where they had been incarcerated. 'They were so old and infirm that they were unable to stand,'[18] reports one notary who recorded the proceedings. These were the men whom Edward's officers arrested when the king finally bowed to the pressure imposed upon him. By that time, as we have noted, younger and more active Templars would have had ample time to escape. And their number, as we shall see, would have been swollen by refugees from elsewhere.

Escape from Persecution

Medieval man did not share our passion for, or precision in, statistics. When chroniclers of the time speak of armies, for example, rough estimates are bandied about, more often than not exaggerated for propaganda purposes. Numerals denoting thousands or even tens of thousands are invoked quite routinely and often quite implausibly, with an often exasperating disregard for accuracy and even credibility. In consequence, there is no reliable or definitive compilation of the Templars' numerical strength at any given point in their history. Nor, for that matter, has any complete list survived (assuming one ever existed outside the Order's own archives) of Templar holdings, in Britain or anywhere else. As we have already noted, official documents and rolls often omit a number of installations – preceptories, manors, estates, houses, farms and other property – that are known from other sources to have been Templar. Thus, for example, the Order's major installations at Bristol and Berwick, both of which almost certainly included wharves and port facilities, do not appear on any official list.

According to medieval accounts, the Temple, at the time of its suppression, numbered many thousands of personnel across Europe. Some reports run as high as twenty thousand, although of these it is doubtful that more than a small percentage were full-fledged mounted knights. At the same time, it was established procedure in the Middle Ages for every knight to be attended by an entourage – an equerry or squire and, in battle, at least three foot-sergeants or men-at-arms; and French records indicate that this policy obtained in the Temple as well. Much of the Order's strength, therefore, would have consisted of fighting men who were not knights.

But the Temple, as might be expected of such an institution, also relied on an immense support staff – bureaucrats, administrators, clerks, a substantial number of chaplains, servants, villeins, artisans, craftsmen, masons – and it is rarely clear how many of these are included in such official records as survive. There are other areas, too, in which no documentation whatever exists, and in which even rough estimates are impossible. It is known, for example, that the Templars possessed a considerable fleet – merchant as well as naval vessels – which operated not only in the Mediterranean, but in the Atlantic as well. Medieval accounts contain numerous passing references to Templar ports, Templar ships, Templar naval resources. There are even documents bearing signatures and seals of Templar naval officers. And yet no detailed information, of any kind, has survived of Templar maritime activity. There is no record anywhere of the fleet's strength, or of what happened to it after the Order was suppressed. Similarly, a late twelfth-century account in England speaks of a woman being received into the Temple as a Sister, and seems quite clearly to imply some sort of feminine wing or adjunct to the Order. But no elaboration or clarification of the matter has ever been found. Even such information as might have been contained in official Inquisition records has long since disappeared or been suppressed.

An exhaustive consideration of both English and Inquisition documents, and a detailed study of the work of other historians, leads us to conclude that in 1307, Templar strength in England numbered some 265 men. Of these, up to twenty-nine would have been full-fledged knights, up to seventy-seven sergeants, and thirty-one would have been chaplains. If the chaplains and other support staff are omitted, the number of fighting Templars comes to at least thirty-two, and possibly as many as 106. Only ten of these were definitely arrested and listed by the Inquisition, though another three Templars in captivity were also probably military men. This leaves something approaching ninety-three military Templars at large – men who escaped completely the clutches of the Inquisition and were never found.[19] That figure does not include fighting men of the Order who escaped persecution in Scotland and Ireland.

The population of Europe in the Middle Ages was a fraction of what it is today, and although such numbers, by modern standards, would appear to be small, in the context of the time they would have been proportionately higher. It must be remembered, moreover, that the effectiveness of medieval armies, even more perhaps than in later times, was determined not by numerical superiority, but by training. At Omdurman in the Sudan in 1898, 23,000 British and Egyptian troops defeated more than 50,000 dervishes, inflicting some 15,000 casualties while losing fewer than 500 themselves. In the action dramatised in the film *Zulu*, 139 British soldiers at Rorke's Drift in 1879 held at bay some 4000 Zulus, inflicting 400 casualties while suffering twenty-five. At the Siege of Malta in 1565, fewer than a thousand Knights of St John, together with their auxiliaries, repelled a Turkish force of 30,000 and inflicted 20,000 casualties. Statistics could be equally lopsided during the Middle Ages, with weight of horses, weight of armour, rigour of discipline and sophistication of tactics proving as decisive as firepower was to be later. In the Holy Land during the Crusades, a force of a dozen fully armoured mounted knights, charging on heavy horses, would function like twentieth-century tanks, easily scattering a force of two or three hundred Saracens. A massed charge of a hundred or so mounted knights could crush two or three thousand adversaries.

In consequence, the prospect of perhaps as many as ninety-three trained Templars at large in Britain was not to be dismissed. With their professional discipline, their up-to-date weaponry and their martial expertise, they could easily have proved decisive against the amateur soldiery and conscripted peasants involved in most European campaigns.

Just such a campaign was then being conducted in Scotland.

4

The Disappearance of the Templar Fleet

Edward II was at first loath to act at all against the Templars in his domains. When external pressures – pressures exerted by Philippe of France, by the Inquisition and by the Pope – at last compelled him to act, he acted sluggishly. The comparative apathy with which the Templars were persecuted in England prevailed in Scotland and Ireland as well.

In Ireland, the Templars owned at least sixteen properties, of which a minimum of six were full preceptories. They are also known to have owned at least four castles and probably another seven. By our estimates, to administer and garrison such holdings would have necessitated a minimum presence of at least ninety men, of whom some thirty-six would have been militarily active.

On 3 February 1308 – nearly four months after the first arrests in France and a month and a half after the first in England – arrests began in Ireland. Altogether, some thirty members of the Order were apprehended and taken to Dublin – approximately one-third of the total strength. There does not appear to have been any particular brutality in Ireland. Certainly there were no burnings, no executions. The Master of Ireland was released on bail, and his subordinates are believed to have been treated with comparable leniency. There are no records of any Irish Templars having been sent to monasteries to do penance. In Ireland, then, by 1314, virtually the full strength of the Order would have been at large, some having escaped the initial arrests, some having been released after interrogation.

Given the prolonged delay before action was taken against them, the Irish Templars would have had ample time and opportunity to make provisions. They clearly seem to have done so. When their lands were seized and their possessions inventoried, virtually no weapons were found. According to one historian, it is 'extremely surprising to find the abodes of a military order so poorly equipped with arms'.[1] In the main house, at Clontarf, there were only three swords. At Kilclogan, there were only two lances, an iron helm and a bow. And yet, with Edward II complaining at this time about Irish arms finding their way to Scotland, there was certainly no shortage of equipment in the country. It would thus seem evident that most Irish Templars not only escaped arrest, but did so with the bulk of their weaponry and equipment.

Templar Refugees

On 6 October 1309 – a full two years after the first arrests in France – Edward ordered his officers to 'arrest all the Templars in Scotland who are still at large, and keep them in safe custody'.[2] In fact, only two were ever arrested, although one of them was the Master of Scotland, Walter de Clifton. But by 1309, Edward was in no position to enforce his decrees in Scotland, most of the country then being in Bruce's hands. In March of that year, Bruce had been declared ruler 'by right of blood' and with the 'consent of the said people he was chosen to be king'. At the time of Edward's decree, he was fighting in Argyll. By the end of the year, he would have two-thirds of Scotland under his control, and the English garrisons at Perth, Dundee and Banff would have to be supplied by sea.

Embroiled in his own guerrilla war against Edward, Bruce was hardly going to honour the English king's edicts. Nor, having been excommunicated, was he going to honour the Pope's – which, as we have seen, would not have been applicable in Scotland anyway. In the circumstances, Bruce would only have welcomed an influx of fugitives who were also professional fighting men. And they would have been only too ready to respond by aligning themselves with his cause.

There is no record of what befell the two Templars arrested in Scotland. Probably they were set free. Under interrogation, however, they testified that a number of their colleagues, including the Preceptor of Balantrodoch, 'threw off their habits' and fled 'across the sea'.[3] On the other hand, the trial of the Templars in Scotland was conducted by none other than Bishop Lamberton of St Andrews. Lamberton, as we have seen, was dextrously playing a complex double game, but his primary allegiances lay with Bruce. He was perfectly capable of acting as a recruiting officer for the person he recognised as his country's rightful king. Fugitive Templars may indeed have escaped by sea, but they could just as readily have sailed up and around Scotland to join Bruce's army in Argyll. Nor need they necessarily have fled by sea at all.

It need not have been just Templars from Scotland who swelled Bruce's ranks. There were also, as we have seen, a sizeable number of knights at large in England who had escaped arrest. They had to go somewhere. It is certainly reasonable to suppose that at least some of them found their way to Scotland — and reasonable to suppose that some of the Irish brethren did so as well. Indeed, one English Templar, at his interrogation, declared explicitly that his colleagues had fled to Scotland. The question, really, is not whether English Templars sought a haven in the north, but how many of them did so.

Whatever the number, which could have been as high as ninety-three, it was in all probability augmented by fugitives from France and elsewhere on the Continent. As we have seen, the Templars in France had sufficient advance warning of the attack upon them to make at least some provisions. Thus the treasure of the Paris preceptory disappeared, as did a number of the Order's high-ranking French dignitaries, who supposedly sailed away on eighteen ships. That the Grand Master and other officials remained does not mean they were unprepared or caught off guard. It merely suggests that they had, until the last moment, every hope of averting the fate that eventually overtook them — every hope, that is, of defending the Order against the accusations levelled against it and of restoring it to the status it had previously enjoyed.

It must be remembered that while Philippe's initial onslaught against the Templars in France was swift and sudden, the process that followed was prolonged. There were to be five years of legal wrangling, negotiation, intrigue, horse-trading and general dithering before the Order was officially dissolved, and seven years before Jacques de Molay was executed. During the whole of this time, large numbers of Templars remained free, wandering about Europe. They had abundant opportunity to make plans, co-ordinate their efforts, organise escape routes and find a refuge.

According to extant charters, there were, at the minimum, 556 full Templar preceptories in France and countless smaller holdings as well. The Order's numerical strength in the country was at least 3200, of whom an estimated 350 were knights and 930 sergeants — a total of 1280 fighting men. During the legal proceedings in France, Inquisition records reveal 620 Templars to have been arrested; if the same percentages apply, about 250 would have been fighting men. This leaves a minimum of 1030 active military members of the Order still at large – Templars who were never arrested, never caught, never found.

A fair number, of course, would have remained in France. Although the account is almost certainly exaggerated, the hills around Lyons were at one point alleged to conceal more than 1500 refugee Templars – a sobering prospect for both the Inquisitors and the French king. But if many Templars remained in France, a sizeable number would have sought refuge abroad. Shortly after the initial arrests, for example, Imbert Blanke, Master of Auvergne, is known to have come to England, apparently to advise English brethren on how to conduct themselves during the impending legal proceedings. Eventually, Imbert was imprisoned in England, but under considerably more relaxed conditions than those his colleagues endured in France. In April 1313, he was sent from the Tower of London to the Archbishop of Canterbury for penance. A month later, he was granted a pension for his support by Edward II. There must have been many Templars who, like Imbert, came to England, but were never detained at all. Some would have come directly across the Channel. A number, in all likelihood, would have come through Flanders, which remained sympathetic to them and maintained constant maritime traffic with the British Isles. As England, during the next seven years, became increasingly unsuitable as a refuge, the fugitives from the Continent, together with their English and Irish brethren, would have gravitated northwards – where, beyond the reach of both Papacy and Inquisition, they could expect immunity.

The Templar Fleet and its Escape Routes

Any mass exodus of knights, especially if it included the Order's treasure as well, would almost certainly have involved the Templar fleet – that fleet which vanished so mysteriously, and about which so little is known. Indeed, the Templar fleet may hold the answers to many of the questions surrounding the last days of the Order. It may also point to a possible Templar presence in Argyll. This is virtually unexplored territory.

By the mid-thirteenth century, the Temple's fleet had become not just a necessity, but a major asset. For the Templars, as for their kindred Order, the Knights of St John, it was much cheaper to transport men, horses and matériel to the Holy Land by their own ships than to hire vessels from local merchants. Moreover, the fleet

7 Kilmory, undated gravestone. Above the warrior's head is a masonic set square. Below is a Templar-style cross forming part of the carved pattern.

8 *above left* The Templar tower, church and preceptory buildings of Garway, Herefordshire, near the Welsh border. It was passed to the Order of St John in the early fourteenth century.

9 *left* Templar Cross, Garway. Originally it stood on a plinth outside the church.

10 *above right* Anonymous Templar gravestone bearing a sword found at Garway. It was used as a lintel during the rebuilding of the church in the early fourteenth century.

11 *right* Garway, figure of the Celtic vegetation god, 'The Green Man', inside the church.

12 *left* Garway, showing the foundations of the original circular Templar church, demolished by the Order of St John, which built a conventional rectangular structure in its place.

13 *below* Bristol, Temple Church, showing the foundations of a circular church of the Templars which was also demolished by the Order of St John in the fourteenth century and was rebuilt in more conventional style.

could be used to transport other personnel and equipment, as well as pilgrims, and this proved a lucrative source of revenue. At one point, the Templars were carrying 6000 pilgrims a year to Palestine from their ports in Spain, France and Italy. Their ships were generally preferred to others because they travelled with an escort of armed galleys. Then, too, the Order 'could be trusted not to sell their passengers into slavery at Moslem ports, as did certain merchants'.[4] And being exempt from customs dues, the Temple's ships also trafficked extensively in such commodities as fabrics, spices, dyes, porcelain and glass. As we have seen, the Templars were licensed to export their own wool.

So active was Templar trade that the civilian shipowners of Marseilles, as early as 1234, sought to ban the Order from their port. From this date on, both the Templars and the Hospitallers were restricted to one ship each, which could make only two voyages a year; they could carry as much cargo as they could hold, but no more than 1500 passengers. Such measures, however, did not curb the maritime activities of either Order. Both simply availed themselves of other ports.

On the whole, the Templar fleet was geared towards operations in the Mediterranean – keeping the Holy Land supplied with men and equipment, and importing commodities from the Middle East into Europe. At the same time, however, the fleet did operate in the Atlantic. Extensive trade was conducted with the British Isles and, very probably, with the Baltic cities of the Hanseatic League. Thus Templar preceptories in Europe, especially in England and Ireland, were generally located on the coast or on navigable rivers. The primary Atlantic seaport for the Templars was La Rochelle, which also had good overland communication with Mediterranean ports. Cloth, for example, could be brought from Britain on Templar ships to La Rochelle, transported overland to a Mediterranean port such as Collioure, then loaded aboard Templar ships again and carried to the Holy Land. By this means, it was possible to avoid the always risky passage through the Straits of Gibraltar, usually controlled by the Saracens.

The personnel of the Paris Temple who eluded Philippe's grasp are unlikely to have escaped by land, for the king's men had the region around Paris fairly well patrolled. (Two Templars who did try to flee northwards were captured at Chaumont, on the upper Marne, just as they were about to leave French territory.) An overland journey all the way to the coast at La Rochelle would have been inordinately difficult, if not impossible. But while the primary Templar port may have been La Rochelle, the Order is known to have maintained a fleet of smaller ships on the Seine, and there were, in fact, a number of Templar houses and preceptories ranged along the river, from Paris to the coast – at least twelve, including one at Rouen and one near the present site of Le Havre. Moreover, the Templars were exempt from tolls and their ships were not subject to search. In the months immediately prior to the first arrests, therefore, both personnel and treasure could easily have been transported down the Seine to the coast. Here, both men and cargo would have been transferred to larger ships sailing up from La Rochelle or any other port. Even after the arrests and persecution had begun, the chief escape routes for fleeing Templars were more likely to have been by river and sea than overland.

But where, having put out from French coastal ports, would the Templar fleet have gone? It must be remembered that no records of any kind survive – and this in itself is indicative, constituting an important clue in its own right. If Philippe had caught, captured or impounded Templar ships, there would certainly be some record. Even if official documentation was censored or suppressed, public knowledge would have been widespread. Such a move could not possibly have been kept secret.

Similarly in Spain and Portugal, a Templar landing could not have passed unnoticed. Granted, Templars sailing from France would have been welcomed by their Spanish and Portuguese brethren. They could have expected a cordial reception in such places as Majorca, where the Order owned the town and port of Pollensa, as well as much other territory, and where the king, Jaime II, was friendly to them. But the seaports of Spain and Portugal were major urban and commercial centres at the time, with a thriving business life and a large civilian population. Amidst the sensation caused by the initial arrests in France, it defies credibility that Templar ships could have put in to some such town as, say, Palma, and left no trace whatever on the historical record. And the Templars themselves, of course, could not afford to attract such attention.

There would, in effect, have been only three possible destinations for the Templar fleet. One, sometimes suggested by historians, would have been somewhere in the Islamic world – either in the Mediterranean or on the Atlantic coast of North Africa. But circumstances argue against this. In the first place, the Templars, in 1307, still hoped to prove themselves innocent of the charges levelled against them. To seek refuge among the 'infidels' would have been tantamount to admitting the accusations of heresy and disloyalty. Moreover, it is again unlikely, if the Templar fleet found a haven under Islam, that Muslim commentators would have left no record. It would, after all, have been a major propaganda coup. Indeed, when small enclaves of Templars in Spain and Egypt did seek refuge there and converted, at least nominally, to Islam, Muslim writers made considerable capital on it. They would hardly have remained silent had the Templar fleet, as well perhaps as the Order's treasure, passed into their camp.

It is sometimes suggested that the Templar fleet might have sought safety in Scandinavia. As we have noted, the two Templars interrogated in Scotland claimed that their brethren escaped by sea, and this has led some historians to assume they went to Denmark, Sweden or, most likely, Norway. Such a possibility cannot be altogether discounted, but it is highly improbable. Scandinavia's population was minuscule at the time, and it would have been difficult to escape notice in any inhabited area. The Templars had no preceptories there, no base from which to operate, no ties, commercial or political, with either people or governments. And after the Order was officially dissolved in 1310, they would have been as liable to arrest and persecution in Scandinavia as elsewhere. Again, too, one would expect there to be some record.

Nevertheless, the fastnesses of the Norse wilderness – no worse, after all, than the regions 'colonised' by the Teutonic Knights – would have provided a refuge of sorts. It might even have appeared attractive if there had been no alternative. But there was an alternative. There was Scotland, a country with whom the Templars already maintained cordial relations, a country whose acknowledged king had been excommunicated, and, what's more, a country crying out for allies, especially trained fighting men. Had the knights sought to devise or contrive an ideal refuge of their own, they could not possibly have done better than Scotland.

Edward's fleet, based on the east coast of England, effectively blocked the established trade routes between Flanders and Scottish ports such as Aberdeen and Inverness. Templar ships, moving northwards from La Rochelle or from the mouth of the Seine, could not have risked negotiating the Channel and the North Sea. Neither could they have proceeded through the Irish Sea, which was also effectively blocked by English naval vessels based at Ayr and at Carrickfergus in Belfast Lough. But one important route was open – from the north coast of Ireland, including the mouth of the Foyle at Londonderry, to Bruce's domains in Argyll, Kintyre and the Sound of Jura. Bruce's close friend and ally, Angus Og MacDonald of Islay, held Islay, Jura and Colonsay, which secured a direct route between north-western Ulster and south-western Scotland. This was the route which for some time had been supplying Bruce with arms and equipment.

If large contingents of Templars from the Continent, and/or parts of the Templar fleet itself, found refuge in Scotland, they can only have done so by this route – from Donegal, from the Foyle, from the north-west coast of Ulster to the Sound of Jura and its environs. But how could a Templar fleet obtain access to this route without negotiating the Irish Sea and risking interception by English ships?

We tend today to think of Ireland as one of the British Isles, whose primary centre is Dublin and whose main ports, except for one or two in the south, are on the east coast, facing the Irish Sea and the British 'mainland'. This, certainly, has been the case since the seventeenth century, but it was not so in the Middle Ages and before. In Bruce's time, Ireland's primary commerce was not with England, but with the Continent. In consequence, Dublin and other such eastern ports were insignificant compared to the major southern harbours in the counties of Wexford, Waterford and Cork. More important still, the west of Ireland, now seen as a remote, denuded and depopulated hinterland, contained at least two ports of genuinely major proportions – Limerick and, most crucial of all, Galway. Limerick and Galway were thriving cities during the Middle Ages, maintaining a booming trade not only with France, but with Spain and North Africa as well. Indeed, some old maps depict Ireland as lying closer to Spain than to England. The trade routes running to Galway from Spain, and from such French coastal centres as Bordeaux and La Rochelle, were as busy and well established as any of the period. From Galway, the route continued northwards, around the coast of Donegal, past the mouth of the Foyle and what today is Londonderry, to the west coast of Scotland. This, almost certainly, would have been the route taken by any escaping Templar ships. It was a safe, convenient and familiar route, and the English fleet had no way of cutting it.

As we have noted, modern sites in the British Isles bearing the prefix 'Temple' are recognised by historians as having formerly been Templar property. As we have also noted, the Templars, given their considerable maritime and commercial activity, tended to build their major installations on the coast or on navigable rivers. Thus, for example, Maryculter in Scotland was on the Dee, Balantrodoch and Temple Liston were on the Firth of Forth. In England, Temple Thornton was on the Tyne, Westerdale on the Esk, Faxfleet on the Humber, and there were extensive port facilities at London, Dover and Bristol. Irish records are decidedly more sketchy, many of them undoubtedly having been lost or destroyed in the upheavals of the ensuing centuries; and in the west of Ireland, where much of the population spoke Gaelic until the twentieth century, the kind of documentation found elsewhere may never have been compiled. Such records as do exist for Ireland display a pattern similar to the kind prevailing elsewhere in the British Isles, with Templar preceptories and installations being sited on the coast or on navigable rivers. But these records show the concentration of Templar holdings to have been along the east coast, from Ulster, to the main base of Clontarf at Dublin, down through Kilcloggan and Templebryan, to Cork. The primary known exception is Limerick, where the Order also had substantial holdings.

What of the west? Nothing is ever said about it, because no one appears to know anything about it. We, however, discovered no fewer than seven additional sites on the north-west coast of Ireland which are not mentioned in any charter, but which, on the basis of all available evidence, do appear to have been Templar. In modern-day Donegal, there is Templecrone near the Isle of Aran and Templecavan on the Malin peninsula. There is Templemoyle near Greencastle on the Foyle. Slightly inland from Donegal Bay are Templehouse, Templerushin and Templecarne. Further inland still, there is Templedouglas. And there may have been an installation of the Order at Lifford, in what today is County Tyrone, just north of Strabane. None of these sites appears to have had any particular religious significance, either Christian or pre-Christian, which might explain the 'Temple' prefix. At most of them, there are ruined chapels of medieval date. Everything indicates that they, too, were formerly Templar holdings. They would not have appeared in the records because they were so isolated from what were then (and in some cases still are) major population centres. Indeed, the ecclesiastical and secular authorities of the time – the Pope in Avignon, Philippe in Paris and Edward in London – may not even have known of their existence. And yet they would have conformed to the established Templar pattern of building: they would have provided valuable ports of call; and they would have guarded the trade routes.

From all this, it would appear that the Templar fleet, escaping the clutches of the French king, would most likely have made its way up the west and round the north coast of Ireland. Very possibly, it made a number of landfalls en route to pick up arms, equipment and perhaps other fugitive brethren. Once having reached the vicinity of the Foyle, the refugees would have been safe in territory held by Bruce's allies. And from the Foyle and the coast of western Ulster, there would have been a direct connection with the established route whereby arms were smuggled to Argyll under the

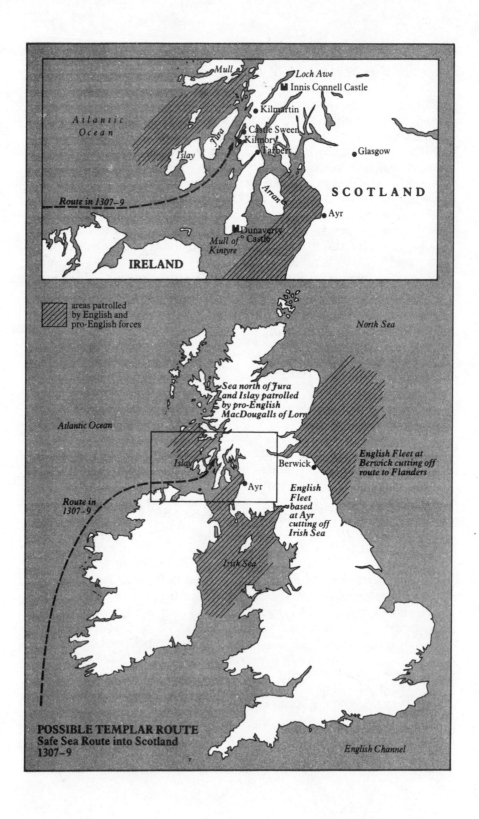

Mull

Loch Awe

■ Innis Connell Castle

● Kilmartin

Castle Sween
Kilmory
Tarbert

Islay

Jura

*Atlantic
Ocean*

Arran

SCOTLAND

● Glasgow

● Ayr

■ Dunaverty
Castle

*Mull of
Kintyre*

Route in 1307–9

IRELAND

areas patrolled
by English and
pro-English forces

North Sea

*Sea north of Jura
and Islay patrolled
by pro-English
MacDougalls of Lorn*

Atlantic Ocean

Islay

Berwick ●

*English Fleet at
Berwick cutting off
route to Flanders*

● Ayr

*English
Fleet
based
at Ayr
cutting off
Irish Sea*

*Route in
1307–9*

Irish Sea

POSSIBLE TEMPLAR ROUTE
Safe Sea Route into Scotland
1307–9

English Channel

auspices and protection of Angus Óg MacDonald. Thus Templar ships, Templar arms and matériel, Templar fighting men and, just possibly, the Templar treasure would have found their way to Scotland, providing vital reinforcements and resources for Bruce's cause.

Legends of Templar Survival

Writing in the mid-nineteenth century, one historian of the Templars states, perhaps a trifle more definitively than can be justified:

Many [Templars], however, were still at large, having success-fully evaded capture by obliterating all marks of their previous profession, and some had escaped in disguise to the wild and mountainous parts of Wales, Scotland and Ireland.[5]

At the end of the century, another historian writes:

The Templars . . . perhaps found a refuge in the little army of the excommunicated King Robert, whose fear of offending the French monarch would doubtless be vanquished by his desire to secure a few capable men-at-arms as recruits.[6]

And a modern historian, writing in 1972, is even more precise:

All but two Scottish brethren escaped; shrewd politicians, they may well have found refuge with the Bruce's guerrillas – certainly King Robert never legally ratified the Scottish Temple's dissolu-tion.[7]

Masonic historians, and Masonically oriented writers, are more explicit still, and more precise in their claims. Thus:

. . . we are told . . . that having deserted the Temple, they ranged themselves under the banners of Robert Bruce, and fought with him at Bannockburn . . . Legend states that after the decisive battle of Bannockburn . . . Bruce, in return for their eminent services, formed these Templars into a new body.[8]

And again:

In 1309 when persecutions began, an inquisition was held at Holyrood, only two knights appeared, the others were legitim-ately occupied in the fighting, having joined Bruce's army, which was marching against the English.[9]

Whether such statements as the latter two, issuing as they do from Masonic sources, are drawing on verifiable information as well as legend is uncertain. In any case, there is no question that legends of a Templar survival in Scotland abound. In fact, there are at least two distinct bodies of legend.

One of these was first promulgated, or at least first broke the surface of history, through the activities of an important eighteenth-century Freemason, Baron Karl von Hund, and the Masonic rite deriving from him – a rite known as the Strict Observance, which purported to be a 'restoration' of the Order of the Temple. According to the Strict Observance, Pierre d'Aumont, Preceptor of Auvergne, together with seven knights and two other preceptors, fled France around 1310, escaping first to Ireland and then, two years later, to Scotland – more specifically, to the island of Mull. On Mull, they are said to have joined forces with a number of other Templars, presumably refugees from England and Scotland, led by a preceptor whose name is cited as George Harris, formerly an officer of the Order at Caburn and Hampton Court; and under the joint auspices of Harris and Pierre d'Aumont, a resolution was made to perpetuate the institution. A list of Templar Grand Masters which Baron von Hund produced shows Pierre d'Aumont succeeding Jacques de Molay.[10]

In Part III of this book, we will examine in detail the plausibility of these assertions, as well as the specific historical context from which they arose and in which they must be placed. We will assess Hund's own credibility and that of the sources from which he claimed to have obtained his information. For the moment, it will be sufficient simply to comment on some of the details in the Strict Observance account.

In certain respects, at any rate, the details are not just unreliable, but demonstrably wrong. For example, the Strict Observance declares Pierre d'Aumont to have been Preceptor of Auvergne. In fact, however, the Preceptor of Auvergne was not Pierre d'Aumont, but Imbert Blanke, who, as we have seen, fled to England in 1306 and got himself arrested. Moreover, it is most improbable that refugee Templars could have found a haven on the island of Mull. Mull, at the time, was owned and occupied by Alexander McDougall of Lorn, one of Edward II's allies and Bruce's fiercest adversaries. Even after Bruce defeated him, he would have had numerous sympathisers on Mull, who would not have been reticent about clandestine Templar activity on the island.

On the other hand, there *were* two sites owned by Bruce's allies where fugitive Templars could indeed have found a refuge, or, at any rate, a safe way-station on their travels. One of these provided a brief refuge for Bruce himself during adverse phases of his campaigns and contained a strongly garrisoned castle which remained unswervingly loyal to him. And both sites were strategically situated on the crucial maritime route between Ulster and Bruce's supply bases in Argyll. These sites were the Mull of Kintyre and the Mull of Oa.

The Strict Observance account may thus be erroneous in some of its particulars, but it is easy to see how such misconceptions could have occurred. On his own admission, Hund heard his account from Scottish informants. Details could well have been garbled in the course of some four and a half centuries. They would almost certainly have been garbled further by transmission and translation. If a modern Englishman can confuse the island of Mull with the Mull of Kintyre or the Mull of Oa, such confusion is all the more understandable on the part of an eighteenth-century German nobleman, knowing nothing of Scottish geography and confronted by a welter of data not even in his own tongue. While the Strict Observance account, therefore, may indeed be mistaken in particulars, its general tenor is eminently plausible. One especially telling detail is the assertion that the fugitive Templars went first to Ireland. This, as we have seen, rings emphatically true; and there would have been no need to include it in a fabricated story.

The second legend of Templar survival first appeared in France around 1804, more than half a century after Hund. Under the Napoleonic regime, an individual named Bernard-Raymond Fabré-Palaprat produced a charter purporting to date from 1324, ten years after the execution of Jacques de Molay. If this charter is to be believed, Jacques, shortly before his death, left instructions for the perpetuation of the Order. To succeed him as Grand Master, he supposedly nominated one of the Templars left behind on Cyprus, a Palestinian-born Christian named John Mark Larmenius. On the basis of the so-called 'Larmenius Charter', Fabré-Palaprat created (or made public) a non-Masonic, neo-chivalric institution, the Ancient and Sovereign Military Order of the Temple of Jerusalem, which is still in existence today. According to unconfirmed statements by its present members, the 'Larmenius Charter', though first made public in 1804, was already in circulation a century before, in 1705, and Fabré-Palaprat's Order is said to date its reconstitution from then.[11]

We ourselves cannot confirm or refute the veracity of the 'Larmenius Charter'. For our purposes, it is of interest primarily because of one statement it contains: 'I, lastly . . . will say and order that the Scot-Templars deserters of the Order, be blasted by an anathema.'[12] This single fulmination is interesting, indeed provocative, and perhaps revealing. If the 'Larmenius Charter' is authentic, and does in fact date from the fourteenth century, the fulmination would seem to confirm the survival of Templar fugitives in Scotland. It suggests further that these fugitives adopted a position opposed to Larmenius and his entourage, who, one gathers, sought exoneration from all charges and some species of reconciliation with the Church. But if, as is more likely, the 'Larmenius Charter' dates from later – from the eighteenth or nineteenth century – it suggests some violent antipathy to the assertions promulgated by Hund and Strict Observance Freemasonry. Or to some other known Templar institution surviving in Scotland at that time.

 Whatever the validity of the legends, there is, as we have seen, no question that at least *some* Templars found their way to Scotland, while others, already in the country, were never caught. The only real question is how many remained at large. Ultimately, however, even the precise numbers do not matter. The point is that the Templars, however numerous or few they might have been, were trained fighting men – the best fighting men of their age, the acknowledged masters of warfare. Scotland was a kingdom desperately struggling for her independence, for the survival of her national and cultural identity. What was more, she lay under Papal interdict and her king was excommunicate. In such circumstances, Bruce would obviously have welcomed whatever help he could get; and such help as the Templars could offer would have been more than welcome. As seasoned veterans, they would have been invaluable in training the Scottish soldiery, in inculcating discipline, in imparting professionalism to men pitted against a numerically superior and better equipped foe. Their expertise in broader strategy and logistics would have been vital. Whether they actually comprised the 'fresh force' that intervened so decisively at Bannockburn will probably never be known. But they need not actually have comprised it. A handful of them would have been sufficient to lead it, and it would still have produced the effect it did on the English army.

5

Celtic Scotland and the Grail Legends

If, in the years following Bannockburn, an enclave of Templars did indeed settle in Argyll and intermarry with the clan system, the region would have constituted a natural habitat for them, and a most congenial one. In certain respects, it might almost have represented something akin to a homecoming. The Templars were, of course, 'a legend in their own lifetime'. In Scotland, however, and particularly in Argyll, there were other legendary antecedents with which the Order, in the eyes of the populace, would have been identified. In effect, Argyll offered a context of legend into which the Templars would have been effortlessly incorporated.

Towards the end of the twelfth century, the first of the so-called Grail Romances appeared in Western Europe. By the beginning of the fourteenth century – by the time of Bruce, that is, and the suppression of the Temple – the Grail Romances as a genre were still much in vogue, and had spawned an immense corpus of collateral literature. The concept of chivalry, as expounded by such works, was then approaching its zenith. Christian rulers self-consciously aspired to the lofty models of Parsifal, Gawain, Lancelot and Galahad – or, at least, sought to purvey such images of themselves to their people. Thus, for example, Edward I endeavoured to portray himself as a latterday Arthur, even to the point of holding 'Round Table' jousts. Thus, on the day before Bannockburn, while the two armies aligned themselves for battle, Bruce and the English knight Henry de Bohun met in single combat – the kind of personalised duel to the death so celebrated in chivalric romance.

The Grail Romances, although condemned by ecclesiastical authorities elsewhere in Europe, enjoyed a particular currency in Scotland. Bruce, it must be remembered, was seeking to re-establish in Scotland a Celtic kingdom whose traditions extended back through David I to the Dalriada. And the Grail Romances contained an important Celtic element, a corpus of Celtic lore and legend not to be found in later literature issuing from Norman England or from the Continent.

In the form that we know them today, the Grail Romances are a peculiarly hybrid genre reflecting a complicated process of cross-fertilisation. As we have discussed in a previous work,[1] they contain an important corpus of Judaeo-Christian material concealed or disguised in elaborate dramatic form. But this material has been grafted on to a body of legend and saga which is uniquely Celtic. Long before the Grail itself appeared in literature, with its specifically Christian import, there were Celtic poems and narratives chronicling a chivalric quest for a mysterious sacred object endowed with magical properties, a remote castle with a crippled or impotent king, an infertile wasteland suffering from the same blight as its ruler. Thus, some recent scholars carefully distinguish between the 'Christian Grail' of the later, better-known romances and the 'pagan Grail' of their precursors. And indeed, it was the confusion of the miraculous cauldron in the earlier works with the more nebulous 'Grail' of the later ones that led to the definition of the Grail as a cup, bowl, chalice or vessel – rather than to the *sang réal*, the blood royal, to which it in fact referred.

On to the foundations of the earlier Celtic sagas, then – the sagas of cauldron and wasteland and castle perilous – a Judaeo-Christian superstructure was added to produce what are now called the Grail Romances. And this Judaeo-Christian superstructure, significantly enough, is repeatedly associated with the Templars. Thus, for example, in *Parzival*, perhaps the single greatest and most important of all the Grail stories, Wolfram von Eschenbach portrays the Templars as 'guardians of the Grail' and of 'the Grail family'. Wolfram also claims to have heard the Grail story from a certain 'Kyot de Provence', who can be identified as Guiot de Provins, a Templar scribe and propagandist.[2] More telling still is the fact that the Grail Romance known as *The Perlesvaus*, second only to Wolfram's version in significance, contains unmistakable allusions to the Order – not only in its depiction of knights in white mantles emblazoned with red crosses presiding over a sacred secret, but also in the very tenor of its thought and values. *The Perlesvaus* abounds with a meticulous, detailed and accurate knowledge of weapons and armour, of techniques of fighting and characteristics of wounds. It is obviously the work not of a troubadour or romancier, but of a fighting man. And so pervasive is the Templar influence in it that the anonymous author is widely believed to have been himself a Templar. In such works as Wolfram's *Parzival* and *The Perlesvaus*, the reader is confronted with a syncretic accretion of two diverse traditions – one Judaeo-Christian, one Celtic. And the 'adhesive', so to speak, the metaphorical framework holding these two components together, is implicitly or explicitly Templar.

By Bruce's time, Celtic tradition, Grail mystique and Templar values had fused into a single, often confusing, amalgam. Thus, for example, there is the well-known Celtic 'cult of the head' – the ancient Celtic belief that the head contained the soul, and that the heads of vanquished adversaries should therefore be severed and preserved. Indeed, the severed head is now regarded as one of the hallmarks of archaic Celtic culture. It figures perhaps most prominently in the myth of Bran the Blessed, whose head, according to tradition, was buried as a protective talisman outside London, face turned towards France. Not only did it protect the city from attack. It also ensured the fertility of the surrounding countryside and warded off plague from England as a whole. In other words, it performed functions strikingly similar to those performed by the Grail in the later romances. It surfaces later as the so-called 'Green Man', the vegetation god and tutelary deity of fertility.

At the same time, the Templars had their own 'cult of the head'. Among the charges preferred against them, and one to which a number of knights pleaded guilty, was that of worshipping a mysterious severed head sometimes known as 'Baphomet'. Moreover, when the officers of the French king burst into the Paris Temple on 13 October 1307, there was found a silver reliquary in the shape of a head, containing the skull of a woman. It bore a label denoting it as 'Caput LVIIIm' – 'Head 58m'.[3] This might at first seem a mere grisly coincidence. But in the list of charges drawn up by the Inquisition against the Templars on 12 August 1308, there appears the following:

> Item, that in each province they had idols, namely heads . . .
> Item, that they adored these idols . . .
> Item, that they said that the head could save them.
> Item, that [it could] make riches . . .
> Item, that it made the trees flower.
> Item, that [it made] the land germinate . . .[4]

These attributes are precisely – so precisely as to be at times verbatim – the attributes ascribed by the romances to the Grail, and by Celtic tradition to the severed head of Bran the Blessed. It is thus clear that both the Grail Romances and the Templars, despite their primary Christian orientation, incorporated crucial residues of Celtic tradition. These residues, baffling and gruesome though they may appear today, would have struck a familiar atavistic chord in the Celtic kingdom Bruce was endeavouring to re-establish.

Thus, although the Celtic prototypes for the Grail Romances did not feature the Grail itself, at least under that name, other components of the later story were certainly present. The Grail itself made its début in a long narrative poem entitled *Le Conte du Graal* by Chrétien de Troyes, writing in the last quarter of the twelfth century. Wolfram's *Parzival* and the anonymous *Perlesvaus*, dating from a quarter of a century or so later, draw on material and sources of information to which Chrétien was not apparently privy; but it is still from Chrétien's poem that these works, and all the other Grail Romances, ultimately, to one degree or another, derive.

Little is known about Chrétien, and little can be gleaned except from the dedications to his works and internal textual evidence. What emerges is meagre enough, but it would seem clear at least that Chrétien worked under the tutelage and sponsorship of aristocratic courts – namely the courts of the counts of Champagne and of Flanders. These courts were closely associated with each other, and were also associated with heterodox religious attitudes, including a skein of heretical Cathare thought. Both courts were also closely associated with the Templars. Indeed, some three-quarters of a century before Chrétien, the Comte de Champagne had been a key figure in the creation of the Order. Hugues de Payens, first Grand Master of the Temple, was a trusted vassal of the Comte de Champagne and seems consistently to have been acting on the count's instructions. Subsequently, the count himself, repudiating his marriage, was taken into the Order, thus (in a curious paradox) becoming the vassal of his own vassal.

Much of Chrétien's early work is dedicated to various members of the court of Champagne, and particularly to the countess, Marie. But his version of the Grail story, composed between 1184 and 1190, is dedicated to Philippe d'Alsace, Comte de Flandres. Chrétien states explicitly that the narrative of the Grail was originally recounted to him by Philippe, who then instructed him to weave whatever romance he could around it.

Unfortunately, Chrétien died before he could finish the work completely. But in what exists of the poem, there are a number of points of interest. For example, it is in Chrétien that Arthur's capital is named for the first time as Camelot. And Chrétien repeatedly designates Perceval by a formula that will later be adopted by

Wolfram and other romanciers, and will eventually come to figure prominently in later Freemasonry – 'the Son of the Widow'. This formula concealed a meaning which was still legible in Chrétien's age, but was subsequently lost.

Most important to note for our particular purposes is that Chrétien, in the Celtic elements of his poem, is drawing on some fund of information other than established English and Welsh sources. Not, of course, that he ignores those sources. On the contrary, he owes much to them. He relies heavily on Geoffrey of Monmouth's *History of the Kings of Britain*, a quasi-legendary account written around 1138 which first brought Arthur to the public consciousness. He also relies heavily on such archaic tales as 'Peredur' and other narratives from the Welsh *Mabinogion*. But there are other aspects of Chrétien's poem which owe nothing to such traditional sources – aspects which are specifically and uniquely Scottish. Indeed, it is clear that Chrétien has some independent source of information about Scotland; and experts conclude it to be from Scotland that Chrétien derived certain key features of his poem's geography and topography.

Thus, for example, Chrétien's hero, 'Perceval le Galois', might be supposed at first to come from Wales. In fact, however, the term 'Gualeis' or 'Galois' was applied, in Chrétien's time, to natives of Galloway in Scotland. The Grail knights, in Chrétien's poem, defend 'les pors de Galvoie' – 'the gates of Galvoie' – this being the land on whose borders they operate. Scholars of the Grail Romances concur that 'Galvoie' must be Galloway.[5]

In Geoffrey of Monmouth, there are references to 'Castellum Puellarum' which, in some of the later Grail Romances, but not Chrétien's, becomes the famous 'Castle Perilous'. Writing in 1338, the commentator and translator Robert of Brunne says that 'Castellum Puellarum' is in fact the real castle of Caerlaverock in Galloway. As one modern biographer of Chrétien observes, Robert of Brunne 'may well be repeating accredited tradition, for in his youth, at Cambridge, he knew the future king Robert the Bruce'.[6] In any case, Caerlaverock was only some ten miles from Annan, the seat of the Bruce family, who had been made lords of Annandale by David I in 1124. The castles at Annan and Caerlaverock were both often said to have 'guarded the door to Galloway'. Although Chrétien does not speak specifically of 'Castellum Puellarum' or 'Castle Perilous', he does speak of a 'Roche de Canguin' – which, according to at least one scholar, 'derives from an embellishment of Caerlaverock'.[7] In Chrétien's poem, it is this site, significantly enough, which 'guarde les pors de Galvoie'.

In Chrétien's poem, Arthur's second residence after Camelot is called 'Cardoeil'. Until 1157, the capital of Scotland was Carlisle, which, in the days of *The Anglo-Saxon Chronicle*, was called 'Cardeol' and then evolved into 'Carduil'. Chrétien also mentions a religious site called 'Mont Dolerous'. This is believed to be Melrose Abbey in Northumberland, founded in 1136 and known in Chrétien's time as 'Mons Dolorosus'. It was here that, nearly two centuries later, Bruce's heart was to be buried.

From this and much similar evidence, it is obvious that Chrétien, in whose work the Grail first appears, is grafting his specifically Christian concept of it on to a corpus of much older material, some of which refers very precisely to Scotland. But why should a romancier working under the patronage of the courts of Champagne and Flanders focus so pointedly on Scottish sites when the Judaeo-Christian superstructure of his poem derived from very different sources?

Chrétien claimed to have received the outlines of the Grail story from Philippe d'Alsace, Comte de Flandres, who told him to make whatever he could of them. And Philippe's contacts with Scotland were numerous and close. As lord of Flanders, he had extensive dealings with Scotland and a considerable knowledge of the country, its people and their traditions. Indeed, throughout the twelfth century, certain ties had been deliberately forged between Scotland and Flanders. During the reigns of David I (1124–53) and Malcolm IV (1153–65), there obtained a systematic policy of settling Flemish immigrants in Scotland. The newcomers were installed in large organised enclaves in upper Lanarkshire, upper Clydesdale, West Lothian and the north of Moray. According to one commentator, the 'Flemish settlement seems a systematic attempt to implant in upper Clydesdale and Moray, at the expense of local aristocracy and church, a new aristocracy'.[8] As we have seen, Bruce's own family is now believed to have been of Flemish, not Norman, descent. A similar origin has been traced for such other prominent Scottish families as Balliol, Cameron, Campbell, Comyn, Douglas, Graham, Hamilton, Lindsay, Montgomery, Seton and Stewart.[9] Some of these families have already figured in our story. They, and others as well, will figure even more prominently later.

The purpose of the Flemish settlement in Scotland seems to have been to build up urban centres in the country. Flanders had already become an urbanised, commercialised region, with great trading cities such as Bruges and Ghent straddling the mercantile routes to the Rhine, the Seine and the British Isles. It also included in its territory Boulogne and Calais. The Scottish monarchy, needing the revenue to be obtained from town rents, looked to Flanders as a model of urban development. Flemish settlers were thus actively encouraged to come to the country and establish metropolitan centres on the Flemish pattern. They were welcomed, too, for their expertise in agriculture, in weaving and in the wool trade.

The association of Scotland and Flanders, begun with David I and Malcolm IV, continued through the reign of Malcolm's successor, William 'the Lion'. When William invaded England in 1173, he was reinforced by a Flemish contingent – a contingent sent to him by Philippe d'Alsace. And in military matters, as well as in urban development, the Scots learned from Flanders. In 1302, the burghers of the Flemish town of Courtrai rose in revolt. Using the so-called 'schilltrom' formation – men formed in a square with long pikes anchored in the ground and pointing outwards – they managed to defeat a large and powerful French army. For the first time in Western Europe, Courtrai broke the hitherto invincible power of the mounted and armoured knight. Bruce learned from the battle. It was precisely the 'schilltrom' formation that he deployed so successfully at Bannockburn, until the mysterious 'fresh force' appeared on the scene to turn the tide.

There was much cross-fertilisation and reciprocal influence between Scotland and Flanders. As a result of the influx of Flemish settlers, Scottish towns assumed certain distinctly Flemish characteristics, while elements of Scotland's ancient Celtic heritage found their way back to Flanders – where they surfaced in (among other things) the Grail Romances. Once they had begun to evolve as a genre, the Grail Romances were carried back to Scotland, where the original Celtic component in them would have been duly recognised and appreciated.

It is not hard to imagine how congenial the exiled Templars would have found Scotland, this setting for the adventures of Grail knights and fictionalised Templars. It was so to speak, 'ready-made' for them. Presenting themselves as 'real-life' Grail knights, they could aid Bruce in his campaigns, and be welcomed as chivalric saviours as well. Where else could they have found a climate so hospitable to survivors of the Order wishing to secularise themselves, integrate themselves and perpetuate themselves, safely insulated from their persecutors elsewhere?

TWO
Scotland and a Hidden Tradition

6

The Templar Legacy in Scotland

One of the fallacies of conventional scholarship is to insist on a rigorous and artificial distinction between 'history' and 'myth'. According to such a distinction, 'history' is regarded as documented fact alone – data which can be subjected to an almost scientific scrutiny, which will stand up to assorted tests and prove thereby that something 'actually happened'. 'History', in this sense, consists of names, dates, battles, treaties, political movements, conferences, revolutions, social changes and other such 'objectively discernible' phenomena. 'Myth', on the other hand, is dismissed as irrelevant or incidental to 'history'. 'Myth' is consigned to the realm of fantasy, to poetry and fiction. 'Myth' is deemed to be the spurious embellishment or falsification of fact, a distortion of 'history', and something therefore to be ruthlessly excised. 'History' and 'myth' must, it is believed, be prised apart before the truth of the past can be revealed.

And yet, for the people who originally created what later ages might call 'myth', there was no such distinction. In his own age, and for centuries after, Homer's *Odyssey*, devoted to the probably fictitious adventures of one man, was deemed no less historically authoritative than the *Iliad*, devoted to a presumed 'actual' occurrence, the Siege of Troy. Events in the Old Testament – the parting of the Red Sea, for instance, or God conferring on Moses the Tables of the Law – are held by many people today to be 'mythic'; but there are also many people, even today, who believe the same events actually to have occurred. In Celtic tradition, the sagas pertaining to, say, Cuchulain and the 'knights' of the Red Branch were believed for centuries to be historically accurate; and even today, there is no way of knowing whether they are indeed so, whether they are greater or lesser embellishments of historical events, or whether they are wholly fictitious. To cite a more recent example, the 'Wild West' of the nineteenth-century United States, as portrayed first by 'dime novels', then by Hollywood, is now generally recognised to be 'mythical'. And yet Jesse James, Billy the Kid, Wild Bill Hickok, Doc Holliday and the Earp brothers *did* exist. The legendary gunfight at the OK Corral *did* actually take place, if not quite in the form usually supposed. Until very recently, the 'myths' woven around such figures and such episodes were virtually inseparable from 'history'. Thus, in the era of Prohibition, men such as Eliot Ness on the one hand, John Dillinger and 'Legs' Diamond on the other, fancied themselves to be re-enacting an historically accurate Western drama of stalwart lawmen and romantic outlaws. And, in the process, they created a new 'history' around which new 'myths' were to be woven.

According to the extent that they inflame the imagination and remain alive in a people's imaginative life, historical events and personages grade imperceptibly into myth. In cases such as King Arthur or Robin Hood, the myth has effectively subsumed whatever historical 'actuality' there may once have been. In the case of Jeanne d'Arc, historical 'actuality', though not eclipsed completely, has receded into the background, while the foreground is dominated by exaggeration, embellishment and pure invention. In more recent instances – Che Guevara, for example, John Kennedy or Marilyn Monroe, John Lennon or Elvis Presley – historical 'actuality' can be discerned among the elements of myth, but cannot ultimately be separated from them; and it is precisely the elements of myth that make us interested in the historical 'actuality'.

It can be argued – and has been argued – that *all* written or recorded history is essentially a form of myth. Any historical account is oriented towards the needs, attitudes and values of the time in which it is composed, not the time to which it refers. Any historical account is necessarily selective, including certain elements, omitting others. Any historical account, if only by virtue of its selectivity, emphasises certain factors and neglects others. To this extent, it is biased; and to the extent that it is biased, it inevitably falsifies 'what actually happened'. If modern media cannot agree on the interpretation of events that occurred only yesterday, the past is subject to far greater latitude of interpretation.

For such reasons as these, post-war novelists – from Carlos Fuentes and Gabriel García Márquez in Latin America to Graham Swift, Peter Ackroyd and Desmond Hogan in England and Ireland – have insisted on a reassessment of what we mean by 'history'. For such novelists, history consists not only of external and provable 'data', but also of the mental context, in which such data are embedded – and within which, in the hands of subsequent generations, they are interpreted. For such novelists, the only true 'history' is the psychic life of a people, a culture, a civilisation – and this includes not only external data, but also the imaginative exaggerations, embellishments and interpretations of myth. Ivo Andrić, the Yugoslavian novelist who won the Nobel Prize in 1961, insists on the historian's need to recognise the underlying 'truth of lies'. The 'lies' of a people or a culture, Andrić maintains – the hyperbole, the exaggeration and embellishment, even the outright falsification and invention – are not purely gratuitous. On the contrary, they bear witness to underlying needs, underlying wants, underlying lacks, underlying dreams and over-compensations; and to that extent they are, in their very falsity, not just true, but also revealing and informative statements containing clues vital to understanding. And to the extent that they serve to crystallise a collective identity or self-definition, they create a new truth – or create something which becomes true.

A simple and all too dismally relevant example should suffice to illustrate the kind of process Andrić describes – the process whereby 'truth' and 'lies', 'history' and 'myth' become entwined so as to create a new historical actuality. In 1688, the Protestant citizens of Londonderry, more out of panic than genuine necessity, shut and barred the city's gates against a contingent of Catholic troops dispatched by James II to garrison the place. This rebellious act produced a predictable reaction on the part of the king; and without either side really having wanted it or intended it, Londonderry found itself besieged. In the sweep of European history, the Siege of Londonderry was a squalid little affair, trivial by comparison with the military operations which, within a decade or so, would be conducted on the Continent. It was also inconsequential, resolving nothing, determining nothing. It was dictated by no military necessity, created no new military necessities, and was not, in any strict military sense, decisive. But on a less tangible level, it was indeed decisive. It shaped and created attitudes, values, orientations. And those attitudes, values, orientations subsequently translated themselves into events.

In reaction not to what 'actually happened' at Londonderry, but to what was believed to have happened, Protestant and Catholic moulds of thought in Ireland congealed. It was in strict accordance with these moulds of thought that the two communities proceeded to act. These actions were to determine the course of Irish affairs for the next century. And when, in 1798, Catholic Ireland rose in revolt, the conduct and course of that revolt were conditioned not by the events of the siege a hundred years before, but by the myths that surrounded those events. Myth thus generated new history. And history – in this case, the 1798 rebellion – generated new myths of its own. These new myths, in their turn, precipitated fresh developments in so-called history, which, also in their turn, fostered fresh myths. The culmination of the process is Northern Ireland today, where the real clash is not so much a clash of religions as a clash of conflicting myths, of conflicting interpretations of history.

The Battle of Blenheim (1704, a mere fifteen years after the Siege of Londonderry) was a genuinely major battle. It was also decisive. It altered the balance of power in Europe and radically transformed the course of European history. But Blenheim, today, lives in people's minds primarily as a stately home in Oxfordshire which also happened to be Churchill's birthplace. The Siege of London-derry, on the other hand, and the 1798 rebellion, and all the other half-mythic and half-historical milestones of Irish history, have been bundled wholesale into the present, where they are regularly celebrated, commemorated, re-enacted, ritualised – and where, in consequence, they are still able to shape attitudes and values, determine tribal identity and polarise communities. Such is the power of myth. And such is the inseparability of myth from what we call history.

History consists not only of facts and events. It also consists of the relationships between facts and events and the interpretation, often imaginative, of such relationships. In any such act of interpretation, a mythic element necessarily comes into play. Myth is not thus distinct from history. On the contrary, it is an inseparable part of history.

Exploitation of the Templar Myth

From their very inception, the Templars mantled themselves in myth, capitalised on myth, exploited myth. The sheer obscurity and mystery surrounding their origins enabled them to surround themselves with an equally potent mystique. This mystique was accentuated by the loyal patronage not only of leading nobles, but also of romanciers such as Wolfram von Eschenbach and Church luminaries such as Saint Bernard. It was easy enough for the

Templars, in the minds of their contemporaries, to become 'legends in their own lifetime', and they did nothing to discourage the process whereby they became so. On the contrary, they often actively encouraged it. Among biblical texts, they constantly invoked Joshua and Maccabees, promoting themselves as latterday avatars of the army that toppled the walls of Jericho, the army that nearly defeated Rome in the years just prior to the Christian era. They encouraged the popular image of themselves as being in some way associated with the Grail Romances, as 'guardians' of that mysterious object or entity known as the Holy Grail.

Amidst the mystique surrounding the Order of the Temple, a number of echoes and images thus became fused. Joshua's army, the Maccabees, the Grail knights merged with yet other historical and/or legendary antecedents – the peers of Charlemagne, the Arthurian Knights of the Round Table and, especially in the British Isles, the Red Branch of Ulster. Nor was martial prowess the only virtue which the mystique surrounding the Temple conferred on them. The Templars appear in *The Perlesvaus* not just as military men, but also as high mystical initiates. This is indicative, for the Templars were only too eager to reinforce the popular image of themselves as magi, as wizards or sorcerers, as necromancers, as alchemists, as sages privy to lofty arcane secrets. And indeed, it was precisely this image that rebounded upon them and provided their enemies with the means of their destruction.

Yet even in the Order's demise, the myth-making process remained active and inseparable from historical actuality. Did Jacques de Molay, the last Grand Master, as he was being burned alive over a slow fire, *really* pronounce a curse on the Pope and the French king, ordering both to join him before God's seat within the year? Whether he did or not, both, within the year, died, in distinctly suspicious circumstances. It is easy enough today to ascribe their deaths to refugee knights or sympathisers drawing on the Order's expertise in poisons; but the medieval mind was only too happy to see some more occult power at work. The French monarchy began to regard itself as accursed, with Jacques de Molay's malediction hanging over it like a sword of Damocles. And that malediction was to remain associated with the French throne regardless of changes of dynasty. Thus, in 1793, when Louis XVI was guillotined, another historical event became entangled with myth and legend: a French Freemason is alleged to have leaped up on to the scaffold, dipped his hand in the king's blood, flicked it out over the crowd and cried, 'Jacques de Molay, thou art avenged!'

In their lifetime, then, the Templars cloaked themselves in legend and myth. In their demise, they spawned new legends, new myths, which were then translated by other people into 'historical fact'. As we shall see, one particularly potent such translation was to be Freemasonry. But there were other, earlier manifestations of the phenomenon – manifestations on which Freemasonry itself was to draw and in which it was itself rooted. Indeed, scarcely had the Order of the Temple been destroyed than it arose again, phoenix-like, from the flames of its own pyre, to assume a new mythic guise.

Within a quarter of a century of the Temple's dissolution, a spate of neo-Templar orders began to appear – and would continue to do so for centuries afterwards. Thus, for example, in 1348, Edward III of England created the Order of the Garter, consisting of twenty-six knights divided into two groups of thirteen each. The Garter, of course, continues to the present day, and is the world's premier order of chivalry. In France in 1352, Jean II created an almost identical institution, the Order of the Star. It was rather more short-lived than the Garter, however, its entire membership being annihilated in 1356 at the Battle of Poitiers. In 1430, Philip, Duke of Burgundy, created the Order of the Golden Fleece. In 1469, Louis XI of France created the Order of St Michael. Its membership was to include such individuals as Claude de Guise, Charles (Connétable) de Bourbon, François de Lorraine, Federico de Gonzaga and Louis de Nevers – as well as commanders and officers of an institution soon to figure prominently in our story, the Scots Guard.

Such orders were, of course, much smaller in number than the Templars, and much less consequential. They never exerted any notable historical influence. They had no land, no preceptories, no holdings of any kind and no revenue. They lacked autonomy, being attached to the person of one or another potentate or sovereign. Although composed initially of fighting men, they were not, strictly speaking, military. They provided no military training, for example; they were organised around no military hierarchy; they did not function as distinct military units or formations, either on or off the battlefield. Ultimately, they were affairs of prestige rather than of real power, vehicles for royal patronage, the domain of courtiers; and their military accoutrements and nomenclature soon became as metaphorical as those of, say, the Salvation Army. But in their inception, in their rites and rituals, in the mystique they sought to arrogate for themselves, they looked to the Temple as a model.

This particular legacy of the Temple was more heraldic than anything else, but there was another legacy which not only transformed the face of European Catholicism, but projected it across the sea – as far westwards as America, as far eastwards as Japan. In 1540, a former military man named Ignatius Loyola, mortified by the advances of Protestantism, resurrected the original Templar ideal of the warrior-monk, the soldier of Christ, and created his own such soldiery. Unlike the Templars, however, Loyola's soldiery would crusade not with the sword (though perfectly prepared to let others wield it on their behalf), but with the word.

Thus was born what Loyola called the Company of Jesus – until the Pope, recoiling from the explicit military connotations of 'Company', insisted it be changed to 'Society'. In their martial structure and organisation, in their far-flung network of 'provinces', in their rigid discipline, the Jesuits were, by Loyola's own admission, modelled on the Templars. Indeed, they often acted as military advisors and ordnance experts, as well as high-level diplomats and ambassadors. Like the Templars, the Jesuits were nominally subject only to the Church; but like the Templars, they often became a law unto themselves. In 1773, in circumstances recalling the suppression of the Temple 461 years before, Pope Clement XIV, 'on secret grounds', suppressed the Jesuits. Subsequently, of course, in 1814, they were resurrected. But even today, the Jesuits are in many respects a self-contained institution, and not infrequently at odds with the Papacy to which they supposedly owe allegiance.

The chivalric orders and the Jesuits were, in different ways, heirs of the Temple who eventually forgot, or deliberately repudiated, their origin. In Scotland, however, a more direct and more tangible heritage of the Templars was to survive, duly acknowledged as such and transmitted by the more concrete channels of soil and family bloodlines. In the first place, collusion, cover-up and wheeling and dealing ensured that the Order's holdings in Scotland were kept intact, retained as a separate unity and administered, at least for a time, by 'defrocked' Templars themselves – and subsequently by some offshoot of them. Templar property in Scotland was not to be dismembered and parcelled out, as it was elsewhere. On the contrary, it was to be held in trust, as if awaiting restoration to its original owners.

Then, too, there was to emerge in Scotland a network of interlocked families who were to provide both a repository and a conduit. To the extent that an authentic Templar tradition survived

93

in Scotland, it survived under the auspices of these families and that of the military formation they sponsored, the Scots Guard, perhaps the most genuinely neo-Templar institution of all. Through the Scots Guard, moreover, and through the families who staffed the Guard with their sons, a new energy was to be imported to Scotland from the Continent. This energy – expressed originally through a spectrum of 'esoteric' disciplines, as well as through stone-masonry and architecture – would fuse with the residue of Templar tradition and breathe fresh life into it. And thus, from the pyres of the old religious-military Order, modern Freemasonry was to be born.

The Templar Lands

In 1312, a month after the official papal dissolution of the Temple, all the lands, preceptories and other installations owned by the Order were granted to their former allies and rivals, the Knights Hospitaller of St John. In the Holy Land, the Hospitallers had been quite as corrupt as the Templars, quite as prone to power-broking, intrigue, factional strife and pursuit of their own interests at the expense of the crusader kingdom's welfare. Like the Templars and, by the mid-thirteenth century, the Teutonic Knights, the Hospitallers were also involved in banking, in commerce, in a broad spectrum of other activities extending far beyond their original brief of warrior-monks. In Europe, however, and especially in their relations with the Papacy, the Hospitallers kept their noses scrupulously clean. They remained proof against any 'infection' by heresy, any transgression that might have rendered them subject to persecution. Neither did they pose a threat to any European monarch.

Undoubtedly, the Hospitallers were as arrogant and autocratic as the Templars and the Teutonic Knights. But their hospital work, and their unswerving loyalty to Rome, more than counteracted such adverse impressions as they made. In consequence, they enjoyed a respectability in both papal and public minds that rival orders did not. Indeed, in the years prior to 1307, there was even talk of 'purifying' the Templars by amalgamating them with the Hospitallers into a single unified order. Between 1307 and 1314, while the Templars' trials were in progress, the Teutonic Knights incurred similar accusations and, fearing similar prosecution, moved their headquarters from Venice to Marienburg, in what is

94

now Poland, far beyond the reach of both papal and secular authority. The Hospitallers remained felicitously placed to benefit from the misfortunes of both their rivals.

Nevertheless, the Hospitallers' acquisition of Templar holdings was not as simple or straightforward as one might think. In some cases, for example, as many as thirty years passed before they actually obtained the property conferred upon them; and by then, of course, the property in question had generally been run down, ruined, made worthless and unviable without investment of considerable capital expenditure. On two occasions – in 1324 and again in 1334 – the Priors of St John resorted to the English Parliament to confirm their right to Templar lands.[1] Even so, it was not until 1340 that they obtained the title to the London Temple. On a number of occasions, too, the Hospitallers found themselves in conflict with secular lords – men who, rather than see it pass into the hands of St John, sought to reclaim property conferred on the Temple by their forebears a century or two before. In many instances, such secular magnates were, if not powerful enough to win the argument, at least able to prolong it through litigation.

Such was the situation in England. In Scotland, matters were even more confused, and often deliberately concealed as well. Perhaps the strongest indication of developments in Scotland lies not in what was said, but in what was left unsaid. Thus, six months after Bannockburn, Bruce issued a charter to the Hospitallers confirming all their possessions in the kingdom.[2] No mention whatever was made of any Templar lands or holdings, even though such lands and holdings should have passed into Hospitaller hands two years before. The Hospitallers were simply confirmed in what they already possessed. Nor, interestingly enough, did the Hospitallers, or the crown, or the secular lords, attempt to lay claim to Templar property. In fact, with but one exception, there is no record of anyone obtaining Templar property, or even endeavouring to obtain it. For the duration of Bruce's lifetime, such property might never have existed, so complete was the silence surrounding it.

In 1338, nine years after Bruce's death, the Grand Master of the Hospitallers requested a list of all Temple properties acquired by his Order everywhere in the world. Every regional or national Prior was instructed to submit an inventory of Templar holdings in his particular sphere of authority. During the last century, a document, quoting the response of the English Prior, was found in the library of the Order of St John at Valetta. After itemising a

substantial number of Templar possessions acquired by the Hospitallers in England, the manuscript says:

> Of the land, buildings . . . churches and all other possessions
> which were Templar in Scotland the reply was nothing of any
> value . . . all were destroyed, burnt and reduced to nothing
> because of the enduring wars which had continued over many
> years.[3]

As of 1338, then, the Hospitallers had still not laid hands on
Templar properties in Scotland. On the other hand, irregularities of
some sort were clearly taking place. For if Templar properties did
not figure in any transactions of the Hospitallers, the Scottish crown
or secular nobles, some of them *were* nevertheless sold – without
being entered in any official records. Thus, for example, before
1329 an officer of the Order of St John, one Rodulph Lindsay, is
reported to have disposed of the Templar lands of Temple Liston.[4]
Yet the transaction is not mentioned in any of the Order's
documents or archives. On what authority, then, was Lindsay
acting? For whom was he functioning as agent?

Lindsay's transaction is only one of a number which have
blurred, for later historians, the whole question of Templar lands in
Scotland during the period in question. As a result, no clear picture
of any sort can be obtained:

> It is . . . unknown how the Templars' properties were handed
> over to the Hospitallers; it seems to have been a ragged piecemeal
> process, and there is evidence that well into the fourteenth
> century the Hospitallers were still having difficulty getting
> possession of former Templar properties.[5]

The same writer concludes: 'There is no period in the history of the
military orders in Scotland more obscure than the fourteenth
century.'[6]

Notwithstanding the obscurities, a certain pattern does emerge:
after 1338, the Hospitallers began to acquire Templar holdings in
Scotland, albeit in a decidedly equivocal way; prior to 1338,
however, no Templar property was passed on, yet with the
exception noted above there is no record anywhere of anything else
happening to it. What is more, the Templar lands, when the
Hospitallers did eventually receive them, were kept separate. They
were not parcelled out, integrated with the Hospitallers' other
holdings and administered accordingly. On the contrary, they
enjoyed a special status and were administered as a self-contained
unit in themselves. They were handled, in fact, not as if St John

actually owned them, but were simply, in the capacity of agents or managers, holding them in trust. As late as the end of the sixteenth century, no fewer than 519 sites in Scotland were listed by the Hospitallers as 'Terrae Templariae' – part, that is, of the self-contained and separately administered Templar patrimony![7]

In fact, the disposition of Templar land in Scotland involved something quite extraordinary – something which has been almost entirely neglected by historians, and which enabled the Temple to sustain at least some degree of, as it were, posthumous existence. For more than two centuries in Scotland – from the beginning of the fourteenth to the middle of the sixteenth – the Templars, it appears, were actually *merged* with the Hospitallers. Thus, during the period in question, there are frequent references to *a single joint Order* – the 'Order of the Knights of St John *and* the Temple'.[8]

It is a bizarre situation, and it raises some tantalising questions. Did the Hospitallers anticipate some future resurrection of the Temple and undertake, perhaps by some secret agreement, to hold Templar property in trust? Or could it be that the Order of St John in Scotland had taken into its ranks enough fugitive Templars to administer their own lands?

Both answers are possible; they are not mutually exclusive. Whatever the truth of the matter, it is clear that Templar lands enjoyed a unique status which has not been officially defined in the historical record. And they continued to do so. In 1346, a Master of the Hospitallers, Alexander de Seton, presided over the regular legal session at the former Templar preceptory of Balantrodoch. By this time, the site had, finally, passed into the hands of the Hospitallers. Nevertheless, it was still being administered separately, possessing a status of its own as part of the Templar patrimony. Two of the charters witnessed by Alexander de Seton survive.[9] They indicate that despite the date, thirty-four years after the suppression of the Templars, 'Temple Courts' were still being held.

'Temple Courts' of the same kind, retaining the same name, were to continue sitting for a good two centuries. Once again, we are confronted with evidence that the Order of St John, though given authority over Templar properties in Scotland, was, for reasons never explicitly stated, unable legally to assimilate them. Once again, we are confronted with the suggestion of an invisible Templar presence looming in the background, waiting for an opportunity to reassert itself and legally reclaim its heritage. And all of Scotland – the monarchy, the wealthy landowners, the Order of St John itself – seems to have colluded in the veiled design.

The Elusive Knight – David Seton

Early in the nineteenth century, a noted genealogical lawyer and antiquarian named James Maidment discovered a chartulary – a roll or bound volume of land deeds – for 'Terrae Templariae' within the Order of St John between 1581 and 1596. In addition to the two known preceptories at Balantrodoch and Maryculter, this document listed three others – at Auldlisten, Denny and Thankerton.[10] It also listed more than 500 other Templar properties, from crofts and fields, flourmills and farms, to castles and four entire townships. Spurred by his discovery, Maidment undertook further research. His final tabulation, transcribed in a manuscript now housed in the National Library of Scotland, lists and names specifically no fewer than 579 Templar holdings![11]

What had happened to this land? How had it been disposed of, and why had records pertaining to it all but vanished from the historical chronicle? At least some answers to these questions can be found in a family which was among the most important and influential in Scotland during Bruce's time. Their name was Seton.

As we have seen, Sir Christopher Seton was married to Bruce's sister. He was present at Bruce's murder of John Comyn and himself killed Comyn's uncle when the latter attempted to intervene. He was also present at Bruce's coronation at Scone in 1306. Subsequently, at the Battle of Methven, he was captured and, on Edward I's orders, executed. A similar fate befell his brother, Sir John Seton. Both, in fact, died alongside Bruce's brother, Neil. In 1320, Christopher Seton's son, Alexander, along with representatives of such other eminent Scottish families as the Sinclairs, signed the Declaration of Arbroath.

For another four hundred years, the Setons were to remain prominent in Scottish affairs and Scottish nationalist activities. It is not therefore surprising, nor even particularly vain, that yet another Seton, George, in 1896, should undertake a comprehensive chronicle of his forebears. In this monumental volume, *A History of the Family of Seton*, the author lists numerous of his ancestors bearing titles ranging from the inconsequential to the illustrious. He also lists numerous other Setons who do not figure in standard noble genealogies. Some of them are humble artisans and burghers. Among this entangled forest of family trees, there is one particularly enigmatic and relevant entry:

c.1560. When the Knights-Templars were deprived of their patrimonial interest through the instrumentality of their

Grand-Master Sir James Sandilands, they drew off in a body, with David Seton, Grand Prior of Scotland (nephew of Lord Seton?), at their head. This transaction is alluded to in a curious satirical poem of that period, entitled:

Haly kirk and her theeves

Fye upon the traitor then,
Quhas has brocht us to sic pass,
Greedie als the knave Judas!
Fye upon the churle quhat solde
Haly erthe for heavie golde;
Bot the tempel felt na loss,
Quhan David Setoune bare the crosse.

David Seton died abroad in 1581 and is said to have been buried in the church of the Scotch Convent at Ratisbon [now Regensburg, near Nuremburg].[12]

It is a tantalising fragment, alluding explicitly to the Temple. It becomes even more tantalising by virtue of its date. Two and a half centuries after the Templars were officially suppressed, the poem suggests, they were still fully operational in Scotland, and undergoing a fresh crisis. But who, precisely, was David Seton? And who, for that matter, was Sir James Sandilands?

The latter, at least, is easy enough to trace. James Sandilands, first Baron Torphichen, was born around 1510, the second son of landed gentry in Midlothian. Sandilands's father was a friend of John Knox, who, after his return to Scotland from Geneva in 1555, resided on the family's estate at Calder. Despite his father's association with a Protestant reformer, the young James Sandilands entered the Order of St John some time shortly before 1537. In 1540, he requested from James V a safe conduct to travel to Malta and obtain there, from the Grand Master, official confirmation of his right to succeed to the Preceptorship of Torphichen on the death of its sitting incumbent, Walter Lindsay. Sandilands's right to succeed Lindsay was duly confirmed by the Grand Master of the Hospitallers, Juan d'Omedes, in 1541. Returning home from Malta, the ambitious young man stopped in Rome to have his newly promised sinecure ratified by the Pope.

Five years later, in 1546, Walter Lindsay died. In 1547, the Master in Malta officially recognised Sandilands as Prior of Torphichen. In the Scottish Parliament, he became known as Lord St John and sat on the Privy Council. By 1557, he was back in Malta, engaged in a prolonged and evidently rather silly dispute with a putative relative, also a member of the Order, over a question of certifiable nobility. To the discredit of both men, the argument culminated in a public brawl, and the putative relative was imprisoned.[13] In 1558, Sandilands returned to Scotland. Here, along with his father, he supported the Reformation and actively opposed the Queen Regent, Marie de Guise – elder sister of François, Duc de Guise, and Charles, Cardinal de Lorraine – who, in 1538, had married James V.

It must have seemed puzzling at first how and why Sandilands could support Protestant reform against a staunchly Catholic ruler, while still remaining a member in good standing of a Catholic military order. He contrived, nevertheless, to accommodate these conflicting allegiances, and his ulterior motives were soon to become outrageously clear. In 1560, by act of the Scottish Parliament, the Pope's authority in the country was abolished, and the Order of St John's rights to the 'Precepterie of Torphephen [sic] Fratibus Hospitalis Hierosolimitani, Militibus Temple Solomonis' were annulled.[14] As Prior of St John, Sandilands was thus obliged to turn over to the crown the properties he administered for the Order. He did not object. Instead, in 1564, he presented himself to the new monarch, Mary Queen of Scots, as:

... present possessor of the Lordship and Preceptories of Torphephen [sic] which was never subject to any Chapter or Convent whatsomever, except only the Knights of Jerusalem and the Temple of Solomon.[15]

On payment of a lump sum of 10,000 crowns plus an annual rent, Sandilands proceeded to negotiate for himself a perpetual leasehold on the properties he had previously administered for the Hospitallers. As part of the transaction, he also obtained the hereditary title of Baron Torphichen.

With an entrepreneurial spirit that any modern yuppie might envy, Sandilands thus effectively swindled the Hospitallers, illicitly disposing of their lands for his own advantage and profiting very handsomely from the deal. It is almost certainly to this affair, or to some aspect of it, that the poem quoted above refers – for the holdings Sandilands disposed of were not just Hospitaller holdings, but also part of the Templar patrimony.

In 1567, Sandilands attended the coronation of James VI, subsequently James I of England. In 1579 he died. His heir was his great-nephew, born in 1574, also named James Sandilands, who became Second Baron Torphichen. But the young man soon found himself financially pressed, and proceeded to sell off the lands he had inherited. By 1604, they had passed into the hands of one Robert Williamson, who, eleven years later, sold them to Thomas, Lord Binning, subsequently Earl of Haddington. They then passed through a number of hands until at last, at the beginning of the nineteenth century, those remaining were purchased by James Maidment.

If Sir James Sandilands is relatively easy to trace and document, David Seton is altogether more elusive. Not only is there much question about who precisely he was; there is even some question about whether he ever actually existed.[16] The only evidence of his existence is the fragment of the poem quoted above, which prompted George Seton to accord him a perplexed footnote in the 1896 family genealogy. And yet scholars have taken the poem seriously enough to accept it as testimony to something which, it would appear, both history and human agencies have conspired to conceal.

As we have seen, the Seton family were among the most distinguished and influential in Scottish history, and were to continue as such for another three centuries. What is not clear is where precisely the mysterious David Seton fits into their family tree. The genealogist of 1896 suggests, plausibly enough, that he was the grandson of George, Sixth Lord Seton, who succeeded to the title in 1513 and died in 1549.[17]

Sandilands, as we have noted, was hostile to Marie de Guise and her marriage to James V. He opposed the dynastic alliance linking the Stuarts with the continental house of Lorraine and its cadet branch, the house of Guise. George Seton was in the opposite camp. In 1527, he had married a certain Elizabeth Hay and had two sons by her, the elder of whom succeeded to the title and became the Seventh Lord Seton, a close friend of Mary Queen of Scots. But in 1539, George Seton married for a second time. His new bride was Marie du Plessis, a member of the entourage who had come to Scotland with Marie de Guise; and Seton's wedding to her thus placed him in intimate association with the royal court. By Marie du Plessis, Seton had three more children, Robert, James and Mary. Mary Seton was to become a maid of honour to Mary Queen of Scots, and was to go down in ballad and legend as one of 'the three Marys' who accompanied the queen to France for her marriage to the Dauphin, later François II, in 1558. Of Robert and James Seton, however, little is known, save that the latter died around 1562 and the former was still alive a year later. Both would have had time to sire children, and genealogists have concluded that David Seton must have been the son of one or other of them. He would thus have been the grandson of the Sixth Lord Seton and the nephew of the Seventh Lord.

If David Seton is so elusive, where did the family's chronicler, writing in 1896, obtain even the meagre information he did? At first we knew of only one earlier printed source, the nineteenth-century historian Whitworth Porter, who had access to the Hospitallers' archives in Valetta. Writing in 1858, Porter vouchsafes only that David Seton is 'said to have been the last Prior of Scotland, and to have retired with the greater portion of his Scottish brethren, about 1572–73'.[18] He adds that Seton died in 1591, ten years later than the date given by the 1896 genealogist, and was buried in the church of the Scotch Benedictines at Ratisbone. Porter also cites the poem, 'Haly Kirk and her Theeves' – with a variant reading of the penultimate line. This line, in the 1896 version, ran: 'Bot the Tempel felt na loss.' Porter quotes it as: 'But the *Order* [our italics] felt na losse.'[19]

It is obvious from this that, even as late as the nineteenth century, the issue was still a sensitive one. 'Tempel' is quite unequivocal. 'Order', however, could as readily denote the Hospitallers as the Templars and, in the context, would seem to do so. Had the 1896 genealogist deliberately tampered with the text? If so, why? If any tampering *did* occur, it would seem more likely in the earlier version. Nothing would have been gained by changing 'Order' to 'Tempel'. But to change 'Tempel' to 'Order' would have exonerated the Knights of St John from the suspicion of harbouring Templars in their midst.

The issue would have remained uncertain, had not an earlier version of the poem turned up, printed in 1843, fifteen years before Whitworth Porter's quotation of it. It draws not on the archives in Valetta, but on Scottish sources. We will have occasion to consider these sources later. For the moment, it is sufficient to note that this 1843 text of the poem – the earliest known – quotes the line precisely as the Seton genealogist was to quote it in 1896: 'But the Tempel felt na loss.'[20]

7

The Scots Guard

Whoever David Seton was, and whatever became of the 'Templars' alleged to have absconded with him, there was already, by that time, another repository for Scottish nobles claiming a Templar legacy. This repository may even have overlapped Seton's elusive cadre. But whether it did or not, it was still to preserve at least some Templar traditions and, albeit obliquely, carry them on into such later developments as Freemasonry. Although uniquely Scottish, this repository was to be based in France. It was thus to pave the way for the refuge which the last Stuarts found in France, and for the kind of Jacobite Freemasonry – specifically Templar-oriented Freemasonry – which coalesced around them.

In the years immediately following Bannockburn in 1314, Scotland and France, united by their common hostility towards England, developed ever closer military connections. In 1326, Bruce and Charles IV of France signed a major treaty renewing the 'auld alliance'. This alliance was to be consolidated by the Hundred Years War. At the nadir of his fortunes, for example, the Dauphin, later Charles VII, planned to flee to Scotland, and would almost certainly have done so had not Jeanne d'Arc appeared to turn the tide of events. Scottish soldiery played a key role in all Jeanne's campaigns, including the famous raising of the Siege of Orléans; and indeed, the Bishop of Orléans at the time was himself a Scot, John Kirkmichael. Jeanne's 'great standard' – the celebrated white banner around which her army rallied – was in fact painted by a Scot, and her commanders at Orléans included Sir John Stewart and two Douglas brothers.[1]

In the aftermath of Jeanne's dramatic series of victories, France, though triumphant, was exhausted and in a state of internal disarray. Domestic order was further threatened by bands of demobilised mercenaries, trained soldiers without a war to fight.

Lacking any other source of livelihood, many of these veterans turned brigand and ravaged the countryside, threatening to disrupt the newly established and still precarious social order. In consequence, the former Dauphin, now Charles VII, proceeded to create a standing army. By this time, the Hospitallers had transferred their resources to maritime operations in the Mediterranean. Charles's army thus became the first standing army in Europe since the Templars, and the first since Imperial Rome to be attached to a specific state – or, more accurately, to a specific throne.

The new French army created by Charles VII in 1445 consisted of fifteen 'compagnies d'ordonnance' of 600 men each – a total of 9000 soldiers. Of these, the Scottish Company – the 'Compagnie des Gendarmes Ecossois' – enjoyed pride of place. The Scottish Company was unchallenged in its status as the army's recognised élite. It was explicitly accorded premier rank over all other military units and formations, and would, for example, pass first in all parades. The commanding officer of the Scottish Company was also granted the rank of 'premier Master of Camp of French Cavalry'.[2] This cumbersome appellation was more than honorary. It conferred on him enormous authority and influence, in the field, in the court and in domestic politics.

But even before the creation of the standing army and the Scottish Company, an even more élite, more exclusive military cadre of Scots had been established. At the bloody Battle of Verneuil in 1424, the Scottish contingents had acquitted themselves with particular bravery and self-sacrifice. Indeed, they were virtually annihilated, along with their commander, John Stewart, Earl of Buchan, and other such nobles as Alexander Lindsay, Sir William Seton and the Earls of Douglas, Murray and Mar. A year later, in recognition of this action, a special unit of Scots was raised to serve as permanent personal bodyguard to the French king. Initially, it consisted of thirteen men-at-arms and twenty archers, a total of thirty-three. A detachment of this cadre was in constant attendance upon the monarch, even to the point of sleeping in his bedchamber.[3]

The élite unit was divided into two sub-formations, the 'Garde du Roi' and the 'Garde du Corps du Roi' – the King's Guard and the King's Bodyguard. Collectively, they were known simply as the Scots Guard. In 1445, when the standing army was raised, the number of men in the Scots Guard was commensurately increased – significantly enough, by multiples of thirteen. In 1474, the numbers were definitively fixed – seventy-seven men plus their commander in the King's Guard, and twenty-five men plus their commander in the King's Bodyguard.[4] With striking consistency, officers and commanders of the Scots Guard were also made members of the Order of St Michael, a branch of which was later established in Scotland.

The Scots Guard were, in effect, a neo-Templar institution, much more so than such purely chivalric orders as the Garter, the Star and the Golden Fleece. Like the Templars, the Guard had a *raison d'être* that was primarily military, political and diplomatic. Like the Templars, the Guard offered both military training and a military hierarchy – as well as an opportunity to 'blood oneself' in battle, to win one's spurs and acquire both experience and expertise. Like the Templars, the Guard functioned as a distinct military formation, in the way that an élite battalion would today. And though they held no lands of their own and never rivalled the Templars in numbers, the Scots Guard were still numerous enough to play a decisive role in the kind of combat prevailing in Europe at the time. They differed from the Templars primarily in the absence of any explicit religious orientation, and in their allegiance not to the Pope but to the French crown. But the Templars' own religious allegiances had always been heterodox and their obedience to the Pope little more than nominal. And the loyalty of the Scots Guard to the French crown was also, as we shall see, rather less fervent than it might have been. Like the Templars, the Guard were to pursue their own policies, their own designs, on behalf of very different interests.

For the better part of a century and a half, the Scots Guard enjoyed a unique status in French affairs. They functioned not just on the battlefield, but in the political arena as well, acting as courtiers and advisors in domestic affairs, as emissaries and ambassadors in international relations. Commanders of the Guard usually doubled in the role of royal chamberlain and often held a number of other posts, both honorary and practical, as well. Not surprisingly, they drew immensely high salaries for the age. In 1461, a captain in the Guard received some 167 *livres tournois* per month, just over 2000 per year.[5] This was equivalent to nearly half the revenue of a noble estate. Officers of the Guard could thus maintain lifestyles of considerable affluence and prestige.

Just as the Templars had recruited from the aristocracy of their age, so the Scots Guard drew their officers and commanders from the most august and distinguished families in Scotland, whose names had figured all through the country's history and are still resonant today – Cockburn, Cunningham, Hamilton, Hay, Mont-gomery, Seton, Sinclair and Stuart (or Stewart). Between 1531 and 1542, there were three Stuarts in the Guard, one of them the unit's captain. Between 1551 and 1553, there were no fewer than five members of the 'Montgommery' (sic) family in the Guard, one of them its captain, and four Sinclairs. In 1587, the time of the elusive David Seton, there were four other Setons, three Hamiltons, two Douglases and a Sinclair. It is clear that the Scots Guard served a special function not only for the French throne, but also for the families who provided their recruits. In effect, the cadre constituted a combination *rite de passage* and training ground for young Scottish nobles – a special vehicle whereby they were initiated into martial skills, politics, court affairs, foreign manners and mores and, it would appear, some species of ritualistic rite as well. In a personal interview, a member of the present-day Montgomery family spoke to us of the pride that he and his relatives still took in their ancestors' affiliation with the Scots Guard. He also informed us that there was, in the family, a species of private order, semi-Masonic, semi-chivalric, to which all males of the Montgomery line were eligible for admission. This order, he said, which apparently dated from around the time of the Scots Guard, was called the Order of the Temple.[6]

In theory, as we have seen, the Scots Guard owed their allegiance to the French throne – or, more specifically, to the Valois dynasty, which at that time occupied the French throne. But the legitimacy of the Valois was also being vigorously challenged at the time by a number of other powerful interests. Chief among these was the house of Lorraine and its cadet branch, the house of Guise. Indeed, much of French history during the sixteenth century revolved around the murderous feud between these rival dynasties. The houses of Guise and Lorraine were ruthlessly determined to depose the Valois – by political means if possible, by murder if necessary – and establish themselves on the throne. By 1610, no fewer than five French monarchs were to have died either by violent means or by suspected poisoning, and the factions of Guise and Lorraine were themselves to be depleted by assassination.

The Scots Guard played an ambiguous role in this internecine strife. In fact, they had been placed in an equivocal position. On the one hand, their nominal allegiance was to the Valois, for whom they constituted a personal bodyguard and the nucleus of an army. On the other hand, it would have been impossible for them not to have some ties with the houses of Guise and Lorraine. In 1538, as we have noted, Marie de Guise had been married to James V of Scotland, forging a crucial dynastic bond between their respective houses. When Marie's daughter, Mary Queen of Scots, ascended the throne, Scotland's monarch was therefore half Stuart, half

Guise-Lorraine; and this was something to which the aristocrats of the Scots Guard could hardly have been indifferent. In 1547, Henri II, the Valois king of France, increased their status and privileges. Notwithstanding this, however, they were often active – and not always secretly – on behalf of Henri's Guise-Lorraine rivals. In 1548, for example, the young Mary Stuart, then aged six, was brought to France under an escort of the Scots Guard. Ten years later, a detachment of the Guard spearheaded the army of François, Duc de Guise, when, in an action that made him a national hero, he wrested the long-contested port of Calais from English hands.

Among the Scottish families contributing to the Guard were, as we have seen, the Montgomeries. In 1549, there were five Montgomeries serving in the unit simultaneously. Between 1543 and 1561, a period of nearly twenty years, the Guard were commanded first by James de Montgomery, then by Gabriel, then by James again. In June, 1559, there occurred one of the most famous and dramatic events of the sixteenth century, whereby Gabriel de Montgomery inscribed for himself, his family and the Guard a permanent place in the history books – and, knowingly or otherwise, struck a major blow for the houses of Guise and Lorraine.

As part of the festivities attending the marriage of two of his daughters, Henri II of France had scheduled a gala tournament, attended by nobles from all over Europe. The king himself was famous for his own love of jousting and was eager to participate personally in the event. The assembled populace and dignitaries watched him enter the lists. He tilted first against the Duc de Savoie, then against François, Duc de Guise. The third combat must have seemed, to the spectators, particularly safe. It pitted the king against his old friend and ostensibly loyal servitor, Gabriel de Montgomery, Captain of the Scots Guard. Because neither adversary was unseated, Henri considered the first clash of lances to be unsatisfactory. Despite the protests of his entourage, he demanded a second combat, and Montgomery consented. The two men charged each other again, and this time the lances splintered as they were supposed to do. But Montgomery 'neglected to throw away the broken shaft', which struck the king's helm, burst open his visor and sent a jagged fragment of wood into his head above the right eye.[7]

There was, of course, wholesale consternation. Half a dozen criminals were promptly decapitated and subjected to similar wounds, which physicians hastened to examine in an attempt to find the best method of treatment. These efforts proved futile, and Henri, after eleven days of agony, died. Many people were suspicious, but Montgomery's action could not be proved anything other than an accident, and he was not officially blamed for the king's death. Tact impelled him to retire from his captaincy of the Scots Guard, however, and he withdrew to his estates in Normandy. Later, in England, he converted to Protestantism. When he returned to France, it was as one of the military leaders of the Protestant faction during the Wars of Religion. Taken prisoner, he was executed at Paris in 1574.

The death of Henri II attracted more attention and commentary than it might otherwise have done, primarily because it had been forecast. It had been forecast twice, in fact – seven years before by Luca Gaurico, a prestigious astrologer,[8] and four years before by Nostradamus, who in 1555 had published the first of his celebrated compilations of prophecy, called *The Centuries*, which contained the ambiguous but suggestive quatrain:

> *Le lyon ieune le vieux surmontera;*
> *En champ bellique par singulier duelle;*
> *Dans cayge d'or les yeux luy crevera,*
> *Deux classes une puis mourir mort cruelle.*[9]

The young lion will master the old
On the martial field by single combat;
In a golden cage [casque] his eyes will be burst open,
Two divisions in one, then a cruel death.

These lines had resonated in many people's minds and hung over the entire tournament. Henri's death in the lists seemed to be vindicating proof of Nostradamus's capacity to 'foresee the future', and established him as Europe's leading prophet, not only for his own age, but in the eyes of posterity as well. Yet we ourselves, along with a number of other recent commentators, have argued that the French king's death at the hands of Gabriel de Montgomery was not an accident at all, but part of an elaborately contrived plan.[10] In the light of such evidence as is now available, Nostradamus's 'prophecy' seems not to have been a 'prophecy' at all, but a species of blueprint for action, perhaps some sort of coded instruction or signal. To or from whom? To or from the houses of Guise and Lorraine, on whose behalf Nostradamus now appears to have been acting as a clandestine agent. And if this is so, Gabriel de Montgomery would have been his co-conspirator – or, at any rate, the instrument chosen by the Guise-Lorraine faction to execute their design, in such a fashion that no one could be charged with criminal intent.

Certainly Henri's death could not have been more opportune for Guise-Lorraine interests. Despite increasingly brazen efforts to turn it to account, however, they failed to capitalise on it as effectively as they desired. For the next decade, virtual anarchy prevailed in France as the warring factions – Valois and Guise-Lorraine – conspired and jockeyed for the throne. In 1563, François, Duc de Guise, was assassinated. The Scots Guard became increasingly public in their support for Stuart interests, which coincided with Guise-Lorraine interests; and they therefore incurred a growing mistrust from the Valois monarchy until Henri II's grandson, Henri III, refused to provide maintenance for them. Although they were eventually reconstituted, they were never to attain anything approaching their former status.

In Scotland and in France, everything was to come to a head at once. In 1587, Mary Queen of Scots was executed by her relative, Elizabeth I. In 1588, the year of the Spanish Armada, François de Guise's son, the new Duc de Guise, along with his brother, the Cardinal de Guise, were both, on the orders of Henri III, assassinated at Blois. A year later, Henri was assassinated in turn by vindictive Guise-Lorraine adherents. Only under Henri IV, a monarch acceptable to all factions, was a semblance of order restored to France.

By that time, however, the houses of Guise and Lorraine had lost two generations of dynamic, charismatic but ruthless young men. The Valois dynasty had fared even worse: it had been extinguished completely and was never again to occupy the French throne. For the next two centuries, France was to be ruled by the Bourbons.

As for the Scots Guard, even when reconstituted, they were greatly reduced in number and, by 1610, had lost virtually all their privileges, becoming simply another regiment in the French army. During the seventeenth century, two-thirds of their personnel were Frenchmen, not Scots. Nevertheless, a vestige of their former prestige still clung to them. In 1612, they were commanded by the Duke of York, subsequently Charles I of England. Interestingly enough, the Guard's rolls for 1624 show three Setons, one of whom is named David.[11] By 1679, he had become a brigadier. The Guard themselves were last to see service in 1747, during the War of the Austrian Succession, at the Battle of Lauffeld.

The Scots Guard, although sadly diminished by events, constituted, as we have seen, something akin to a neo-Templar institution. It also served as a crucial conduit of transmission. The nobles comprising the Guard were heirs to original Templar traditions.

They were the means by which these traditions were returned to France and planted there, to bear fruit some two centuries later. At the same time, their contact with the houses of Guise and Lorraine exposed them in France to another corpus of 'esoteric' tradition. Some of this corpus had already found its way back to Scotland through Marie de Guise's marriage to James V; but some of it was also to be brought back by the families constituting the Scots Guard. The resulting amalgam was to provide the true nucleus for a later order – the Freemasons.

8

Rosslyn

Some three miles south of Edinburgh lies the village of Roslin. It consists of a single street with a parade of shops and houses and, at the end, two pubs. The village begins at the edge of a steep wooded gorge, the valley of the North Esk. Seven miles away, near where the North Esk joins the South, lies the former Templar preceptory of Balantrodoch, now simply called Temple.

The valley of the North Esk is a mysterious, seemingly haunted place. Carved into a large, moss-covered rock, a wild pagan head gazes at the passer-by. Further downstream, in a cave behind a waterfall, there is what appears to be another huge head with cavernous eyes – perhaps a weathered carving, perhaps a natural product of the elements. The path leading through the valley is crossed by numerous ruined stone buildings and passes by a cliff-face with a dressed stone window. Behind this window is a veritable warren of tunnels, sufficient to conceal a substantial number of men and accessible only by a secret entrance: one had to be lowered down a well. According to legend, Bruce found refuge here during one of the many crises that beset his campaigns.

Perched on the very edge of the gorge is an eerily strange edifice, Rosslyn Chapel. One's first impression is that it appears to be a cathedral in miniature. Not that it is particularly small. But it is so overloaded, so dripping with Gothic carvings and floridly intricate embellishments, that it seems somehow to be a truncated part of something greater – like a fragment of Chartres, transplanted to the top of a Scottish hill. It conveys a sense of amputated lushness, as if the builders, after lavishing their most dazzling skills and costly materials upon the structure, simply stopped abruptly.

In fact, they did. They ran short of money. Rosslyn Chapel was originally intended to be part of something much greater, the 'Lady Chapel' of a vast collegiate church, a full-sized cathedral on the

French scale. In the absence of funds, the project was never realised. From the existing west wall, massive blocks of stone jut forth, awaiting others which never arrived.

The interior of the chapel is a fevered hallucination in stone, a riotous explosion of carved images and geometrical configurations piled on top of one another, flowing into one another, overlapping one another. Motifs that anticipate those of Freemasonry abound. One finds oneself in what appears to be a petrified compendium of 'esoterica'.

As one would expect of such a place, Rosslyn Chapel is a focus for secrets and for legends. The most famous of these pertains to the extraordinary pillar at the east end of the structure, now called 'the Apprentice Pillar'. An account printed in 1774 speaks of:

> ... a tradition that has prevailed in the family of Roslin from father to son, which is, – that a model of this beautiful pillar having been sent from Rome, or some foreign place; the master-mason, upon viewing it, would by no means consent to work off such a pillar, til he should go to Rome, or some foreign part, to take exact inspection of the pillar from which the model had been taken; that, in his absence, whatever might be the occasion of it, an apprentice finished the pillar as it now stands; and that the master, upon his return, seeing the pillar so exquisitely well finished, made enquiry who had done it; and, being stung with envy, slew the apprentice.[1]

Above the west door of the chapel, there is the carved head of a young man with a gash on his right temple. This is said to be the head of the murdered apprentice. Opposite him is the head of a bearded man, the master who killed him. To his right, there is another head, that of a woman, called 'the Widowed Mother'. It is thus made clear that the unnamed precocious youth was – to use a phrase familiar to all Freemasons – a 'Son of the Widow'. As we have noted, the same phrase was used to designate Perceval or Parzival in the Grail Romances.

The Masonic connotations of the chapel and its symbolism can hardly be coincidental, for Rosslyn was built by the family which, perhaps more than any other in Britain, became associated with later Freemasonry – the Saint-Clairs or, as they are now known, the Sinclairs.

Sir William Sinclair and Rosslyn Chapel

As we have seen, noble families such as the Hamiltons, the

Montgomeries, the Setons and the Stuarts contributed successive generations of their sons to the Scots Guard. So, too, did the Sinclairs. In the late fifteenth century, three Sinclairs were serving in the Guard at the same time. In the mid sixteenth century – the period of Gabriel de Montgomery – there were no fewer than four Sinclairs in the unit. Altogether, between 1473 and the death of Mary Stuart in 1587, the rolls of the Scots Guard testify to the enrolment of ten members of the family from Scotland. And, of course, there was also the French branch of the family, the Norman Saint-Clair-sur-Epte, which was particularly active in the French politics of the age.

While certain members of the Sinclair family were pursuing military and diplomatic careers on the Continent, others were equally busy at home – as, indeed, they had been since Bruce's time. In the early years of the fourteenth century, William Sinclair had been Bishop of Dunkeld. Along with Bishops Wishart of Glasgow, Lamberton of St Andrews, Mark of the Isles and David of Moray, William Sinclair had been one of the five leading Scottish ecclesiastics to rally around Bruce and his cause. The bishop's nephew, also named William, had been one of Bruce's closest friends and retainers. On Bruce's death in 1329, it was Sir William Sinclair, along with Sir James Douglas, who embarked with his heart for the Holy Land, only to die in Spain.

In the late fourteenth century, a hundred years before Columbus, another Sinclair was to embark on an even more audacious exploit. Around 1395, Sir Henry Sinclair, Earl (or 'Prince', as he is sometimes styled) of Orkney, together with the Venetian explorer Antonio Zeno, attempted to cross the Atlantic. Certainly he reached Greenland, where Zeno's brother, also an explorer, claimed to have discovered a monastery in 1391; recent studies suggest he may even have reached what was later to be called the New World.[2] According to certain accounts, there is some intriguing evidence to indicate that he intended making for Mexico.[3] If this is true, it would explain why, when Cortés arrived in 1520, he was identified by the Aztecs not only with the god Quetzalcoatl, but also with a blond-haired blue-eyed white man who had allegedly preceded him long in the past.

'Prince' Henry's grandson, Sir William Sinclair, was also active at sea. The husband of Sir James Douglas's niece, and brother-in-law to Sir James himself, he had been appointed Grand Admiral of Scotland in 1436, and was subsequently to become Chancellor as well. But his greatest renown, which was to link him ever after with Masonic and other esoteric traditions, lay in the sphere of architecture. It was under Sir William's auspices that, in 1446, the foundations for a large collegiate church were laid at Rosslyn.[4] In 1450, the structure was formally dedicated to St Matthew and work proper began. While it proceeded, another William Sinclair – probably the nephew of Rosslyn's builder – became the first member of his family to enrol in the Scots Guard and rose to prominence in the unit.

The building of Rosslyn Chapel was to take forty years. It was finally completed in the 1480s by Sir William's son, Oliver Sinclair, a close associate of Lord George Seton, who swore fealty to Oliver Sinclair for life at this time. Oliver Sinclair never proceeded with the rest of the church, probably because, by now, as it appears, Sinclair energies were being diverted elsewhere. Sir William's grandson, also named Oliver, was a military officer, close confidant and Master of the Royal Household to James V. In 1542, he commanded the Scottish army at Solway Moss, where he was captured. On giving his parole to aid the English cause, he was released, but seems not to have held to his oath. In 1545, he was ordered to return to prison in England – whereupon he proceeded to disappear from history, presumably going to ground in the Scottish hinterlands or perhaps abroad.

Oliver's brother, Henry Sinclair, was Bishop of Ross. In 1541, he was appointed Abbot of Kilwinning – a name which was later to figure crucially in Freemasonry. In 1561, he was appointed to the Privy Council of Mary Queen of Scots. Not surprisingly, he maintained intimate contacts with the Guise and Lorraine factions in France, spending much of his time in Paris. His and Oliver's younger brother, John, also became a bishop. John, too, was a counsellor to Mary Queen of Scots and in 1565 performed her marriage to Henry Stewart, Lord Darnley, at Holyrood.

The Sinclairs were thus at the heart of Scottish affairs in the fifteenth and sixteenth centuries. They moved in the same circles as families like the Setons and the Montgomeries. Like the Setons and the Montgomeries, they were close to the Stuart monarchy, contributed personnel to the Scots Guard and maintained intimate links with the Guise and Lorraine factions in France. Indeed, their links with the Guise and Lorraine factions would probably have been even closer by virtue of the French branch of the family. At the same time, and more even than the other Scottish houses, the Sinclairs were already becoming associated with what subsequent Freemasonry would come to regard as its pedigree.

As we have noted, the foundations for Rosslyn Chapel were laid in 1446 and the actual work commenced four years later. These are among the few definitive and confirmed facts. Our information

14 The remains of Rosslyn Castle, near Edinburgh, home of the Saint-Clairs (now Sinclairs) since the twelfth century. It was destroyed in 1650 by General Monk.

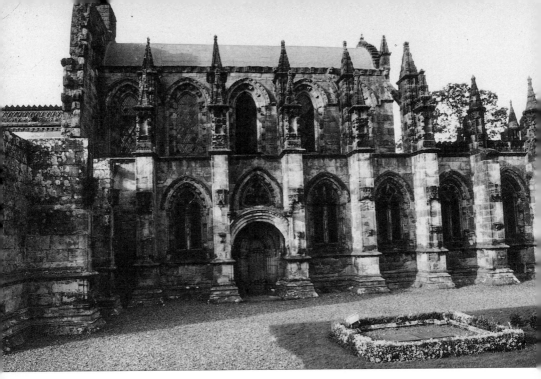

15 Rosslyn Chapel, orginally intended to be the Lady Chapel of a much larger cathedral. The chapel's foundations were laid in 1446 and work continued on it for about forty years. Its sealed vaults contain the bodies of all the barons of Rosslyn – said to be laid out in their armour rather than placed in coffins.

16 The head of the murdered apprentice, Rosslyn Chapel. The story tells of the master-mason, jealous of the apprentice's skill at building a stone pillar, who killed the young mason with a blow to the forehead. The story has many obvious parallels with the Freemasonic legend of the death of Hiram Abiff, builder of the Temple.

17 The Apprentice Pillar, Rosslyn Chapel, one of three pillars on a raised and separated stage at the east of the chapel. It was for building this, according to legend, that the apprentice was killed.

18–19 Rosslyn Chapel. Examples of the prevalent Celtic vegetation god, 'The Green Man', which pervades all the more conventional secular and Christian decoration of the chapel.

concerning almost everything else, though not implausible and certainly not disproved, we owe to later tradition – later in some cases by a century and a half, in other cases by three or more.

According to this later tradition, Sir William Sinclair, in preparation for the building of his chapel, imported stonemasons and other artisans from the Continent.[5] The town of Roslin itself was supposedly built to house and accommodate the new arrivals. Tradition also has it:

> ... that in 1441 James II, King of Scotland, appointed St Clair Patron and protector of Scottish Masons; that the Office was hereditary; that after his death, circa 1480, his descendants held annual meetings at Kilwinning, ... the nomination of Craft Office-Bearers remained a prerogative of the Kings of Scotland; that it was neglected by James VI when he became King of England ...[6]

It is important to note that 'Masonry' in this context does not imply Freemasonry as we know it today. On the contrary, it refers to the guild or guilds of professional workers and builders in stone. As we shall see, these men were not all just simple artisans, unlettered and untutored manual labourers. But neither were they mystical philosophers who, in between construction projects, met in secret conclaves, conducted clandestine initiations with passwords and meaningful handshakes, and discussed the mysteries of the cosmos. In the terminology that was later to arise, these men were held to be practitioners of 'operative Masonry' – in other words, the practical application of mathematics and geometry to the art of architecture.

Sir William Sinclair's appointment in 1441, then, attests simply to his involvement in the art of building – and perhaps in the mathematical and geometric principles associated with architecture. But this in itself is unusual. Ordinarily, a lord, a monarch, a municipality or some other patron would commission an entire team of architects and masons, who undertook the whole of the work themselves. The head of this team, called 'the Master of the Work', would base his plan on a particular geometry, and all subsequent construction would be made to harmonise with that basic pattern. The 'Master' would arrange for wooden templates to be cut to his design, and the stonemasons would proceed in accordance with the templates.

At Rosslyn, however, Sir William Sinclair appears to have designed his own chapel and acted as 'Master of the Work' himself. In the early eighteenth century, the stepson of a later Sinclair – who had access to all the family's charters and archives before they were destroyed by fire in 1722 – writes that:

> . . . it came into his [Sir William Sinclair's] minde to build a house for Gods service, of most curious worke, the which, that it might be done with greater glory and splendor, he caused artificers to be brought from other regions and forraigne kingdomes . . . and to the end the worke might be the more rare; first he caused the draughts to be drawn upon Eastland boards, and made the carpenters to carve them according to the draughts thereon, and then gave them for patterns to the masons, that they might thereby cut the like in stone.[7]

Sir William would thus appear to have been considerably more knowledgeable and technically expert than the typical noble of his time; and his appointment as 'Patron and protector of Scottish Masons' would appear to have been more than just honorary. And thus, as subsequent charters attest, the appointment may have been conferred by the king, but it was also conferred – or, at any rate, ratified – by the masons themselves. As one such charter states: 'The lairds of Roslin has ever been patrons and protectors of us and our privileges.'[8] And a letter dating from the late seventeenth century declares:

> The Lairds of Roslin have been great architects and patrons of building for many generations. They are obliged to receive the Mason's word which is a secret signal masons have throughout the world to know one another by . . .[9]

In 1475, while Rosslyn was still under construction, the stone-masons of Edinburgh were granted a charter of incorporation as a guild and proceeded to draw up trade regulations. Taking its name from the place where the charter was ratified, this seemingly routine medieval transaction later became known as the 'Incorporation of Mary's Chapel'.[10] But routine though it may have been, it came to enjoy considerable significance for later Freemasonry. When such Freemasonry surfaced in Scotland, it revolved initially around a lodge known as 'Lodge No. 1', also referred to as 'Mary's Chapel'.

Subsequent charters of incorporation followed, but the next relevant document does not appear until more than a century later. In 1583, William Schaw, a confidant of James VI (later James I of England), received from the king the post of Master of Work and 'General Warden of the Masons'. A copy of his statutes, dating from 1598 and inscribed in his own hand, survives today in the oldest minute book of Mary's Chapel Lodge No. 1 in Edinburgh.[11]

Schaw's appointment, of course, did not imply any challenge to, or usurpation of, the status of the Sinclairs. That was an internal matter among masons themselves and had already become one of their accepted principles. Schaw's appointment, on the other hand, was a wholly external matter, establishing him as an official in the royal administrative apparatus, rather like a Permanent Secretary today. He would have acted, in effect, as a kind of liaison or ombudsman between masons and the crown.

Schaw's tenure terminated in 1602. Shortly before or shortly after that date, another important document was issued, known as the 'Saint Clair Charter'. The text laments that: '. . . our hail craft has been destitute of ane patron and protector and overseer, which has gendrid many false corruptions and imperfections'.[12] From this, it would seem that the Sinclairs, whatever their hereditary status, had been lax, negligent or worse. And yet the charter proceeds to reaffirm the old allegiance by acknowledging the William Sinclair of the time, and his heirs, as overseers, patrons and judges of the craft and its members. The signatures appended to this statement come from lodges already in existence at Edinburgh, Dunfermline, St Andrews and Haddington.

In 1630, a second 'Saint Clair Charter' was drawn up. It repeated the tenets of the previous charter and elaborated on them. The attached signatures bear witness to new lodges in Dundee, Glasgow, Ayr and Stirling.[13] There are thus palpable indications of a growing dissemination of lodges and, at the same time, of a process of increasing centralisation. And there is also, of course, something significant in the reaffirmation of the long-standing link between masonry and the Sinclairs, whatever the latter's past negligence may have been. One can only conclude from this that the family's association with the craft derived either from what was then common knowledge or from a tradition so firmly established and deeply rooted it could not be altered. One can also conclude that both masonry and the Sinclairs, at the beginning of the seventeenth century, found it desirable to promulgate their affiliation. Masonry had, by then, acquired a certain prestige which – as any observer at the time could have divined – was destined to increase. Association with it, for reasons soon to be made clear, was conferring ever more prestige. And yet nobody, not even the other prominent Scottish families, ever presumed to challenge the Sinclair claim or tried to arrogate it for themselves. The Setons, the Hamiltons, the Montgomeries and other such families, including the Stuarts, were all to become deeply involved in what was already emerging as Freemasonry. Indeed, according to a manuscript dating from 1658, one

John Mylne, 'Master of the Lodge at Scone, and at his Majesty's own desire, entered James VI as "frieman, meason and fellow craft"'.[14] Pride of place, however, continued to be accorded to the Sinclairs.

Rosslyn and the Gypsies

The Sinclairs were not only hereditary patrons and protectors of masonry. They had also, during the sixteenth century, established themselves as patrons and protectors of gypsies, who 'enjoyed the favour and protection of the Roslin family as late as the first quarter of the seventeenth century'.[15] Legislation against gypsies in Scotland had always been harsh, and during the Reformation it became more so. In 1574, the Scottish Parliament decreed that all gypsies apprehended should be whipped, branded on the cheek or ear, or have the right ear cut off.[16] Further, even more severe, legislation was introduced in 1616. By the end of the seventeenth century, gypsies were being deported *en masse* to Virginia, Barbados and Jamaica.

In 1559, however, Sir William Sinclair was Lord Justice General of Scotland under Queen Mary. Although his efforts do not appear to have been notably successful, he nevertheless opposed the measures then being implemented against gypsies. Availing himself of his judicial status, he is said to have intervened on one critical occasion and saved a particular gypsy from the scaffold. From then on, the gypsies became annual visitors to the Sinclair estates, which offered them a welcome refuge. Every May and June, they would congregate in the fields below Rosslyn Castle, where they would perform their plays. Sir William Sinclair is even said to have made available two towers of the castle for them to occupy during their stay in the vicinity. These towers came to be known as 'Robin Hood' and 'Little John'.[17] The designations are significant, for *Robin Hood and Little John* was a favourite May-tide play performed by English and Scottish gypsies at the time; and like the gypsies, it had been officially banned, the Scottish Parliament decreeing on 20 June 1555 that 'no one should act as Robin Hood, Little John, Abbot of Unreason or Queen of May'.[18]

Gypsies had, of course, long been credited with 'second sight'. Towards the beginning of the seventeenth century, this faculty became increasingly attributed to Freemasons as well. One of the earliest and most famous references to Freemasonry as we know it today appears in a 1638 poem by Henry Adamson of Perth, called 'The Muses Threnodie'. This poem contains the oft-quoted lines:

> For we be brethren of the Rosie Crosse;
> We have the Mason word, and second sight,
> Things for to come we can foretell aright . . .[19]

This, certainly, is the first known suggestion that Freemasons were endowed with 'occult powers'. The powers in question are unmistakably gypsy; and the common denominator between gypsies and Freemasonry was Sir William Sinclair.

More important for the evolution and development of Freemasonry, however, is the fact that the gypsies came to Rosslyn to perform plays. Indeed, one prominent authority on the subject has stated that the troupes received every May and June at Rosslyn were not gypsies at all, but 'in reality a company of strolling players'.[20] Whether they were gypsies or not, the fact remains that they regularly performed, at the home of Scotland's Chief Justice, a play banned by law.

Why should it have been banned? In part, of course, because the subject matter itself – the endorsement of a legendary 'outlaw' – would have been seen as 'subversive'. In part, because the austere Calvinist Protestantism then being promulgated in Scotland by John Knox regarded – as Cromwell's Puritans were to do in England a century later – all theatre as 'immoral'. But the primary reason becomes evident from the phraseology of the decree whereby the play was banned. 'No one should act as Robin Hood, Little John, Abbot of Unreason or Queen of May.' The 'Abbot of Unreason' is, naturally, the Friar Tuck of legend; the 'Queen of May' is the figure more generally known as Maid Marion. But both of these figures were originally very different from what later traditions have made of them. In fact, Robin Hood, all through the Middle Ages in England and Scotland, was only secondarily the 'outlaw' of subsequent story. Pre-eminently, he was a species of 'fairy' derived ultimately from the old Celtic and Saxon fertility god or vegetation deity, the so-called 'Green Man', while in popular folklore Robin Hood was interchangeable with 'Green Robin', 'Robin of the Greenwood', 'Robin Goodfellow', Shakespeare's Puck in *A Midsummer Night's Dream*, who, at the summer solstice, presides over fertility, sexuality and nuptials.

The Robin Hood legend provided, in effect, a handy guise whereby the fertility rites of ancient paganism were introduced back into the bosom of nominally Christian Britain. Every May Day, there would be a festival of unabashedly pagan origin. Rituals would be enacted around the 'May Pole', traditional symbol of the archaic goddess of sexuality and fertility. On Midsummer's Day, every village virgin would become, metaphorically, Queen of the May. Many of them would be ushered into the 'greenwood' where they would undergo their sexual initiation at the hands of a youth playing the role of Robin Hood or Robin Goodfellow, while Friar Tuck, the 'Abbot of Unreason', would officiate, 'blessing' the mating couples in a parody of formal nuptials. By virtue of such role-playing, the borders separating dramatic masque and fertility ritual would effectively dissolve. May Day would be, in fact, a day of orgy. Nine months later, it would produce, throughout the British Isles, its annual crop of children. It was in these 'sons of Robin' that many such family names as Robinson and Robertson first originated.

In the context of the time, then, a play entitled *Robin Hood and Little John* – a play enacted every May and June at Rosslyn, whether by gypsies or by a troupe of strolling performers, which involved an orgiastic 'Abbot of Unreason' and a Venus-like Queen of the May – would not have been conventional drama as we conceive it today. On the contrary, it would have been a pagan fertility rite, or a dramatisation of a pagan fertility rite, which Christians of every stamp – whether Calvinist or Roman Catholic – could only have found scandalous and sinful. But this was what 'theatre' usually meant or implied for the rural populace of the age. It is hardly surprising, therefore, that the sombre, self-righteous Puritan legislators of sixteenth-century Scotland and seventeenth-century England should have waxed sanctimonious about such 'theatre'.

What is significant is that the Sinclairs not only sanctioned, but welcomed and protected, these practices. And Rosslyn not only provided an ideal milieu for them. It might, to all intents and purposes, have been designed specifically for them. The dominant theme of the chapel, underlying all the elaborate Christian overlay, is unabashedly pagan and Celtic. The figure that occurs most frequently is the 'Green Man' – a human head with vines issuing from its mouth and sometimes its ears, then spreading wildly, in tangled proliferation, over the walls. Indeed, the 'Green Man' is everywhere in Rosslyn Chapel, peering out at every turn from liana-like tendrils which he himself engenders. His head – for there is never a body attached to it – is like the heads the Templars were accused of worshipping, or the severed heads of ancient Celtic tradition, both of which were talismans of fertility. Rosslyn thus invokes both the Templars and the archaic Celtic kingdom of Scotland which Bruce sought to restore.

At Rosslyn Chapel, a number of critical elements, in some cases from very diverse sources, converged. Residues and deep-rooted traditions from the past were brought together with current, at times precociously innovative, developments. There must, for example, have been a productive interaction between the Sinclairs, the 'operative' stonemasons who built under their auspices and the gypsies or travelling players who performed under their protection. The fusion of such elements was a crucial step in the eventual coalescence of Freemasonry. But other elements – the old chivalric Templar legacy, for instance – had yet to be re-assimilated. And certain supremely important new elements had still to be added.

For the rural populace, as we have seen, the idea of 'theatre' was represented by such works as *Robin Hood and Little John*. In the urban centres of Britain, however, there was another kind of theatre, more familiar to us today and more readily accorded a legitimate place in cultural tradition. This was the miracle or mystery play, which first began as early as the twelfth century and attained its fullest development during the fourteenth and fifteenth. Ultimately deriving from the Mass and liturgical sources, the miracle play was a combination of drama and pageant. Most miracle plays were embedded in sequences or cycles, four of which survive today – those of York, Chester, Wakefield and one other sometimes ascribed to Coventry. Moving from the precincts of the church out into the market place, these cycles sought, on feast days, to involve the entire populace of a town in a re-creation and re-enactment of biblical material. Episodes from scripture – the murder of Abel, for example, Noah and his ark, the Nativity and even the Crucifixion – would be portrayed in simplified, easily digested dramatic form. God and Jesus would both often appear 'on stage'. Evil – generally in the form of a clownish Devil or buffoon – would be duly castigated. Sometimes topical issues would be raised and contemporary sources of grievance satirised. Performances would be staged on large wagons, like modern carnival floats, located at various points around the town, and spectators would move from one point to the next as though through the stations of the cross in church. The performers would be the members of the various guilds – the Tanners, Plasterers, Shipwrights, Bookbinders, Goldsmiths, Mercers, Butchers, Ostlers – and each guild would be responsible for depicting a specific biblical episode.

In an important article published in 1974, the Reverend Neville Barker Cryer has demonstrated how the miracle plays were a major source of the rituals later to be found in Freemasonry, providing material which would otherwise have been amorphous with a dramatic structure and form.[21] Certainly the guilds of 'operative' stonemasons were particularly active in the staging of miracle plays. Because much of their work had consisted of building churches, abbeys and other religious houses, they enjoyed a uniquely close relationship with the ecclesiastical establishment. This made them more familiar than other guilds with liturgical techniques of dramatisation, as well as with certain bodies of biblical material.[22] And as the Reformation curtailed the programme of religious building, the guilds of stonemasons had more opportunity to develop their skills in ritual drama, gradually evolving their own rites which became ever more divorced from taboo Catholicism.

As we have noted, each guild in a town was traditionally responsible for dramatising specific bodies of biblical material, specific incidents and episodes from scripture. In some instances, the assignment of particular subject matter to a particular guild would have been more or less arbitrary. It would have been difficult, for example, to find something in scripture of unique relevance to, say, the glovemakers or, as they were called, Gaunters. On the other hand, there *were* certain biblical narratives of unique relevance to the stonemasons. Moreover, their proximity to the ecclesiastical establishment would have enabled them to choose, and eventually to monopolise, the narratives they wished to perform. The Reverend Cryer suggests that something of this sort was indeed the case. Masonic guilds would gradually have arrogated to themselves the prerogative of dramatising material of particular pertinence to their own highly specialised work – such as the building of Solomon's Temple.[23] And thus the central mythic drama of later Freemasonry – the murder of Hiram Abiff – would first have been enacted by stonemasons in a miracle play.[24]

9

Freemasonry:
Geometry of the Sacred

Freemasonry is itself profoundly uncertain of its own origins. In the four centuries or so of its formal existence, it has endeavoured, sometimes desperately, to establish a pedigree. Masonic writers have filled numerous books with efforts to chronicle the history of their craft. Some of these efforts have been not just spurious, but, on occasion, positively comical in their extravagance, naïveté and wishful thinking. Others have not just been plausible, but have opened important new doors of historical research. In the end, however, most such research has culminated in uncertainty; and, not infrequently, it has provoked more questions than it answered. One problem is that Freemasons themselves have too often sought a single coherent heritage, a single unaltered skein of tradition extending from pre-Christian times to the present day. In fact, Freemasonry is rather like a ball of twine ensnarled by a playful kitten. It consists of numerous skeins, which must be disentangled before its various origins can be discerned.

Masonic legend argues that Freemasonry, at least in England, descends from the Saxon King Athelstan. Athelstan's son is said to have joined an already existing fraternity of masons, become an enthusiastic mason himself and, by dint of his status, obtained a 'free charter' for his brethren. As a result of this royal recognition, a masonic conclave is supposed to have been convened at York and the regulations drafted which formed the basis of English Freemasonry.

Subsequent Masonic historians have exhaustively investigated this account. The consensus is that little or no evidence exists to support it. But even if it were true, it would still leave the most important questions unanswered. Where did the masons allegedly patronised by Athelstan and his son come from? Where did they learn their craft? What was so special about it? Why should it have commanded from the throne the protection it reportedly did?

Certain Masonic writers have sought to answer such questions by invoking the so-called 'Comacine Masons'. According to these writers, there existed, during the latter days of the Roman Empire, a college of architects initiated into what would later be called Masonic mysteries. When Rome fell, the college, based at Lake Como, is said to have escaped and quietly to have perpetuated its teachings through successive generations; its adepts, during the Dark Ages, are said to have found their way to various centres across Europe, including Athelstan's court.

Neither of these two accounts is altogether implausible. Some sort of building programme does appear to have been pursued during Athelstan's reign, to which York bears testimony. It was perhaps the most ambitious programme of its sort in Europe at the time, and may well have involved some new, or newly rediscovered, technical or technological expertise. Moreover, early Bibles have been found, dating from Saxon England, which depict God in the characteristically Masonic role of architect. And there is indeed some evidence that some sort of architectural college did exist on an island in Lake Como during the latter days of the Roman Empire. It is perfectly possible that some of this college's teachings were preserved and later disseminated across Western Europe.

But neither Athelstan and his son, nor the Comacine Masons, serve to account for one of the most salient aspects of later Freemasonry – the fact that it contains a major skein of Judaic tradition filtered through Islam. The corpus of legends central to Freemasonry – including, of course, the building of Solomon's Temple – derives ultimately from Old Testament material, both canonical and apocryphal, as well as from Judaic and Islamic commentaries upon it. It is worth looking at the most important of these legends – the murder of Hiram Abiff – in some detail.

The Hiram story is rooted in the context of the Old Testament. It figures in two books, I Kings and II Chronicles. According to I Kings V: 1–6:

> Hiram the king of Tyre sent an embassy to Solomon, having learnt that he had been anointed king in succession to his father and because Hiram had always been a friend of David. And Solomon sent this message to Hiram . . . 'I therefore plan to build a temple . . . so now have cedars of Lebanon cut down for me . . .'[1]

There then follows a detailed account of the construction of the Temple by both Solomon's builders and Hiram's. The levy of manpower raised for the project is said to be in the charge of one Adoniram – a variant spelling, it would appear, of the name of Hiram himself. After the Temple itself is finished, the Israelite monarch wishes to adorn it with two great bronze pillars and other embellishments. Accordingly, in I Kings VII: 13–15:

> King Solomon sent for Hiram of Tyre; he was the son of a widow of the tribe of Naphtali but his father had been a Tyrian, a bronzeworker. He came to King Solomon and did all this work for him: He cast two bronze pillars . . .

In II Chronicles II: 3–14 there is a slightly different account:

> Solomon then despatched this message to Huram king of Tyre, . . . 'I am now building a house for the name of Yahweh my God . . . So send me a man skilled in the use of gold, silver, bronze, iron, scarlet, crimson, violet, and the art of engraving too; he is to work with my skilled men . . .' . . . Huram king of Tyre replied . . . 'I am sending you a skilled craftsman, Huram-abi, the son of a Danite woman by a Tyrian father. He is skilled in the use of gold, silver, bronze, iron, stone, wood . . . in engraving of all kinds, and in the execution of any design . . .'

In its treatment of the Temple's master builder, the Old Testament is cursory enough. But Freemasonry – drawing on other sources and/or inventing some of its own – elaborates on the meagre details and develops them into what, in the framework of a conventional organised religion, would constitute a full-fledged and self-contained theology. The story, when it appears in its final form, contains small variations in its particulars, similar to the variations in the Gospels; but its general tenor remains consistent from lodge to lodge, rite to rite and age to age.

The protagonist of the legend is usually known as Hiram Abiff or, probably more accurately, Adoniram. 'Adoniram' is manifestly derived from 'Adonai', the Hebrew word for 'Lord', in much the same way that 'Kaiser' and 'Czar' are derived from 'Caesar'. The master builder would thus have been 'Lord Hiram' – though it has also been suggested that 'Hiram' was not a proper name at all, but a title, perhaps denoting the king or someone connected with the royal house. 'Abiff' is a derivation from the word for 'father'. 'Hiram Abiff' might thus be the king himself, the symbolic father of his people, or he might be the king's father – the ex-king or 'retired' king, who might have abdicated after a stipulated number of years.

In any case, the point is that he would appear to be connected by blood with the royal house of Phoenician Tyre, and is obviously a 'master' versed in the secrets of architecture – the secrets of number, shape, measure and their practical application through geometry. And modern archaeological research confirms that Solomon's Temple, as it is described in the Old Testament, bears an unmistakable resemblance to the actual temples built by the Phoenicians. It is even possible to go a step further. Tyrian temples were erected to the Phoenician mother goddess Astarte (who, subjected to a forcible sex change by the early Church Fathers, entered Christian tradition as the male demon Ashtaroth). In ancient Tyre, Astarte was known by the sobriquets 'Queen of Heaven' and 'Star of the Sea' or 'Stella Maris' – formulae which were also, of course, hi-jacked by Christianity and conferred upon the Virgin. Astarte was worshipped conventionally 'on the high places'; hilltops and mountains – Mount Hermon, for example – abounded with her shrines. And whatever his nominal allegiance to the God of Israel, Solomon was one of her worshippers. Thus, in I Kings III: 3:

> Solomon loved Yahweh: he followed the precepts of David his father, except that he offered sacrifice and incense on the high places.

I Kings XI: 4–5 is even more explicit:

> When Solomon grew old his wives swayed his heart to other gods; and his heart was not wholly with Yahweh his God as his father David's had been. Solomon became a follower of Astarte, the goddess of the Sidonians . . .

Indeed, the famous 'Song of Solomon' itself is a hymn to Astarte, and an invocation of her:

> Come from Lebanon, my promised bride,
> come from Lebanon, come on your way.
> Lower your gaze, from the heights of Amana,
> from the crests of Senir and Hermon.[2]

All of which raises questions about Solomon's Temple, constructed by a Phoenician master builder. Was it indeed dedicated to the God of Israel, or was it dedicated to Astarte?

In any case, Hiram, adept of architecture, is brought by Solomon from Tyre to preside over the building of the Temple – so that 'Solomon's Temple' is ultimately, strictly speaking, 'Hiram's Temple'. In reality, of course, the immense manpower involved in so ambitious an undertaking would have consisted primarily, if not exclusively, of slave labour. In Masonic ritual and tradition, however, at least some of the builders are depicted as free men, or free masons, presumably Tyrian professionals who are paid for their work. They are organised into three grades or degrees – apprentices, fellows and masters. Because they are so numerous, Hiram cannot possibly know all of them personally. In consequence, each grade or degree is given its own word. Apprentices are given the word 'Boaz', after one of the two immense brass pillars or columns supporting the Temple's porch. Fellows are given the word 'Jachin', after the second pillar or column. Masters are given, at least initially, the name 'Jehovah'. Each of these three words is also accompanied by a particular 'sign', or placement of the hands, and a particular 'grip', or handshake. When wages are distributed, each worker presents himself to Hiram, gives the word, sign and grip appropriate to his rank and receives the appropriate payment.

One day, as Hiram is praying in the precincts of his nearly completed edifice, he is accosted by three villains – fellows according to some accounts, apprentices according to others – who hope to obtain the secrets of a superior degree not yet their due. Hiram having entered through the western door, the villains block his exit and demand from him the secret word, sign and grip appropriate to a master. When he refuses to divulge the information they desire, they attack him.

Accounts vary as to which blow he receives at which door, as well as which implement inflicts which wound. For our purposes, it is sufficient that he receives three blows. He is struck on the head with a maul or a hammer. He is hit with a level on one temple and with a plumb on the other. Historically, accounts vary also as to the sequence of these injuries – as to which inaugurates the assault and which constitutes the *coup de grace*. The first wound is received at either the north or the south door. Trailing blood, which leaves a distinctive pattern on the floor, Hiram staggers from exit to exit, receiving an additional blow at each. In all accounts, he dies at the east door. This, in a modern lodge, is where the Master stands to officiate. It is also, of course, where the altar of a church is always placed.

Mortified by what they have done, the three villains proceed to conceal the Master's body. According to most accounts, it is hidden on a nearby mountainside, buried under loose earth. A sprig of acacia – the sacred plant in Freemasonry – is uprooted from an adjacent clump and thrust into the grave so as to make the soil look undisturbed. But seven days later, when nine of Hiram's subordinate masters are searching for him, one of them, climbing the mountainside and seeking a handhold to pull himself upwards, seizes the sprig of acacia, which comes away in his grip. This, of course, leads to the discovery of the murdered man's body. Realising what has happened, and fearing that Hiram may have divulged the master's word before he died, the nine masters resolve to change it. The new word, they agree, will consist of whatever any of them should chance to utter as they disinter the corpse. When Hiram's hand is clasped by the fingers and the wrist, the putrefying skin slips off like a glove. One of the masters exclaims 'Macbenae!' (or any of several variants thereof), which, in some unspecified language, is said to mean 'The flesh falls from the bone', or 'The corpse is rotten', or simply 'The death of a builder'. This becomes the new master's word. Subsequently, the three villains are discovered and punished. Hiram's body, exhumed from the mountainside, is reinterred with great ceremony in the precincts of the Temple, all the masters wearing aprons and gloves of white hide to show that none of them has stained his hands with the dead man's blood.[3]

As we have said, over the last 250 years alternative versions of the story have varied slightly in the sequence of events or in some of the specific details. There are also variations in Solomon's supposed conduct throughout the affair. Sometimes his role is heavily emphasised; sometimes it is played down. But in their essentials, all versions of the legend conform to the outline delineated above. What lurks behind the narrative is another question, which lies beyond the confines of this book, belonging more properly to studies in anthropology, comparative mythology and the origin of religions. In the wake of Sir James Frazer's pioneer work in *The Golden Bough*, commentary has proliferated. Some scholars, as well as certain Masonic writers, have argued that the whole of the Hiram story – like many other narratives in ancient myth and, for that matter, in the Bible too – was a deliberate distortion, a veil intended to mask one of the most archaic and widespread of rituals, that of human sacrifice. It was certainly not uncommon, in the Middle East of biblical times, to consecrate a building with a sacred corpse – a child, a virgin, a king or some other personage of royal blood, a priest or a priestess, a builder. Tomb and shrine were often one and the same. In later epochs, the victim would already be dead, or would be replaced by an animal; but in the beginning, a human being was often deliberately killed, ritually sacrificed, in order to sanctify a site with his or her blood. The story of Abraham and Isaac is only one of numerous indications that the ancient Israelites subscribed to such practices. And indeed, residues of the tradition persisted well into Christian times, with churches frequently being erected on the burial sites of saints – or saints being buried, if not actually killed, in order to consecrate churches. In his novel *Hawksmoor*, published in 1984, Peter Ackroyd depicts a series of early eighteenth-century London churches being built on sites of human sacrifice. What some readers and reviewers regarded as the fantasy of a horror story rests in fact on a long-established principle. At the time of which Ackroyd is writing, Freemasons were almost certainly privy to this principle, even if they never actually implemented it.

In any case, and whatever the atavistic residues concealed within it, the core of the Hiram story is not a latterday fabrication, but a narrative of very great antiquity. As we have noted, there is little enough of it in the Old Testament proper, but there are elaborations and variations among the earliest of Talmudic legends and Judaic apocrypha. Why it should become so important later – why, indeed, Hiram should come to assume the proportions of a veritable Christ-figure – is, of course, another question. But by the Middle Ages, the architect or builder of Solomon's Temple had already become significant to the guilds of 'operative' stonemasons. In 1410, a manuscript connected with one such guild mentions the 'king's son of Tyre', and associates him with an ancient science said to have survived the Flood and been transmitted by Pythagoras and Hermes.[4] A second, admittedly later, manuscript, dating from 1583, cites Hiram and describes him as both the son of the King of Tyre and a 'Master'.[5] These written records bear testimony to what must surely have been a widespread and much older tradition. Such a tradition may account for the parallels between the King of Tyre's son and Athelstan's – both royal princes, both reputed architects, master builders and patrons of masons.

It is not clear precisely when the Hiram story first became central to Freemasonry. Almost certainly, however, it contributed in some measure to the institution's beginnings. Looking back to Sir William Sinclair's Rosslyn Chapel, and the head of 'the murdered apprentice', it is possible to see in his wound an injury identical to the one allegedly inflicted on Hiram, while the woman's head in the chapel is known as 'the Widowed Mother'. Here, then, are motifs from the Hiram story long antecedent to modern Freemasonry.

According to later Freemasonic writers, the skull-and-crossbones was long associated with both the Templars and with the murdered Master. For how long it had in reality been so remains unknown.

During the seventeenth and eighteenth centuries, the skull-and-crossbones was used as a device to denote Hiram's grave – and, by extension, the grave of any Master Mason. As we have seen, legend has it that Bruce, on exhumation of his grave, was said to have been found buried with his leg-bones crossed beneath his skull. The skull-and-crossbones was also an important part of the regalia of the Freemasonic degree known as 'Knight Templar', and it figures prominently among the graves at Kilmartin and elsewhere in Scotland, along with other specifically Masonic emblems.

In Freemasonry today, the death of Hiram is ritually re-enacted by every aspirant to the so-called Third Degree, the Degree of Master Mason. But there is now one crucial addition: the Master is resurrected. 'To go through the Third Degree' means to die ritually and be reborn. One acts the part of Hiram; one becomes the Master and experiences his death; one is then, according to the phraseology employed, 'raised' a Master Mason. There is an interesting echo of this rite in an episode pertaining to the prophet Elijah in I Kings XVII: 17–24. On a visit to Sidon, near the city gate, Elijah finds a widow gathering firewood and is taken into her house. During his sojourn with her, her son – the 'son of a widow' – becomes ill and dies. Elijah 'stretched himself on the child three times', crying for God's succour – whereupon 'the soul of the child returned to him again and he revived'.

There is one curious footnote to this survey of the Hiram story. Until the eighteenth century, it was kept rigorously secret and seems to have been part of the arcane lore confided only to initiated brethren. Around 1737, however, in France, paranoia about Freemasonry and its secrecy set in (and has continued to the present day). Police raids ensued. Certain individuals appear to have infiltrated lodges in order to report on the activities conducted there. A few Freemasons defected or leaked information. As a result, there began to appear the first in an ongoing series of 'exposures', all of which have proved signally anticlimactic. Nevertheless, they cast the Hiram legend more or less into public domain, rendered it familiar to non-Freemasons and divested it of much of its portentous mystique.

In 1851, the French poet Gérard de Nerval, having returned from a tour of what was then an exotic Middle East, published a massive 700-page memoir, *Voyage en Orient*. In this opus, Nerval not only recounted his own experiences (some of them semi-fictionalised); he also included travelogue, commentaries on manners and mores, legends he had encountered, folk-tales and stories he had heard.

Among the latter, there is the fullest, most detailed and most evocative version of the Hiram story ever to appear in print, either before or after. Nerval not only recited the basic narrative, as it is outlined above. He also divulged – for the first time, to our knowledge – a skein of eerie mystical traditions associated in Freemasonry with Hiram's background and pedigree.[6]

What is particularly curious is that Nerval makes no mention of Freemasonry whatsoever. Pretending that his narrative is a species of regional folk-tale, never known in the West before, he claims to have heard it, orally recited by a Persian raconteur, in a Constantinople coffee-house.

In another writer, such apparent naïveté might be plausible, and there would be no particular reason to query his assertions. But Nerval was part of a literary circle which included Charles Nodier, Charles Baudelaire, Théophile Gautier and the young Victor Hugo, all of whom were steeped in arcana and esoterica. It is not clear whether Nerval was himself a Freemason. He may not have been. He may, in the murky subterranean world of occult sects and secret societies, have had other allegiances. But there can be no question whatever that he knew what he was doing – that he knew his narrative (even if he *did* hear a version of it in a Constantinople coffee-house) was not a quaint Middle Eastern folk-tale, but the central myth of European Freemasonry. Why Nerval chose to divulge it, and why he divulged it in the manner he did, remains a mystery, rooted in the complex politics of the mid-nineteenth-century French 'occult revival'. But his weird, haunting and evocative retelling of the Hiram legend is the most complete and detailed version we have, or are likely ever to have.

The Architect as Magus

The Hiram legend represents a strand of Judaic tradition in Freemasonry. In certain of its versions, however, including Gérard de Nerval's, it also incorporates Islamic elements and influences; and, as we have seen, Nerval claimed to have obtained his version from Islamic sources. How, then, did it find its way into the heart of medieval Christian Europe? And why should it have been so important to the builders of Christian religious edifices? Let us begin by considering the second of these questions.

Judaism forbade the making of graven images. Islam inherited and perpetuated that taboo. Under both Judaism and Islam, a cultural heritage evolved which was inimical to representational art

– to any depiction of natural forms, including, of course, that of man himself. The kind of decoration one associates with Christian cathedrals is not to be found in the synagogue or the mosque.

In part, this interdict derives from the fact that any attempt to depict the natural world, including the human form, was deemed to be blasphemous – an attempt by man to compete with God as creator, even to usurp and displace God as creator. God alone was held to possess the prerogative of creating forms out of nothingness, creating life out of clay. For man to create a replica of such forms, and a replica of life, out of wood, stone, pigment or any other substance, was a trespass on the divine prerogative – and, of necessity, a parody or travesty of it.

But there was also a deeper theological justification behind this apparently over-literal dogma – a justification which overlapped, and may even have been influenced by, ancient Pythagorean thought. God, in both Judaism and Islam, was One. God was a unity. God was everything. The forms of the phenomenal world, on the other hand, were numerous, manifold, multifarious and diverse. Such forms bore witness not to the divine unity, but to the fragmentation of the temporal world. If God was to be discerned in the creation at all, it was not in the multiplicity of forms, but in the unifying principles running through those forms and underlying them. In other words, God was to be discerned in the principles of shape – determined ultimately by the degrees in an angle – and by number. It was through shape and number, not by representation of diverse forms, that God's glory was held to be manifest. And it was in edifices based on shape and number, rather than on representational embellishment, that the divine presence was to be housed.

The synthesis of shape and number is, of course, geometry. Through geometry, and the regular recurrence of geometric patterns, the synthesis of shape and number is actualised. Through the study of geometry, therefore, certain absolute laws appeared to become legible – laws which attested to an underlying order, an underlying design, an underlying coherence. This master plan was apparently infallible, immutable, omnipresent; and by virtue of those very qualities, it could be construed, easily enough, as something of divine origin – a visible manifestation of the divine power, the divine will, the divine craftsmanship. And thus geometry, in both Judaism and Islam, came to assume sacred proportions, becoming invested with a character of transcendent and immanent mystery.

Towards the end of the first century BC, the Roman architect Vitruvius had enunciated what were to become some of the most basic premises for later builders. He had recommended, for example, that builders be organised into mutually beneficial societies or *collegia*'. He had insisted, 'Let the altars look to the east',[7] as, of course, they do in Christian churches. More important still, he had established the architect as something more than a mere technician. The architect, he said, 'should be ... a skilful draughtsman, a mathematician, familiar with historical studies, a diligent student of philosophy, acquainted with music ... familiar with astrology ...'.[8] For Vitruvius, in effect, the architect was a species of magus, conversant with the sum of human knowledge and privy to the creation's underlying laws. Paramount among these laws was geometry, on which the architect was obliged to draw in order to construct temples 'by the help of proportion and symmetry ...'.[9]

In this respect, too, then, Judaism and Islam were to converge with classical thought. For was not architecture the supreme application and actualisation of geometry – an application and actualisation that went further even than painting and rendered geometry three-dimensional? Was it not in architecture that geometry in effect became incarnate?

It was thus in structures based on geometry, with no embellishment to distract or deflect the mind, that God's presence was to be accommodated and worshipped. The synagogue and the mosque, therefore, were both based not on decoration, but on geometric principles, on abstract mathematical relationships. And the only ornamentation allowed in them was of an abstract geometrical kind – the maze, for example, the arabesque, the chessboard, the arch, the pillar or column and other such 'pure' embodiments of symmetry, regularity, balance and proportion.

During the Reformation, the taboo against representational art was to be adopted by some of the more austere forms of Protestantism. This was particularly so in Scotland. But medieval Christianity, under the hegemony of the Catholic Church, had no such inhibitions or prohibitions. Nevertheless, Christendom was quick to seize upon the principles of sacred geometry, and utilised them to augment its own attempts to embody and do homage to the divine. From the period of the Gothic cathedrals on, sacred geometry in architecture and in architectural adornment went hand in hand with representational art as an integral component of Christian churches.

In the Gothic cathedral, indeed, geometry was the single most important factor. As we have noted in the building of Rosslyn Chapel, the construction of any such edifice was conducted under the direction of the so-called 'Master of the Work'. Each such master would devise his own unique geometry, with which everything that followed had to harmonise. A study of Chartres has revealed, during the course of its construction, the imprint of nine separate masters.[10]

Most masters were essentially proficient craftsmen and draughtsmen, whose skills were wholly technological. Some of them, however – two, it is believed, out of the nine at Chartres – were obviously versed in something more.[11] Their work reflects a metaphysical, spiritual or, in the language of Freemasonry, 'speculative' character which attests to a high degree of education and sophistication – attests to men who were thinkers and philosophers as well as builders. As we have noted, one manuscript, dating from 1410, speaks of a 'science' whose secrets were revived after the Flood by Pythagoras and Hermes. From references of this kind, it is clear that certain masters, at least, had access to Hermetic and Neo-Platonic thought well before such thought, during the Renaissance, came into vogue in Western Europe. But prior to the Renaissance, such thought – heterodox as it was, and drawing on non-Christian sources – would have been extremely dangerous to its adherents, who were therefore compelled to secrecy. In consequence, an 'esoteric' tradition of 'initiated' masters would have arisen within the guilds of 'operative' stonemasons. Here, then, were the seeds of what was later to be called 'speculative' Freemasonry.

Within this 'esoteric' tradition of 'initiated' masters, sacred geometry was of paramount importance – a manifestation, as we have seen, of the divine. For such masters, a cathedral was more than a 'house of God'. It was something akin to a musical instrument, an instrument tuned to a particular and exalted spiritual pitch, like a harp. If the instrument were tuned correctly, God Himself would resonate through it, and His immanence would be felt by all who entered. But how *did* one tune it correctly? How and where did God specify His design requirements? Sacred geometry provided the general principles, the underlying laws. But there was one Old Testament context in which, it was believed, God had very precisely and specifically instructed His worshippers, had drawn up His own blueprints. This context was the building of Solomon's Temple. And thus the building of the Temple came to assume supreme importance for the stonemasons of the Middle Ages. Here, God had actually *taught* the practical application of sacred geometry through architecture. And His chief pupil, Hiram of Tyre, was therefore adopted as the model to which every true master builder must aspire.

The Hidden Knowledge

This is *why* the Hiram story came to assume the importance that it did. There remains the question of *how* it and its various embellishments find their way into the heart of Christian Europe. How, for that matter, did sacred geometry as a whole – compounded of Pythagorean, Vitruvian, Hermetic, Neo-Platonic, Judaic and Islamic thought – find its way to the West? In order to answer these questions, one must look at the periods in history when such bodies of teaching might have been most influentially transmitted and assimilated – periods when Christianity was most exposed to 'alien' influences and, sometimes deliberately, sometimes by a form of osmosis, absorbed them.

The first such period was in the seventh and eighth centuries, when Islam, impelled by the militant energy characteristic of a new faith, swept through the Middle East, traversed the coast of North Africa, crossed the Straits of Gibraltar, overwhelmed the Iberian peninsula and advanced into France. The subsequent Islamic rule in Spain reached its apotheosis in the tenth century, and thus coincides with Athelstan's reign in England. Although there is no documentation on the matter, it is certainly possible that some of the principles of sacred geometry and architecture filtered northwards from Spain and France. The armies of Islam may have been halted by Charles Martel at the Battle of Poitiers in 732, but ideas are always more difficult to repulse than armies.

In 1469, Ferdinand of Aragón married his cousin, Isabelle of Castile. From this union, modern Spain was born. In an access of apostolic zeal, Ferdinand and Isabelle embarked on a programme of 'purification', whereby their united domains were to be systematically purged of all 'alien' – that is, Judaic and Islamic – elements. What ensued was the era of the Spanish Inquisition and the *auto-da-fé*. As Carlos Fuentes has said, Spain, at this point, banished sensuality with the Moors and intelligence with the Jews and proceeded to go sterile.[12] But during the seven and a half centuries between the Battle of Poitiers and the reign of Ferdinand and Isabelle, Spain was a veritable repository for 'esoteric' teachings. Indeed, the first major 'esotericist' in Western tradition was the Majorcan Raymond Lull, or Lully, whose work was to exert an enormous influence on later European developments. But even apart from Lull, it was accepted that individuals seeking 'esoteric' or mystical initiation had to make a statutory pilgrimage to Spain. In *Parzival*, Wolfram von Eschenbach claims his story to have derived ultimately from Spanish sources. Nicolas Flamel, probably the most celebrated of the early Western alchemists, is said to have learned the secrets of transmutation from a book obtained in Spain.

For seven and a half centuries, then, Spain was to remain a source of 'esoteric' inspiration. From Spain, material continued to filter into the rest of Europe, sometimes in a trickle, sometimes in a flood. But the Spanish influence, important though it might be, was soon to be eclipsed by other, more dramatic contacts between Christendom and its rival faiths. The first of these was, of course, the Crusades, during which tens of thousands of Europeans in the Holy Land became steeped in the very creeds they had marched to extirpate. During the Crusades, the Sicilian court of the Hohenstauffen Emperor Friedrich II became a veritable clearing-house for Judaic and Islamic currents of thought. The Templars were another major conduit – perhaps *the* major conduit – for such currents. Although nominally 'knights of Christ', the Templars, in practice, maintained cordial relations with both Islam and Judaism, and are even said to have harboured ambitious plans for reconciling Christianity with its two rival faiths.

The Templars built extensively. Using their own teams of masons, they constructed their own castles and preceptories. Templar architecture was usually Byzantine in its characteristics, reflecting influences from beyond Rome's sphere of control. As we have seen, two graves of Templar master masons were found at Athlit in Israel – probably the oldest known 'masonic' graves in the world.

The Templars sponsored their own guilds. They also acted as patrons and protectors for other guilds of craftsmen and stonemasons – and appear, on occasion, to have become members of such guilds themselves.[13] On occasion, too, skilled artisans would be taken in as 'associates' of the Temple. They would live in self-contained villages attached to preceptories and enjoy many of the Order's privileges, including exemption from tolls and taxes. In Europe, moreover, the Templars were self-appointed guardians of the roads, ensuring safe passage for pilgrims, travellers, merchants – and builders. Given this broad spectrum of activities, it is hardly surprising that principles of sacred geometry and architecture should find their way to Western Europe under Templar auspices.

But if the Templars were a conduit for such principles, they could only have been so for a limited period of time – for no more (and probably less) than the two centuries of their existence. Nor, as we have stressed repeatedly, must the Templars be inflated into something they were not. Some of the Order's functionaries may indeed have been as well-educated as, say, their equivalents in the ecclesiastical hierarchy; some may indeed have been versed in the arcana of sacred geometry and architecture; but the majority of Templars were mere rude soldiers, as untutored and unsophisticated as most other nobles of their age. From their superiors, such men might have learned that the guilds of 'operative' stonemasons possessed technological secrets meriting respect, but they would not have known what those secrets were – still less have been capable of understanding them. With the official dissolution of the Order, moreover, much was undoubtedly lost. In Scotland particularly, refugee Templars, cut off from their former superiors, would have been left with only empty forms to observe. They might have regarded the art of building with deference, but its significance for them would have been more symbolic and ritualistic than practical; they are hardly likely to have understood much about it. Indeed, any Templars surviving in Scotland would probably have been like certain later kinds of Freemasonry, mechanically perpetuating a corpus of traditions and observances without really appreciating what they signified.

If there was a connection between the Templars and the guilds of 'operative' stonemasons in Scotland, it would, in any case, have exhausted itself by the fifteenth century – would have worn thin and become diluted. But just at that point, there was to be a transfusion of fresh inspiration from elsewhere, which regenerated the application of sacred geometry to architecture and imparted a new impetus to both. In 1453, Constantinople and the last surviving remnants of the old Byzantine Empire fell to the Turks. The result was a massive influx into Western Europe of refugees, together with the treasures, accumulated during the previous thousand years, of Byzantine libraries – texts on Hermeticism, Neo-Platonism, Gnosticism, Cabbalism, astrology, alchemy, sacred geometry, all the teachings and traditions which had originated in Alexandria during the first, second and third centuries and been constantly augmented and updated. And then, in 1492, as we have seen, Ferdinand and Isabelle of Spain inaugurated a ruthless extirpation of Islam and Judaism from their domains. This, too, produced an exodus of refugees who found their way eastwards and northwards, bringing with them the entire corpus of Iberian 'esotericism', which had been filtering piecemeal into Christendom since the seventh and eighth centuries.

The impact of these developments was overwhelming. It transformed Western civilisation. Scholars and historians concur that the influx of ideas from Byzantium and Spain was probably the single most important contributing factor to the cultural phenomenon now known as the Renaissance.

The Byzantine material found its way initially to Italy, where men such as Cosimo de'Medici immediately pounced upon it. Academies were established to study and propagate it. Translations – the earliest and most famous by Marsilio Ficino – were commissioned and disseminated.[14] Exegeses – by Pico della Mirandola, for instance – were written and similarly diffused. From Italy, during the next hundred years, a wave of 'esotericism' was to spread across the rest of Europe. Sacred geometry, now regarded as a form of 'talismanic magic', was applied no longer just to architecture, but – in the works of Leonardo and Botticelli, for example – to painting as well. It was soon to suffuse other arts, including poetry, sculpture, music and, particularly, the theatre.

Not that architecture was thereby diminished. On the contrary, it acquired an even more exalted status than before. The dissemination of Neo-Platonism – the syncretic mystical teachings which had coalesced in immediately post-Christian Alexandria – imparted a renewed significance to the older classical thought of Plato himself. And in Plato, Renaissance scholars, excitedly seeking relevant connections, found a principle crucial to the later crystallisation of Freemasonry. In Plato's *Timaeus*, there appears the earliest known equation of the Creator with the 'Architect of the Universe'. The Creator, in the *Timaeus*, is called '*tekton*', meaning 'craftsman' or 'builder'. '*Arche-tekton*' thus denoted 'master craftsman' or 'master builder'. For Plato, the '*arche-tekton*' crafted the cosmos by means of geometry.[15]

As we have seen, the corpus of 'esoteric' material from Constantinople found its way initially to Italy. Of the corpus from Spain forty years later, much also reached Italy, but much found its way to the Low Countries, the Spanish dominions of Flanders and the Netherlands. Here, it generated a Flemish Renaissance which paralleled the Italian. And by the beginning of the sixteenth century, the strands originating in Italy and the Low Countries had converged under the patronage of the houses of Guise and Lorraine. Thus, for example, the first French edition of the seminal *Corpus hermeticum*, published in 1549, was dedicated to Charles de Guise, Cardinal of Lorraine – brother of Marie de Guise, who married James V of Scotland and bore Mary Queen of Scots.

The houses of Guise and Lorraine were already steeped in 'esoterica'. Indeed, Cosimo de'Medici's interest in Byzantine 'esoterica' had owed much to the encouragement of his scholarly colleague, René d'Anjou, duke of Lorraine in the mid-fifteenth century – who had spent time in Italy and fostered the transplantation of Italian Renaissance thought in his own domains. Sheer geographical proximity dictated that material from Flanders should find its way into those domains as well. By the early sixteenth century, then, and despite their ostensible Catholicism, the Guise and Lorraine families had become assiduous sponsors for works of European 'esotericism'. From them – via Marie de Guise's marriage to James V, via the Scots Guards and via such families as the Stuarts, Setons, Hamiltons, Montgomeries and Sinclairs – it was to be carried back to Scotland. Here – where the old Templar legacy had prepared the ground and guilds of 'operative' stonemasons under Sinclair patronage were evolving their own mysteries – it was to find fertile soil. And here we find Marie de Guise writing of Sir William Sinclair that:

> . . . we bind . . . us to the said Sir William, in likwis that we sall be leill and true maistres to him, his counseil and secret shewen to us we sall keip secret.[16]

The Hidden Knowledge in France and England

The Guise and Lorraine families were, as we have seen, ruthlessly ambitious. Not only did they come within a hair's-breadth of gaining the French throne. They also had their eyes on the Papacy, and would almost certainly have attained it had not their intrigues, and their blunders, in French politics compromised their credibility and drained their resources. In order to facilitate their designs on the throne of St Peter, they undertook to present themselves as a bulwark of Catholic Europe – 'defenders of the faith' against the Reformation and the rising tide of Protestantism in Germany, Switzerland and the Low Countries. In consequence, they adopted and pursued a public policy of fervent Catholicism, often fanatical in intensity. One manifestation of this policy was the notorious Holy League, an alliance of Catholic princes and potentates dedicated to eradicating Protestantism from the Continent. To outsiders, the Holy League seemed a testimony to Guise and Lorraine piety. To the Guise and Lorraine families themselves, however, the Holy League was simply a matter of political expediency – the blueprint for a structure intended ultimately to supplant or subsume the Holy Roman Empire. And, of course, there was little point in wresting control of the Papacy if the Papacy were powerless. In order to render it worth the taking, the Papacy had to be strengthened and, so far as possible, its old medieval hegemony over Europe restored.

Unfortunately for the Guise and Lorraine families, the policy and public image that furthered their designs on the Continent were counter-productive in Britain. Both England and Scotland had, by then, become Protestant. For England in particular, the primary threat was soon to be embodied by Catholic Spain, whose ruler, Philip II, married Mary Tudor four years before her death in 1558. Anything even faintly 'Papist' was anathema in England, and the Holy League was perceived as a menace, not just to Protestantism on the Continent, but in the British Isles as well. By virtue of their zealous support for the Church, François de Guise and his family became, in English eyes, ogres, exceeded in terms of menace only by the Spanish monarch.

'Esoteric' thought was enthusiastically taken up in England. It was embraced by poets such as Sidney and Spenser, for example, and figures in *Arcadia* and *The Faerie Queene*; it was also embraced by Marlowe and by Francis Bacon. But to the extent that it was associated with Catholic houses on the Continent, it could not be dealt with publicly or explicitly. It was often treated obliquely, allegorically. Its existence was largely subterranean, confined to small scholarly cabals, circumscribed aristocratic circles and what we would now call 'secret societies'.[17] These organisations were often militantly anti-'Papist', and actively opposed to the blatant political and dynastic ambitions of the Guise and Lorraine families on the Continent. But they were simultaneously steeped in the corpus of 'esoteric' material which had filtered back to Scotland from the Guise and Lorraine families and there found such fertile soil.

The career of the Scottish philosopher Alexander Dickson exemplifies the way in which such material, amidst the complicated political cross-currents of the period, was transmitted.[18] Born in 1558, Dickson graduated from St Andrews in 1577 and spent the next six years in Paris. On his return, he published a book dedicated to Queen Elizabeth's favourite, Robert Dudley, Earl of Leicester. This book drew heavily on the early work of the prominent Italian 'esotericist', Giordano Bruno – whose defiance of Rome was to lead him to the stake in 1600, and who, before his death, nominated Dickson as his successor.[19] And yet in 1583, despite his close association with Bruno, whom Rome regarded as an arch-heretic, and despite moving in circles very close to the throne of Elizabeth, Dickson was in Paris, vociferously proclaiming his support for Mary Queen of Scots and associating with personages connected with the Holy League. And though his friendship with Sidney appears to have been genuine enough, he was also a spy, supplying the French ambassador with secret English documents, including some which Sidney had drawn up. By 1590, Dickson was in Flanders, conducting clandestine missions for Catholic potentates. By 1596, he was rumoured to be working with James Beaton, Scottish ambassador to France, and with Charles de Guise, Duc de Mayenne, then head of the Holy League. Also connected with this group was Lord George Seton, whose son Robert was created Earl of Winton in 1600, and married Margaret Montgomerie, an alliance which was to lead, along a cadet line of the family, to the earldom of Eglinton. Beaton, formerly Archbishop of Glasgow, had been conspiring with the Guise and Lorraine families since at least 1560. In 1582, while Dickson was still in Paris, Beaton and Henri, Duc de Guise, were plotting to invade England with an army supplied by Spain and the Papacy. On the night before her execution in 1587, Mary Queen of Scots named Beaton and Henri de Guise among her executors.

Alexander Dickson typifies the way in which 'esoteric' and political allegiances had become entangled, sometimes working in tandem, sometimes diametrically opposed. Dickson, however, was a relatively minor figure compared with England's real 'arch-magus' of the age, Dr John Dee. And yet Dee, too, had to thread a precarious path between warring factions, Catholic and Protestant interests, the aspiration to 'esoteric' knowledge and the more immediately pressing demands of state. Nor did he escape as unscathed as Dickson. Although his Protestant allegiances were never, like Dickson's, in doubt, he came repeatedly under suspicion, was once imprisoned and was consistently harassed.

Born in Wales in 1527, physician, philosopher, scientist, astrologer, alchemist, Cabbalist, mathematician, diplomatic emissary and spy, Dee was one of the most dazzlingly brilliant men of his age, the epitome of the so-called 'Renaissance man'. He is widely believed to have provided Shakespeare with the prototype for Prospero in *The Tempest*, and his influence, both during his lifetime and afterwards, was enormous. It was Dee who gathered the diverse strands of 'esoterica' and synthesised them in a fashion that prepared the way for later developments. It was through Dee and his work that England, during the seventeenth century, was to become a major centre for 'esoteric' studies. And it was Dee who, in effect, set the stage for the emergence of Freemasonry.

As a young man still in his twenties, Dee was already lecturing at continental universities – Louvain, for example, and Paris – on principles of geometry. During the critical period of Guise and Lorraine plots and counterplots, he was moving unchecked about the Continent, establishing currency for himself in all quarters. In 1585–6, he was in Prague – which, under the liberal, pacifist and supposedly 'eccentric' Holy Roman Emperor Rudolf II, had become the new centre for 'esoteric' studies. He enjoyed the patronage of the emperor and returned with material which would enable England, in that respect, to supplant Prague. Among his most important later disciples were to be Inigo Jones and Robert Fludd – who, as a young man, worked as tutor in mathematics and geometry to the then Duc de Guise and his brother.

Dee was instrumental in disseminating Vitruvian principles of architecture and geometry. In 1570, moreover, fifteen years before his journey to Prague, he published a preface to an English translation of Euclid. In this preface, he extolled the 'supremacy of architecture among the mathematical sciences'.[20] He spoke of Christ as 'our Heavenly Archemaster'.[21] He echoed Vitruvius's portrait of the architect as a species of magus:

> I thinke, that none can justly account themselves Architects, of the suddeyne. But they onely, who from their childes yeares, ascendying by these degrees of knowledges, beyng fostered up with the atteyning of many languages and Artes, have wonne to the high Tabernacle of Architecture . . .[22]

And, in a passage of crucial relevance to later Freemasonry, he invoked Plato:

> And the name of *Architecture*, is of the principalitie, which this Science hath, above all other Artes. And *Plato* affirmeth, the *Architect* to be *Master* over all, that make any worke . . .[23]

During most of Dee's lifetime, 'esoteric' thought in England had, as we have seen, remained underground or had been taken up only in certain rarefied circles. In Scotland, it had prospered; but because of Marie de Guise and Mary Queen of Scots, everything Scottish was suspect in English eyes. In consequence, Dee and other English adherents of 'esoterica' could not yet forge the crucial link with developments in Scotland.

By the beginning of the seventeenth century, however, the situation had dramatically changed. In 1588, Philip II's Armada had been decisively defeated and Spain was seen as less and less of a threat to English security. The possibility of the Guise and Lorraine families establishing a foothold in Britain had receded with the execution of Mary Queen of Scots. And the assassination, a year later, of the young Duc de Guise and his brother had effectively cut the heart out of the family, crippling its dynastic and political ambitions. By 1600, it was an all but spent force, and the Holy League, too, was crumbling.

Moreover, 'esoteric' thought was no longer associated so exclusively with the houses of Guise and Lorraine, or even, for that matter, with Catholic interests. One of its most important new patrons was, as we have seen, the Holy Roman Emperor Rudolf II, who declared himself to be neither Catholic nor Protestant, but Christian;[24] he never persecuted Protestants, he became increasingly estranged from the Papacy, and, on his deathbed, he refused the last rites of the Church. By 1600, in fact, 'esoteric' thought had begun to flourish energetically and publicly in Protestant principalities. In the Netherlands, in the Palatinate of the Rhine, in the kingdoms of Württemburg and Bohemia, it was soon to be used as an instrument of propaganda against Rome. Thus purged of any taint of the Guise and Lorraine families, it could safely break surface in England.

In 1603, moreover, when the Guise and Lorraine families were no longer able to exploit the situation, James VI of Scotland – a Stuart monarch with Guise-Lorraine blood – became James I of England. At this point, from the perspective of posterity, one can virtually hear a 'click' as the requisite historical components at last slip into place. With the union of England and Scotland under a single sovereign, noble Scottish families began to play a role in English affairs, and two of them – the Hamiltons and the Montgomeries – crossed the Irish Sea to establish the Ulster Plantation. Through such families, something of the old Templar mystique, and that of the Scots Guard, began to seep into England and Ireland. And the new king, it must be remembered, was a patron and possibly a member of the guilds of 'operative' stonemasons. He brought with him from the north their traditions, as well as the 'esoteric' heritage of his Guise-Lorraine forebears. All of these elements, conjoined to the work of John Dee and his disciples, were to coalesce into philosophical or, as it is called, 'speculative' Freemasonry. All of them had now become not only respectable and legitimate, but associated with the throne as well. The old Templar sword and the trowel of the master-builder were to become, in effect, adjuncts of the Stuart arms.

There was to be one further current of influences before Freemasonry crystallised into its modern form. On the Continent, as we have noted, 'esoteric' teaching was now being promoted by Protestant princes, especially in Germany, and was being used as an instrument of propaganda against the twin bastions of Catholicism, the Papacy and the Holy Roman Empire. It had, by now, begun to call itself 'Rosicrucianism', and Frances Yates has labelled this phase of its dissemination 'the Rosicrucian Enlightenment'.[25] Anonymous pamphlets began to appear, extolling an 'Invisible College' or clandestine confraternity allegedly derived from a mythical founder, Christian Rosenkreuz. These pamphlets militantly attacked the new Holy Roman Emperor and the Pope; they extolled the spectrum of 'esoteric' teaching; they forecast the imminent advent of a new Golden Age, in which all social and political institutions were to be regenerated and an epoch of Utopian harmony was to begin, free of the tyranny, both secular and spiritual, of the past.

In England, the chief exponent of 'Rosicrucian' thought was John Dee's disciple, Robert Fludd – who, along with Francis Bacon, was among the conclave of scholars commissioned by King James to produce an English translation of the Bible. But while Fludd may have endorsed 'Rosicrucian' ideas, they certainly did not originate with him, nor is he believed to have had any hand in the authorship of the anonymous 'Rosicrucian Manifestos'. Those manifestos are now thought to have been composed, in part if not in their entirety, by a German writer from Württemburg, Johann Valentin Andrea.[26] And they are thought to have been associated preeminently with the court at Heidelberg of Friedrich, Count Palatine of the Rhine.

In 1613, Friedrich married Elizabeth Stuart, daughter of James I of England. Four years later, the nobles of the Kingdom of Bohemia offered Friedrich the crown of their country, and his acceptance of it precipitated the Thirty Years War, the most bitter and costly conflict to be fought on European soil prior to the twentieth century. In the early years of the fighting, most of Germany was overrun by Catholic armies and German Protestantism was threatened with extinction. Thousands of refugees – among them the philosophers, scientists and 'esotericists' who embodied the 'Rosicrucian Enlightenment' – fled to Flanders and the Netherlands, and thence to the safety of England. To facilitate the escape of these fugitives, Johann Valentin Andrea and his colleagues in Germany created the so-called 'Christian Unions'.[27] The Unions, which constituted a species of lodge system, were intended to preserve intact the corpus of 'Rosicrucian' doctrine by organising its proponents into cells and smuggling them to safe havens abroad. Thus, from the 1620s on, German refugees began to arrive in England, bringing with them both 'Rosicrucian' ideas and the organisational structure of the Christian Unions.

By James I's time, as we have seen, a lodge system had already been established within the guilds of 'operative' stonemasonry and had begun to proliferate across Scotland. By the end of the Thirty Years War, a system had filtered down to England. In its general structure, it seems to have coincided most felicitously with that of Andrea's Christian Unions; and it proved more than ready to accommodate the influx of 'Rosicrucian' thought. German refugees thus found a spiritual home in English masonry; and their input of 'Rosicrucian ideas' was the final ingredient necessary for the emergence of modern 'speculative' Freemasonry.

In the years that followed, developments proceeded on two fronts. The lodge system consolidated itself and proliferated further, so that Freemasonry became an established and recognised institution. At the same time, certain of the individuals most active in it formed themselves into an English version of the 'Invisible College' of the 'Rosicrucians' – a conclave of scientists, philosophers and 'esotericists' in the vanguard of progressive ideas.[28] During the English Civil War and Cromwell's Protectorate, the 'Invisible College' – now including such luminaries as Robert Boyle and John Locke – remained invisible. In 1660, however, with the restoration of the monarchy, the 'Invisible College' became, under Stuart patronage, the Royal Society. For the next twenty-eight years, 'Rosicrucianism', Freemasonry and the Royal Society were not just to overlap, but virtually to be indistinguishable from one another.

20–22 Rosslyn Chapel. Three of a series of symbolic figures at the extreme east of the chapel; the photograph on the right shows an angel indicating the breast and right calf, relevant to later Freemasonic ritual.

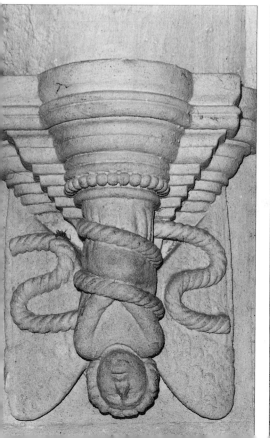

23 *opposite* Christ as the Divine Architect. From the mid-thirteenth-century *Bible moralisée*.

24 *above* The Creator as Divine Architect of the Universe, as depicted in the early fourteenth-century *Holkham Bible*. This concept orginates with Plato's *Timaeus*.

25 Gravestone of a Templar Mason from the Knights Templar castle of Athlit, Israel. The grave must pre-date the abandoning of the castle by the Order in 1291.

THREE

The Origins of Freemasonry

10

The Earliest Freemasons

In its present form, Freemasonry dates specifically from the seventeenth century. Indeed, it is a unique product of seventeenth-century thought and circumstances, a synthesis of the multifarious ideas and perceptions brought about by the convulsions in Western religion, philosophy, science, culture, society and politics. The seventeenth century was a period of cataclysmic change, and it was as a response to this that Freemasonry crystallised. Freemasonry was to act as a kind of adhesive, a binding agent which served to hold together, in a way that the Catholic Church no longer could, the diverse elements and components of a fragmenting world, a fragmenting world-view.

It is to the seventeenth century that Freemasonry itself generally looks for its own origins – or, at any rate, looks for the first emergence of the structure that has filtered down to us today. Thus, Freemasonic writers and historians have delved exhaustively into seventeenth-century affairs, endeavouring to trace the gradually spreading network of lodges, to chart the process whereby certain rites spawned other rites and various illustrious personalities became involved. Of necessity, we will have to address ourselves, albeit cursorily, to the same material. It is not the purpose of this book, however, to attempt any such catalogue. We have no wish to overlap what can readily be found in the copious histories of Freemasonry, and what, though relevant enough to Freemasons themselves, is irrelevant to non-brethren. Our purpose must be to attempt some species of 'overview' – to trace the 'main thrust', the general spirit and energy of Freemasonry, as it suffused and eventually, we would argue, transformed English society.

As we have seen, Freemasonry, in the years prior to the English Civil War and Cromwell's Protectorate, became closely associated with 'Rosicrucianism'. We have already quoted (p. 119) from a poem, composed in 1638, by Henry Adamson of Perth. If artistic quality is any gauge, Adamson may well have been a preincarnation of William McGonagall, acknowledged master of illiterature. Weirdly enough, Adamson's poem also pertains to the collapse of a bridge over the Tay. It is worth quoting here in fuller detail:

> Just by this time we see the bridge of Tay
> O happie sight indeed, was it that day;
> A bridge so stately, with elleven great arches,
> Joining the south and north, and commoun march is
> Unto them both, a bridge of squared stone . . .
>
> . . . and in the year threescore thirteene
> The first down-fall this Bridge did ere sustaine,
> By ruin of three arches nixt the town
> Yet were rebuilt. Thereafter were thrown down
> Five arches in the year fourscore and two . . .
>
> Therefore I courage take, and hope to see
> A bridge yet built, although I aged be
> More stately, firme, more sumptuous, and more fair,
> Than any former age could yet compare:
> Thus *Gall* assured me it would be so,
> And my good *Genius* truely doth it know:
> For what we do presage is not in grosse,
> For we be brethren of the *Rosie Crosse*;
> We have the *Mason word*, and second sight,
> Things for to come we can foretell aright;
> And shall we show what mysterie we meane,
> In fair acrosticks CAROLUS REX, is seene . . .[1]

In 1638, then, Adamson and other self-styled 'brethren of the Rosie Crosse' did not hesitate to arrogate to themselves 'the Mason word and second sight', and there is no record of any Freemasons ever objecting to this claim. It is also worth noting in passing the status accorded by the poem to Charles I.

As the Thirty Years War rocked the Continent, as Catholic victory threatened continental Protestantism with extinction, Britain generally, and the Stuart monarchy in particular, loomed increasingly as a bastion, a bulwark, a refuge. Driven from his seat at Heidelberg, Friedrich, Count Palatine of the Rhine, and his wife Elizabeth, daughter of James I, found a haven at The Hague. Here, they established a new 'Rosicrucian' court-in-exile, to which German refugees thronged and from which they were shunted on to England – where the father, and then the brother, of their Stuart protectress seemingly reigned secure, shielded by the moat of the Channel.

Then civil war erupted in England, Parliament aligned itself against the monarchy, a king was executed and Cromwell's dour Protectorate was established. Although not as horrific as the Thirty Years War on the Continent, the conflict in England (which can be regarded as a kind of offshoot or tributary of the Thirty Years War) was certainly trauma enough. England may not have been threatened with a reimposed Catholic hegemony; but she was subjected to another form of religious control, perhaps even more fanatical, certainly more intolerant, uncompromising and austere. In works such as *Paradise Lost*, Milton could get away with veiled Neo-Platonism (although even he ran repeatedly foul of the regime). But in the climate of the Protectorate, Freemasonry, with its spectrum of heterodox religious, philosophical and scientific interests, kept a prudently low profile. And the 'Invisible College' remained invisible.

Later Freemasons consistently stress an absence of any political interest or allegiance on the part of their predecessors. Freemasonry is repeatedly said to have been apolitical, from its very inception. We would argue that this position is of later development, and that the Freemasonry of the seventeenth century – and much of the eighteenth as well – was indeed politically *engagé*. Its roots lay in families and guilds bound in ancient allegiance to the Stuarts and the Stuart monarchy. It had found its way from Scotland down to England under the auspices of James I, a Scottish king who was himself a Freemason. The old 'Sinclair Charters' explicitly acknowledge the patronage and protection of the crown. And in a manuscript from the mid-seventeenth century, it is demanded of Freemasons:

> . . . that you bee true men to the Kinge without any treason or falsehood and that you shall noe no treason or falsehood but you shall amend it or else give notice thereof to the Kinge.[2]

By virtue of this injunction, Freemasons were bound in fealty to the monarchy.

The absence of any vociferous pro-Stuart statements during the first three-quarters of the seventeenth century can hardly be taken as proof of political apathy, indifference or neutrality on the part of

Freemasonry. Prior to the Civil War, there would have been no need for any such statements: the Stuart claim to the English throne appeared secure, and loyalty to the dynasty would have been too self-evident, too taken for granted, to require explicit declaration. During the Protectorate, on the other hand, any formal declaration of Stuart loyalties would have been exceedingly dangerous. Specific individuals might, of course, profess their adherence to the monarchy, provided they did not challenge the authority of Parliament or of Cromwell's regime; but it is scarcely to be credited that Cromwell would have sanctioned a semi-secret network of lodges to disseminate political views which he found inimical. Freemasonry was already under a cloud of suspicion by virtue of the relaxed, tolerant and eclectic contrast it presented to the government's austere puritanism. To have declared a Stuart allegiance would have been tantamount to institutional suicide, and individual Freemasons would have incurred the attention of the notorious witchfinder-generals. In consequence, Freemasonry, to the extent that it can be traced at all during the Protectorate, is studiously, even strenuously, non-commital.

In short, then, Freemasonry, during the Civil War and the Protectorate, never repudiated its adherence to the Stuart monarchy. It simply remained prudently silent. Behind this silence, the old allegiances remained firmly intact. And it is hardly coincidental that in 1660, with the Stuart restoration and Charles II's assumption of the throne, Freemasonry – both in its own right and through the Royal Society – should come into its own.

But if Freemasons remained loyal to the Stuart monarchy, they were still capable of protesting – by force of arms if necessary – against Stuart abuses. In 1629, Charles I had dissolved Parliament. In 1638, annoyed by the consequences of the king's autocratic action, the leading nobles, ministers and burghers of Scotland drew up what they called the 'National Covenant'. This Covenant protested against the monarch's arbitrary rule and reaffirmed Parliament's legislative prerogatives. The signatories pledged themselves to mutual defence and began to raise an army. Of particular prominence among the so-called 'Covenanters' was the Earl of Rothes. In an entry in his diary, dated 13 October 1637, there is the first known reference to 'the Masone word'.[3]

In August 1639, a Covenanter-controlled Parliament convened in Edinburgh. Provoked by this act of defiance, Charles mobilised his army and prepared to advance against Scotland. Before he could do so, however, the Scottish army, under the Earl of Montrose, moved south, defeated an English contingent and, in August 1640, occupied Newcastle. A truce was concluded, but the Scots remained in Newcastle until June 1641, when peace was officially signed.[4]

Against the background of the events of 1641, while the Covenanters' army occupied Newcastle, there occurred what Freemasons themselves regard as a landmark in their history – the first recorded initiation on English soil. On 20 May 1641, Sir Robert Moray – 'Mr. the Right Honerabell Mr. Robert Moray, General Quarter Mr. to the armie off Scotlan'' – was inducted, at or near Newcastle, into the old Mary's Chapel Lodge of Edinburgh.[5] For Moray to have been inducted into the Lodge implies, of course, that the Lodge, and indeed some species of lodge system, was already in existence and fully operational. As we have seen, this had in fact been the case for some time. General Alexander Hamilton, who was present at Moray's induction, had himself been inducted the year before.[6] Nevertheless, Moray is often regarded by later commentators as 'the first full-fledged Freemason'. But if he was not quite that, he was certainly important enough to warrant the attention of scholars, and to bring Freemasonry out of the shadows and into an increasingly intense limelight.

Although the precise date is not known, Moray was born at the beginning of the seventeenth century into a well-established Perthshire family, and died in 1673. As a young man, he saw military service in France with a Scottish unit – believed to have been the by then resuscitated Scots Guard – and rose to the rank of lieutenant-colonel. In 1643, a year and a half after his Masonic initiation, he was knighted by Charles I, then returned to France and resumed his military career, becoming a full colonel in 1645. In the same year, he became a secret envoy authorised to negotiate a treaty between France and Scotland whereby Charles, deposed in 1642, would have been restored to the throne. In 1646, he was involved in another plot to secure the king's escape from parliamentary custody. Around 1647, he married Sophia, daughter of David Lindsay, Lord Balcarres. Like the Sinclairs, Setons and Montgomeries, with whom they were associated, the Lindsays had long been among the noble Scottish families steeped in 'esoteric' tradition. Lord Balcarres himself was known as an Hermeticist and practising alchemist. His wife was the daughter of Alexander Seton of the Seton-Montgomery branch of the family, which was to play a key role in later Freemasonry. It was into this circle that Moray, by virtue of his marriage, entered – though it is worth noting that his induction into Freemasonry pre-dated his marriage by some six years.

On the execution of Charles I, Moray resumed his military and diplomatic career in France. He was a close confidant of the future Charles II and held a number of official posts under the exiled monarch-in-waiting. In 1654, he and his brother-in-law, Alexander Lindsay, who had succeeded to the Balcarres title, were with Charles in Paris. Then, between 1657 and 1660, he was in exile at Maastricht, devoting his time primarily, as he wrote, 'to chemical pursuits'.

Shortly after the Restoration, Moray's brother, Sir William Moray of Dreghorn, became Master of Works – that is, Master of 'operative' masons – to the newly reinstated king. Moray himself returned to London and held a number of judicial appointments, even though he never actually sat on the bench. In 1661, he became Lord of Exchequer for Scotland, and in 1663 the country's Deputy-Secretary. For the next seven years, he, the king and the Duke of Lauderdale were effectively to govern Scotland on their own – although Moray maintained close relations with the Scottish branch of the Hamilton family as well. He remained, until his death, one of the king's closest advisors. 'Charles had great confidence in him, and his counsels were uniformly for prudence and moderation.'[7] The king often visited him privately at his laboratory in Whitehall and described him as 'head of his own church'.[8] Among his associates at this time, all of whom spoke of him in glowing terms, were Evelyn, Huygens and Pepys. According to the *DNB*, 'the disinterestedness and elevation of his aims were universally admitted. He was devoid of ambition; indeed, as he said, he "had no stomch for public employments".'[9]

According to another of Moray's contemporaries, he was 'a renowned chymist, a great patron of the Rosicrucians, and an excellent mathematician'.[10] It was in this capacity that he was to make his most enduring claim on posterity. For Moray was not only one of the founders of the Royal Society. He was also its guiding spirit and, so Huygens says, its 'soul'.[11] In Frances Yates's words, 'Moray did more than, probably, any other individual to foster the foundation of the Royal Society and to persuade Charles II to establish it by patronage . . .'[12] For the duration of his life, Moray was to regard the Royal Society as perhaps his greatest achievement, and 'watched assiduously over its interests'.

Given the fact that so few records of seventeenth-century Freemasonry survive, one can only deduce its interests, activities and orientation by the prominent individuals associated with it. Moray provides just such a gauge. He would appear to be typical and representative of seventeenth-century Freemasonry. If he is indeed so, the Freemasonry of the time can be characterised as a fusion of traditions filtered down through the Scots Guard and through noble Scottish families like the Lindsays and Setons; of 'chemistry' or alchemy and 'Rosicrucianism' filtering across from the Continent; and of the spectrum of scientific and philosophical interests which prevailed in the 'Invisible College' and subsequently the Royal Society.

It might, of course, be argued that Moray was an exception, a highly eclectic and idiosyncratic individual, not, in fact, a typical representative of Freemasonry at all. But the annals of Freemasonry for the time cite one other truly prominent figure, and he displays precisely the same spectrum of interests, influences and preoccupations as Moray. This figure, known today perhaps primarily for the museum which bears his name, was Elias Ashmole.

Ashmole was born in Lichfield in 1617. During the Civil War, he was active on the royalist side, then, in 1644, retired to his native town, where the deposed Charles I had appointed him commissioner of excise. His official duties brought him frequently to Oxford. Here, he came under the influence of Captain (later Sir) George Wharton, who instilled in him a lifelong fervour for alchemy and astrology. By 1646, Ashmole was moving in London's astrological circles, but he maintained close contacts with the 'Invisible College', which began, in 1648, to meet in Oxford. It included at that time Robert Boyle, Christopher Wren and Dr John Wilkins (another founder member of the Royal Society).[13]

Ashmole had in his possession at least five original manuscripts by John Dee, and in 1650 edited one of them, a treatise on alchemy, for publication under the anagrammatic pseudonym of James Hasolle. Other Hermetic and alchemical works followed, which influenced both Boyle and later Newton, while Ashmole himself became a well-known frequenter of 'Rosicrucian' circles. In 1656, an English translation of an important German 'Rosicrucian' text was published with a dedication: 'To . . . the only Philosopher in the present age: . . . Elias Ashmole'.[14]

Charles II was deeply interested in alchemy, and Ashmole's work on the subject had impressed him. In the new king's first appointment as restored monarch, Ashmole was installed in the post of Windsor Herald. His favour with the court steadily increased, and numerous other offices were conferred upon him. So, too, before long, were international accolades. Since 1655, he had been engaged on his magnum opus, a history of the Order of the Garter – and, in passing, of every other chivalric institution in the West. This work, still regarded as the definitive text in its field, was published in

1672, receiving immense acclaim not only in England but abroad as well. In 1677, Ashmole bestowed on the University of Oxford the antiquarian museum he had inherited from a friend, together with his own additions to it. Oxford, in exchange, was obliged to house the collection – which, according to a contemporary source, consisted of twelve wagonloads. Extravagantly praised and eulogised, hailed as one of the sages of his epoch, Ashmole died in 1692.

Ashmole had been initiated as a Freemason in 1646, five years after Moray. The event is noted in his own diary:

> 1646. Oct. 16. 4 H 30' p.m. I was made a Freemason at Warrington in Lancashire with Coll: Henry Mainwaring of Karincham in Cheshire. The names of those who were then of the Lodge, Mr. Rich. Penket, Warden, Mr. James Collier, Mr. Rich. Sankey, Henry Littler, John Ellam, Rich. Ellam and Hugh Brewer.[15]

Thirty-six years later, in 1682, Ashmole's diary records another lodge meeting, this time in London, at the Masons' Hall, and the list of those in attendance includes a number of prominent gentlemen in the City.[16] Ashmole's diary thus bears witness to a number of things – to his own continued allegiance to Freemasonry over thirty-six years, to the spread of Freemasonry across England, and to the calibre of the people associated with it by the 1680s.

Frances Yates notes it as a point of significance that, 'the two persons of whom we have the earliest certain membership of masonic lodges were both foundation members of the Royal Society'.[17] Together with Moray, Ashmole was indeed one of the Royal Society's founders. All through the Civil War and Cromwell's Protectorate, he was, like Moray, a fervent royalist, passionately dedicated to the restoration of the Stuart monarchy. And much more flagrantly than Moray, Ashmole displayed a preoccupation with chivalry and chivalric orders. In his history of the Garter, he addressed himself to the Templars – and became the first writer on record since the suppression of the Order to speak favourably of them. It is through Ashmole – noted antiquarian, expert on chivalric history, prominent Freemason, co-founder of the Royal Society – that one can discern what must have been a prevailing attitude towards the Templars in seventeenth-century Freemasonic and 'Rosicrucian' thought. Indeed, it is with Ashmole that the 'rehabilitation' of the Templars, at least so far as the general public is concerned, effectively begins. But Ashmole was not alone.

In 1533, the German magus, philosopher and alchemist Heinrich Cornelius Agrippa von Nettesheim first published his famous opus, *Of Occult Philosophy*. This work is one of the landmarks of 'esoteric' literature, and it consolidated Agrippa's reputation as the supreme 'magician' of his age – the real prototype, more than any historical Georg or Johann Faustus, for the figure in Marlowe's play and Goethe's dramatic poem. In the original Latin edition of his work, Agrippa mentions the Templars in passing. His comments reflect what, in the absence of any contrary evidence or tradition in Germany at the time, was the prevailing view of 'the destestable heresy of the Templars'.[18]

In 1651, the first English translation of Agrippa's work was published. It contained a short dedicatory poem of praise by the alchemist and 'natural philosopher' Thomas Vaughan – a friend and disciple, as we shall see, of Moray – and was sold in a bookshop in the churchyard of St Paul's. Agrippa's reference to the Templars had, in the original Latin, consisted of a few words in a text of more than 500 pages. And yet the anonymous English translator was sufficiently offended or embarrassed by this reference to change it. The English edition therefore refers to the 'detestable heresy' not of the Templars, but 'of Old Church-Men'.[19] It is thus clear that by 1651, two years after the death of Charles I, the 'rehabilitation' of the Templars was already under way. There were certain interests in England, reflected by the translator of Agrippa's work and presumably by his anticipated readership, who were not prepared to see the Templars vilified – not even in passing, not even by so august a figure as the archmagus of Nettesheim.

The Restoration of the Stuarts and Freemasonry

If Moray was the guiding spirit and the 'soul' of the Royal Society, Dr John Wilkins was its driving force and organisational mastermind. Wilkins was closely associated with the 'Rosicrucian' court of Friedrich, Count Palatine of the Rhine, and Elizabeth Stuart. Subsequently, he served as chaplain to their son, who was sent to England for schooling. Eventually, Wilkins became Bishop of Chester. In 1648, he published his most important work, *Mathematicall Magick*, which drew heavily on the work of Robert Fludd and John Dee and extolled both in its preface. In the same year, Wilkins began to convene the meetings at Oxford, to which the Royal Society itself officially traces its origins. It was at Oxford, as we have seen, that Ashmole made the acquaintance of the group.

The meetings at Oxford continued for eleven years, until 1659, after which they were moved to London. On the Restoration in 1660, Moray approached the reinstated monarch for royal sponsorship. The Royal Society was duly established in 1661, with the king as its official patron, and also a Fellow. Moray was the organisation's first President. Among the other founding members were Ashmole, Wilkins, Boyle, Wren, the diarist John Evelyn and two especially important 'Rosicrucian' refugees from Germany, Samuel Hartlib and Theodore Haak. In 1672, Isaac Newton became a Fellow; in 1703, he was elected President and remained so until his death in 1727.

During and immediately following Newton's presidency, the overlap between the Royal Society and Freemasonry was to be particularly marked. The Royal Society at this time included the famous Chevalier Ramsay, who will soon figure prominently in our story. It included James Hamilton, Lord Paisley and Seventh Earl of Abercorn, joint author of the acclaimed *Treatise on Harmony* and a Grand Master of English Freemasonry. Most importantly of all, perhaps, it included John Desaguliers, a close friend of Newton's, who became a Fellow in 1714 and then Curator. In 1719, Desaguliers became the third Grand Master of England's Grand Lodge, and he was to remain one of the most eminent figures in English Freemasonry for the next twenty years. In 1731, he was to initiate François, Duc de Lorraine, subsequently husband of the Empress Maria Theresa of Austria. In 1737, he was to initiate Frederick, Prince of Wales, to whom he was chaplain.[20]

But the Royal Society, in the years immediately following the Restoration, was only one conduit for Freemasonry and Free-masonic thought. The spectrum of activities embraced by seventeenth-century Freemasonry included science, philosophy, mathematics and geometry, Hermetic, Neo-Platonic and 'Rosicruc-ian' thought. The same preoccupations are conspicuous in the work of some of the most consequential literary figures of the period – the twin brothers Thomas and Henry Vaughan, for example, and the so-called 'Cambridge Platonists', Henry More and Ralph Cud-worth. No records survive to confirm that these individuals were actually initiated members of specific lodges. At the same time, they could not reflect more accurately and precisely the thrust and orientation of Freemasonry's concerns. Henry More's circle in-cluded the distinguished physician, scientist and alchemist Francis van Helmont. Thomas Vaughan, noted as an alchemist and 'natural philosopher', became a close personal friend, disciple and protégé of Sir Robert Moray.

Earlier, during the Civil War, Vaughan and his brother had been active on the royalist side. Under Cromwell's Protectorate, Thomas Vaughan had translated – using the pseudonym of Eugenius

Philalethes – a number of 'esoteric' and Hermetic works from the Continent, including the famous 'Rosicrucian Manifestos'. Vaughan's close connections with Moray suggest that, even if he wasn't a Freemason himself, he was close to the mainstream of Freemasonic thought; and his interests were echoed by his brother Henry, who, so far as posterity is concerned, has proved the more eloquent spokesman. Henry Vaughan's poetry – which ranks with that of Andrew Marvell and George Herbert – can be regarded as a summation of the currents and influences which characterised seventeenth-century Freemasonry.

But while More and the Vaughan brothers created lasting testaments in literature, perhaps the most impressive monument to seventeenth-century Freemasonry endures today in London's architecture. In 1666, the Great Fire levelled 80 per cent of the old city, including eighty-seven churches, and necessitated a virtually complete reconstruction of the capital. This entailed a prodigious and concentrated effort on the part of the 'operative' guilds of stonemasons. 'Operative' masonry was thus catapulted to public consciousness, with its handiwork and skills prominently and majestically on display in such structures as St Paul's, St James, Piccadilly, and the Royal Exchange. As the new city took shape before the eyes of the populace, a hitherto unprecedented prestige accrued to its architects and builders; and much of this rubbed off on to adherents of 'speculative' Freemasonry, who were quick to stress their kinship with their 'operative' brethren. The most important figure in this context was, of course, Sir Christopher Wren. Wren, as we have seen, was an habitué of the 'Invisible College' that met at Oxford and subsequently became a founding member of the Royal Society. He is alleged to have become Grand Master of Freemasonry in England in 1685.[21] At the same time, he was not just a thinker but also a practising architect. He thus constituted a crucial – perhaps *the* crucial – link between 'speculative' Freemasonry and the 'operative' guilds.

In philosophy and religion, then, in the arts, in the sciences, most manifestly in architecture, Freemasonry, in the period immediately following the Restoration, entered upon halcyon days. But if it prospered during this time, it also exerted a beneficial and constructive influence. Indeed, one could argue that – with its increasing dissemination and its progressively more public nature – it did much to heal the wounds of the Civil War.

This is not to say, of course, that it lacked detractors. In 1676, for example, *Poor Robin's Intelligence*, a short-lived satirical broadsheet, printed the following mock advertisement:

These are to give notice, that the Modern Green-ribbon'd Caball, together with the Ancient Brother-hood of the Rosy-Cross; the Hermetick Adepti and the Company of Accepted Masons, intend all to dine together on the 31st November next, at the Flying-Bull in Windmill-Crown-Street . . .[22]

But such light-hearted lampoons could scarcely do Freemasonry any harm. If anything, they functioned like modern gossip columns, stimulating public interest and probably enhancing the very prestige they purported to tarnish. This applied equally to the work of Dr Robert Plot, custodian of the Ashmolean Museum in Oxford, who, in 1686, published his *Natural History of Staffordshire*. Plot sought to mock, if not actually condemn, Freemasonry. Instead, he furnished Freemasonry with precisely the kind of advertisement that most conduced to its appeal – and, at the same time, provided posterity not just with a valuable source book, but also with a testimony to how influential the institution had become:

To these add the *Customs* relating to the *County*, whereof they have one, of admitting Men into the *Society of Free-Masons*, that in the *moorelands* of the *County* seems to be of greatest request, than any where else, though I find the *Custom* spread more or less all over the *Nation*, for here I found persons of the most eminent quality, that did not disdain to be of this *Fellowship*. Nor indeed need they, were it of that *Antiquity* and *honor*, that is pretended in a large *parchment volum* they have amongst them, containing the *History* and *Rules* of the craft of *masonry*. Which is there deduced not only from *sacred writ*, but *profane story*, particularly that it was brought into *England* by *St Amphibal*, and first communicated to S. *Alban*, who set down the *Charges* of *masonry*, and was made paymaster and Governor of the *Kings* works, and gave them *charges* and *manners* as St *Amphibal* had taught him. Which were after confirmed by King *Athelstan*, whose youngest son *Edwyn* loved well masonry, took upon himself the *charges*, and learned the *manners*, and obtained for them of his Father, a *free-Charter*. Whereupon he caused them to assemble at *York*, and to bring all the old *Books* of their *craft*, and out of them ordained such *charges* and *manners*, as they then thought fit: which *charges* in the said *Schrole* or *Parchment volum*, are in part declared: and thus was the *craft* of *masonry* grounded and confirmed in *England*. It is also there declared that these *charges* and *manners* were after perused and approved by King *Hen.* 6. and his *council*, both as to *Masters* and *Fellows* of this right Worshipfull *craft*.[23]

Dr Plot goes on, at considerable length, to describe what he knows of Freemasonic rituals, lodge meetings and initiation procedures, as well as the integrity with which 'operative' stonemasons conduct their building. At the very end of his account, in one fragment of an immensely convoluted sentence, he launches his attack:

> ... but some others [practices] they have (to which they are *sworn* after their fashion), that none know but themselves, which I have reason to suspect are much worse than these, perhaps as bad as this *History* of the *craft* it self; than which there is nothing I ever met with, more false or incoherent.

It is a lame fashion in which to conduct an attack. Most of Plot's readers, not surprisingly, ignored (or never reached) his concluding sally and warmed instead to everything that preceded it – the ancient and illustrious pedigree claimed by Freemasonry, the involvement of 'persons of the most eminent quality', the benefits of membership, the mutual support, the good works, the prestige attached to building and architecture. After all this, the castigation at the end must have seemed a mere spasm of petulance and possibly of pique at not being accepted as a Freemason himself.

As we have seen, then, Freemasonry, in the period between 1660 and 1688, basked in a kind of Golden Age. It had already established itself, perhaps even more effectively than the Anglican Church, as a great unifying force in English society. It had already begun to provide a 'democratic' forum where 'king and commoner', aristocrats and artisans, intellectuals and craftsmen, could come together and, within the sanctum of the lodge, address themselves to matters of mutual concern. But this situation was not to last. Within a quarter of a century, Freemasonry was to suffer the same traumatic divisions as English society itself.

I I

Viscount Dundee

Around 1661, Charles II's younger brother, James, Duke of York, converted to Catholicism. He did so quietly, without any fanfare, and there were, in consequence, no very vigorous objections. But in 1685, Charles II died and his brother ascended the throne as James II. Immediately, the new monarch began proselytising on behalf of his religion. Favours were conferred on the Jesuits. Payments were offered to individuals in high places if they converted. The civil, judicial and military establishments were filled with Catholic appointees. As head of the Church of England, moreover, James was able to appoint pro-Catholic bishops, or, if he so desired, leave sees vacant.

Prior to 1688, James had sired two daughters, Mary and Anne, both of whom had been raised as Protestants. It was generally assumed that one or the other of them would become his heir and that England would again have a Protestant sovereign. On the basis of this assumption, James's Catholicism was tolerated as a transient phase – distasteful, but preferable to the kind of traumatic civic upheaval that had occurred forty years before.

In 1688, however, James fathered a son, who, by right of succession, would take precedence over his female heirs; and England was thus confronted with the prospect of a Catholic dynasty. Three years before, moreover, in France, Louis XIV had revoked the Edict of Nantes, which had guaranteed freedom of religion to Protestants. French Protestants were suddenly, after being left in peace for nearly a century, subjected to renewed persecution and deportation. Fearing the possibility of a similar fate, English Protestants were provoked to resistance.

Friction between Parliament and the king increased. Then James demanded that the Anglican clergy read a declaration of tolerance for Catholics and other dissenters, and seven bishops refused to comply. They were indicted for their disobedience by royal decree, but in a patent snub of the king's authority, they were acquitted. On the same day, Parliament offered the throne to James's fervently anti-Catholic daughter, Mary, and her husband, William, Prince of Orange. The Dutch prince accepted the invitation. On 5 November 1688, he landed at Torbay to become the new king of England.

Fears of another full-fledged civil war on English soil proved mercifully unfounded. James chose not to fight and, on 23 December, decamped, going into exile in France. In March of 1689, however, he landed in Ireland with French troops and military advisors. Here he summoned his own parliament and proceeded to raise an army from his Irish Catholic subjects under the command of Richard Talbot, Earl of Tyrconnell.

Sporadic fighting ensued. Londonderry was besieged by James's Catholic troops on 19 April and held out until 30 July, when it was relieved. But it was not until a year later that the armies of William and James met in pitched battle. At the River Boyne, on 1 July 1690, James was disastrously defeated and went into permanent exile in France. His supporters continued the conflict for another year, until 12 July 1691, when they were again defeated at the Battle of Aughrim. The shattered Catholic forces fell back on Limerick, were besieged there and at last, on 3 October, capitulated. Thus ended England's 'Glorious Revolution' and, with it, the rule of the Stuart dynasty. Throughout the events that cost him his throne, James, according to one historian, 'had displayed political ineptitude of almost heroic proportions'.[1]

Insofar as it was a 'revolution' at all, that of 1688 had been reasonably civilised. Strictly speaking, it was less a 'revolution' than a *coup d'état* – and a bloodless one at that, so far, at least, as England proper was concerned. Nevertheless, it rent British society as dramatically as the Civil War had done earlier in the century. For the second time in less than fifty years, a Stuart monarch had been deposed, and this occasioned much soul-searching, both individual and collective. Whatever the transgressions of one particular king, there were many in England who felt the Stuart monarchy possessed a legitimacy, a native pedigree, an intrinsic 'Britishness', which the Dutch house of Orange – Britain's arch-enemy only a quarter of a century before – did not. In Scotland, loyalty to the ancient ruling house took precedence ultimately over all religious affiliations. In Ireland, of course, James's embrace of Catholicism had especially endeared him to the populace. The fissures created in English society were mirrored by those which opened up among the noble Scottish families so entwined in our story. At the Siege of Londonderry, for example, there were Hamiltons on both sides. Lord James Sinclair remained 'loyal to the crown', whoever happened to be wearing it, while his brother was in prison and his son, an officer in the Scots Guard, died at the Battle of the Boyne.

In Scotland, the Stuart cause was to be championed primarily by John Grahame of Claverhouse, created First Viscount Dundee by James II in 1688. Like many of the other noble Scottish houses, the Grahames of Claverhouse could claim blood kinship with the Stuarts and thereby descent from Bruce: in 1413, Sir William Grahame had married James I of Scotland's sister, the great-granddaughter of Marjorie Bruce and Walter the Stewart. Later, a member of the family had married the sister of Cardinal Beaton, the arch-conspirator on behalf of Guise and Lorraine interests. For the most part, however, the family's history was undistinguished – 'a record of nonentities dowered with a competence'.[2]

John Grahame of Claverhouse, Viscount Dundee, was born in 1648. He was a well-educated man, having graduated with an MA from the University of St Andrews in 1661. Subsequently, he was to serve both Charles II and James II. Between 1672 and 1674, he was a volunteer in France with the Duke of Monmouth and with John Churchill, later Duke of Marlborough. In 1683, he was at court in England with Charles and, two years later, with James. In 1684, the latter conferred on him the estate of Dudhope Castle, and he married Lady Jean Cochrane, daughter of Lord William Cochrane, a prominent Freemason. In 1686, he was promoted Major-General of Horse. Among his closest friends was Colin Lindsay, Third Earl of Balcarres, grandson of the alchemist.

In April 1689, just as Catholic armies in Ireland were laying siege to Londonderry, Claverhouse, having mustered pro-Stuart forces in Scotland, raised the standard of King James in Dundee. On 27 July, his troops met those of the Williamite commander, Major-General Hugh Mackay, at the Pass of Killiecrankie, about thirty miles from Perth. There was much preliminary manoeuvring, but the battle, when it finally commenced, lasted approximately three minutes. Mackay's soldiers managed to discharge one volley before they were overwhelmed by Claverhouse's charge. At the very moment that the Williamite line disintegrated, Claverhouse, galloping at the head of his victorious men, fell from his horse, shot fatally through the left eye – a curious echo of the lance thrust with which Gabriel de Montgomery had killed Henri II of France a century and a quarter before. With Claverhouse gone, the Stuart cause in Scotland faltered from lack of leadership. The army straggled on, advancing to Dunkeld, where they were defeated. In May of the following year, a second defeat at Cromdale put an end to organised resistance in Scotland – at least for a generation.

'There is,' according to one historian, 'a persistent tradition that at Killiecrankie Dundee was the victim of foul play.'[3] There is indeed evidence to suggest that Claverhouse did not die 'in battle' – that he was deliberately murdered, amidst the confusion of the charge, by two men acting for King William who had joined his army and infiltrated his staff. That in itself would not be particularly extraordinary. On the contrary, it would have been pretty much in keeping with the conventions of the time to assassinate a dangerous enemy. What is relevant to our enquiry is not whether Claverhouse died in combat or by an assassin's hand, but the fact that his body, when found on the field, reputedly bore a Templar cross.

Master of the Scottish Templars?

According to the 'esoteric' historian A. E. Waite:

It has been said that . . . Dom Calmet has lent the authority of his name to three important statements: (1) that John Claverhouse, Viscount Dundee, was Grand Master of the ORDER OF TEMPLARS in Scotland; (2) that when he fell at Killiecrankie on July 27, 1689, he wore the Grand Cross of the Order; (3) that this Cross was given to Calmet by his brother. If this story be true we are brought at once into the presence of a Templar survival or restoration which owes nothing to the dreams or realities of Chevalier Ramsay . . . and nothing . . . to masonry itself . . . We know that evidence is wanting at every point for the alleged perpetuation of the old Templar Order in connection with Masonry and that the legends of such perpetuation bear all the traces of manufacture . . . But if a Grand Cross of the Temple was actually and provably found on the body of Viscount Dundee, it is certain that the ORDER OF THE TEMPLE had survived or revived in 1689.[4]

Waite wrote these words in 1921, before much of the evidence we have outlined here became available. Waite, for example, was unaware of the Scots Guard as a possible repository for Templar traditions. He was also unaware of the intricate network of family connections whereby such traditions may have been preserved. Nevertheless, the tenor of his statement remains valid. If Claverhouse was wearing a *bona fide* Templar cross, which was indeed pre-1307, it would constitute impressive proof that the Order was still operating, or had been resurrected, in Scotland in 1689. Unfortunately, Waite gives no source whatever for the story he quotes. For that, one must look elsewhere.

In 1920, a year before Waite's account, the following reference appeared in the journal of Quatuor Coronati, the premier Freemasonic research lodge in the United Kingdom:

> In 1689 at the battle of Killiecrankie . . . Lord Dundee lost his life as a leader of the Scottish Stuart Party. According to the testimony of the Abbé Calmet he is said to have been Grand Master of the Order of the Temple in Scotland.[5]

This statement can be found earlier, when a researcher into Freemasonry, John Yarker, writes in 1872:

> . . . and that Lord Mar was Grand Master of the Scottish Templars in 1715, in succession to Viscount Dundee, who was slain at Killiecrankie, in 1689, bearing the Cross of the Order, as we are informed by Dom Calmet.[6]

Prior to Yarker, the story appeared in a booklet published in 1843. The author is anonymous, but may have been the Scottish poet and academic, W. E. Aytoun:

> We find, from the testimony of the Abbé Calmet, that he had received from David Grahame, titular Viscount of Dundee, the Grand Cross of the Order worn by his gallant and ill fated brother at the battle of Killiecrankie. 'Il étoit,' says the Abbé, 'Grand Maitre de l'ordre des Templiers en Ecosse.'[7]

We are left with three crucial questions. Who was Lord Mar – Claverhouse's successor, according to Yarker, as Grand Master of the Scottish Templars? Who was the Abbé Calmet, apparently the all-important source of the story? Who was Claverhouse's elusive brother, David, who allegedly passed the cross from the dead viscount to the French abbé?

John Erskine, Earl of Mar, was a well-known Jacobite leader. He became earl in 1689, the year of Killiecrankie. Initially, he opposed the Stuart cause and as late as 1705 was acting for the crown as Secretary of State for Scotland. During the next ten years, he changed allegiances so frequently that he earned the nickname of 'Bobbing John'. By 1715, however, he had finally committed himself to the exiled Stuarts and, in that year, took a prominent part in the rebellion on their behalf. With the suppression of the revolt, he lost his estates and went into exile with James II in Rome. In

1721, he was appointed 'Jacobite Minister to the French Court' – that is, the Stuarts' ambassador to France. In Paris, he became a close friend of Chevalier Ramsay – one of the chief propagators, as we shall see, of eighteenth-century Freemasonry.

Dom Augustin Calmet was one of the most renowned and respected scholars and historians of his age, known particularly for his versatility in languages. Born in 1672, he became a Benedictine monk in 1688, aged sixteen. In 1704, he held an important post at the Abbey of Munster, on the French side of the Rhine. In 1718, he became abbot of St Léopold, in Nancy, in 1728 abbot of Senones, where he died in 1757. His works were voluminous. They included commentaries on all the books of both the Old and New Testaments, a massive history of the Bible as a whole, a history of the Church in Lorraine, an introduction to the prestigious *Histoire ecclesiastique* of Cardinal Fleury and – in a dotty digression from such lofty labours – a standard text on vampires. From Calmet's published letters, it is clear that between May 1706 and July 1715 he was living in Paris and moving largely in the circles of Jacobite exiles.[8]

David Grahame, Claverhouse's younger brother, is decidedly more difficult to trace. He is known to have fought at Killiecrankie and to have survived the battle, only to be taken prisoner three months later. In 1690, however, he somehow managed to escape his captors, and next appears in France, where James II conferred on him the Dundee title formerly held by his brother. As Viscount Dundee, he is cited in a regimental list of the Scots Brigade serving at Dunkerque in June 1692, under Major-Generals Buchan and Canon. Among the other officers on this list there appear Sir Alexander M'Lane, father of Sir Hector Maclean; John Fleming, Sixth Earl of Wigtoun; James Galloway, Third Baron Dunkeld; and James Seton, Fourth Earl of Dunfermline. The last of these had been particularly close to Claverhouse, had commanded his cavalry at Killiecrankie, and was one of the funeral party which secretly removed from the field, and possibly interred, the dead commander's body.

David Grahame appears in another French army list of 1693. The last known reference to him anywhere is in an anti-Jacobite pamphlet published in London in 1696. According to this pamphlet, he and other prominent exiles have been given important posts in the French army. After that, David Grahame simply vanishes from history. 'This is curious,' one historian observes, 'since as Third Viscount he would have been an important person.'[9] When we contacted the French army's Historical Service, we received a reply from General Robert Bassac, who reported that he had found no reference to any David Grahame. He did, however, find:

> ... a certain Viscount Graham of Dundee as an officer in the regiment D'Oilvy [i.e. Ogilvie, Earl of Airlie] in 1747. This regiment had been raised by David, Comte d'Airley, and formed out of the remnants of the corps defeated at Culloden. Perhaps he was a son or a nephew.[10]

The Scots Brigade stationed at Dunkerque in 1692 may perhaps provide an additional clue to David Grahame's fate. In May of that year:

> ... the Scotch officers, considering that, by the loss of the French fleet, King James's restoration would be retarded for some time, and that they were burdensome to the King of France, being in garrisons on whole pay without doing duty ... humbly entreated King James to have them reduced into a company of private sentinels, and chose officers amongst themselves to command them.[11]

The unit was reconstituted accordingly. Its list of officers included two Ramsays, two Sinclairs, two Montgomeries and a Hamilton. It was initially transferred to the south of France, then, in 1693, to Alsace, not far from the Abbey of Munster. In 1697, it was again fighting in the vicinity of this abbey, where, by 1704, Dom Calmet had been appointed to the post of 'sous-prieur'. There were thus two contexts in which Calmet could conceivably have come into contact with Grahame. The first was in Alsace between 1693 and 1706. The second was in Paris after May of 1706, when Calmet was frequenting Jacobite circles there.

On the basis of this background information, it is worth looking at the story again. The thrust of it is as follows:

1 John Claverhouse, Viscount Dundee, was 'Grand Master' of some sort of Templar or neo-Templar organisation in Scotland which had survived, in some coherent form, at least as late as 1689;
2 Following Claverhouse's death at Killiecrankie, he was succeeded in the 'Grand Mastership' by the Earl of Mar;
3 When Claverhouse's body was recovered from the field of Killiecrankie, he was found to be wearing or carrying some species of original – that is, pre–1307 – Templar regalia referred to as 'the Grand Cross of the Order';

4 This device, having passed into the hands of his brother, David, was then confided to the Abbé Calmet.

If the story thus outlined is true, it constitutes the most important evidence of a Templar survival in Scotland since the late sixteenth century, when the elusive David Seton allegedly rallied the Order around him after its lands had been illicitly disposed of by Sir James Sandilands.

The story does, however, pose certain questions. If the Scottish Templars were indeed affiliated with the Stuart cause, why was Claverhouse succeeded as Grand Master by the Earl of Mar – who seems at the time to have supported the English Parliament and not to have become a firm Jacobite until 1715? And why, if the Templar regalia was indeed important, was it not passed to the next Grand Master, whoever he was, rather than to a French priest, scholar and historian? To answer these questions, one must resort to hypothesis and speculation. Yet if the story of Claverhouse's Templar cross were entirely fabricated, it would not, in all probability, contain the contradictions it does. Imagination and invention are free to untrammel themselves from such contradictions, in a way that history is not.

In any case, and whatever the questions posed by the story, it is certainly plausible. Dom Calmet would have had nothing to gain from making it up, except perhaps as a tale on which to dine out; and if that were the case, he would have made more of it than he did. Calmet, moreover, is generally accepted as an impeccably reliable witness. If Claverhouse did indeed have a cross or some other regalia of Templar origin, it would, most likely, have passed into his brother's hands; and his brother, as we have seen, had sufficient opportunity to confide it to the French priest. For a piece of original Templar regalia to have survived would not have been unusual. We ourselves have personally seen and handled other such effects, which have been carefully and lovingly preserved in Scotland; we have seen and handled an original rule of the Order, dating from before 1156. The sheer existence of these items bears eloquent witness to how much has eluded the researches of historians.

But there is one other crucial fragment of evidence to support the story of Claverhouse's Templar cross. As we have seen, the Templar patrimony in Scotland survived intact within the Order of St John until 1564, when Sir James Sandilands, its appointed administrator, contrived to turn it into his own secular property. In the fifteenth century, Claverhouse's ancestor, Robert Grahame, had married the daughter of the Constable of Dundee. By this marriage, he became brother-in-law to John Sandilands, Sir James's grandfather. The Grahame and Sandilands families were thus linked; and an item held in trust by the latter could easily have found its way into the former's hands.

12

The Development of Grand Lodge

It is difficult to say precisely how much Freemasonry, as it evolved in Scotland, owed to the old Templar heritage and Templar traditions. At the beginning of the eighteenth century, whatever link there may have been between them was long lost, and no new link had yet been forged. Freemasonry had not yet publicly attempted to claim a Templar pedigree for itself. And while Claverhouse and his brother are extremely likely to have been Freemasons, no documentation survives to confirm that they were. If a Templar cross was indeed passed from Claverhouse to his brother and thence to the Abbé Calmet, this may attest some species of Templar survival, but it constitutes no direct connection with Freemasonry. When the Templar mystique surfaced again, it was to do so primarily, as we shall see, in France. Freemasonry, in the mean time, had come to play a much more central role in English affairs.

Under William and Mary, Protestantism regained its supremacy in England. By an act of Parliament which obtains to the present day, all Catholics were precluded from the throne, as was anyone married to a Catholic. Thus a repetition of the circumstances which had precipitated the 1688 revolution was effectively forestalled.

In 1702, eight years after his wife, William of Orange died. He was succeeded by Queen Anne, his sister-in-law and James II's younger daughter. She, in turn, was succeeded in 1714 by George I, grandson of Elizabeth Stuart and Friedrich, Count Palatine of the Rhine. When George died in 1727, the throne passed to his son, George II, who reigned until 1760. For sixty years following William's accession in 1688, the exiled Stuarts clung tenaciously to their dream of regaining the kingdom they had lost. The deposed James II died in 1701, to be succeeded by his son, James III, the so-called 'Old Pretender'. He in turn was succeeded as claimant by his son, the 'Young Pretender', Charles Edward, 'Bonnie Prince Charlie'. Under these three monarchs-in-exile, Jacobite circles on the Continent were to remain hotbeds of conspiracy and political intrigue. Nor were they ineffectual. In 1708, a projected Stuart invasion of Scotland was mounted, supported by French troops and transported by French ships. England, with most of her troops committed to the War of the Spanish Succession, was ill-equipped to counter this threat, and the invasion would very likely have proved successful but for a combination of bad luck, Jacobite dithering and French apathy. In the event, the whole project foundered, but seven years later, in 1715, Scotland rose in a full-scale revolt under the Earl of Mar – who, as we have seen, was alleged to have succeeded Claverhouse as Grand Master of the latterday Templars. Also joining in the rebellion was Lord George Seton, Earl of Winton, whose title was forfeited as a result and the earldom allowed to lapse, while he himself was condemned to death. In 1716, however, he escaped from the Tower of London and joined the exiled Stuart pretenders in France. He remained active in Jacobite affairs for the rest of his life, and in 1736 he became Master of an important Jacobite Masonic lodge in Rome.[1] The revolt was put down, but only at considerable cost, and the exiled Stuarts were to remain a threat for another thirty years. Only after the invasion and full-scale military operations of 1745–6 was this threat at last to recede.

The 1688 revolution had introduced a number of modern, much-needed reforms, including, and not least, a Bill of Rights. At the same time, however, British society had been grievously split. Nor was it simply a matter of those who supported the Stuarts fleeing the country *en masse* and leaving it entirely to their rivals. On the contrary, Stuart interests continued to be well represented in English affairs. Not all Stuart adherents were prepared to sanction force. Not all were prepared to defy Parliament. Many, despite their loyalties, were to prove conscientious civil servants under William and Mary, under Anne, under the Hanoverians. Such was the case, for example, with Sir Isaac Newton. But if William and Mary, and Anne, were reasonably popular monarchs, the Hanoverians were not; and there were many in England who publicly, unabashedly, without actually slipping into official treason, inveighed against the detested German sovereigns and agitated for a return of the Stuarts, whom they regarded as the country's rightful dynasty.

It was among these Stuart sympathisers that the modern-day Tory Party originated and came of age. The early eighteenth-century Tories had arisen in the late 1670s out of the old, pre-Civil War cavalier class. Most were High Church Anglican or Anglo-Catholic. Most were landowners and sought to concentrate power in the hands of landed gentry. Virtually all of them esteemed the crown above Parliament and insisted on the Stuarts' hereditary right to the throne.

Their opponents, nicknamed Whigs, had also risen to prominence during the 1670s. The Whigs consisted mostly of the newly consolidated mercantile and professional classes, and were active in commerce, in industry, in finance and banking, in the army. They encouraged religious diversity and included many dissenters and free-thinkers. They extolled the power of Parliament over that of the crown. And, as Swift says, they 'preferred . . . the monied interest before the landed'.[2] Subscribing, implicitly or explicitly, to the 'Puritan work ethic', they represented the triumphantly emergent middle class, whose leadership, first in the Commercial, then in the Industrial Revolution, was to determine the course of British history and establish money as supreme arbiter. They had no particular affection for the Hanoverians, but were prepared to tolerate the German rulers as a price of their own burgeoning success.

The fissures in British society were to be reflected in Freemasonry itself. According to extant records, Freemasonry, after the 1688 revolution, continued ostensibly as before. Lodges continued not just to meet, but also to proliferate. It is likely that many older lodges, or the senior members of newer lodges, were pro-Stuart or Tory, but there is no evidence to suggest that Freemasonry, at this point, actually served as a vehicle for Jacobite espionage, conspiracy or propaganda. So far as possible, most lodges in England seem to have remained – or tried to remain – studiously aloof from politics. And inevitably, as more and more Whigs rose to prominence and assumed important positions in the country's social and commercial affairs, they found their way into the lodge system, putting their own pro-Hanoverian stamp on to Freemasonry.

As we have seen, however, Freemasonry, from its very inception, had been inextricably linked with the Stuarts. Freemasons, during the seventeenth century, were not only required to 'be true to the Kinge', but also, and actively, to root out and inform against conspirators – thus becoming, in effect, part of the Stuarts' administrative apparatus and machinery. Such allegiances ran deep. It is not surprising, therefore, that the main thrust of Freemasonry should have remained attached to the Stuart line, should have followed that line into exile and, from abroad, worked to further its interests in England. During the first third or so of the eighteenth century, Freemasonic lodges might be either Whig or Tory, Hanoverian or Jacobite; but it was the Tories in England and the Jacobites abroad who possessed more of the institution's history and heritage. They constituted the mainstream, while other developments were but tributaries.

In England, prominent Freemasons like the Duke of Wharton were also professed Jacobites. Abroad, most of the Jacobite leaders – General James Keith, for example, the Earl of Winton (Alexander Seton), and the Earls of Derwentwater (first James, then his younger brother Charles, Radclyffe) – were not only Freemasons, but also instrumental in the dissemination of Freemasonry throughout Europe. After the suppression of the 1745 rebellion, a number of illustrious Freemasons were to be sentenced to death for their service to the Jacobite cause – Derwentwater, who had formerly been Grand Master of French Freemasonry, and the Earls of Kilmarnock and Cromarty, who had been Grand Masters of Scottish Freemasonry. Only the latter escaped execution at the Tower.

According to one historian:

> There is no question but that the Jacobites had a crucial influence on the development of Freemasonry – to such an extent, indeed, that later witnesses went so far as to describe Freemasonry as a gigantic Jacobite conspiracy.[3]

We would argue that the Jacobites did not just have 'a crucial influence on the development of Freemasonry'. We would argue that they were, at least initially, its chief custodians and propagators. And when Grand Lodge – subsequently to become the primary repository of English Freemasonry – was created in 1717, it was created in large part as a Whig or Hanoverian attempt to break what had hitherto been a virtual Jacobite monopoly.

The Centralisation of English Freemasonry

Grand Lodge of England was created on 24 June 1717 – St John's Day, the day formerly held sacred by the Templars. There were, initially, four London lodges which, in a manifest thrust towards centralisation, chose to amalgamate into one organisation and elect a Grand Lodge as a governing body. They quickly drew more lodges into their fold, and by 1723 the original four lodges had increased in number to fifty-two.[4]

The usual explanation for the coalescence of Grand Lodge is astonishingly bland – or disingenuous. According to one writer, it 'came into being for the frankly social purpose of providing an occasion at which the members of a few London lodges could meet'.[5] One is also told that the period was one of general enthusiasm for clubs and societies, and that the dissemination and proliferation of English Freemasonry was a consequence of this enthusiasm. And yet there is no comparable movement towards centralisation among the various dining and drinking clubs of the time, or the burgeoning antiquarian, bibliographical and scientific societies. It is specifically in Freemasonry that the emphasis is not just on proliferation, but, even more crucially, on centralisation. Thus, for example, of the fifty-two lodges comprising Grand Lodge in 1723, at least twenty-six appear to have *pre-dated* Grand Lodge's foundation in 1717. Their entry into the historical record, in other words, results not from their proliferation, but from their preparedness to centralise.

According to J. R. Clarke, a Freemasonic historian writing in 1967, 'I think that in 1717 there was a much more serious reason for the co-operation: it was made necessary by the political state of the country.'[6] Clarke goes on to stress the effusive demonstrations of pro-Hanoverian allegiance at the inaugural meeting of Grand Lodge – the drinking of loyal toasts to King George, the singing of loyal songs. And he rightly concludes that such an exaggerated display of patriotic fervour must be seen as an attempt to prove that Freemasons were not Jacobites – a display which would hardly have been necessary were there not some reason to suspect that they were.

Historians today tend to think of the Scottish rebellion of 1715 and the foundation of Grand Lodge in 1717 as two distinct events, separated by a full two years. In fact, however, the 1715 rebellion was not finally and completely suppressed until the execution of Lords Kenmuir and James Derwentwater in February 1716, and the plans for the amalgamation which formed Grand Lodge were made well before the event – during the previous summer or autumn of 1716.[7] The Scottish rebellion and the foundation of Grand Lodge were not therefore separated by two years, but by a mere six to eight months. And there would appear, quite patently, to have been a causal connection between the two. It is as if the pro-Hanoverian establishment, envious of the network which Freemasonry provided for its Jacobite rivals, deliberately sought to foster a parallel network of its own – as if it sought to compete, very much in the enterprising free-market spirit of early Georgian England. Nor was

Grand Lodge above co-opting material from its rivals in order to augment its appeal.

This is apparent in the vexed, complicated and controversial issue of Freemasonic 'degrees', or what might be called stages of initiation. Freemasonry today is divided into three 'Craft' degrees and a number of 'optional' 'higher degrees'. The three 'Craft' degrees – Entered Apprentice, Fellow Craft and Master Mason – come under the jurisdiction of United Grand Lodge of England. The 'higher degrees' do not. They come under the jurisdiction of other Freemasonic bodies, such as the Ancient and Accepted Scottish Rite Supreme Council or the Grand Chapter of the Royal Arch. Most English Freemasons today will work through the three degrees offered by Grand Lodge, then continue on to their choice among the various 'higher degrees' – rather in the way that a student, graduating with a BA in English Literature from one university, might move to another university to work for a BA in French or German Literature. In the early to mid-eighteenth century, however, this was not permitted. For an English Freemason of the time, who did not want his loyalty to the crown impugned, only the degrees offered by Grand Lodge were available. The 'higher degrees', being an almost exclusively Jacobite preserve, were not; and the Freemasonic authorities offering such 'higher degrees' were considered suspect at best, treasonous at worst. Argument still rages about the matter, but it is widely acknowledged today that what are now called 'higher degrees' not only originated in Jacobite Freemasonry, but, in fact, had been there all along. In other words, they do not appear to have been later inventions, but to have been incorporated in a 'Store of Legend, Tradition and Symbolism of wide extent' of which Grand Lodge, in 1717, selected only a portion.[8] And, according to one Freemasonic historian:

> ... what our Jacobite Brethren did was to take still other portions of the same Store, adapting them in a manner which to them seemed perfectly justifiable to the service of that Cause which for them was Sacred ... The Cause ... has passed away, but, freed from all political associations, many of the Degrees remain.[9]

In other words, the 'higher degrees' seem to have involved aspects of Freemasonic ritual, tradition and history which were simply not known or available to Grand Lodge – or which would have been too politically volatile for Grand Lodge to accommodate, and which had therefore to be repudiated. After 1745, however, when the Stuarts had finally and definitively ceased to be a threat and the Hanoverian grip on the throne was secure, Grand Lodge, albeit grudgingly, began to recognise the 'higher degrees'. And indeed, certain aspects of the 'higher degrees', purged now of any potentially controversial elements, were eventually appropriated and incorporated into extensions of Grand Lodge's own system. Out of this, which entailed a merger with a parallel and rival alternative Grand Lodge, there finally arose, in 1813, United Grand Lodge.[10]

Most English Freemasonic history today has been written by scholars working under the auspices of United Grand Lodge. They present Jacobite Freemasonry and the proliferation of 'higher degrees' as schismatic and heretical — deviations from the mainstream of which they themselves are representative. In fact, however, this would appear to be precisely the opposite of what actually occurred, with Jacobite Freemasonry apparently forming the original mainstream and Grand Lodge the deviation — which, by dint of historical circumstance and vicissitude, eventually became the mainstream itself. One is reminded of the origins of Christianity and the process whereby Pauline thought, originally a schism or heretical deviation from Jesus's own teachings, supplanted those teachings and became the new orthodoxy — while Nazarean thought, the original repository of the teachings, was labelled a form of heresy.

Like Pauline thought, Grand Lodge seems to have begun as a deviation of the mainstream. Like Pauline thought, it displaced the mainstream and became the mainstream itself. But like Pauline thought, it did not always have things easy, and it continued to be suspect in the eyes of the secular authority it sought to appease. As a Masonic historian observes: 'to be a member of the Fraternity of Freemasons at that period was to invite the suspicion that one was also a Jacobite . . .'[11]

The Influence of English Freemasonry

The Duke of Wharton, Grand Lodge's Grand Master in 1722, did little to encourage either public or official confidence. Not only was he a vociferous Jacobite. Three years before, he had co-founded the famous (or notorious) Hell Fire Club, which originally met in the Greyhound Tavern near St James. In this undertaking, he was joined by another figure soon to be prominent in Freemasonry, George Lee, Earl of Lichfield, whose father had died fighting for the Stuarts at the Boyne and whose mother, Charlotte Fitzroy, was an illegitimate daughter of Charles II. Lee himself was thus of Stuart blood and a cousin of two other illegitimate grandchildren of

Charles II, James and Charles Radclyffe, successively Earls of Derwentwater. Not surprisingly, he, too, played an active role in Jacobite affairs. In 1716, his machinations had effected the escape of Charles Radclyffe and thirteen others from Newgate Prison, where they had been incarcerated for their part in the 1715 rebellion. James Radclyffe had already been executed.

Predictably enough, the authorities cracked down. In 1721, an edict was issued against 'certain scandlous clubs or societies'. Quietly, though only temporarily, the Hell Fire Club was closed down. Aware of the suspicion it attracted, Grand Lodge felt obliged to assure, or reassure, the government that it was 'safe'. In 1722:

> . . . a select Body of the Society of Free Masons waited on . . . the Lord Viscount Townsend [brother-in-law of Robert Walpole, the Prime Minister] . . . to signify to his Lordship, that being obliged by their Constitutions, to hold a General Meeting now at Midsummer, according to annual Custom, they hoped the Administration would take no Umbrage at that Convocation, as they were all zealously affected to His Majesty's Person and Government. His Lordship received this Intimation in a very affable Manner, telling them he believed they need not be apprehensive of any Molestation from the Government, so long as they went on doing nothing more dangerous than the ancient secrets of the society; which must be of a very harmless Nature, because, as much as Mankind love Mischief, no Body ever betray'd them.[12]

And yet it was at this 1722 convocation – amidst charges of irregularity – that Wharton managed to get himself elected Grand Master. Subsequently, he was accused of attempting to 'capture Freemasonry for the Jacobites'.[13] The following year, he was succeeded by the pro-Hanoverian Earl of Dalkeith and left abruptly, 'without any ceremony'.[14] If there were ever any minutes for the period of his or his predecessors' Grand Masterships, they disappeared. Officially, Grand Lodge's minutes begin on 25 November 1723, under Dalkeith's Grand Mastership.

In September 1722, an ambitious if rather half-baked Jacobite plot was exposed – to foment a rising in London, capture the Tower and hold it until the rebels could be joined by an invasion force from France. Among the conspirators implicated in this plot was Dr John Arbuthnot, a prominent Freemason and former Royal Physician to Queen Anne. Arbuthnot's closest friends included a number of other distinguished Freemasons, among them Pope and Swift – who, though not involved in the plan, suffered some degree of stigma by association. The September plot undid much of the credibility Grand Lodge had endeavoured to establish for itself earlier in the year and dictated the need for fresh assurances.

In 1723, as if to allay once and for all any suspicion of subversive political activity, there appeared the famous *Constitutions* of James Anderson. Anderson, a minister of the Scots Church in St James and chaplain to the staunchly pro-Hanoverian Earl of Buchan, was a member of the immensely influential Horn Lodge, which included such pillars of the establishment as the Duke of Queensborough, the Duke of Richmond, Lord Paisley and, by 1725, Newton's associate, John Desaguliers.[15] Such credentials and connections effectively placed Anderson above suspicion. In 1712, moreover, he had printed some virulent anti-Catholic sermons, extolling Queen Anne and invoking God:

> ... that he may disappoint the vain hopes of our common Adversaries by continuing the Protestant reformed Religion amongst us, and securing further the Protestant Succession to the Crown in the Line and House of Hanover ...[16]

Later, in 1732, Anderson was to publish another pro-Hanoverian work, *Royal Genealogies*. Among its subscribers were the Earl of Dalkeith, the Earl of Abercorn, Colonel (later General) Sir John Ligonier, Colonel John Pitt, Dr John Arbuthnot, John Desaguliers and Sir Robert Walpole.

Anderson's *Constitutions* became, in effect, the Bible for English Freemasonry. It enunciates what were to become some of the now familiar and basic tenets of Grand Lodge. The first article, in its sheer vagueness, remains to this day a point of debate, interpretation and contention. In the past, Freemasons had been obliged to declare their allegiance to God and the Church of England, but, Anderson writes, 'tis now thought more expedient only to oblige them to that Religion to which all men agree, leaving their particular opinions to themselves . . .'[17] The second article states explicitly: 'A Mason . . . is never to be concerned in Plots and Conspiracies against the Peace and Welfare of the Nation.'[18] According to the sixth article, no arguments pertaining to religion or politics are to be countenanced in the lodge.

The *Constitutions* did not entirely allay all suspicion. As late as 1737, a long letter appeared in two London journals, warning that Freemasonry was dangerous to English society because it was secretly serving the Stuart cause. Portentous allusions were made to certain 'special' lodges which were privy to crucial information and withheld it from ordinary Freemasons. These lodges – which 'admit . . . even Jacobites, Nonjurors, and Papists' – were said to be recruiting on behalf of Stuart interests. The anonymous author admitted that many Freemasons were loyal supporters of the Crown, but then asked: 'how can We be sure that those Persons who are known to be well-affected are let into all their mysteries?'[19]

By then, however, such paranoia had become the exception rather than the rule. With Anderson's *Constitutions*, Grand Lodge became respectable, an increasingly unimpugnable social and cultural adjunct of the Hanoverian regime which was to extend, eventually, up to the throne. In Scotland, in Ireland and on the Continent, other forms of Freemasonry, as we shall see, continued active. In England, however, Grand Lodge established something approaching a monopoly; and its political orthodoxy was never subsequently to be seriously in doubt. Indeed, so integrated had Grand Lodge become in English society that its nomenclature had already begun to permeate the language and remains with us to this day. Phrases such as 'standing foursquare', 'on the level', 'taking a man's measure', subjecting a person to 'the third degree' and many others certainly derive from Freemasonry.

By the 1730s, Grand Lodge had begun to take a burgeoning interest in North America and to 'warrant' lodges there – that is, to sponsor lodges as affiliates of itself. In 1732, for example, General James Oglethorpe founded the colony of Georgia and became, two years later, Master of Georgia's first Freemasonic lodge. Oglethorpe's own political allegiances were ambiguous. Most of his family were active Jacobites. Three of his sisters were particularly militant on behalf of the Stuart cause, as was his elder brother, exiled for seditious activity. In the 1745 rebellion, Oglethorpe himself commanded British troops in the field, and displayed such apathy in his operations that he was court-martialled. Although he was acquitted, there seems little doubt that he shared his family's sympathies. Nevertheless, his venture in Georgia met with approval from both the Hanoverian regime and Grand Lodge. Not only did Grand Lodge warrant the lodge he had founded. It also 'strenuously recommended' that its English membership take up 'a generous collection' on behalf of their Georgia offshoot and affiliate.[20]

Thus, by the third decade of the eighteenth century, English Freemasonry, under the auspices of Grand Lodge, had become a bastion of the social and cultural establishment, including, among its more illustrious brethren, Desaguliers, Pope, Swift, Hogarth and Boswell, as well as Charles de Lorraine, future husband of the Austrian Empress Maria Theresa. As we have seen, it had begun as a deviation from the mainstream, and then – so far at least as England was concerned – become the mainstream itself. In some respects, the Freemasonry of Grand Lodge may have been 'less complete' than that of the Jacobites, less privy to ancient secrets, less heir to original traditions. And yet despite all this, or perhaps precisely because of it, the Freemasonry of Grand Lodge performed a social and cultural function that its rivals did not.

Grand Lodge suffused the whole of English society and inculcated its values into the very fabric of English thought. Insisting on a universal brotherhood which transcended national frontiers, English Freemasonry was to exert a profound influence on the great reformers of the eighteenth century – on David Hume, for example, on Voltaire, Diderot, Montesquieu and Rousseau in France, on their disciples in what was to become the United States. It is to Grand Lodge, and to the general philosophical climate fostered by it, that much of what is best in English history of the age can be ascribed. Under the aegis of Grand Lodge, the entire caste system in England became less rigid, more flexible, than anywhere else on the Continent. 'Upward mobility', to use the jargon of sociologists, became increasingly possible. Strictures against religious and political prejudice served to encourage not just tolerance, but also the kind of egalitarian spirit that so impressed visitors from abroad: Voltaire, for example, later a Freemason himself, was so enthused by English society that he extolled it as the model to which all European civilisation should aspire. Anti-Semitism became more discredited in England than anywhere else in Europe, with Jews not only becoming Freemasons, but also gaining an access hitherto denied them to social, political and public life. The burgeoning middle class was given room and latitude to manoeuvre and expand in a way that it could not elsewhere, and hence to catapult Britain to the forefront of commercial and industrial progress. Charitable works, including the often stressed solicitude for widows and orphans, disseminated a new ideal of civic responsibility and paved the way for many subsequent welfare programmes. One might even argue that the solidarity of the lodge, together with its invocation of the medieval guilds, anticipated many of the features of later trade unionism. And finally, the process whereby masters and grand masters were elected implanted in English thinking a healthy distinction, soon to bear fruit in America, between the man and the office.

In all these respects, English Freemasonry constituted a kind of adhesive, holding together the fabric of eighteenth-century society. Among other things, it helped to provide a more temperate climate than obtained on the Continent, where grievances were eventually to culminate first in the French Revolution, then in the upheavals of 1832 and 1848. As we shall see, this climate was to extend to the British colonies in North America and to play a crucial role in the foundation of the United States. Thus, the form of Freemasonry promulgated by Grand Lodge was to supplant its own origins. In doing so, it was to emerge as one of the most genuinely important and influential phenomena of the century – and one whose significance has all too often been overlooked by orthodox historians.

13

The Masonic Jacobite Cause

While Grand Lodge was thriving, pro-Jacobite lodges in England were driven increasingly underground. Some certainly persisted, particularly in the north-east, around Newcastle and the Radclyffe family estates at Derwentwater;[1] but the prevailing climate afforded them little latitude for expansion or development. The same obtained for Scotland, where much evidence pertaining to Freemasonry between 1689 and 1745 was lost, deliberately or otherwise, in the tumult of events. Ireland, however, was a different matter.

As early as 1688, Freemasonry was well-known in Ireland. In that year, a Dublin orator, seeking to capture the attention of his audience, did so by referring to a man 'being Freemasonized the new way' – implying, of course, that there was also an 'old way'.[2] In the same year, there was a minor scandal when a notorious individual named Ridley, known as an anti-Catholic spy and informer, was found dead with what was referred to as a 'Mason's Mark' upon his body – though there is no indication of what this 'Mark' was, how it was affixed or imprinted, or whether it had anything at all to do with his death.[3]

Documentation on the early history of Grand Lodge of Ireland is patchy, all minute books prior to 1780 having been lost, and all records prior to 1760. Whatever information can be obtained derives from external sources, such as newspaper reports and letters. The evidence available indicates that Irish Grand Lodge was formed around 1723 or 1724, six or seven years after its English rival. The first Grand Master was the Duke of Montague, who, in 1721, had presided over Grand Lodge of England. Montague was a godson of George I and staunchly pro-Hanoverian. Not surprisingly, given the depth and pervasiveness of Stuart allegiances in Ireland, he got up numerous noses, and Irish Grand Lodge was plagued by internal squabbles. Between 1725 and 1731, there is a total lacuna in its history, and later commentators have concluded it must have been hopelessly split between Hanoverian supporters and Jacobites.

In March 1731, there appears to have been some consolidation under the Grand Mastership of the Earl of Ross. A month later, Ross was succeeded by James, Lord Kingston. He, too, in 1728, had presided over the Grand Lodge of England but after 1730, when English Grand Lodge ratified certain unspecified changes, 'confined his zeal to Irish Freemasonry'.[4] Kingston was to personify the orientation of Irish Grand Lodge. He had a Jacobite past and came from a Jacobite family. His father had been a courtier to James II and had followed the deposed king into exile, returning to Ireland in 1693 to be first pardoned, later arrested and charged with recruiting military personnel for the Stuart cause. In 1722, Kingston himself had incurred similar accusations.[5]

Irish Grand Lodge was thus to remain a repository for aspects of Freemasonry which the Grand Lodge of England repudiated or disowned. And it was to the Freemasonry of Irish Grand Lodge that the numerous British regiments passing through Ireland or stationed there in garrison were to be exposed. When the network of regimental field lodges began to proliferate through the British Army, most of them, at least initially, were warranted by Irish Grand Lodge. This was to be immensely important, but its effects were not to become apparent for another quarter of a century.

In the mean time, the original mainstream of Freemasonry had moved with the exiled Stuarts to the Continent. It was in France, in the period immediately prior to 1745, that the most consequential developments were to occur. And it was in France that Jacobite Freemasonry was to become integrated – or perhaps re-integrated – with the old Templar heritage.

The Earliest Lodges

Freemasonry seems to have come to France with contingents of the defeated Jacobite army between 1688 and 1691. According to one eighteenth-century account, the first lodge in France dates from 25 March 1688, and was established by an infantry regiment, the Royal Irish, which had been formed by Charles II in 1661, had accompanied him to England on his restoration and had then gone into exile again with James II. Subsequently, in the eighteenth century, this unit came to be known as the 'Regiment d'Infantrie Walsh' after its commanding officer.[6] The Walshes were a prominent family of exiled Irish shipowners. One member of the family, Captain James Walsh, provided the ship which carried James II to safety in France. Later, Walsh and his kinsmen founded a major shipbuilding concern at St Mâlo, which specialised in furnishing the French navy with warships. At the same time, they remained fervently loyal to the Jacobite cause. Two generations later, Walsh's grandson, Anthony Vincent Walsh, together with Dominic O'Heguerty, another influential merchant and shipowner, was to provide the vessels on which Charles Edward Stuart launched his invasion of England. In recognition of this service, Anthony Walsh was created an earl by the exiled Stuarts and his title was officially recognised by the French government.

In France, the Irish military men responsible for the transplantation of Freemasonry moved, naturally enough, in the same circles as pro-Stuart refugees from Scotland – such as David Grahame, the brother of John Claverhouse, Viscount Dundee, alleged to have been found after Killiecrankie with a Templar cross. If Freemasonry had previously, for a time, lost contact with the skein of Templar tradition, that contact was re-established in France during the first quarter of the eighteenth century. And France was to provide fertile soil for both Freemasonry and the Templar mystique.

In many respects, it had been a Frenchman, René Descartes, who, early in the seventeenth century, first embodied what was to become the prevailing mentality of the eighteenth. In France, however, the combined pressures of Church and state had proved inimical, and the impetus of Cartesian thought had passed to England, where it manifested itself through men such as Locke, Boyle, Hume and Newton, as well as through such institutions as the Royal Society and Freemasonry itself. It was therefore to England that progressive-minded French thinkers, such as Montesquieu and Voltaire, looked for new ideas. They and their countrymen were to prove particularly receptive to Freemasonry.

But if Freemasonry first came to France in 1688, some thirty-five years were to elapse before the first authoritatively documented native French lodge was established. This was formed in 1725 according to most sources, in 1726 according to one other which may be more reliable.[7] Its primary founder was Charles Radclyffe, Earl of Derwentwater, whose elder brother, James, had been executed for his part in the 1715 rebellion. Radclyffe's co-founders included Sir James Hector MacLean, chief of the MacLean clan; Dominic O'Heguerty, the wealthy expatriate merchant and shipowner who, along with Anthony Walsh, provided vessels for Charles Edward Stuart's expedition in 1745; and an obscure man, said to be a restaurateur, whose name appears on surviving documents as 'Hure' or 'Hurc'. One writer has persuasively argued that this may be a corruption of 'Hurry'.[8] Sir John Hurry had been beheaded at Edinburgh in 1650 for his loyalty to the Stuarts. His family had remained militantly Jacobite and were ennobled by Charles II; and it may well have been one of his exiled children or grandchildren who, together with Radclyffe, MacLean and O'Heguerty, established the first French lodge.

By 1729, French lodges were already proliferating within the framework of specifically Jacobite Freemasonry. Not to be outdone by the 'competition', the Grand Lodge of England began, in that year, to establish its own affiliated lodges in France. For a time, the two separate systems of Freemasonry pursued parallel and rival courses of development. Although it never managed to impose a monopoly, the Jacobite system gradually gained the ascendancy. Out of it there eventually evolved, in 1773, the most important Freemasonic body in France, the Grand Orient.

One of the most prominent Jacobite lodges in France was the Lodge de Bussy. The street in which this lodge was situated, the rue de Bussy (now the rue de Buci), ran directly into the square in front of St Germain des Prés. The other street running into the square was the rue de Boucheries, where the lodge founded by Radclyffe was located. The two lodges, in other words, were within yards of one another, and the neighbourhood was effectively a Jacobite enclave. The French Jacobites were soon to cast their nets further afield. In September 1735, for example, the Lodge de Bussy initiated Lord Chewton, son of the Earl of Waldegrave, British Ambassador to France (himself a member of the 'Horn' Lodge since 1723) and the Comte de St Florentin, Secretary of State to Louis XV.[9] Among those present were Desaguliers, Montesquieu and Radclyffe's cousin, the Duke of Richmond.[10] Later in the same year, the Duke of Richmond established a lodge of his own at his château of Aubigny-sur-Nère.

Although Radclyffe had co-founded the first recorded lodge in France, he was not Grand Master. According to the oldest surviving documents, the first Grand Master, appointed in 1728, was none other than the former Grand Master of the Grand Lodge of England, the Duke of Wharton.[11] Becoming ever more militant in his Jacobite sympathies, Wharton, after being supplanted in Grand Lodge, had gone to Vienna, hoping to persuade the Austrian Habsburgs to mount an invasion of England on behalf of the Stuarts. His subsequent peregrinations took him to Rome and then to Madrid, where he founded the first lodge in Spain.[12] While in

Paris, he appears to have stayed for a time with the Walsh family. On his return to Spain, he was succeeded as Grand Master of French Freemasonry by Sir James Hector MacLean, Radclyffe's colleague. In 1736, MacLean in turn was succeeded by Radclyffe, the *eminence grise*, who emerged from the wings to assume his position centre-stage.[13]

Radclyffe was one of two major personalities in the dissemination of Freemasonry throughout France. The other was an eclectic, peripatetic individual named Andrew Michael Ramsay. Ramsay was born in Scotland some time during the 1680s. As a young man, he joined a quasi-'Rosicrucian' society called the 'Philadelphians', and studied with a close friend of Isaac Newton.[14] He was later to be associated with other friends of Newton, including John Desaguliers. He was also a particularly close friend of David Hume, and they exercised a reciprocal influence on each other.

By 1710, Ramsay was in Cambrai, studying with the man he regarded as his mentor, the liberal mystical Catholic philosopher François Fénelon. On Fénelon's death in 1715, Ramsay came to Paris. Here, he became an intimate of the French regent, Philippe d'Orléans, who inducted him into the neo-chivalric Order of St Lazarus;[15] from then on, Ramsay was to be known as 'Chevalier'. When precisely he made Radclyffe's acquaintance is not known, but by 1720 he was affiliated with the Jacobite cause and served, for a time, as tutor to the young Charles Edward Stuart.

In 1729, despite his Jacobite connections, Ramsay returned to England. Here, an apparent lack of qualifications notwithstanding, he was promptly admitted to the Royal Society. He also became a member of another prestigious organisation, the fashionable 'Gentlemen's Club of Spalding', which included the Duke of Montague, the Earl of Abercorn, the Earl of Dalkeith, Desaguliers, Pope, Newton and François de Lorraine. By 1730, he was back in France and increasingly active on behalf of Freemasonry, and increasingly associated with Charles Radclyffe.

On 26 December 1736 – the date on which Radclyffe assumed the Grand Mastership of French Freemasonry – Ramsay gave a speech which was to become one of the major landmarks in Freemasonic history, and a source of endless controversy ever since.[16] This speech, which was presented again in a slightly modified version for the general public on 20 March 1737, became known as Ramsay's 'Oration'.[17] There was an ulterior political motive behind it. France at the time was ruled by Louis XV, then aged twenty-seven. The real governing power in the country, however, as Richelieu had been a century before, was the king's chief advisor, Cardinal André Hercule de Fleury. Fleury, tired of war, was anxious to establish a lasting peace with England. In consequence, he was hostile to the hotbed of anti-Hanoverian conspiracy which Jacobite Freemasonry in France had come to be. The Stuarts, for their part, hoped to dissuade Fleury from his desired détente and to keep France, the traditional supporter of the Scottish royal house, firmly allied to their dream of regaining the English throne. Ramsay's 'Oration' was intended, at least in part, to allay Fleury's antipathy towards Freemasonry and to win him over, with the eventual aim of establishing Freemasonry in France under royal patronage. He hoped to initiate Louis XV. With the French king thus involved, Freemasonry would constitute a united Franco-Scottish front, and another invasion of England could be contemplated, another attempt made to restore the Stuarts to the English throne. These objectives prompted Ramsay to reveal more than anyone had previously done of the attitudes and orientation of early eighteenth-century Jacobite Freemasonry – and, at the same time, to divulge more than anyone previously had of its alleged history.

In a statement plundered almost verbatim from Fénelon, Ramsay declared: 'The world is nothing but a huge republic of which every nation is a family and every individual a child.'[18] This statement did not make much impression on Fleury, a Catholic nationalist monarchist cardinal who did not like Fénelon anyway. But it was to prove enormously influential among later political thinkers, not only in France, not only elsewhere in Europe, but in the American colonies as well. Ramsay went on: 'The interests of the Fraternity shall become those of the whole human race.'[19] And he condemned Grand Lodge, as well as other non-Jacobite forms of Freemasonry, as 'heretical, apostate and republican'.

Ramsay stressed that the origins of Freemasonry lay in the mystery schools and sects of the ancient world:

> The word Freemason must therefore not be taken in a literal, gross, and material sense, as if our founders had been simple workers in stone, or merely curious geniuses who wished to perfect the arts. They were not only skilful architects, desirous of consecrating their talents and goods to the construction of material temples; but also religious and warrior princes who designed to enlighten, edify, and protect the living Temples of the Most High.[20]

But though they may have derived from the mystery schools of antiquity, they were, Ramsay asserted, fervently Christian. In Catholic France at the time, it would, of course, have been

imprudent to specify the Templars by name. But Ramsay emphasised that Freemasonry had its beginnings in the Holy Land, among
'the Crusaders':

> At the time of the Crusades in Palestine many princes, lords, and
> citizens associated themselves, and vowed to restore the Temple
> of the Christians in the Holy Land, and to employ themselves in
> bringing back their architecture to its first institution. They
> agreed upon several ancient signs and symbolic words drawn
> from the well of religion in order to recognise themselves
> amongst the heathen and Saracens. These signs and words were
> only communicated to those who promised solemnly and even
> sometimes at the foot of the altar, never to reveal them. This
> sacred promise was therefore not an execrable oath, as it has been
> called, but a respectable bond to unite Christians of all nationali-
> ties in one confraternity. Some time afterwards our Order formed
> an intimate union with the Knights of St John of Jerusalem. From
> that time our Lodges took the name of Lodges of St John.[21]

Needless to say, the Knights of St John, such as they were in the
early eighteenth century, never acknowledged any affiliation of this
kind. Had they survived as an accredited public institution, the
Templars, just possibly, might have done. Ramsay, for his part,
charting the purported history of Freemasonry, quickly moved
from the Holy Land back to Scotland and the Celtic kingdom
immediately prior to Bruce:

> At the time of the last Crusades many Lodges were already
> erected in Germany, Italy, Spain, France. James, Lord Steward
> of Scotland, was Grand Master of a Lodge established at Kil-
> winning, in the West of Scotland, MCCLXXXVI, shortly after
> the death of Alexander III, King of Scotland, and one year
> before John Baliol mounted the throne. This lord received
> as Freemasons into his Lodge the Earls of Gloucester and
> Ulster, the one English, the other Irish.[22]

And finally, in an unmistakable reference to the Scots Guard,
Ramsay declared that Freemasonry 'preserved its splendour among
those Scotsmen to whom the kings of France confided during many
centuries the safeguard of their royal persons'.[23]

The implications and significance of Ramsay's 'Oration' will be
considered shortly. For the moment, it is sufficient to note that the
attempt to win Cardinal Fleury's sympathy and support backfired.
Two years before, in 1735, the police had acted against Freemasonry in Holland. In 1736, they had done so in Sweden. Now,

within a few days of Ramsay's second 'Oration', Fleury ordered the French police to follow suit. An immediate investigation of Freemasonry was ordered. Four months later, on 1 August 1737, the police report was completed. Freemasonry was declared to be innocent of 'indecency', but potentially dangerous 'by virtue of the indifference of the Order towards religions'.[24] On 2 August, Freemasonry was interdicted in France and the Grand Secretary arrested.

In a series of police raids, numerous documents and membership lists were confiscated. Fleury and his advisors must surely have been shocked by the extraordinary number of high-ranking nobles and churchmen who proved already to be Freemasons. The chaplain of the Garde du Corps, the King's Bodyguard, for example, turned out to be a member of the Jacobite Grand Lodge Bussi-Aumont, as the old Lodge de Bussy had come to be called. So, too, was the Guard's quartermaster. Indeed, virtually all members of the lodge were officers, officials or intimates of the court.[25]

Rome was already alarmed, and there can be little doubt that Fleury applied pressure to his ecclesiastical colleagues and superiors. Even before the investigation in France was completed, Pope Clement XII acted. On 24 April 1738, a Papal Bull, 'In eminenti apostolatus specula', forbade all Catholics to become Freemasons under threat of excommunication. Two years later, in the Papal States, membership in a lodge was punishable by death.

According to one authority on the subject, the first effect of Clement's Bull may have been to force Radclyffe's removal as Grand Master of French Freemasonry.[26] Within a year, he was replaced by a French aristocrat, the Duc d'Antin. The duke in turn was succeeded in 1743 by the Comte de Clermont, a prince of the blood. It is thus clear that the Papal Bull had a fairly minimal effect in dissuading French Catholics from becoming Freemasons. On the contrary, after the promulgation of the Bull some of the most illustrious names in France became involved. Even the king seems to have been on the point of joining a lodge.[27] The Pope, it would appear, accomplished nothing, save to topple the Jacobites from their former position of supremacy in French Freemasonic affairs. From the time of the Papal Bull on, the Jacobites were to play a progressively less influential role in French Freemasonry, and ceased completely to affect its evolution and development. Eventually, as we have noted, Grand Orient was to emerge as the chief repository of Freemasonry in France.

In certain quarters, the Church's attitude must have seemed – and must still seem – puzzling. Most of the Jacobite leaders, after all, had either been born Catholic or become converts. Why, then, should the Pope have acted against them – particularly when doing so meant Freemasonry falling increasingly under the anti-Catholic influence of the English Grand Lodge? With hindsight, the answer to that question is much clearer than it probably was to many people – Catholics, Freemasons or both – at the time. The point is that Rome feared, not entirely without justification, that Freemasonry, as an international institution, stood a reasonable chance of offering a philosophical, theological and moral alternative to the Church.

Prior to the Lutheran Reformation, the Church had provided, with whatever qualified success, a species of international forum. Potentates and princes, though their nations might war with each other, were still nominally Catholic and acted under the Church's umbrella; their people might sin, but they sinned according to the context and definition established by Rome. As long as the Church's umbrella remained in place, it ensured that channels of communication remained open between belligerents and that, in theory at least, Rome could act as arbiter. With the Reformation, of course, the Church was no longer able to function in that capacity, having lost her authority among the Protestant states of northern Europe. But she still enjoyed considerable currency in Italy, in southern Germany, in France, in Spain, in Austria and the domains of the Holy Roman Empire.

Freemasonry threatened to offer the kind of international forum that Rome had provided prior to the Reformation: to furnish an arena for dialogue, a network of communications, a blueprint for European unity that transcended the Church's sphere of influence and rendered the Church irrelevant. Freemasonry threatened to become, in effect, something like the League of Nations or United Nations of its day. It is worth repeating Ramsay's statement in his 'Oration': 'The world is nothing but a huge republic of which every nation is a family and every individual a child.'

Freemasonry may not have been any more successful in fostering unity than the Church had been, but it could hardly have been less so. A few years after Clement's Bull, for example, Austria and Prussia were at war. Both Frederick the Great, King of Prussia, and François, Emperor of Austria, were Freemasons. By virtue of this common bond, the lodge offered an opportunity for dialogue, and at least a prospect of peace. It was in an effort – futile, in the event, and even, it might be argued, counter-productive – to preclude such developments that Rome acted against Freemasonry. The Jacobites, and Jacobite Freemasonry on the Continent, were incidental casualties of much broader considerations. And their fall from prominence was probably, in the end, more costly to Rome than leaving their status intact would have been.

As we have seen, the Papal Bull, intended to exclude Catholics from Freemasonry, proved signally ineffectual. Indeed, it was precisely in the Roman sphere of influence that Freemasonry, during the next half century, was to spread most vigorously and to assume some of its wilder, more exotic and extravagant permutations. It was patronised more enthusiastically by Catholic potentates – François of Austria, for example – than by anyone else. And it was to prove most influential precisely within such bastions of Roman authority as Italy and Spain. By casting Freemasonry as a villain, Rome in effect turned it into a refuge and rallying point for her own adversaries.

In England, Grand Lodge became progressively more divorced from both religion and politics. It fostered a spirit of moderation, tolerance and flexibility, and often worked hand in hand with the Anglican Church, many of whose clergy were themselves Freemasons and found no conflict of allegiance. In Catholic Europe, on the other hand, Freemasonry became a repository for militantly anti-clerical, anti-establishment, eventually revolutionary sentiment and activity. True, many lodges remained bulwarks of conservatism, even reaction. But many more played a vital part in radical movements. In France, for example, prominent Freemasons such as the Marquis de Lafayette, Philippe Égalité, Danton and Sieyès, acting in accordance with Freemasonic ideals, were prime movers in the events of 1789 and everything that followed. In Bavaria, in Spain, in Austria, Freemasonry was to provide a focus of resistance to authoritarian regimes, and it functioned prominently in the movements culminating with the revolutions of 1848. The whole of the campaign leading to the unification of Italy – from the revolutionaries of the late eighteenth century, through Mazzini, to Garibaldi – could be described as essentially Freemasonic. And from the ranks of nineteenth-century European Freemasonry there emerged a figure who was to cast the sinister shadow of terrorism not only over his own age, but over ours as well – a man named Mikhail Bakunin.

14

Freemasons and Knights Templar

Despite papal injunctions, Jacobite Freemasonry pursued its own course, still steadfastly aligned to the Stuart cause and the dream of restoring the Stuarts to the British throne. More explicitly than ever before, the Jacobites began to use Freemasonry, and the proliferating network of lodges on the Continent, first for recruitment, and then, after their defeat, for support of distressed exiled brethren. In 1746, for example, an English Jacobite arrived in France bearing letters which urged all Freemasons to come to his aid.[1]

But if the Jacobites thus exploited Freemasonry for political purposes, they also publicly re-integrated it with elements of its own origins and heritage – elements which had been 'winnowed out' by Grand Lodge. Influenced by Fénelon, Ramsay reinvested Jacobite Freemasonry with a mystical character. More important, he reintroduced, in his 'Oration', a specifically chivalric dimension, stressing the role of the 'Crusaders'. Later, he was to speak of the endeavour to reinstate the Stuarts as nothing less than a 'crusade'.[2] In letters exchanged between lodges at this time, there was much talk of 'innovations introduced ... which aimed at transforming the Fraternity from an "Ordre de Société" to an "Ordre de Chevalerie".'[3] Pamphlets and even police reports began to speak of 'the new chevaliers' and 'this order of chivalry'.[4]

If Grand Lodge was evolving into a social adhesive, Jacobite Freemasonry aspired to something markedly more dramatic, more romantic, more grandiose – a new generation of mystical knights and warriors charged with the exalted mission of reclaiming a kingdom and restoring a sacred bloodline to its throne. The parallels to the Templars were too obvious to be ignored, and it was only a matter of time before they were invoked explicitly as precursors of Freemasonry.

It is not clear precisely when – within the privacy of lodges whose records, if they ever existed, have long been lost – the connections between Freemasonry and the Templars were first made explicit. Very likely it was as early as 1689, when David Claverhouse arrived in France allegedly with the Templar cross recovered from his brother's body and passed it on to the Abbé Calmet. But while one can only speculate about this, there is no question that by the 1730s, under the auspices of Radclyffe and Ramsay, the Templar heritage was being promulgated. In 1738, shortly after Ramsay's 'Oration', the Marquis d'Argens published an article on Freemasonry. In this work, he speaks of Jacobite lodges attempting to arrogate a specifically Templar pedigree to themselves.[5] And during the course of the next decade, the Templars – so far at least as all forms of Freemasonry other than Grand Lodge were concerned – became increasingly the focus of attention. In 1743, for example, the so-called 'Vengeance' or 'Kadosh' degree is believed to have been introduced at Lyons – vengeance to be exacted by Freemasonry for the death of the last Templar Grand Master, Jacques de Molay.[6] We have already noted how potent this motif was to become.

The man chiefly responsible for publicising the Templar heritage within Freemasonry was a German nobleman, Baron Karl Gottlieb von Hund. Having first joined a lodge in Frankfurt, Hund, very much a man of the world, travelled widely in Freemasonic circles. Between December 1742 and September 1743, he was in Paris. Early in the 1750s, he began to advertise an ostensibly 'new' form of Freemasonry which claimed, quite specifically, a Templar origin. When pressed to justify himself, Hund declared that during his nine-month visit to Paris he had been introduced to 'Templar Freemasonry'. He arrived six months before Ramsay's death, three years before Radclyffe's. He had, he said, been initiated into 'higher degrees' and dubbed 'Chevalier Templier' by an 'unknown superior' identified to him only under the appellation of 'Eques a Penna Rubra' – 'Knight of the Red Feather'. This ceremony, he declared, had been performed in the presence of, among others, a certain Lord Clifford (probably the young Lord Clifford of Chudleigh, related by marriage to Radclyffe) and the Earl of Kilmarnock. Not long after his induction, Hund said, he was presented to Charles Edward Stuart in person, whom he was led to believe was one of the 'unknown superiors', if not indeed the secret Grand Master, of the whole of Freemasonry.[7]

26 *above* Ruined church of Temple, near Edinburgh, formerly known as Balantrodoch, the headquarters of the Order of the Temple in Scotland.

27 *below left* Seventeenth-century grave at Temple showing masonic dividers and set square.

28 *below right* Seventeenth-century grave at Temple with skull-and-crossbones flanked by masonic tools.

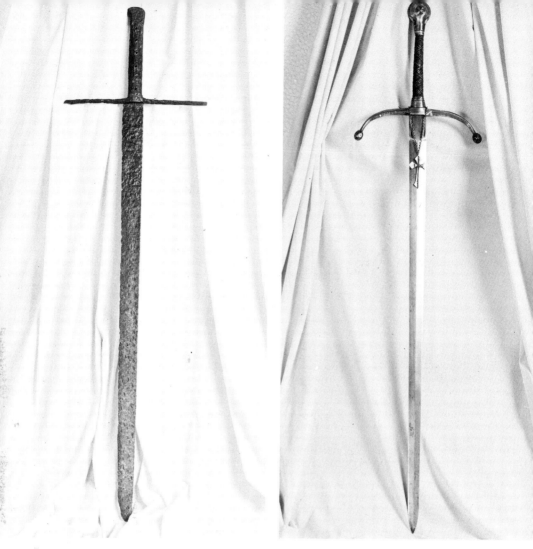

29–30 The above swords (*left* mid- to late-fifteenth-century sword, probably of German origin; *right* mid-seventeenth-century blade, nineteenth-century hilt), currently in a private collection (Stella Templum Scotorum), have long been in Scottish Jacobite Templar ownership. One of them is known to have been used by the Earl of Kilmarnock and his colleagues to initiate Baron von Hund into the Jacobite Order of the Temple, 1743.

31 *opposite* Personal ceremonial sword of Alexander Deuchar, Master of the Scottish Templars (*Militia Templi Scotia*) from 1810 to 1835. Deuchar gathered a large collection of regalia and documents relating to early Scottish Templarism and Freemasonry.

32 English Masonic Knights Templar star jewels, *c*.1830. A candidate for
admission must already be both a Master Mason, 'exalted' into the Royal
Arch, and a Christian. It is thus distinguished from the religious freedom
allowed by 'Craft' Freemasonry as promulgated by United Grand Lodge of
England.

The form of Freemasonry to which Hund had been introduced was subsequently to become known under the name of 'Strict Observance'. Its name derived from the oath it demanded – an oath of unswerving and unquestioning obedience – to the mysterious 'unknown superiors'. The basic tenet of the Strict Observance was that it had descended directly from the Knights Templar. Members of the Strict Observance felt they were legitimately entitled to refer to themselves as 'Knights of the Temple'.

To his own embarrassment, Hund, when pressed for further information and evidence, was unable to support his claims. As a consequence, many of his contemporaries dismissed him as a charlatan and accused him of having fabricated the account of his initiation, his meeting with 'unknown superiors' and with Charles Edward Stuart, his mandate to disseminate the Strict Observance. To these charges, Hund could only reply plaintively that his 'unknown superiors' had abandoned him. They had promised to contact him again, he protested, and to give him further instructions, but had never done so. To the end of his life, he continued to affirm his integrity, maintaining that he had been deserted by his original sponsors.

With the wisdom of historical hindsight, it is now clear that Hund was a victim not so much of any deliberate betrayal as of circumstances beyond everyone's control. He had been initiated in 1742, when Jacobite currency was still good, when the Stuarts enjoyed considerable prestige and influence on the Continent, when there seemed a reasonable prospect of restoring Charles Edward to the British throne. Within three years, however, all that was to change.

On 2 August 1745, Bonnie Prince Charlie, without the French support originally promised him, landed in Scotland. At a council of war, it was decided by one vote to advance southwards, and the Jacobite forces embarked on a march intended to bring them to London. They entered Manchester and on 4 December reached Derby. But few volunteers rallied to them – a mere 150 men in Manchester – and the spontaneous uprisings they expected on their behalf never occurred. After two days in Derby, it became painfully obvious that the only option was retreat. With Hanoverian troops in pursuit, the Jacobites fell back, and their situation, during the four months that followed, continued to deteriorate. At last, on 16 April 1746, they were cornered by the army of the Duke of Cumberland at Culloden and, in less than thirty minutes, were virtually annihilated. Charles Edward Stuart fled into ignominious exile again, and spent the rest of his life in obscurity. Of the prominent Jacobites who survived the battle, many were deported, banished or driven into voluntary exile. Some, including the Earl of Kilmarnock, were executed. So, too, was Charles Radclyffe, captured in a French ship off the Dogger Bank. The Jacobite dream of restoring the Stuarts to the British throne was extinguished for ever.

It is hardly surprising, therefore, that Hund's 'unknown superiors', who were all prominent Jacobites, never contacted him again. Most of them were dead, in prison, in exile or lying very low. There was no one of sufficient prestige left to help him vindicate his claims, and he was left to promulgate Strict Observance Freemasonry on his own. But he certainly does not seem to have been a charlatan, or to have fabricated his account of his induction into 'Templar Freemasonry'. Indeed, there has only recently come to light some telling evidence in his favour.

The Identity of Hund's Hidden Master

Part of Hund's evidence concerning the pedigree of Strict Observance consists of a list of Grand Masters of the original Knights Templar from their inception in 1118.[8] Until very recently, there had been numerous such lists, none of which concurred with any of the others and all of which had been academically suspect. It was not until 1982 that we ourselves were able to produce what can now be regarded as a definitive list of the early grand masters (until the loss of Jerusalem).[9] This list was compiled with the aid of information and documentation which were not available or accessible in Hund's time, so that he cannot possibly have drawn on the same sources as we did. And yet, except for the spelling of a single surname, he produced a list, reputedly received from his 'unknown superiors', which concurred precisely with our own. Hund's list can only have come from 'inside sources' – from sources who were indeed privy to Templar history and/or records in a way that no 'outsider' at the time could have been.

A second, particularly important piece of evidence in Hund's favour involves the identity of the 'Knight of the Red Feather', who, he claimed, had dubbed him a 'Knight of the Temple' in 1742. Until now, the identity of this individual has remained a mystery and in some quarters he has been regarded as pure fiction. Hund himself, as we have seen, at first thought the 'Knight of the Red Feather' to have been Charles Edward Stuart. Other commentators have suggested the Earl of Kilmarnock, Grand Master of Jacobite

Freemasonry in France at the time; but in making this suggestion, they have forgotten, or chosen to ignore, Hund's assertion that Kilmarnock was present in the room at the same moment as the pseudonymous individual. We ourselves, in a previous work, suggested that the 'Knight of the Red Feather' might have been Radclyffe, whom Hund did *not* say was present. Now, however, it is possible to establish, almost definitively, who the 'Knight of the Red Feather' actually was.

In 1987, we obtained access to the papers of a group called 'Stella Templum', which had, over two hundred years or more, maintained an archive of Jacobite Templar material.[10] In it was a letter dated 30 July 1846 – nineteen days short of the hundredth anniversary of the Earl of Kilmarnock's execution at the Tower of London on 18 August 1746. The signature on the letter appears to be that of one 'H. Whyte', and beneath it there is a wax seal in the form of a Templar cross. The addressee is simply called 'William'. The text refers to certain regalia, including, it would appear, the actual sword with which Hund was initiated:

> Observe that the blade and other articles are now in your charge. The Earl was not able to take them. Mr Grills and I think your care the best. Poor old Kilmarnock – God bless him – received the blade from Alexander Seton/The Knight of the Red Feather.
>
> I know not what will happen now, God willing you and Gardner will continue 100 years.
>
> Remember K. next month on the 18th.[11]

If this letter can be believed – and there is certainly no reason whatever to doubt its authenticity – the writer knew the 'Knight of the Red Feather' to be one Alexander Seton.

Alexander Seton was more generally known as Alexander Montgomery, Tenth Earl of Eglinton. In 1600, Robert Seton was created First Earl of Winton. He had married Lady Margaret Montgomery, daughter and heiress of Hugh Montgomery, Third Earl of Eglinton, and the Eglinton title was inherited by the younger of their sons, his descendants assuming the surname of Montgomery. Thus the Alexander Seton in question was in fact Alexander Montgomery, who was particularly active in Jacobite Freemasonry on the Continent. When Chevalier Ramsay died in 1743, for example, his death certificate was signed by Alexander Montgomery (Earl of Eglinton), Charles Radclyffe (Earl of Derwentwater), Michael de Ramsay (the Chevalier's cousin), Alexander Home and George de Leslie.[12]

Why should it have been Alexander Montgomery (Seton), rather than Radclyffe, Ramsay, Kilmarnock, Charles Edward Stuart or anyone else, who dubbed Baron von Hund a 'Knight of the Temple'? Undoubtedly because he was descended from the family around whom, in the person of the elusive David Seton, the original survivors of the Templars in Scotland had rallied when their patrimonial lands were illicitly disposed of by Sir James Sandilands in 1564. And if the information we received from a contemporary member of the family is accurate, an 'Order of the Temple' has persisted among the Montgomeries to the present day.

In the aftermath of the 1745 rebellion, Jacobite Freemasonry as such, with its specific political orientation and allegiance to the Stuart bloodline, effectively died out. Variations of it, however, purged of political content and tempered by the moderation of the Grand Lodge of England, survived. They survived in part through the so-called 'higher degrees' offered by such institutions as Irish Grand Lodge. Most important, however, they survived within the Strict Observance promulgated by Hund – of which the highest degree was that of 'Knight Templar'. The Strict Observance was to spread throughout Europe. More significant still, however, it was to find fertile soil among the colonists – many of them Jacobite refugees or deportees – of what was to become the United States.

FOUR

Freemasonry and American Independence

15

The First American Freemasons

Not surprisingly, perhaps, there is more myth, legend and rumour associated with the origins of Freemasonry in America than there is hard fact or reliable information. According to some traditions, a form of Freemasonry or proto-Freemasonry came to the New World as early as the Jamestown settlement of 1607 and established itself in Virginia, working to promote the kind of idealised society outlined twenty years later by Francis Bacon in such works as *The New Atlantis*. This possibility cannot entirely be discounted. The 'Rosicrucian' thinkers of the early seventeenth century were obsessively aware of the opportunities America offered for the idealised social blueprints that figured so prominently in their work. So, too, were the members of the 'Invisible College' which eventually became visible in the form of the Royal Society. It would be most surprising if at least something of their ideas did not find its way across the Atlantic. In any case, the first transplantations of Freemasonry to America, when and wherever they occurred, would have been as inevitable, as routine, as predictable and, initially, as devoid of major consequence as the transplantation of other English attitudes and institutions. No one could have foreseen the significance these transplantations would quickly assume.

So far as authoritative documentation is concerned, the first known Freemason to settle in the American colonies was one John Skene. Skene is listed as a Mason of an Aberdeen lodge in 1670 and in 1682 emigrated to North America.[1] He settled in New Jersey, where he later became deputy governor. But the Freemasonry he brought with him would have existed in a vacuum in New Jersey. There were no brethren with whom Skene might have consorted, no existing Freemasonic framework into which he might have fitted.

Nor did he create any of his own. No record, at any rate, survives to suggest otherwise.

Skene had become a Freemason before ever going to America. The first American-based settler to become a Freemason was Jonathan Belcher, who, on a visit to England in 1704, was initiated into an English lodge.[2] Belcher returned to the colonies a year later, becoming in time a prosperous merchant and eventually, in 1730, governor of Massachusetts and New Hampshire. By that time, Freemasonry was starting to establish itself solidly in the colonies, and Belcher's son was to become particularly active in its dissemination.

There must have been many cases similar to those of Skene and Belcher – men who were already Freemasons when they emigrated to the colonies, men already settled in the colonies who, on visits to England, were inducted into lodges. And in 1719, there is even a record of a ship called the *Freemason* plying the American coastal trade.[3] But there is no record whatever of any American-based lodges prior to the late 1720s. On 8 December 1730 Benjamin Franklin printed in his newspaper, *The Pennsylvania Gazette*, the first documented notice about Freemasonry in North America. Franklin's article, which consisted of a general account of Freemasonry, was prefaced by the statement that 'there are several Lodges of FREE MASONS erected in this Province . . .'[4]

Franklin himself became a Freemason in February 1731,[5] and Provincial Grand Master of Pennsylvania in 1734. That same year, he ushered into print the first Freemasonic book to be published in America, an edition of Anderson's *Constitutions*. In the mean time, the first recorded American lodge had been founded in Philadelphia. Its earliest surviving documents, labelled as its 'second' book of records, date from 1731, so that the first book, assuming there was one, must have covered at least the previous year.[6]

Many of the earliest lodges in America – including, very possibly, some whose records have not survived and which we therefore have no means of knowing about – were, in Freemasonry's own language, 'irregular'. In order to become 'regular' or 'regularised', a lodge had to be 'warranted' – had to receive a charter, that is, from a superior governing body, a Grand Lodge or, so to speak, mother lodge. Thus, for example, the Grand Lodge of England would issue warrants to its own offshoots, or new lodges, in the American colonies. But warrants could also be issued by other bodies, such as Grand Lodge of Ireland, which offered the so-called 'higher degrees' and other features characteristic of Jacobite Freemasonry, which had been divested after 1745 of its specifically political, specifically pro-Stuart orientation, yet retained its uniquely chivalric quality.

The first officially warranted or chartered lodge on record in America is St John's Lodge of Boston, founded in 1733 and chartered by the Grand Lodge of England.[7] In the same year, as we have seen, Grand Lodge was also raising money to send to its brethren in Oglethorpe's colony of Georgia, although no records of specific lodges, warranted or unwarranted, survive prior to 1735, when one was established in Savannah. In the mean time, Massachusetts, in 1733, had already warranted a Provincial Grand Lodge, under the Grand Mastership of Henry Price. The Deputy Grand Master was Andrew Belcher, son of Jonathan Belcher who had been initiated in England in 1704.[8] Between 1733 and 1737, the Grand Lodge of England warranted Provincial Grand Lodges in Massachusetts, New York, Pennsylvania and South Carolina. In Georgia, New Hampshire and other future states, there were one or more local lodges but no Provincial Grand Lodge. From Virginia, no records survive, but there are supposed to have been lodges warranted not by the Grand Lodge of England, but by the quasi-Jacobite Grand Lodge of York.

Military Lodges

At the same time that Freemasonry – almost entirely under the auspices of the Grand Lodge of England – was spreading through the colonies, there occurred another development which was to have a much more profound effect on American history. Since 1732, Freemasonry had also been spreading through the British Army in the form of regimental field lodges. These lodges were mobile, carrying their regalia and accoutrements in trunks along with the regimental colours, silver and other purely military paraphernalia. Often, the colonel commanding would preside as the lodge's original master and might then be succeeded by other officers. The regimental field lodges were to have a profound effect on the army as a whole. They provided, as we shall see, a channel of communication for the redress of grievances. And just as civilian lodges brought together men of diverse backgrounds and social classes, so the field lodges brought together officers and men, subalterns and more senior commanders. One consequence of this was the creation of a climate in which dynamic young soldiers – such as James Wolfe, for example – could advance themselves, regardless of caste.

The first lodge in the British Army was created in the 1st Foot, later the Royal Scots, in 1732.[9] By 1734, there were five such regimental lodges. By 1755, there were twenty-nine. Among the regiments possessing their own field lodges were those later to be known as the Royal Northumberland Fusiliers, the Royal Scots Fusiliers, the Royal Inniskilling Fusiliers, the Gloucestershire Regiment, the Dorset Regiment, the Border Regiment and the Duke of Wellington's (West Riding).

Of particular significance is the fact that these lodges were *not* chartered by the Grand Lodge of England. On the contrary, they were chartered by Irish Grand Lodge, which offered the 'higher degrees' characteristic of Jacobite Freemasonry. Moreover, these lodges were chartered prior to 1745, when the 'higher degrees' first began to be purged of their Jacobite orientation.

At the same time, of course, Freemasonry had also established itself in the upper echelons of military command and administration, and included some of the most prominent figures of the day. The Duke of Cumberland, for example, younger son of George II, was a Freemason. So, too, it seems, was General Sir John Ligonier, the most important British military commander of the 1740s. During the Jacobite rebellion of 1745, Ligonier commanded the British Army in the Midlands. A year later, he was transferred to the Continent, where he played a key role in operations during the War of the Austrian Succession. Ligonier's precise Freemasonic affiliations have not been definitively established, but he appears, as early as 1732, on the list of subscribers to James Anderson's work, along with such prominent Freemasons as Desaguliers, the Earl of Abercorn and the Earl of Dalkeith, all three former Grand Masters of Grand Lodge.

Among Ligonier's subordinates was the man who would emerge as perhaps the single most important British commander of the age, the future Lord Jeffrey Amherst – who will figure conspicuously in this narrative. Amherst was commissioned in the 1st Foot Guards (now the Grenadier Guards) under Ligonier, whose aide-de-camp he became. Before going on to greater things in America, he served with Ligonier on the Continent during the War of the Austrian Succession. In 1756, he became lieutenant-colonel of the 15th Foot (later the East Yorkshire Regiment), where the field lodge, established two years before, continued to function under his auspices.[10] Subsequently, he was to become colonel of the 3rd Foot (the Buffs or East Kent Regiment) and the 60th Foot (known then as the Royal Americans, later as the King's Royal Rifle Corps and now as the Royal Greenjackets). In both units, field lodges were established under his aegis.[11]

Amherst's sponsor – the man who paid for his commission – had been a family friend, Lionel Sackville, First Duke of Dorset, an associate of the Duke of Wharton, together with whom he became a Knight of the Garter in 1741. Sackville had two sons. The elder, Charles, Earl of Middlesex, founded a Freemasonic lodge in Florence in 1733.[12] Along with Sir Francis Dashwood, he also co-founded the Dilettanti Society, which had many Masonic members. By 1751, both he and Dashwood were members of a prominent entourage of Freemasons attached to the court of Frederick, Prince of Wales, who was himself a Freemason.[13]

Sackville's younger son, George, was equally active in Free-masonic affairs. By 1746, he was colonel of the 20th Foot (later the Lancashire Fusiliers), and took a particular interest in the regiment's field lodge, even becoming its official Master.[14] One of his two wardens was Lieutenant-Colonel Edward Cornwallis (twin brother of a later Archbishop of Canterbury), who in 1750 was made governor of Nova Scotia and founded the first lodge there. Among Cornwallis's subordinates was the young Captain James Wolfe, who had already established a reputation for brilliance and audacity under the Duke of Cumberland, then under Sir John Ligonier on the Continent. Subsequently, of course, working in close concert with Amherst, Wolfe was to play a decisive role in the course of North American history.

George Sackville himself, in the mean time, had become, by 1751, Grand Master of Irish Grand Lodge.[15] Eight years later, during the Seven Years War, he was to be charged with cowardice at the Battle of Minden, court-martialled and dismissed from the service. His friendship with George III, however, enabled him to retain his status in governmental quarters. By 1775, under the title of Lord Germain, he was Colonial Secretary. It was in this capacity that he served through the American War for Independence.

The French and Indian War

Events were soon to bring American Freemasonry and that of the British Army together on a hitherto unprecedented scale. Substantial contingents of British regulars, both officers and men, were soon to be working in close concert with the colonists, training them in military procedures and operations and, in the process, transmitting other things as well – not least the corpus of 'higher degree' (formerly Jacobite) Freemasonry. And this Freemasonry

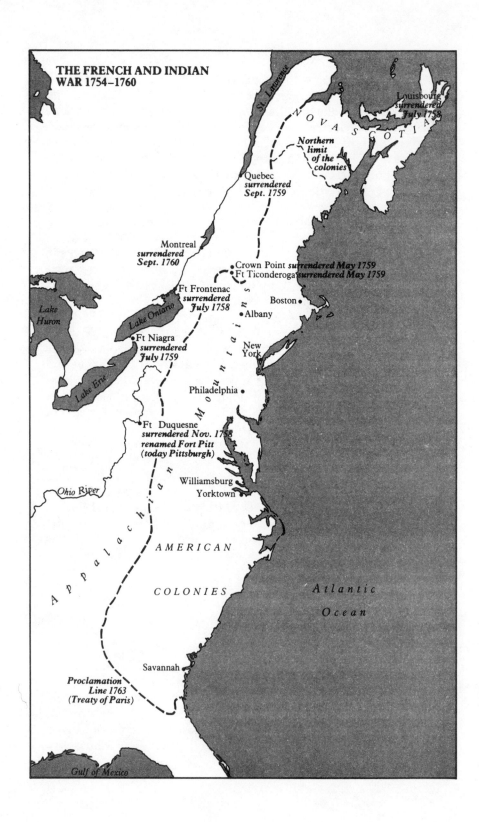

THE FRENCH AND INDIAN WAR 1754–1760

Louisbourg *surrendered July 1758*

St. Lawrence

N O V A · S C O T I A

Northern limit of the colonies

Quebec *surrendered Sept. 1759*

Montreal *surrendered Sept. 1760*

Crown Point *surrendered May 1759*
Ft Ticonderoga *surrendered May 1759*

Lake Huron

Ft Frontenac *surrendered July 1758*

Lake Ontario

Boston

Albany

Ft Niagra *surrendered July 1759*

Lake Erie

New York

Philadelphia

M o u n t a i n s

Ft Duquesne *surrendered Nov. 1758 renamed Fort Pitt (today Pittsburgh)*

Williamsburg
Yorktown

Ohio River

A M E R I C A N

A
p
p
a
l
a
c
h
i
a
n

C O L O N I E S

Atlantic Ocean

Savannah

Proclamation Line 1763 (Treaty of Paris)

Gulf of Mexico

was to provide an ideal conduit for the kind of rapport and sense of fraternity that tends generally to develop among comrades-in-arms.

There had, of course, been military operations in America before, where British and French interests had been clashing since the beginning of the eighteenth century. During the War of the Spanish Succession (1701–14), a joint French and Spanish attack on Charleston, in South Carolina, was successfully repulsed. Small-scale skirmishing between British and French colonists also occurred around the Canadian border, the French territory called Acadia being captured and re-christened Nova Scotia. A quarter of a century later, during the War of the Austrian Succession (1740–8), there were again operations in America, this time on a slightly larger scale. In 1745, colonists from New England seized the French fortress of Louisbourg on Cape Breton Island, which guarded the entrance to the St Lawrence. Again, however, operations in North America were peripheral, mere footnotes to the more important campaigns being conducted in Europe. They involved extremely small numbers of regular troops, relatively junior officers and were little more than skirmishes.

In 1756, however, the Seven Years War erupted in Europe; and this time, large-scale military and naval operations spread much further afield – extending, indeed, not only as far as America, but to India as well. British troops were once again to be engaged in campaigns on the Continent, but in relatively modest numbers compared to the forces of France, Austria and Prussia. The British Army's principal theatre of activity was to be North America; and the rivers and forests of the New World were to witness clashes between sizeable, highly trained and well-drilled European armies on a scale that would have seemed inconceivable half a century before.

Between 1745 and 1753, the English population of North America had swollen dramatically, and not just with exiled or refugee Jacobites. As early as 1754, Benjamin Franklin proposed a plan for the union of all the colonies, which the British government rejected. But if political centralisation was denied, organisation, communication and trade developed rapidly, and need for expansion westwards became increasingly pressing. When colonists from Virginia began moving into the Ohio Valley of western Pennsylvania, however, they threatened the link between French territory in Canada, on the St Lawrence, and that on the Mississippi; and when a contingent of colonial militia under the young George Washington was dispatched into the region to build a fort, full-scale fighting broke out. The first four years of the war were marred by military disasters, some of them serious enough to send shock waves reverberating back to England. In April 1755, a British column – both regulars and colonial militia – under General Edward Braddock was ambushed by French troops and their Indian allies near Fort Duquesne. The column was virtually annihilated, Braddock was fatally wounded and Washington, his aide-de-camp, barely escaped. A sequence of additional reverses ensued. One after another, British forts throughout what is now upstate New York were lost, and a massive, European-style general assault intended to recapture Fort Ticonderoga was repulsed with appalling casualties. Among them was the commander himself, General James Abercrombie, and Lord George Howe, one of the most promising younger officers in the British Army at the time. Prior to his death, Howe had been one of the leading innovators in the kind of irregular warfare that was coming to characterise operations in North America. Along with Amherst and Wolfe, he was instrumental in helping the army adapt itself from the rigid manoeuvres of the European battlefield to the more flexible, more modern tactics dictated by the rivers and forests of the wilderness in which it now had to fight.

According to a prominent military historian:

[Howe] threw off all training and prejudices of the barrack yard, joined the irregulars in their scouting parties . . . and adopted the dress of his rough companions and became one of themselves. Having thus schooled himself he began to impart the lessons he had learned . . . He made officers and men alike . . . throw off all useless encumbrances; he cut the skirts off their coats and the hair off their heads, browned the barrels of their muskets, clad their lower limbs in leggings to protect them from briars, and filled the empty spaces in their knapsacks with thirty pounds of meal, so as to make them independent for weeks . . .[16]

Howe's death at Ticonderoga deprived the British Army of one of its most resourceful, imaginative and audacious figures, a man who displayed the potential of a great commander. But Ticonderoga was to be the last serious British reverse of the war. In England, William Pitt, later Earl of Chatham, had become Secretary of State and embarked on a massive re-shuffle of both the army and the Royal Navy. Old-fashioned, hidebound and doctrinaire officers were sacked, demoted or passed over, and commands were handed out to a host of younger, more dynamic, more flexible and more innovative men. In North America, the most important of these were James Wolfe, then aged thirty-one, and Amherst, ten years older – who, on the advice of his old superior, Sir John Ligonier, was appointed major-general and commander-in-chief. Among Wolfe's and Amherst's most prominent subordinates were Thomas Desaguliers, son of the distinguished Freemason, and William Howe, younger brother of George and later a central figure in the American War for Independence.[17]

As commander-in-chief, Amherst was better placed than Lord George Howe had been to introduce new techniques and tactics to the army. He adopted Howe's innovations and created a number of others as well – rifle or sharpshooter regiments clad in dark green, ranger units for scouting and guerrilla operations, light infantry. One light infantry regiment, designed specifically for scouting and skirmishing, was clad in dark brown skirtless coats with no lace or adornment of any kind. Some troops were even dressed in Indian apparel.

A number of colonial officers learned their trade from Amherst – officers who would later rise to prominence during the American War for Independence. It was from Amherst that such men as Charles Lee, Israel Putnam, Ethan Allen, Benedict Arnold and Philip John Schuyler acquired both the discipline of the professional soldier and the tactics specifically adapted to warfare in North America. And while Washington had by then resigned his commission, he, too, knew, and was profoundly influenced by, Amherst.

In July 1758, Amherst and his entourage of gifted young subordinates recaptured Louisbourg, taken initially during the War of the Austrian Succession, then lost. Three and a half months later, another British column captured Fort Duquesne, razed it to the ground and re-built it as Fort Pitt – the site now of Pittsburgh. During the following year, Amherst advanced through upstate New York, capturing one fort after another, including Ticonderoga. In September 1759, Wolfe, with William Howe leading the advance column, accomplished one of the most audacious feats in military history, proceeding up the St Lawrence by ship, then scaling the sheer cliffs of the Heights of Abraham outside the citadel of Quebec with 4000 troops. In the battle that ensued, both Wolfe and the French commander, the Marquis de Montcalm, died, but the tide had now turned. Desultory operations continued for another year; then, in September 1760, Montreal, besieged by Amherst and William Howe, capitulated, and France ceded her North American colonies to Britain.

The influx of British regulars into North America brought with it an influx of Freemasonry – particularly the kind of 'higher degree' Freemasonry warranted by Irish Grand Lodge. Of the nineteen line regiments under Amherst's command, no fewer than thirteen had practising field lodges.[18] Lieutenant-Colonel John Young – who commanded a battalion of the 60th Foot, one of the regiments under Amherst's personal colonelcy, at both Louisbourg and Quebec – had, as early as 1736, been appointed Deputy Grand Master of Grand Lodge of Scotland by Sir William St Clair of Rosslyn.[19] In 1757, he had become Provincial Grand Master for all Scottish lodges in America and the West Indies. In 1761, Young was succeeded in the 60th Foot by Lieutenant-Colonel (subsequently Major-General) Augustine Prevost. In the same year, Prevost became Grand Master of all lodges in the British Army warranted by another Freemasonic body, the Ancient and Accepted Scottish Rite.[20]

In 1756, one Colonel Richard Gridley was authorised 'to congregate all Free and Accepted Masons in the Expedition against Crown Point [subsequently taken by Amherst] and form them into one or more lodges'.[21] When Louisbourg fell in 1758, Gridley formed another lodge there. In November 1759, two months after Wolfe's capture of Quebec, the six field lodges of the troops occupying the citadel convened a meeting. It was decided that since 'there were so many lodges in the Quebec garrison', they should form themselves into a Grand Lodge and elect a Grand Master.[22] Accordingly, Lieutenant John Guinet of the 47th Foot (later the Lancashire Regiment) was elected Grand Master of the Province of Quebec. He was succeeded a year later by Colonel Simon Fraser, commander of the 78th Foot, the Fraser Highlanders.[23] Fraser, significantly enough, was the son of Lord Lovat, who, as a prominent Jacobite, had taken a major part in the 1745 rebellion and acquired the dubious distinction of being the last man ever executed on Tower Hill. In 1761, Simon Fraser was succeeded as Quebec's Provincial Grand Master by Thomas Span of the 47th Foot. Span was followed in 1762 by Captain Milborne West of the same regiment, and West, in 1764, became Provincial Grand Master for the whole of Canada.

One of the most interesting aspects of all this is the comparatively junior rank, quotidian background and general obscurity of the men holding such exalted offices. Most of them were not aristocrats, never rose to positions of public prominence, never even advanced themselves significantly or conspicuously in the army. They were basically 'ordinary soldiers'. From the appointments of the likes of Lieutenant Guinet and Captain West, one can discover something of the way in which the regimental field lodges functioned, how they pervaded the entire military chain of command and why they enjoyed such popularity. A subaltern like Lieutenant

Guinet would have been in daily contact with the rank-and-file, who, within the framework of the lodge, could deal with him as an equal. At the same time, as Provincial Grand Master of Quebec, he would have presided over officers who, in the military hierarchy, were far superior. The field lodges thus created a fluidity of interaction and communication which, in the context of the time, was an extraordinary and probably unique social phenomenon.

Not surprisingly, the Freemasonry so prevalent in Amherst's army was transmitted to the colonial officers and units serving with it. American commanders and personnel pounced on whatever opportunities arose to become not just comrades-in-arms, but also fellow Freemasons. Fraternal bonds were thus forged between regular British troops and their colonial colleagues. Lodges proliferated, Freemasonic ranks and titles were conferred like medals, or like promotions. Men such as Israel Putnam, Benedict Arnold, Joseph Frye, Hugh Mercer, John Nixon, David Wooster and, of course, Washington himself not only won their military spurs. They were also – if they were not already brethren – inducted into Freemasonry.[24] And even those who did not themselves become practising Freemasons were still constantly exposed to the influence of Freemasonry, which spilled over from the British Army to merge with the fledgling lodges already established in the colonies. By this means, Freemasonry would come to suffuse the whole of colonial administration, society and culture.

But it was not just Freemasonry in itself – not just the rites, rituals, traditions, opportunities and benefits of Freemasonry. It was also an ambience, a mentality, a hierarchy of attitudes and values for which Freemasonry provided a particularly efficacious conduit. The Freemasonry of the age was a repository for an imaginatively stirring and potent idealism, which it was able, in a fashion uniquely its own, to disseminate. Most colonists did not actually read Locke, Hume, Voltaire, Diderot or Rousseau, any more than most British soldiers did. Through the lodges, however, the currents of thought associated with such philosophers became universally accessible. It was largely through the lodges that 'ordinary' colonists learned of that lofty premise called 'the rights of man'. It was through the lodges that they learned the concept of the perfectibility of society. And the New World seemed to offer a species of blank slate, a species of laboratory in which social experiment was possible and the principles enshrined by Freemasonry could be applied in practice.

16

The Emergence of
Masonic Leaders

One of the key questions about the American War for Independence is how and why Britain contrived to lose it. For the war was not so much 'won' by the American colonists as 'lost' by Britain. Britain alone, quite independently of the colonists' efforts, had the capacity to win or lose the conflict; and by not actively choosing to win it, she lost it more or less by default.

In most conflicts – the War of the Spanish Succession, for example, the Sevens Years War, the wars of the Napoleonic era, the American Civil War, the Franco–Prussian War, the two world wars of our own century – victory or defeat by one or another combatant can be explained in military terms. In most such conflicts, the historian can point to one or more specific factors – certain tactical or strategic decisions, certain campaigns, certain battles, certain logistic considerations (such as supply lines or volume of industrial production), or simply the process of attrition. Any of these factors, the historian can say, either individually or in combination, brought about the collapse of one of the combatants, or rendered it untenable for one of the combatants to continue fighting. In the American War for Independence, however, there are no such factors to which the historian can satisfactorily point. Even the two battles usually regarded as 'decisive' – Saratoga and Yorktown – can be regarded as 'decisive' only in terms of American morale, or perhaps, with the wisdom of hindsight, in terms of intangible 'watersheds'. Neither of these engagements crippled, or even seriously impaired, Britain's capacity to continue fighting. Neither involved more than a fraction of the British troops deployed in North America. The war was to continue for four years after Saratoga, during which time the British defeat was redressed by a series of victories. And when Cornwallis surrendered at Yorktown, the bulk of the British forces in North America was still intact, still well-placed to continue operations elsewhere, still strategically and numerically in a position of advantage. There was, in the American War for Independence, no conclusive victory comparable to Waterloo, no ineluctable 'turning point' comparable to Gettysburg. It seems almost as if everyone simply got tired, became bored, lost interest, decided to pack up and go home.

In American history textbooks, certain standard explanations are routinely presented as military explanations for the British defeat – because, of course, any such military explanation amounts to a testimonial of American prowess at arms. Thus, for example, it is often suggested, if not quite explicitly stated, that the whole of colonial North America was up in arms, confronting Britain with a hostile continent arrayed against her – a situation akin to that of Napoleon's or Hitler's invasion of Russia, with an entire people united to repel the aggressor. More often still, it is maintained that the British Army was out of its element in the wilderness of North America – was untrained and unadapted to the kind of irregular guerrilla fighting employed by the colonists and dictated by the terrain. And it is often generally maintained that the British commanders were incompetent, inept, lazy, corrupt, out-thought and out-manoeuvred. It is worth looking at each of these assertions individually.

In fact, the British Army was not confronted by a continent or a people passionately united against it. Of the thirty-seven news-papers in the colonies in 1775, twenty-three were in favour of the rebellion, seven were loyal to Britain and seven were neutral or uncommitted. If this can be taken to reflect the attitudes of the populace, fully 38 per cent were not prepared to support independence. In reality, a substantial number of colonists remained actively attached to what they regarded as the mother country. They voluntarily spied, voluntarily furnished information, accommodation and supplies to British troops. Many of them actually resorted to arms and campaigned, alongside British regular units, against their colonial neighbours. In the course of the war, there were no fewer than fourteen regiments of 'Loyalists' affiliated with the British Army.

Neither is it tenable to argue that the British Army was unsuited and untrained for the kind of warfare being waged in North America. In the first place, and contrary to popular impressions, most campaigning of the conflict did not involve irregular fighting at all. Most of it involved set-piece battles and sieges of precisely the kind being fought in Europe, precisely the kind at which the British Army, and the Hessian mercenaries within it, excelled. But even when irregular warfare was employed, British troops were at no disadvantage. As we have seen, Amherst, Wolfe and their subordinates, a mere twenty years before, had employed precisely that kind of warfare in wresting North America from France. In fact, the British Army had pioneered the sort of fighting sometimes dictated by the forests and rivers in which the techniques and formations of the European battlefield were out of place. Hessian troops might indeed have been vulnerable to such tactics, but British units like the 60th Foot – Amherst's old rifle regiment – could outdo (and often outdid) the colonists at their own game, a game which, after all, most of the colonists' military leaders had learned from *British* commanders.

There remains the charge of incompetence and ineptitude on the part of the British commanders. So far as one of those commanders is concerned – Sir John Burgoyne – the charge is probably valid. As for the three primary commanders, however – Sir William Howe, Sir Henry Clinton and Lord Charles Cornwallis – it is not. In fact, Howe, Clinton and Cornwallis were quite as competent as their American counterparts. All three of them won more victories against the colonists than they lost – and larger, more substantial victories. All three of them had previously demonstrated their skill, and would have occasion to demonstrate it again. Howe, in particular, had played a prominent role in the war against the French twenty years before – had learned irregular tactics from his brother who died at Ticonderoga, had served under Amherst at Louisbourg and Montreal, had led Wolfe's troops up the Heights of Abraham at Quebec. And between 1772 and 1774, he was responsible for the introduction of light infantry companies into line regiments. Clinton had been born in Newfoundland, had grown up in Newfoundland and New York, had served in the New York militia before joining the Guards and seeing action on the Continent, where his rise in the military hierarchy has been described as 'meteoric'. Cornwallis also distinguished himself during the Seven Years War. Subsequently, during the fighting in Mysore, he was to win a string of victories that gave Britain control of southern India – and, in the process, was to act as mentor to the young Sir Arthur Wellesley, later Duke of Wellington. And during the 1798 rebellion in Ireland, Cornwallis proved himself not just a skilled strategist, but also a wise and humane man, who had constantly to curb the over-zealous brutality of his subordinates. These were not, in short, inept or incompetent commanders.

But if the British high command during the American War for Independence was not incompetent or inept, it was – to a degree never satisfactorily explained by historians – strangely dilatory, desultory, apathetic, even torpid. Opportunities were blandly ignored which would have been seized or pounced upon by far less efficient men. Operations were conducted with an almost somnambulistic, lackadaisical air. The war, quite simply, was not pursued with the kind of ruthlessness required for victory – the kind of ruthlessness displayed by the same commanders when pitted against adversaries other than the American colonists.

In fact, Britain did not lose the war in North America for military reasons at all. The war was lost because of other, entirely different factors. It was a deeply unpopular war, much as the war fought in Vietnam by the United States two centuries later was to be. It was unpopular with the British public, with most of the British government, with virtually all the British personnel directly involved – soldiers, officers and commanders. Clinton and Cornwallis both fought under duress, and with extreme reluctance. Howe was even more adamant, repeatedly expressing his anger, his unhappiness and his frustration about the command with which he had been saddled. His brother, Admiral Howe, felt the same way. The colonists, he declared, were 'the most oppressed and distressed people on earth'.[1]

Amherst's position was more militant still. At the outbreak of hostilities, Amherst was fifty-nine – fifteen years older than Washington, twelve years older than Howe, but still perfectly capable of conducting operations. Following his successes in the Seven Years War, he had become governor of Virginia, and had further developed his skills in irregular warfare during the Indian rebellion led by Chief Pontiac. When the American War for Independence began, he was commander-in-chief of the British Army, and had been chafing against the bureaucracy and tedium of his 'desk job'. Had Amherst taken command in North America, and (together with his old subordinate, Howe) campaigned with the vigour he had displayed against the French twenty years before, events would unquestionably have fallen out differently. But Amherst exhibited the same distaste as those who did grudgingly take the field; and his superior rank permitted him the luxury of refusal. The first offer came in 1776, and Amherst declined it. In January 1778, he was approached again. This time he was not even asked. The king, George III, actually appointed him commander-in-chief in America and demanded that he take control of the war there. Threatening to resign his commission, Amherst refused the king's direct order. Attempts to persuade him by members of the government proved equally futile.

For Amherst, for Howe, for most of the other British commanders, as for the bulk of the British public at large, the American War for Independence was perceived as a kind of civil war. In effect, they found themselves, to their own discomfiture, pitted against adversaries whom they could only regard as fellow Englishmen – often linked to them not just by language, heritage, customs and attitudes, but also, in many cases, by actual family ties. But there was even more to it than that. As we have seen, Freemasonry, in eighteenth-century Britain, was a network pervading the whole of society, and particularly the educated classes – the professional people, the civil servants and administrators, the educators, the men who shaped and determined public opinion. It also engendered a general psychological and cultural climate, an atmosphere which suffused the mentality of the age. This was especially true in the military, where the field lodges constituted a cohesive structure binding men to their units, to their commanders and to one another. And it was even more true among 'ordinary soldiers', who lacked the ties of caste and family which obtained in the officer class. During the American War for Independence, most of the military personnel involved, commanders and men on both sides, were either practising Freemasons themselves or were steeped in the attitudes and values of Freemasonry. The sheer prevalence of field lodges ensured that even non-Freemasons were constantly exposed to the institution's ideals. It could not fail to be apparent that many of those ideals were embodied by what the colonists were fighting for. The principles on behalf of which the colonists declared and then fought for independence were – incidentally, perhaps, but still pervasively – Freemasonic. And thus, for the British high command, as well as for the 'rank-and-file', they were engaged in a war not just with fellow Englishmen, but also with Freemasonic brethren. In such circumstances, it was often difficult to be ruthless. This is not to suggest, of course, that British commanders were guilty of treason. They were, after all, professional soldiers, and were prepared, however reluctantly, to do their duty. But they were at pains to define their duty as narrowly as possible, and to do nothing more.

The Influence of Field Lodges

There are, unfortunately, no rolls, membership lists or other forms of documentation to establish definitively who among the British high command were practising Freemasons. As a rule, most military men were initially inducted into field lodges, and field lodges were notoriously lax both in keeping records, and in returning such records as were kept to their parent lodge. Having once been chartered or warranted, a field lodge would usually tend to lose contact with its sponsoring body. This was particularly true of lodges warranted by Irish Grand Lodge, which had enough trouble with its own records; and it was Irish Grand Lodge, as we have seen, that warranted most of the early field lodges. In some cases, too, field lodges would warrant other field lodges, and the original parent lodge would never be informed. And as regiments were disbanded or amalgamated, field lodges would migrate, mutate, transplant themselves, sometimes obtain new warrants from different sponsoring bodies. Even outside the military, documentation was often appallingly patchy. All three brothers of George III, for example, are known to have been Freemasons; one of them, the Duke of Cumberland, eventually became Grand Master of the English Grand Lodge. Records exist, however, only for the induction of Henry, Duke of Gloucester, on 16 February 1766.[2] There is no indication of when, where or by whom the Duke of York, who at that time was already a Freemason, was initiated, although one historian says limply that he was 'initiated abroad'.[3] If data are so haphazard and erratic in the case of a royal prince, they are all the more so in the case of military commanders.

Not surprisingly, therefore, it cannot be ascertained whether Howe, Cornwallis and Clinton were indeed practising Freemasons. There are certainly abundant grounds, however, for concluding that they were. Of the four regiments in which Howe served before becoming a general officer, three had field lodges; and as colonel, he would have had to condone, if not preside over, their activities. As we have seen, moreover, Howe served under Amherst and Wolfe, in an army where Freemasonry was rampant. During the American War for Independence, his statements and attitudes concur precisely with those of known Freemasons. And of the thirty-one line regiments under his command in North America, twenty-nine possessed field lodges.[4] Even if Howe himself was not a Freemason, he could not but have absorbed something of Freemasonry's influence.

The same applies to Cornwallis, who enjoyed a particularly close rapport with Howe. Cornwallis served in two regiments before becoming a general officer and was colonel of one of them. Both had field lodges. As we have seen, Cornwallis's uncle, Edward, subsequently a lieutenant-general, had become governor of Nova Scotia and, in 1750, founded a lodge there. And indeed, the whole Cornwallis family, during the eighteenth and nineteenth centuries, was one of the most prominent in English Freemasonry.

In Clinton's case, the evidence is rather more ambiguous. Prior to becoming a general officer, he did not serve in line regiments, but in the Guards, who did not have field lodges until later. On the other hand, he was aide-de-camp, during the Seven Years War, to Ferdinand, Duke of Brunswick, one of the most active and influential Freemasons of the age. Ferdinand had been inducted in Berlin in 1740. In 1770, he became Provincial Grand Master, under the auspices of the English Grand Lodge, for the Duchy of Brunswick. A year later, he joined the Strict Observance. In 1776, he co-founded a prestigious lodge in Hamburg along with Prince Karl of Hesse. In 1782, he instigated the Convent of Wilhelmsbad, a major congress for the whole of European Freemasonry. As Ferdinand's aide-de-camp, Clinton would unquestionably have been exposed to Freemasonry and its ideals. Moreover, a record survives of a 'St Johns Day' festival celebrated by the Master and brethren of Lodge No. 210 on 25 June 1781, while the British Army was in occupation of New York. According to this record, toasts were drunk:

> To the King and the craft,
> The Queen . . . with masons' wives
> Sir Henry Clinton and all loyal Masons
> Admiral Arbuthnot . . . and all distressed Masons
> Generals Knyphausen and Reidesel . . . and visiting Brethren
> Lords Cornwallis and Rawdon . . . with Ancient Fraternity.[5]

Thus Freemasonry pervaded both the British Army and the rebellious colonies. It must be stressed at this point, however, that the evidence which follows does *not* attest to any kind of coherent, organised 'Freemasonic conspiracy'. Most historians of the American War for Independence have tended, so far as Freemasonry is concerned, to fall into one of two camps. Certain fringe writers, for example, have sought to portray the war exclusively as a 'Freemasonic event' – a movement engineered, orchestrated and conducted by cabals of Freemasons in accordance with some carefully calculated grand design. Such writers will often cite lengthy lists of Freemasons – which proves little more than that they have lengthy lists of Freemasons to cite, and there is certainly no shortage of such lists. On the other hand, most conventional historians circumvent the Freemasonic aspect of the conflict entirely. Philosophers such as Hume, Locke, Adam Smith and the French *philosophes* are regularly enough invoked; but the Freemasonic milieu which paved the way for such thinkers, which acted as a kind of amniotic fluid for their ideas and which imparted to those ideas their popular currency, is neglected.

In fact, there was no Freemasonic conspiracy. Of the fifty-six signatories of the Declaration of Independence, only nine can definitely be identified as Freemasons, while ten others may possibly have been. Of the general officers in the Continental Army, there were, so far as documentation can establish, thirty-three Freemasons out of seventy-four.[6] Granted, the known Freemasons were, as a rule, more prominent, more instrumental in shaping the course of events than their unaffiliated colleagues. But not even they were working in any kind of concert towards any kind of prearranged grand design. It would have been impossible for them to do so. The movement which culminated in American independence was, in effect, an ongoing and constant exercise in improvisation – and in what today would be called a kind of *ad hoc* 'damage control'. Unexpected *faits accomplis* had to be confronted, accepted, contained and turned to account one step at a time – until the next *fait accompli* dictated a new sequence of impromptu adaptations and adjustments. In this process, Freemasonry tended, on the whole, to act as a restraining and moderating influence. In 1775, for example, a number of militant radicals were already agitating for a complete severing of ties with Britain. As a Freemason, however, General Joseph Warren, subsequent commander of colonial troops at Bunker Hill, was issuing statements that anticipate those of Ulster Unionists today – that he was defying Parliament, but remained loyal to the crown. Washington held precisely the same position; and even as late as December 1777, a year *after* the Declaration of Independence, Franklin was prepared to renounce all thoughts of independence if the grievances which had precipitated the war were redressed.[7] It is thus as foolish to speak of 'Freemasonic conspiracies' as it is to discount Freemasonry altogether. Ultimately, the currents of thought disseminated by Freemasonry were to prove more crucial and more pervasive than Freemasonry itself. The republic which emerged from the war was not, in any literal sense, a 'Freemasonic republic' – was not, that is, a republic created by Freemasons for Freemasons in accordance with Freemasonic ideals. But it did embody those ideals; it was profoundly influenced by those ideals; and it owed much more to those ideals than is generally recognised or acknowledged. As one Masonic historian has written:

... Freemasonry has exercised a greater influence upon the

establishment and development of this [the American] Government than any other single institution. Neither general historians nor the members of the Fraternity since the days of the first Constitutional Conventions have realised how much the United States of America owes to Freemasonry, and how great a part it played in the birth of the nation and the establishment of the landmarks of that civilisation . . .[8]

17

The Resistance to Britain

As we have seen, the 'orthodox' or 'official' form of English Freemasonry, as exemplified by Grand Lodge, offered at most only the first three 'craft' degrees. The so-called 'higher degrees', so far as can be determined, were initially unique to the older Jacobite Freemasonry. Following the 1745 rebellion, 'higher degree' Freemasonry did not die out. It simply lost its specifically Jacobite, specifically political orientation and continued to function. Purged of its Stuart affiliations, it was no longer perceived as subversive by Grand Lodge, who began, albeit grudgingly, to accord official recognition to the 'higher degrees'. It soon became increasingly respectable for loyal, upstanding and civic-minded Englishmen, through specialised study, to work for such 'higher degrees' as the Mark Degree, the Royal Arch or Royal Ark Mariner. They did so under a variety of auspices, including Grand Lodge of Ireland, Grand Lodge of Scotland and the Strict Observance created by Baron von Hund. As we have seen, it was Hund who, for the first time so far as public record is concerned, claimed for Freemasonry a Templar ancestry.

Prior to the Seven Years (or French-Indian) War, most of the Freemasonry in North America was orthodox pro-Hanoverian, warranted by Grand Lodge. During the Seven Years War, however, 'higher degree' Freemasonry, by means of regimental field lodges, was transplanted on a large scale to the American colonies and quickly took root. Boston – the soil from which the American Revolution was to spring – exemplifies the process of transplantation and the friction that sometimes arose from it.

St Andrew's Lodge of Boston

Freemasonry had begun in Massachusetts in 1733, when Henry

Price, acting on authority from the Grand Lodge of England, became Grand Master of Massachusetts's own Provincial Grand Lodge, St John's. His deputy Grand Master, as we have seen, was Andrew Belcher, son of the provincial governor. By 1750, there were two other lodges based in Boston. Both they and their parent lodge, St John's, met at a tavern called the 'Bunch of Grapes', at the junction of what today are State and Kilby Streets; and British regiments with warrants from Grand Lodge also met on the premises. Subsequently, St John's was to warrant more than forty lodges under its umbrella. Meanwhile, in 1743, Grand Lodge of England had named a distinguished Boston merchant, one Thomas Oxnard, Provincial Grand Master of North America.[1] Boston thus became, in effect, the Freemasonic capital of Britain's transatlantic colonies.

But in 1752, an 'irregular' lodge, without an official warrant, was found to be operating at another tavern, the 'Green Dragon' – re-named Freemasons' Hall in 1764. When the scandalised members of St John's complained, the 'irregular' lodge duly applied for a warrant of its own – not from the Grand Lodge of England, however, but from Grand Lodge of Scotland, which offered 'higher degrees'. The warrant was not forthcoming until 1756, when British troops and their regimental field lodges, chartered by both Irish and Scottish Grand Lodge, began to arrive in America. The 'irregular' lodge was then warranted under the name of St Andrew's.[2] Soon, however, it began to warrant new lodges of its own and claimed for itself, therefore, the status of a Provincial Grand Lodge – under the authority of Grand Lodge of Scotland. There were thus two rival Provincial Grand Lodges in Boston: St John's, under the aegis of the Grand Lodge of England, and St Andrew's, under the aegis of Grand Lodge of Scotland. Not surprisingly, things became acrimonious, tempers flared, a 'them and us' situation developed and a miniaturised civil war of Freemasonic insult ensued. St John's looked askance at St Andrew's and, with vindictive passion, repeatedly 'passed resolutions against it'. Whatever they entailed, these resolutions produced no effect and St John's proceeded to sulk, petulantly forbidding its members to visit St Andrew's. In squabbles of this sort, some of Boston's most eminent citizens expended considerable time, energy and passion.

Ignoring the strictures against it, St Andrew's continued to meet and to gain recruits – sometimes, indeed, pilfering them from St John's. And on 28 August 1769, St Andrew's conferred, for the first time anywhere in the world, a new Freemasonic degree – specifically called the Knight Templar Degree.[3] Where precisely this degree came from is unclear. Although no definitive documentation exists, it is believed to have been brought to Boston by the 29th Foot, later the 1st Battalion of the Worcestershire Regiment, whose field lodge had been warranted by Grand Lodge of Ireland ten years before. In any case, the Templar pedigree arrogated by the Jacobites, and promulgated by Hund, was now beginning to gain adherents beyond their particular rites. From Boston, the Freemasonic degree of Knight Templar was to be carried back to England and Scotland.

But the bestowal of the first known Knight Templar degree was not to be St Andrew's sole claim to distinction. By 1773, it had assumed a position in the vanguard of what were now rapidly escalating events. At that time, its Grand Master was Joseph Warren, whom Grand Lodge of Scotland had appointed Grand Master for the whole of North America. Among the other members of the lodge were John Hancock and Paul Revere.[4]

For some eight years prior to 1773, friction between Britain and her American colonies had been assuming increasingly ominous proportions. Virtually bankrupted by the Seven Years War, Britain had sought to replenish her treasury at the colonies' expense, by imposing a series of ever more stringent tax measures. Each such measure had naturally provoked new resistance and angry opposition in the colonies. In 1769, the Virginia Assembly, prompted by Patrick Henry and Richard Henry Lee (both alleged Freemasons), had formally condemned the British government and been dissolved by the provincial governor. In 1770, the famous 'Boston Massacre' had occurred, when a British sentry and his colleagues, surrounded by a hostile crowd, fired a volley into it and killed five people. In 1771, an uprising in North Carolina had to be quelled by troops, and thirteen rebels were executed for treason. In 1772, two prominent Freemasons, John Brown and Abraham Whipple, had attacked a customs ship off Rhode Island and burned it.[5]

The situation came to a head with the Tea Act, passed to save the East India Company from bankruptcy. By virtue of this act, the East India Company was authorised to unload much of its huge tea surplus in the colonies, duty-free. This enabled it to undersell both legitimate tea merchants and colonial smugglers, and thus to monopolise the tea trade. In effect, the colonists were coerced into buying only the East India Company's tea – and more of it than they wanted or needed.

On 27 November 1773, the first of three East India Company merchant ships, the *Dartmouth*, arrived in Boston with an immense cargo of tea. On 29 and 30 November, mass meetings were held in protest, and the *Dartmouth* was unable to unload. For more than a fortnight, she remained stranded in port. Then, on the night of 16 December, a group of colonists (variously estimated at between sixty and two hundred) clumsily and provocatively disguised themselves as Mohawk Indians, boarded the ship and dumped its entire cargo – 342 chests of tea worth some £10,000 – into Boston Harbour. This was the famous 'Boston Tea Party'. It was more of a mischievous prank than an act of revolution. In itself, it neither involved nor precipitated violence. There was not to be any shooting in earnest for another fourteen months. All the same, the 'Tea Party' effectively marks the beginning of the American War for Independence.

At the time of the 'Tea Party', St Andrew's lodge was meeting regularly in what was called the 'Long Room' of Freemasons' Hall, formerly the 'Green Dragon' tavern. The lodge shared this room, and much of its membership, with a burgeoning number of politically-oriented secret societies and quasi-Masonic clandestine fraternities dedicated to opposing British fiscal legislation. Among the organisations that met in the 'Long Room' were the 'Long Room Club' (which included St Andrew's Grand Master, Joseph Warren), the 'Committee of Correspondence' (which included Warren and Paul Revere and synchronised local opposition with opposition in other American cities such as Philadelphia and New York) and the 'North End Caucus' (which included a good many Freemasonic brethren, including Warren).[6] Another, even more militant, organisation was the 'Sons of Liberty' and its inner nucleus, the so-called 'Loyal Nine', who advocated violence and had been fomenting riots, demonstrations and other forms of civil disobedience since 1765. Prominent among the 'Sons of Liberty' was Samuel Adams, who is not known to have been a Freemason. Neither did the 'Sons of Liberty' meet at the 'Long Room' of Freemasons' Hall. Again, however, its membership overlapped that of St Andrew's lodge. Paul Revere, for example, was particularly active in the 'Sons of Liberty'. At least three of the 'Loyal Nine' were also Freemasonic brethren of St Andrew's.[7]

The record of meetings of St Andrew's lodge immediately prior to the 'Boston Tea Party' is revealing. On 30 November 1773, for example, the second day of mass protest at the *Dartmouth*'s arrival, the lodge met, but only seven members were present. According to the Minute Book, it was 'motioned and seconded that the Lodge be adjourned to Thursday Evening next, on account of the few Brethren present. N.B. Consignees of the Tea took up the Brethren's time.'[8]

On the Thursday stipulated, 2 December, fifteen members and one visitor attended the lodge, and officers for the following year were elected. A week later, on 9 December, the date scheduled for the regular monthly meeting, fourteen members and ten visitors were present, but official business was postponed until the following week, the 16th. That night was the night of the 'Boston Tea Party'. Only five members attended the lodge. Beneath their names in the Minute Book, it is stated: 'Lodge closed (on account of the few Members present) until to Morrow Evening.'[9]

Contrary to some subsequent claims and legends, the 'Tea Party' does not appear to have been planned at St Andrew's lodge. In fact, it appears to have been planned by Samuel Adams and the 'Sons of Liberty'. But there is no question that at least twelve members of the lodge were involved in the 'Party'. Not only that. Twelve other participants afterwards became members of St Andrew's.[10]

The 'Tea Party', moreover, could not have occurred without the active collusion of two detachments of colonial militia who were supposed to be guarding the *Dartmouth*'s cargo. Of these men, the captain of the first detachment, Edward Proctor, had been a member of St Andrew's lodge since 1763.[11] Three of his men – Stephen Bruce, Thomas Knox and Paul Revere – were also members of the lodge, and three others were members of the 'Loyal Nine'. In the second detachment of militia, three more men were members of St Andrew's. Altogether, nineteen members out of forty-eight in the two militia detachments are known to have collaborated in dumping the *Dartmouth*'s tea. Of these nineteen, six, including the detachment commander, were members of St Andrew's and three more were members of the 'Loyal Nine'.[12]

The Continental Army

The day after the 'Tea Party', Paul Revere rode to New York, where news of what had happened was published and gleefully circulated among the other colonies. When the news reached London three months later, the reaction was swift and misguidedly drastic. A law was passed, the Boston Port Bill, which placed an embargo on all trade with Boston, and the port was effectively closed. The city – and, by extension, the whole of Massachusetts – was lifted out of the hands of civil administration and placed under what amounted to martial law. A military man, General Thomas Gage, was appointed governor of Massachusetts. A year later, in 1775, Gage received substantial reinforcements of British regulars under the command of Sir William Howe.

The slowness of transatlantic communication was still impeding the development of events, but they had already begun to assume a momentum of their own. On 5 September 1774, the First Continental Congress was convened in Philadelphia under the presidency of Peyton Randolph, a prominent attorney and Provincial Grand Master of Virginia.[13] The Boston delegates included Samuel Adams of the 'Sons of Liberty' and Paul Revere. But contrary to later tradition, there was no unanimity of views or objectives. Few of the representatives at this point desired, or even contemplated, independence from Britain. Such measures as the Congress passed were essentially economic, not political. They were also highly provisional, a combination of stop-gap and bluff. Thus, for example, the 'Continental Association' was formed, nominally to end or curb all trade with Britain and the rest of the world, to seal off the colonial economy and render it entirely self-sufficient. Such a design was hardly feasible in practice; but the enunciation of it could justifiably be expected to galvanise Parliament.

Parliament, however, 3500 miles away and with little understanding of or interest in the realities of the situation, invariably responded, when galvanised, in the wrong way, with the wrong measures. The situation continued to deteriorate, and when the Massachusetts Provincial Congress met in February 1775, it announced plans for armed resistance. Parliament responded by declaring Massachusetts to be in a state of rebellion. Amidst the increasingly inflammatory rhetoric that followed, Patrick Henry, in a speech to Virginia's Provincial Assembly, made his famous statement: 'Give me liberty, or give me death.'[14]

But the crisis was already passing beyond the domain of rhetoric – and even of civic or economic action. On 18 April 1775, 700 British troops were dispatched to seize a depot of militia arms stored at Concord, outside Boston. Paul Revere embarked on his famous ride to warn of their advance, and they were confronted at Lexington by seventy-seven armed colonists. A skirmish ensued – 'the shot heard round the world' – and eight colonists were killed, ten wounded. *En route* back to Boston with the confiscated cache of weapons, the British column was harassed by an estimated 4000 colonial marksmen and sustained 273 casualties killed and wounded. The colonists lost ninety.

On 22 April, the Third Provincial Congress of Massachusetts convened, with Joseph Warren, Grand Lodge of Scotland's Grand Master for North America, as president. Warren authorised the mobilisation of 30,000 men. At the same time, he wrote, in his 'Address to Great Britain':

> Hostilities are at length commenced in this colony by the troops under the comand of General Gage . . . These, brethren, are marks of ministerial vengeance against this colony for refusing, with her sister colonies, a submission to slavery; but they have not yet detached us from our royal sovereign. We profess to be his loyal and dutiful subjects . . . nevertheless, to the persecution and tyranny of his cruel ministry we will not tamely submit.[15]

Most of the non-Freemasons among the defiant colonists – men such as John and Samuel Adams – were already demanding more radical measures. As we have noted, however, Warren, in declaring his continued allegiance to the crown, if not to Parliament, expressed the position of most Freemasons. And it was this position that prevailed when, on 10 May 1775, the Second Continental Congress convened – first under the presidency of Peyton Randolph, then, when he died, under John Hancock of St Andrew's lodge – and authorised the raising of a full-fledged army. George Washington, a prominent Freemason under the Virginia Grand Mastership of Randolph, was appointed commander-in-chief. At least one historian has suggested that he owed his appointment to his Freemasonic connections.[16] Certainly there were more experienced military men available – although virtually all of them were Freemasons too. Indeed, during the early days of the war, the high command of the Continental Army was dominated by Freemasons. It is worth digressing to consider, albeit briefly, some of their biographies.

Among those who might well have been appointed supreme commander in Washington's stead was General Richard Montgomery. Montgomery had been born in Ireland, near Dublin. During the French–Indian War, he served as a regular officer in the British Army under Amherst. At the Siege of Louisbourg, he was in the 17th Foot, subsequently the Leicestershire Regiment, which formed part of Wolfe's brigade. Settling in the colonies after the war, Montgomery married the daughter of Robert R. Livingston – who, in 1784, was to become Grand Master of New York's Provincial Grand Lodge and who, in 1789, administered the oath whereby Washington became first president of the United States. Montgomery is believed to have been inducted into the field lodge of the 17th Foot during the Louisbourg campaign. Certainly his status as a Freemason was well known among his contemporaries. 'Warren, Montgomery and Wooster!' was a frequent Freemasonic toast, commemorating three distinguished brethren who were among the first to die in the conflict.[17]

General David Wooster had been a colonel, then a brigadier, during the French–Indian War. He served under Amherst at Louisbourg and is believed to have joined a field lodge there with Lord Blayney, subsequently Grand Master of English Grand Lodge. As early as 1750, Wooster had organised the Hiram Lodge No. 1 in New Haven and become its first Master.[18]

General Hugh Mercer had served as a surgeon's mate in the rebel Jacobite army of Charles Edward Stuart. After Culloden, he escaped to Philadelphia where, ten years later, he served under Braddock and was wounded at Fort Duquesne. A year later, he was in the strongly Freemasonic 60th Foot. When Fort Duquesne was rebuilt as Fort Pitt, Mercer was placed in command of it with the rank of colonel. A long-standing Freemason, he was in the same Fredericksburg lodge as Washington.[19]

General Arthur St Clair had been born in Caithness and was descended from Sir William Sinclair, the builder of Rosslyn Chapel. Like Montgomery, St Clair joined the British Army, served in the 60th Foot during 1756–7, then with Wolfe's brigade under Amherst at Louisbourg. A year later, he was with Wolfe at Quebec. In 1762, he resigned his commission and settled in the colonies. He is known to have been a Freemason, though no details of his induction or lodge affiliation have survived.[20]

General Horatio Gates had also served as a regular officer in the British Army. He, too, had fought under Amherst at Louisbourg. He was one of Washington's closest personal friends and married the daughter of the Provincial Grand Master for Nova Scotia. His precise Freemasonic affiliations are uncertain, but he is known to have been an habitué of Provincial Grand Lodge of Massachusetts.[21]

General Israel Putnam had served under Lord George Howe and was with him at his death in the disastrous frontal assault on Fort Ticonderoga. Subsequently, Putnam served under Amherst. He had been a Freemason since 1758, when he joined a field lodge at Crown Point shortly after Amherst's capture of the fort.[22]

General John Stark had seen action, along with Lord George Howe, in the irregular guerrilla unit known as 'Rogers' Rangers'. Subsequently, he was with Howe at Ticonderoga, then with Amherst. He may have become a Freemason at that time, but no conclusive evidence of his affiliation exists prior to 1778.[23]

This is a sampling of what amounts, in effect, to something like a litany. The list could easily be prolonged. General John Nixon was with Lord George Howe at Ticonderoga, then with Amherst at Louisbourg, as was General Joseph Frye. General William Maxwell was with George Howe at Ticonderoga, then with Wolfe at Quebec, as was General Elias Dayton. All were Freemasons.

One man who deeply resented Washington's appointment – so much so that it eventually led him to treason – was Benedict Arnold. Arnold, too, had served under Amherst and is believed to have become a Freemason at that time. In 1765, he joined David Wooster's Hiram Lodge No. 1 in New Haven.[24] Arnold's friend, Colonel Ethan Allen, had served with George Howe at Ticonderoga, then with Amherst. In July 1777, he received the first or 'Entered Apprentice' degree from a lodge in Vermont, but seems not to have advanced any further.[25]

18

The War for Independence

On the same day that the Second Continental Congress convened, Ethan Allen, along with Arnold, who was then his lieutenant, launched a surprise attack on Ticonderoga, the fort so bitterly contested a generation before. Stores of weapons and munitions were captured, including artillery. Five weeks later, the colonists, working secretly during the night, pre-empted British plans to fortify Boston by erecting their own emplacements on two ridges overlooking the city, Breed's Hill and Bunker Hill. Their nominal commander was Brigadier Artemus Ward, another veteran of the French–Indian War, but their guiding spirit was Joseph Warren of St Andrew's Lodge.

General Thomas Gage was subsequently to be blamed for what happened next, but the real responsibility lay with Sir William Howe, who commanded in the field. It was Howe who had the authority, once the true nature of the situation became clear, to revoke the plan of battle or adhere to it and suffer the inevitable cost. For a veteran subordinate of Amherst and Wolfe, Howe behaved strangely indeed.

Despite the stifling heat, Howe ordered his troops to advance, in close ranks, with full equipment weighing more than a hundred pounds per man, directly into the face of the colonists' fire and to take the emplacements by storm, with the bayonet. The colonists' fire, loosed in well-disciplined volleys learned from the British Army during the French–Indian War, was withering, and it took Howe's soldiers four assaults to carry the position. When they did – having sustained more than 200 killed and nearly 800 wounded out of some 2500 men engaged – they were not disposed to be gentle. Warren died on a British bayonet, and those of his colleagues who did not flee were annihilated. The colonists' losses were in excess of 400.

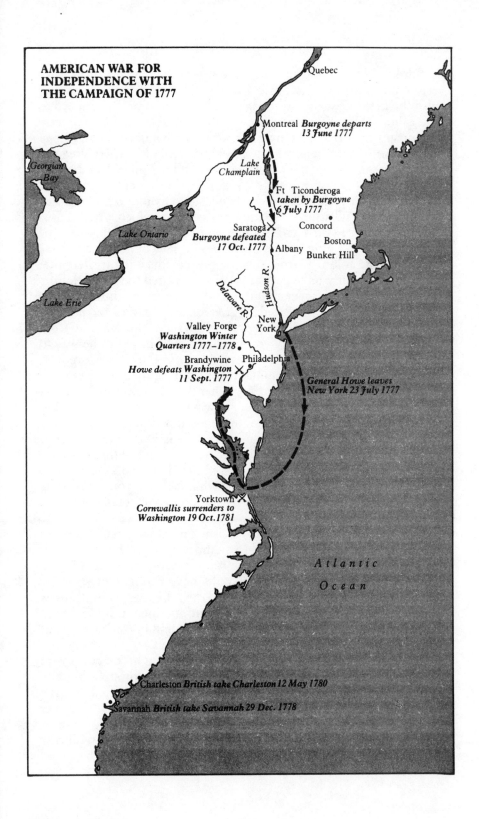

AMERICAN WAR FOR INDEPENDENCE WITH THE CAMPAIGN OF 1777

Quebec

Montreal *Burgoyne departs 13 June 1777*

Lake Champlain

Georgian Bay

Ft Ticonderoga *taken by Burgoyne 6 July 1777*

Concord

Lake Ontario

Saratoga *Burgoyne defeated 17 Oct. 1777*

Albany

Boston

Bunker Hill

Lake Erie

Delaware R.

Hudson R.

New York

Valley Forge *Washington Winter Quarters 1777–1778*

Brandywine *Howe defeats Washington 11 Sept. 1777*

Philadelphia

General Howe leaves New York 23 July 1777

Yorktown *Cornwallis surrenders to Washington 19 Oct.1781*

Atlantic Ocean

Charleston *British take Charleston 12 May 1780*

Savannah *British take Savannah 29 Dec. 1778*

Bunker Hill is important because it was the first major face-to-face confrontation between colonials and British regulars. It was also the first full-scale, full-fledged battle of the war, as opposed to the minor skirmishing at Lexington and Concord. But it is also important by virtue of Howe's curious behaviour and conduct of the action. Howe, it must be remembered, had learned irregular tactics under his elder brother George, under Amherst and under Wolfe. Throughout his military career, both before and after Bunker Hill, he eschewed the costly, wasteful frontal assault against an entrenched position – the kind of assault in which, after all, his elder brother had died at Ticonderoga in 1758. At Bunker Hill, he had a number of alternatives open to him. He could perhaps have dislodged the colonists from their emplacements with artillery fire. He could certainly have cut them off and waited them out, letting them succumb to hunger, thirst and shortage of ammunition. He could probably have deployed his grenadier companies and his light infantry in the kind of imaginative ways he had learned from Amherst and Wolfe twenty years before – and in which he was to deploy them on subsequent occasions later in the war. Moreover, having fought alongside colonial troops during the French–Indian War, Howe knew, better than any other British officer in Boston at the time, how tough they could be, how well-drilled and disciplined in the British Army's own techniques of volley firing.

In doing what he did at Bunker Hill, it is almost as if Howe, having repeatedly stated his reluctance to fight against the colonists, were sending a signal to his masters in London: 'You want me to fight? Very well, I'll fight. But this is what it'll cost you. This is the kind of mess you'll be getting us into. Do you really want to continue such lunacy?'

This would not have been cynicism on Howe's part. Neither would it have been the wanton squandering of a thousand men simply to make a point. On the contrary, Howe, knowing full well what Britain was getting into, would have thought in strategic terms. And thinking in strategic terms, he might well have concluded it worth the sacrifice of a thousand men if, by so doing, he could avert the loss of many times that number in subsequent engagements.

But even if this were the lesson Howe sought to convey to London, it failed to register. True, he might have thought initially that he had got his way – he himself was exculpated for the casualties at Bunker Hill; Gage was blamed and the British Army evacuated Boston. But Howe then found himself in the position he least wanted to occupy – replacing Gage, saddled with the responsibilities of commander-in-chief and obliged to continue operations against the colonists. He was never again to squander troops as he had at Bunker Hill. On the contrary, he repeatedly, in the campaigns that followed, went out of his way to spare lives, both those of his own men and those of the colonists. But his behaviour was to be no less equivocal, no less ambiguous.

The British Spy Network

Despite the loss of blood at Bunker Hill, or perhaps because of it, the colonists, guided largely by the Freemasons among them, still sought to avert a complete rupture with Britain. On 5 July, the Continental Congress adopted the so-called 'Olive Branch Petition' to George III, appealing for a peaceful settlement of differences. This was followed a day later by yet another resolution, declaring that the colonies did not desire independence but would 'not yield to enslavement'. On 23 August, however, the 'Olive Branch Petition' was summarily rejected and the king declared Britain's North American colonies to be in open rebellion. Events had thus assumed a momentum of their own and were escalating beyond what all the major factions had anticipated or desired.

On 9 November, a special committee – the 'Committee of Congress for Secret Correspondence' – was appointed to establish a network of contacts among 'our friends abroad'. This committee consisted of Robert Morris, John Jay, Benjamin Harrison, John Dickinson and Benjamin Franklin.[1] It was to operate extensively through Freemasonic channels and to lead to the creation of an elaborate spy network. At the same time, and quite coincidentally, it was to overlap a British spy network which ran parallel to it and also operated through Freemasonic channels. Both networks were to be based primarily in Paris, which became the centre for a vast web of espionage, intrigue and shifting allegiances.

Franklin, as we have seen, was a Freemason of long standing, having been initiated nearly half a century before, in 1731. In 1734 and again in 1749, he had been Grand Master of Pennsylvania. In 1756, he had been inducted into the Royal Society, still at that time strongly oriented towards Freemasonry. Between 1757 and 1762, and again between 1764 and 1775, he had spent considerable time abroad, in England and in France. In 1776, as the conflict in the colonies became a full-fledged war for independence, Franklin became, in effect, the American ambassador to France, and was to serve in this capacity until 1785. In 1778, in Paris, he was to become a member of a particularly important French lodge, 'Neuf Soeurs' or 'Nine Sisters', which was also to include such luminaries as John Paul Jones (first initiated in Scotland in 1770) and Voltaire. A year later, on 21 May 1779, Franklin became Master of 'Neuf Soeurs', a post to which he was re-elected in 1780.[2] In 1782, he became a member of a more elusive and mysterious Freemasonic conclave, the 'Royale Loge des Commandeurs du Temple a l'Ouest de Carcassonne' ('Royal Lodge of Commanders of the Temple West of Carcassonne').[3]

From the 1750s until 1775, Franklin was Deputy Postmaster-General for the American colonies. In this capacity, he had become particularly friendly with his opposite numbers, the joint British Postmasters-General, Sir Francis Dashwood and the Earl of Sandwich. Dashwood's Freemasonic affiliations are unclear. It is probable that he was a member of the lodge founded in Florence in 1733 by his close friend, Charles Sackville, Earl of Middlesex. Both he and Sackville were also members of the coterie of Freemasons attached to Frederick, Prince of Wales. Subsequently, he was to create what amounted to a private Freemasonic lodge of his own.[4]

In 1732, Dashwood had co-founded a quasi-Masonic society, the Dilettanti. While travelling abroad between 1739 and 1741, he had moved in Jacobite circles, becoming a close friend and, for a time, staunch supporter of Charles Edward Stuart. This brought him into contact with prominent Jacobites in England, such as George Lee, Earl of Lichfield, who had helped his cousin, Charles Radclyffe, escape from Newgate Prison and who, along with the Duke of Wharton, another fervent Jacobite and influential Freemason, had co-founded the original 'Hell Fire Club'. In 1746, Dashwood co-created, along with the Earl of Sandwich and two others, the ironically named 'Order of Saint Francis', which has since become known, in the popular mind and for later historians, by the same name as Wharton's and Lichfield's earlier organisation. Indeed, it is now Dashwood who is generally associated, erroneously, with the 'Hell Fire Club' – although his 'Franciscans' *were* involved in pretty much the same kind of neo-pagan orgiastic activities.

In 1761, Dashwood became Member of Parliament for Weymouth and Melcombe Regis. In 1762, he was Chancellor of the Exchequer under the Earl of Bute. A year later, he became Lord le Despencer and Lord Lieutenant of Buckinghamshire, as well as commander of the Buckinghamshire militia, in which one of his subordinates was another maverick and already notorious MP, John Wilkes. He became joint Postmaster-General in 1766. His first colleague in this post was Willis Hill, Lord Hillsborough, a co-founder, along with the Duke of Wharton and the Earl of Lichfield, of the original 'Hell Fire Club'. Hill was then succeeded by the Earl of Sandwich.

Sandwich had met Dashwood around 1740 and the two were to become lifelong friends. Not surprisingly, Sandwich became a member first of Dashwood's 'Dilettanti', then of the 'Order of Saint Francis'. He remained Postmaster-General until 1771, when he became First Lord of the Admiralty, a post he occupied through most of the American War for Independence. He did so with protuberant ineptitude, earning even from so cautious and restrained a source as the *Britannica* the statement: 'For corruption and incapacity Sandwich's administration is unique in the history of the British Navy.'[5]

During the summers of 1772, 1773 and 1774, Franklin stayed at Dashwood's home in West Wycombe.[6] They collaborated on an abridgement of the Book of Common Prayer:

> The Preface and Services were Dashwood's work edited by Franklin, the Catechism and the Psalms were Franklin's work and edited by Dashwood. The finished text was printed at Dashwood's expense . . .[7]

And Franklin -- that 'snuff-coloured little man' as D. H. Lawrence called him, sanctimonious author of *Poor Richard's Almanac*, proponent of temperance, frugality, industry, moderation and cleanliness while primly exhorting his readers not to 'use venery' -- became a member of Dashwood's 'Franciscans'. A paragon of moral rectitude at home, Franklin, in England, would apparently let his wig down, and the caves under Dashwood's estate at West Wycombe would become a boudoir for the cavortings of libidinous Postmasters-General.

To judge by a letter from Sandwich to Dashwood in September 1769, they had not much else to do:

> I am allmost [sic] ashamed to write to you upon Post Office business having been so idle for the whole summer; but indeed there is so little business that requires our attendance, and we have the good fortune to agree so perfectly well in every thing that requires an opinion, that there is very little occasion we should put ourselves to any inconvenience by a personal attendance.[8]

In fact, however, there was more to the matter than that. Because it afforded access to virtually all letters, all communications, the position of Postmaster-General was also traditionally that of spymaster. And during the American War for Independence, their experience as Postmasters-General was to stand both Dashwood and Franklin in good stead.

In his dual role of spymaster and colonial ambassador to France, Franklin established his centre of operations in Paris. He was accompanied here by two other appointees of the Congressional Committee for Secret Correspondence, Silas Deane and Arthur Lee. Lee's brother was based in London. So, too, was Franklin's sister, who is also believed to have been engaged in espionage. She had long been a good friend of Howe's brother, Admiral Lord Richard Howe, commander of naval operations in the colonial theatre. In 1774, she had brought Franklin and the admiral together, ostensibly to play chess, and they frequently discussed the colonists' grievances.[9] In 1781, an open letter was published by one 'Cicero', who accused the Howe brothers of belonging to a 'faction' which conspired to facilitate the colonists' bid for independence. 'Washington's whole conduct,' 'Cicero' charged, '. . . demonstrated a confidence which could arise from nothing short of certain knowledge.'[10] He explicitly accused Admiral Howe of 'having secret intrigues with Doctor Franklin'.[11] The admiral replied in a newspaper, declaring that 'Cicero' 'is perfectly right as to the fact though a little deceived in his inferences'.[12] At the same time, however, he admitted that he *had* withheld knowledge of his meetings with Franklin from the naval high command – which suggests that he might indeed have had something to hide.

One of the most important agents for the colonists in England was Dashwood's former friend, fellow MP and associate club member, John Wilkes. Wilkes had become an active Freemason in 1769 and by 1774 was Lord Mayor of London. In this capacity, he was publicly vociferous on behalf of the colonists' cause. But since the late 1760s, he had also been the secret British representative of the Boston-based 'Sons of Liberty', who had played so crucial a role in the 'Tea Party'.[13] Throughout the war, Wilkes was clandestinely raising money for the Continental Army and remitting it to Franklin in Paris. From Paris, it was either passed on to North America or used to purchase arms and matériel. Oddly enough, a letter of 1777 suggests that although Wilkes's network was penetrated, nothing was ever done about it.[14]

The British spy network, also run from Paris, was officially under the auspices of William Eden, Lord Auckland, another eminent man whose Masonic history has eluded investigators. In 1770 he had become Grand Steward of Grand Lodge, but no details exist of when, where or by whom he was initiated.[15] Auckland's network operated in large part through sea captains trading between France and North America – including those who carried dispatches between Franklin and Congress. As late as 10 December 1777, one of these captains, a man from Maryland named Hynson, reported to Auckland of Franklin that 'whenever Great Britain would show a disposition for peace he would be the first to give up this independence'.[16] According to Franklin, Silas Deane was of like mind. Hynson said that Franklin had misgivings, however, about Arthur Lee, who 'lived in a higher stile than he had ever done and had a great deal of pride'.[17] Lee would not want to lose his status and was content to see the war continue.

Apart from his maritime agents, Lord Auckland had one of particular importance in Paris. This was Dr Edward Bancroft, a distinguished naturalist and chemist. Before the war, Bancroft had been a close friend of Franklin's; in 1773, Franklin had sponsored his nomination as a Fellow of the Royal Society. He was also a close friend of Silas Deane's. Not knowing that Bancroft was a British agent, Deane, on being dispatched to Paris, promptly sent for him. Bancroft or his masters staged a charade whereby he appeared to be forced to 'flee' England in order to join Deane in France. Here he became not only Deane's confidant, but Franklin's as well.[18] By 1777, he had even become Franklin's private secretary! And in 1779, he became a member of the prestigious 'Neuf Soeurs' lodge, of which Franklin in that year was Master.[19]

Through Bancroft, the British government was kept apprised not only of the colonists' activities, but also of French plans for entering the war. In theory, at least, Britain could therefore have anticipated and moved to thwart such developments as the French contribution to the colonial victory at Yorktown. But with Lord Sandwich as First Lord of the Admiralty, and with Admiral Lord Richard Howe commanding the fleet in North American waters, the Royal Navy displayed the same dilatory conduct as the army's high command.

In retrospect, it is clear that the intelligence Bancroft provided was sound. In 1785, Parliament was to reward him by giving him a period of monopoly over the import of a certain vegetable dye used for printing calico, a process which he had pioneered. Nevertheless, the king, who personally read all intelligence reports, did not trust him and suspected him of being a double agent for the colonists.[20] Of especially questionable character was a clandestine mission Bancroft undertook to Ireland in 1779. In March 1780, Lord Stormont, the British ambassador to France, wrote to the king that a secret Irish delegation, consisting of allied Catholics and Independents, had arrived in Paris the previous December and met with Louis XVI. According to Stormont:

. . . they propose that Ireland shall be an Independent Kingdom, that there shall be a sort of Parlt. but no king, that the Protestant Religion shall be the established Religion . . . but that the Roman Catholics shall have the fullest Toleration. The Delegates are closely connected with Franklin who my informer thinks carries on a correspondence by means of His, Franklin's, sister, a Mrs. Johnstone now in London who has a small lodging in Fountain Court in the Strand.[21]

From these seeds, some twenty years later, a new quasi-Masonic organisation was to spring, the Society of United Irishmen, under the aegis of such men as Lord Edward Fitzgerald and Wolfe Tone. Their activities were to culminate in the Irish rebellions of 1798 and 1803.

In the mean time, the British spy network under Lord Auckland continued to penetrate – but not exploit – that of the colonists. In this process, Sir Francis Dashwood, as Postmaster-General, was of particular importance. Again and again, Dashwood intercepted the colonists' correspondence and communiqués and passed them on to Auckland. But what is most extraordinary is that, during the whole of this time, Dashwood and Franklin appear to have maintained personal contact, by their own secret channels of communication. Thus, for example, one of Dashwood's agents, a certain John Norris, reports in a letter dated 3 June 1778: 'Did this day Heliograph Intelligence from Dr Franklin in Paris to Wycombe.' At least one commentator has concluded from this that Franklin was actually a British agent![22] If that were the case, however, something of the contacts between Dashwood and Franklin would unquestionably have surfaced among Lord Auckland's papers – or those of some other British authority's, or even the king's. The fact that it doesn't suggests the contacts were not sanctioned by, or known to, British Intelligence. In all likelihood, Dashwood and Franklin – who were, after all, old friends and colleagues – were playing a harmless game of their own, exchanging gossip, irrelevant tittle-tattle and/or simple disinformation. Although Dashwood was opposed to the war, there is no suggestion that he was engaged in treason. On the contrary, he appears to have discharged his duties – if only to the minimal degree required of him – conscientiously enough. In this respect, his behaviour is strikingly similar to that of British military and naval commanders.

The Declaration

In North America, the momentum of events had accelerated

dramatically. By the time the Congressional Committee for Secret Correspondence was formed, the colonists had already embarked on an ambitious and misguided offensive. A substantial force under General Richard Montgomery attempted to invade Canada. On 13 November 1775, they managed to capture Montreal. But Montgomery, despite having served under Wolfe and Amherst, then made the mistake of trying to take Quebec by storm. The colonists' assault was repulsed with heavy casualties, the contingent was decimated and Montgomery himself was killed. But the British commander in Canada, Sir Guy Carleton, was a close friend of Howe's, and shared Howe's diffidence about the war. Not only did Carleton not bother to pursue the shattered colonial forces. He also released the prisoners he had captured.

At the beginning of 1776, the more moderate Freemasonic-oriented factions in the Continental Congress still prevailed. Their position had been enunciated once again the previous December, when Congress again defied Parliament but continued to affirm allegiance to the crown. Now, however, the mood began to change and more radical elements began to gain the ascendancy. Thomas Paine's pamphlet, 'Common Sense', did much to polarise attitudes and convert many hitherto loyal colonists to the principle of independence from the mother country. On 7 June, Arthur Lee's brother, Richard Henry Lee, proposed officially that the colonies should become 'free and independent states'. By then, too, Franklin's embassy had begun to bear fruit. Louis XVI of France had pledged a million livres of munitions, and a comparable commitment was elicited from Spain, Britain's other major continental antagonist. These contributions were to sustain the colonial army for nearly two years.

On 11 June, Congress appointed a committee to draft a declaration of independence. Of the five men on this committee, two – Franklin and Richard Montgomery's father-in-law, Robert Livingston – were Freemasons, and one, Roger Sherman, is believed, though not confirmed, to have been.[23] The other two – Thomas Jefferson and John Adams – were not, despite subsequent claims to the contrary. The text of the declaration was composed by Jefferson. It was submitted to Congress and accepted on 4 July 1776. The nine signatories who can now be established as proven Freemasons, and the ten who were possibly so, included such influential figures as Washington, Franklin and, of course, the president of the Congress, John Hancock.[24] The army, moreover, remained almost entirely in Freemasonic hands. As we have seen, the Freemasons in Congress and the military initially resisted total independence. Once the die had been cast, however, they were to set about getting their own particular ideals enshrined in the institutions of the emergent republic. As we shall see, it is in the Constitution that the influence of Freemasonry is most discernible.

When it was first promulgated, the Declaration of Independence must have appeared both a quixotic gesture and a forlorn hope. Certainly the situation of the colonists at the time was far from promising, and was soon to become bleaker still. In March, Howe had indeed evacuated Boston – only to land, on 22 August, in New York. At the Battle of Brooklyn (sometimes called the Battle of Long Island), he lost 65 killed and 255 wounded while inflicting more than 2000 casualties on his adversaries. Instead of pursuing the defeated colonists, however, he allowed them to escape. In the campaign that followed, he displayed the same lassitude. At Harlem Heights, for example, opposite where Columbia University now stands, he procrastinated for four weeks before ordering the assault that carried the colonists' position. When Fort Washington was captured, Hessian troops began bayoneting prisoners, and Howe lost his temper with the German mercenaries.

But not even Howe's gentlemanly conduct could spare the Continental Army from what followed. Forced to evacuate Brooklyn, Washington withdrew to Manhattan, only to be dislodged from there in turn, and on 15 September, Howe occupied New York. Subsequent engagements compelled Washington to retreat through New Jersey, then across the Delaware into Pennsylvania. By that time, the Continental Army had been reduced from 13,000 men to 3000. At Fort Lee alone, it had lost 140 cannon. Again, however, Howe displayed a curious diffidence, contriving to procrastinate and mark time while his beleaguered quarry escaped. It is significant that during the following year – the year of Washington's most severe defeats – he, not Howe, was on the offensive. Howe did not seek him out; he sought out Howe. When he did, Howe reacted cursorily – almost like a man swatting away a fly and going back to sleep.

Thus, on 26 December 1776, Washington made his famous crossing of the Delaware and fell in a surprise attack on a detachment of Hessians at Trenton. Eluding the main British force under Cornwallis, he then, on 3 January 1777, won a second victory, at Princeton, against a smaller contingent. Instead of responding, however, Howe, whose army was vastly superior in both numbers and supplies, simply abandoned New Jersey and moved into Pennsylvania. On 11 September, he brushed aside Washington's assault at Brandywine. Instead of pursuing, however, he proceeded to occupy Philadelphia – whence the Continental Congress had hastily fled – and establish winter quarters. Three weeks later, on 4 October, Washington attacked again, at Germantown. Again, Howe repulsed him, this time inflicting particularly heavy casualties. His army plagued by disease, desertion, low morale and lack of supplies, Washington withdrew into his own winter quarters at Valley Forge. With gentlemanly good sportsmanship, Howe left him alone to lick his wounds and rebuild his shattered army.

In this process of rebuilding the Continental Army, Freemasonry was to play a particularly significant role. Lured by the dreams which Freemasonry had helped to inculcate, professional soldiers from abroad crossed the Atlantic and rallied to the colonists' cause. There was, for example, Baron Friedrich von Steuben, a Prussian veteran recruited by Franklin and Deane, who became Washington's drill-master. Bringing with him the discipline and professionalism of Frederick the Great's army, Steuben, almost single-handedly, turned the raw colonial recruits into an efficient fighting force. There was also the Frenchman Johann de Kalb, another veteran of European battlefields, who was to become perhaps the most competent and reliable of Washington's subordinate commanders. There was Casimir Pulaski, a passionately committed Pole, destined to die of his wounds at the Siege of Savannah. From Poland, too, came Tadeusz Kosciuszko, who constructed the elaborate fortifications for West Point and became the colonists' leading military architect and engineer. Finally, of course, there was the twenty-year-old Marquis de Lafayette, whose status and charismatic personality compensated for his lack of military experience and had a dramatic effect on morale, while his diplomatic activity was to prove crucial. Indeed, he was probably more responsible than anyone else for bringing France into the war, and this, in turn, made possible the final victory at Yorktown. With the exception of Kosciuszko, on whom no relevant information survives, all of these men were known or probable Freemasons. Lafayette and Steuben in particular saw themselves as contributing to the foundation of the ideal Freemasonic republic.

The Débâcle of Saratoga

With the defeats at Brandywine and Germantown and the demoralising winter at Valley Forge, 1777 was an especially disastrous year for Washington. To the north of his sphere of operations, however, there occurred what was to prove, with the wisdom of hindsight, the single most critical engagement of the war. Washington played no direct part in it. Neither did Howe. But Howe, by virtue of that very fact, once again demonstrated the curious diffidence and apathy so characteristic of him throughout the conflict. Indeed, the evidence suggests he may, in this instance, have been demonstrating something more.

As we have seen, the war was extremely unpopular. It was unpopular with British commanders in North America – the Howe brothers, Cornwallis and Clinton – and it was unpopular with members of both parties at home. Edmund Burke, for example, was eloquently outspoken against repression of the colonies. So, too, was Charles Fox. William Pitt, Earl of Chatham, who had presided over the conquest of North America from the French twenty years before, made a number of impassioned speeches in Parliament calling for conciliation – and died as he was concluding one of them. Pitt's son, then serving as aide to Sir Guy Carleton in Canada, had been ordered by his father to resign his commission rather than fight against the colonists. The Earl of Effingham also resigned. Admiral Augustus Keppel, who succeeded Sandwich as First Lord of the Admiralty, publicly declared that he would not engage in operations against men whom he regarded as compatriots. As far as is known, no such public statement was made by George Rodney, the greatest naval commander of the age; but it is clear that Rodney felt the same way, studiously avoiding any action in American waters until the war had been decided, and only then moving into the Caribbean to inflict a dramatic defeat on the French fleet. And, as we have seen, Amherst, commander-in-chief of the army and acknowledged master of campaigning in North America, similarly refused to take the field. In Canada, Sir Guy Carleton shared the diffidence of his friend, Sir William Howe. Among the upper echelons of the British establishment, military, naval and civic, resistance to the war was virtually unanimous – as was antipathy to its chief propagator in England, Lord George Germain. There was only one notable exception, one man who both curried favour with Germain and advocated a ruthless suppression of the colonists – Sir John ('Gentleman Johnny') Burgoyne.

A dandy and a minor playwright in England, Burgoyne, prior to the outbreak of hostilities in 1775, had seen no previous service in North America. For him alone among the British commanders, North America was an alien world. During the Seven Years War, he had been based in England, participating in a series of half-hearted raids on the French coast. Subsequently, he had raised his own regiment of light cavalry and taken his men to Portugal, where they fought as volunteers in that country's conflict with Spain. Having routed the Spanish forces at Villa Velha in 1762, Burgoyne returned to England with a reputation for resourcefulness and dash. He never became a Freemason.

At the time of Bunker Hill, he was serving under Howe in Boston. Then, in February 1776, he was appointed second-in-command to Sir Guy Carleton at Quebec and saw action in Canada during the abortive invasion by Richard Montgomery. Burgoyne vigorously disapproved of the apparent 'hesitancy' with which Carleton, like Howe to the south, conducted operations. As we have seen, Carleton released the prisoners captured in the assault on Quebec. On another occasion, he released an additional 110 colonial captives, including one general, gave them food and shoes and allowed them to return home. In at least one instance, he also deliberately issued orders that allowed the retreating colonists to escape. For Burgoyne, such behaviour was inexcusable. He was contemptuous of anyone and anything 'foreign' and, alone among the British commanders, he applied that adjective to the colonists. He regarded them as something between vermin and spoiled children sorely in need of what a later age would call 'a short sharp shock'. Haughtily insensitive to their grievances, he had no compunction whatever about suppressing them as ruthlessly as circumstance allowed. They did not merit, as far as he was concerned, the gentlemanly treatment of Carleton and Howe.

In November 1776, Burgoyne returned to England, where he curried further favour with his friend and patron, Lord George Germain. Through Germain's offices, he also became a personal confidant of the king. This enabled him to go behind the backs of his superiors in North America and sell his own ambitious plan for ending the war at a single stroke. He himself would implement the plan and reap the glory that accrued.

The plan required elaborate orchestration, choreography and timing. It entailed a sizeable British column under Burgoyne's own command striking southwards from Canada, advancing down towards Albany through the old forts at Ticonderoga and Crown Point – the hilly, heavily-wooded terrain through which Amherst and Wolfe had fought their way twenty years before, but of which Burgoyne himself had no experience whatever. Howe, meanwhile, would effectively be deprived of independent command. He would lead his forces, then based around Manhattan, northwards to link up with Burgoyne at Albany. Thus:

. . . two armies, one from the north in Canada and one from the south, should march to a juncture, cutting the colonies into two separate sections, after which the separated areas could be conquered individually.[25]

In effect, the whole of New England would have been cut off from the colonies to the south. According to one commentator, Burgoyne was confident that he 'would secure . . . glory, position, honour, and a favoured place in history'.[26]

Burgoyne's plan was certainly ambitious. Whether it might have succeeded in more competent hands is questionable; and even if it *had* succeeded, the value of the results might well have been negligible, since by 1777 the major theatres of operations had shifted far to the south, and New England had become strategically irrelevant. Nevertheless, Germain and the king bought the idea. Sir Guy Carleton was to be replaced by Burgoyne as commander-in-chief in Canada and was notified accordingly in March 1777. Carleton promptly resigned but remained in Quebec long enough to outfit Burgoyne and see him on his way. Burgoyne, after their previous quarrels, was surprised by the readiness with which Carleton co-operated. Sir Guy, Burgoyne wrote, 'could not have shown . . . more zeal than he did to comply with and expedite my requisitions and desires'.[27] In fact, Carleton was simply in a hurry to get Burgoyne out of his hair and absolve himself of the whole matter. But Carleton also recognised, as we shall see, that the faster Burgoyne embarked on his march, the more certainly he would be marching to his doom. Knowing full well what must happen, Carleton was expediting not the success of Burgoyne's enterprise, but its inevitable ruin.

The success of Burgoyne's plan hinged ultimately on the co-operation of Howe, who was engaged at the time in operations around Manhattan. In order for the plan to succeed, Howe had to carry out his part of it by moving northwards with his army and linking up with Burgoyne at Albany. Burgoyne assumed that Lord Germain, his friend and patron back in England, would issue the requisite orders compelling Howe's compliance, personal objections notwithstanding. Certainly that responsibility did rest with Germain; and it is Germain, therefore, who has usually taken the blame for what followed.

Unquestionably, Germain *was* partially culpable, partially guilty of negligence. The generally accepted story is that he was anxious to go on holiday. Not wanting to keep his coach waiting in the road, he hurriedly signed Burgoyne's orders; but as Howe's had not yet been properly copied, he simply neglected them. So, at any rate, wrote the Earl of Shelburne, in what has come to be one of the standard indictments of Germain:

> Among many singularities he had a particular aversion to being put out of his way on any occasion; he had fixed to go into Kent or Northamptonshire at a particular hour, and to call on his way at his office to sign the dispatches, all of which had been settled, to both these Generals. By some mistake those to General Howe were not fair copied, and upon his growing impatient at it, the office, which was a very idle one, promised to send it to the country after him, while they dispatched the others to General Burgoyne, expecting that the others could be expedited before the packet sailed with the first, which, however, by some mistake sailed without them, and the wind detained the vessel which was ordered to carry the rest. Hence came General Burgoyne's defeat, the French declaration, and the loss of the thirteen colonies. It might appear incredible if his own secretary and the most respectable persons in office had not assured me of the fact; what corroborates it, is that it can be accounted for no other way.[28]

Lord Shelburne, in this account, is not wholly correct. What happened *can* be accounted for in another way – or, at any rate, in a way that adds a complementary dimension to Shelburne's version. For while Germain may indeed have neglected to sign the requisite orders personally, they *were* nevertheless signed and sent to Howe. They were signed by a man named D'Oyley, a Deputy Secretary at the War Office. Howe is known to have received them, on 24 May 1777.[29] That they did not bear Germain's personal signature is beside the point. Howe should still, in theory, have been obliged to act in accordance with them.

What is more, Howe *already knew* what he was supposed to be doing:

> Granting that Lord George was a difficult man to like or respect, nonetheless his inexcusable negligence in not making certain his orders reached Sir William at New York are only one side of the calamitous error ... On the other side was General Howe's positive knowledge that as Burgoyne marched south the Americans were closing in around him.[30]

Indeed, so positive was Howe's knowledge that he even provided Burgoyne with intelligence to that effect. Howe:

... told Burgoyne that the American northern army was about to be reinforced by 2500 fresh troops. Howe also knew ... that the rebel General Israel Putnam, with 4000 more troops, was at Peekskill, between Clinton at New York City, and Burgoyne at Fort Edward.[31]

A brief scrutiny of the precise sequence of events reveals the way in which Howe and Carleton jointly contrived to ensure Burgoyne's failure – and, through the unexpected additional boon of Germain's negligence, to foist the whole of the blame on to him. At the beginning of 1777, Howe, as we have seen, decided to abandon New Jersey to Washington and advanced on the colonial capital of Philadelphia. He notified Germain of his intentions and Germain, on 3 March, approved.[31] On 26 March, however, there occurred the *contretemps* described above. Germain issued official orders for Burgoyne to march south and for Howe to link up with him at Albany. These orders were dispatched, with Germain's signature, to Burgoyne. They were dispatched, according to the War Office, with D'Oyley's signature, to Howe, who received them on 24 May.[32] But a full seven weeks before, on 2 April, Howe had already written to Carleton in Canada that he would not be able to offer much assistance to Burgoyne 'as I shall probably be in Pennsylvania'.[33] In other words, Howe, seven weeks before receiving his orders, already knew what he would be expected to do and had already decided not to do it. Carleton received Howe's letter *before* Burgoyne began his advance southwards from Quebec on 13 June. Yet Carleton not only neglected to warn Burgoyne, but even hastened Burgoyne on his way – with a 'zeal' that the gratified Burgoyne found surprising. It is thus clear that Howe and Carleton, taking advantage of the slowness of communication and the general vagueness of orders, contrived to exculpate themselves while allowing Burgoyne to march to a defeat which was a foregone conclusion. And Germain, on his part, by continuing to be vague, unwittingly aided them in their subsequent self-exoneration.

On 18 May, Germain wrote to Howe. Weirdly enough, he endorsed Howe's advance on Philadelphia – 'trusting, however, that, whatever you may meditate, it will be executed in time for you to co-operate with the army ordered to proceed from Canada ...'.[34] It is extraordinary that Germain can have been so naïve as to think that Howe could possibly advance southwards into Pennsylvania *and* then manage to march north to link up with Burgoyne in time. Howe himself was not so naïve. He did not even pretend to make haste. On the contrary, he moved in a downright leisurely fashion. When Germain's letter reached him on 16 August, he was on a ship in the Chesapeake Bay, *en route* for Philadelphia. On that same day, the Hessians in the vanguard of Burgoyne's column made contact with the colonists at Bennington and were wiped out:

> When Howe decided to abandon Burgoyne . . . it is difficult to imagine how he expected Burgoyne to reach Albany . . . there can be little doubt that, with or without Germain's orders, Sir William Howe must have had some inkling that Burgoyne was marching straight into very serious trouble, and yet did nothing to make certain Burgoyne would not be badly, even fatally, mauled.[35]

On 30 July, Burgoyne, advancing through the forested wilderness of upstate New York, had dispatched a worried letter to Germain complaining that he had no idea of Howe's intentions. This seems to have been his first intimation of danger. On 20 August, four days after the defeat at Bennington, he dispatched a second letter. By that time, Howe was already marching into Pennsylvania. On 30 August, Howe wrote bluntly to Germain that he had 'not the slightest intention of helping Burgoyne'.[36] On 11 September, as we have seen, he defeated Washington at Brandywine. On 27 September, he occupied Philadelphia and, a week later, on 4 October, trounced Washington again, even more soundly, at Germantown. Burgoyne, in the mean time, was sinking ever more deeply into the morass of his own making. On 7 October, three days after Germantown, his column clashed with the colonists' main force under General Horatio Gates. Repulsed, and suffering heavy casualties, Burgoyne fell back on his camp at Saratoga, only to be dislodged from there by Gates's counter-attack. At last, on 17 October, completely surrounded, with all routes of retreat cut off and no hope of assistance or relief, Burgoyne surrendered with nearly 6000 men. Five days later, Howe, ensconced in his winter quarters at Philadelphia, wrote to Germain, referring to his letter of 2 April (and taking some retrospective liberty with its phraseology): 'I positively mentioned that no direct assistance could be given by the southern army.'[37]

From this sequence of events, it is clear that Howe, as early as March, had made up his mind not to go to Burgoyne's aid. He even said as much in his letter to Carleton. Yet neither man, though both knew full well what the consequences would almost certainly be, made any attempt to avert them. Howe, who was obviously opposed to Burgoyne's expedition, never sought to remonstrate with his masters in London, never asserted his authority as commander-in-chief to argue that the plan was misconceived. And Carleton, by hastening Burgoyne on his way, even abetted the eventual outcome. Both men were able to exculpate themselves by taking advantage of the slowness of communications and Germain's long-recognised incompetence – as well as by responding to the unwitting vagueness of the orders issued to them with a deliberate vagueness of their own.

There is bound to have been one other protagonist in the drama whom later historians have completely overlooked. Amherst, it must be remembered, was commander-in-chief of the army at the time. He was a veteran of the very terrain through which Burgoyne proposed to march; he could readily assess both the dangers and Burgoyne's ineptitude. He was not only Howe's former commander in the field, but also an old friend, and any complaint from Howe would certainly have received a sympathetic hearing. All orders, in theory, should have passed through Amherst's hands. Indeed, strictly speaking, they should have been issued through him, rather than through Germain. At very least, he would had had to be privy to what was happening. And yet Amherst, during the whole sequence of events that culminated with Saratoga, seems to have refined himself out of existence. There is no record of Howe complaining to him – or, for that matter, of their exchanging letters of any kind. There is no record of his offering a single comment, a single suggestion, a single word of advice. There is no record of his issuing any orders whatever. His sheer invisibility calls attention to itself. If there was indeed a tacit readiness on Howe's and Carleton's parts to see Burgoyne fail, Amherst must also have been involved and, at very least, have acquiesced.

In any case, and whatever Amherst's role or non-role, the conclusions are inescapable. There can be little doubt that Howe and Carleton *wanted* Burgoyne to fail. The real question is why. Was it simply personal animosity towards Burgoyne, a spiteful desire to see him discredited? That is most unlikely. Granted, both Howe and Carleton disliked Burgoyne intensely and probably justifiably. But it is hardly conceivable that they would have countenanced the sacrifice of an army to satisfy a personal grudge – especially as that sacrifice would serve only to make their own tasks more difficult. Whatever their personal feelings for Burgoyne, they would not have abandoned him to his fate *unless it made sense to do so in broader terms* – made sense in accordance with some general political perspective on the war. And given Howe's and Carleton's perspective on the war, it did make precisely such sense. Historians have tended to see Howe's abandonment of Burgoyne as either a monstrous blunder resulting from crossed signals, or as an act of outrageous and mystifying negligence. In fact, however – and this is a crucial point – it was perfectly consistent with the way in which Howe (and Carleton, and Cornwallis) had conducted, and were to conduct, operations throughout the course of the conflict.

Burgoyne's disaster also gave Howe an opportunity he had been seeking for some time – an excuse to resign his command without any personal stigma. Within a month of the Battle of Saratoga, he did so. A month later, his brother, Admiral Richard Howe, followed suit.

In purely military terms, Saratoga, as we have noted, was not in itself decisive. It did not cripple the British war effort. It did not deplete the manpower available in the war's major theatres of operations. It did not impede the capacity to campaign on the part of other British commanders. On the contrary, Howe's forces were still intact and the overall strategic position was no worse than it had been before. Had Howe wished to do so, he could still have crushed Washington.

But in non-military terms, Saratoga was indeed decisive and did mark the real turning point in the American War for Independence. In the first place, it provided the colonists with a major transfusion of morale precisely when such a transfusion was most desperately needed. In the second place, it prompted France not just to recognise the rebellious colonies as an independent republic, but also to enter the war on their side. This was to make a very crucial strategic difference. It was to bring regular French troops to North America. It was to pit the Royal Navy against a fleet of comparable strength in North American waters and thereby challenge, even if only temporarily, the British naval blockade. Through the spectre of operations on the Continent, it was to keep pinned down in England quantities of troops who, in theory at least, might otherwise have been dispatched to the colonies. It was to force Britain to extend herself as far afield as Gibraltar, Minorca and India. It was, in sum, to stretch British resources – military, naval and economic – in a way that made the war increasingly counter-productive.

These consequences, however, took time to bite. Until they did, the conflict continued. It continued, in fact, for another four years. On 8 January 1778, Franklin, Silas Deane and Arthur Lee in Paris negotiated a formal treaty of alliance with France. But in North America proper, the situation of the colonists remained desperate. In May, Howe was replaced by Sir Henry Clinton, with Lord

Cornwallis technically under him but often exercising an independent command. Washington's army became, in effect, a lame duck. It was to suffer two more winters as severe as the one at Valley Forge and was to be plagued, after each, by crippling mutinies. Neither Clinton nor Cornwallis, however, made any attempt to exploit the situation. In the mean time, the focus of operations shifted to the south.

In December 1778, British forces captured Savannah, and held it, in October of the following year, against a determined assault by the colonists. For most of 1779, operations were negligible, but in May 1780, Clinton captured Charlestown, South Carolina, inflicting on the colonists their worst defeat of the war. At the same time, Benedict Arnold entered into secret negotiations with Clinton to turn West Point and the Hudson Valley over to British hands. On 16 August 1780, Cornwallis clashed with Horatio Gates, the victor of Saratoga, at Camden, in southern New Jersey. The colonists were again defeated, Baron de Kalb – Gates's second-in-command – dying in the battle. Gates himself fled the field, and was never able subsequently to outlive the ignominy. Campaigning became more and more desultory. With the exception of one further British victory at Guildford Courthouse on 15 March 1781, it degenerated into guerrilla skirmishing. Finally, on 7 August 1781, Cornwallis, who had been raiding in Virginia, established his base at Yorktown and allowed himself to get pinned down there. On 30 August, a French fleet wrested temporary control of the approaches and disembarked forces under Lafayette and Baron von Steuben. Some three weeks later, Washington's army arrived and Cornwallis, with 6000 troops, found himself besieged by 7000 colonials and nearly 9000 French. He held out until 18 October, then surrendered – even though Clinton, with 7000 reinforcements, was less than a week's march away. It is obvious that by this time the British high command had lost all interest in the war. As Cornwallis's soldiers surrendered, their commander, in a fit of wry, whimsical good humour, ordered his bands to play a tune called 'The World Turned Upside Down'. It was rather like saying, with a rueful smile, 'Fair cop!'

Like Saratoga, Yorktown was not in itself militarily decisive. Clinton's army was still intact; and in April 1782, Admiral Rodney cornered the French fleet in the West Indies and utterly destroyed it. Had Britain wished to pursue the war, she could have choked off further French aid to North America. But on 27 February, Parliament had already voted down any further action against the colonists and negotiations for peace began. They took nearly a year, during which all operations were suspended except against remnants of the French fleet at sea. At last, on 4 February 1783, the new British government proclaimed a formal end to hostilities. On 3 September, the Treaty of Paris was signed, whereby the rebellious colonies were recognised as an independent republic, the United States. By November, the last contingents of the British Army had withdrawn from the new nation's soil and the Continental Army had been disbanded. On 23 December, Washington resigned his commission as commander-in-chief.

INTERLUDE

Masonic Loyalties

The influence of Freemasonry on the course of the American War for Independence was both direct and oblique, general and particular. In some cases, it served as a conduit for political, even revolutionary, activity. Thus, for example, St Andrew's lodge in Boston played an important role in the 'Boston Tea Party' and also, in John Hancock, provided the Continental Congress with a president. Freemasonry imparted its attitudes and values to the newly formed Continental Army and may well have had something to do with the appointment of Washington as commander-in-chief. It constituted, as well, a ready-made fraternal bond with volunteers from abroad, such as Steuben and Lafayette.

In a less direct, less quantifiable fashion, it helped to create a general atmosphere, a psychological climate or ambience which helped shape the thinking not only of active brethren such as Franklin and Hancock, but of non-Freemasons as well. Without eighteenth-century Freemasonry, the principles at the very heart of the conflict – liberty, equality, brotherhood, tolerance, the 'rights of man' – would not have had the currency they did. True, those principles owed much to Locke, Hume, Adam Smith and *les philosophes* in France. But most, if not all, of those thinkers were either Freemasons themselves, moved in Freemasonic circles or were influenced by Freemasonry.

But Freemasonry also filtered down to 'grass roots' level. Not only did it help shape the ideals underlying the American War for Independence. Not only did it affect the thinking of the politicians and statesmen, the high-level planners and decision-makers. Not only did it colour the attitudes of men like Howe, Carleton, Cornwallis, Washington, Lafayette and Steuben. It also suffused the 'rank-and-file' of the war, the 'ordinary soldiers', who found in it a unifying bond and a principle of solidarity. This was particularly true for the Continental Army, where, in the absence of regimental traditions, Freemasonry formed the basis for '*élan vital*' and '*esprit de corps*'. In the British Army, too, however, Freemasonry forged bonds not just between soldiers, but also between soldiers and their officers. Thus, for example, the field lodge of the 29th Foot, later the Worcestershire Regiment, included two lieutenant-colonels, two lieutenants and eight privates.[1] The lodge of the 59th Foot, later the East Lancashire Regiment, included a lieutenant-colonel, a major, two lieutenants, a surgeon, a music master, three sergeants, two corporals and three privates.[2]

Nor was the influence of Freemasonry confined to the personnel within each of the armies involved. It also obtained between adversaries. The American War for Independence abounds with anecdotes testifying to the way in which Freemasonic loyalties conditioned, and even on occasion transcended, all others.

Among the British Army's closest Indian allies during the war were the Mohawks, under their famous chief, Joseph Brant. Brant's sister, prior to the conflict, had married Sir William Johnson, Provincial Grand Master of New York and an associate of Amherst. On a visit to London in 1776, Brant was himself initiated as a Freemason. Later that year, during the colonists' abortive invasion of Canada, a certain Captain McKinstry was captured by some of Brant's tribesmen, bound to a tree and surrounded with brushwood which the Indians prepared to set alight. When McKinstry made a 'Masonic appeal', Brant recognised it and ordered him released. He was turned over to a British lodge in Quebec, which arranged his repatriation.[3]

Among the prisoners-of-war taken in Howe's capture of New York was a local Freemason named Joseph Burnham. Burnham managed to escape and, fleeing on foot, sought refuge one night on the planks that formed part of the ceiling of a local lodge. The planks, not having been nailed, gave way, and Burnham landed with a crash among the conclave of startled British officers in the room below. Recognition signs were exchanged and the British officers 'made a generous contribution for Brother Burnham, who was afterwards transported with secrecy and expedition to the Jersey shore'.[4]

On another occasion, Joseph Clement, a British Freemason from the 8th Foot (later the Liverpool Regiment), was serving with a ranger detachment when, after a skirmish, he saw an Indian preparing to scalp a colonial prisoner. Making a Freemasonic sign to Clement, the prisoner appealed for his protection. Clement ordered the Indian away, then had the prisoner transported to a nearby farmhouse, where he was nursed back to health, then sent home. Some months later, in upstate New York, Clement was himself captured and lodged in a local jail. His custodian, it transpired, was the very man whose life he had previously saved, and that night 'a friend came to him and intimated that at dawn the jail door would be upon the latch, and that outside a horse would be waiting so that he might escape to the frontier'.[5]

If this kind of rapport existed among officers and men, it also existed among commanders. On 16 August 1780, Cornwallis, as we have seen, clashed with colonial forces under Horatio Gates and Baron de Kalb at the Battle of Camden. When the colonial position collapsed, Gates fled the field, outstripping his troops in his flight. Kalb, traditionally considered a Freemason, was mortally wounded. He was found by Cornwallis's second-in-command, Francis Rawdon, Earl of Moira, who, a decade later, became acting Grand Master of the Grand Lodge of England. Kalb was taken to Moira's tent, where Moira looked after him personally for three days. When Kalb died, Moira arranged for a Freemasonic funeral.[6]

Within both armies, Freemasonry functioned as a kind of court of appeal for favours and the redress of grievances. To take one example from after the war, the field lodge of the 14th Dragoons in 1793 drew up a petition requesting that its parent lodge, Grand Lodge of Ireland, 'intercede with the Lord Lieutenant or the Commander in Chief' on behalf of a certain J. Stoddart, the regimental quartermaster. The petition was accordingly sent to Colonel Cradock, commander of the regiment and a fellow Freemason, 'with the request of this Grand Lodge – that he will kindly use his friendly and Brotherly influence in behalf of the said Brother Stoddart'.[7]

Throughout the American War for Independence, there are accounts of the warrants and regalia of field lodges being captured by one side or the other and duly returned. In one instance, the regalia of the 46th Foot – later the 2nd Battalion of the Duke of Cornwall's Light Infantry – was captured by colonial troops. On the instructions of George Washington, it was sent back, under a flag of truce, with the message that he and his men 'did not make war upon institutions of benevolence'.[8] On another occasion, the warrant of the 17th Foot – later the Leicestershire Regiment – was similarly captured. It, too, was returned, with a letter from General Samuel Parsons. This letter is eloquently typical of the spirit fostered by Freemasonry in both armies and all ranks:

Brethren,

When the ambition of monarchs, or the jarring interests of contending States, call forth their subjects to war, as Masons we are disarmed of that resentment which stimulates to undistinguished desolation, and, however our political sentiments may impel us in the public dispute, we are still Brethren, and (our professional duty apart) ought to promote the happiness and advance the weal of each other.

Accept, therefore, at the hands of a Brother, the Constitution of the Lodge 'Unity, No. 18' held in the 17th British Regiment, which your late misfortunes have put it in my power to restore to you.

I am, your Brother and obedient servant,
Samuel H. Parsons[9]

19

The Republic

In November 1777, shortly after Saratoga, the Continental Congress had agreed, at least in a general way, on the form of government to be adopted for the fledgling republic. This form was to be a federation of states, each of which had formally to ratify the proposed Articles of Confederation. Squabbles about boundaries delayed the process, and the Articles of Confederation were not ratified by all thirteen colonies until the beginning of March 1781, seven months before the British surrender at Yorktown. But another six years were to elapse before things advanced significantly further.

Between 1783 and 1787, there was a lacuna – as if the colonists, dazed by what they had accomplished, required a pause in which to regain breath and take stock of the situation. Their population, it transpired, was some 211,000 less than it had been before the war. Most of this decline was caused by settlers loyal to the crown fleeing back to England or, more frequently, to Canada.

At last, on 25 May 1787, the Constitutional Convention opened in Philadelphia and commenced its efforts to devise the machinery of government for the new nation. The first voice to make itself heard in any significantly influential way was a characteristically Freemasonic one, that of Edmund Randolph. Most of Randolph's family had remained loyal to the crown and returned to England in 1775. Randolph himself, however, a member of a Williamsburg lodge, had become Washington's aide-de-camp. Subsequently, he was to become Attorney-General, then governor, of Virginia, and Grand Master of Virginia's Grand Lodge.[1] During Washington's presidency, he was to serve as the first Attorney-General of the United States, then the first Secretary of State.

During the Constitutional Convention, Washington, though elected to preside, took no part in the debates, and it is probable that

Randolph, to some degree at least, acted as his mouthpiece or proxy. Randolph proposed that the Convention not just review or revise or modify the Articles of Confederation which had, until then, held the newly independent colonies together. He proposed that a new basis for central government be established. This proposal was adopted, and work began to forge the loose confederation of former provinces into a single nation.

History had, of course, seen republics before. Indeed, the concept of a republic dated from classical times – from ancient Greece and from Rome in the period prior to the Empire. But, as the delegates to the Constitutional Convention were only too painfully aware, all such previous republics had been subject to problems as chronic as those which had plagued monarchies. Chief among these perhaps was the propensity of republican governments to fall into the hands of dictatorial individuals or dynasties, who would then become as tyrannical as any sovereign or royal house, sometimes even more so. By virtue of this propensity, the very concept of the republic had become badly discredited among eighteenth-century social philosophers. Even among the most enlightened thinkers of the age, there were profound misgivings about whether republicanism was a viable form of government. Hume, for example, had dismissed it as a 'dangerous novelty'.[2] Odious though absolute monarchy might be, he said, it was still preferable.[3] To such problems, the delegates at the Constitutional Convention now addressed themselves. They did so by devising and emphasising two principles which, taken together, comprised a unique development in the political institutions of the age.

The first of these principles was that power was to be vested in the office, not in the man, and that the man was to be replaced in office at regular intervals by vote. An individual might occupy a political or governmental position, would discharge the responsibilities attendant upon it, but could not become inseparable from it. This, granted, was hardly a new principle. Again, however, and desirable though it might sound in theory, it had so frequently been abused in practice as to have become discredited. In matters of government especially, the theoretical separation of man from office had betrayed itself too often, and too monstrously, to inspire anything but cynicism. Men such as Locke, Hume and Adam Smith did not even deign to mention it. And yet Freemasonry was one of the few eighteenth-century institutions in which the principle *did* function effectively and enjoyed a degree of respectability. Masters and grand masters were elected from and by their peers for a stipulated tenure. They did not exercise autocratic power. On the contrary, they could be, and often were, held accountable. And when they were deemed unworthy of the office to which they had been elected, they could be impeached or deposed – not by revolution, 'palace coup' or any other violent means, but by established administrative machinery. Nor would the dignity of the office be diminished.[4]

In order to ensure the separation of man from office, the Constitutional Convention devised the second of its guiding principles, and the one that represented a unique contribution to the political history of the epoch. According to a system of so-called 'checks and balances', power was to be equally distributed between two distinct and autonomous governmental bodies – the Executive, in the form of the Presidency, and the Legislature, in the form of the two houses of Congress. By virtue of its autonomy, each of these bodies would be able to forestall any excessive concentration of power in the hands of the other. And the separation of man and office would be guaranteed in both by regular and legally obligatory elections similar to those which obtained in the lodge system. Such elections were not uncommon elsewhere in the eighteenth century, but they applied only to the legislative branch of government, which was often powerless and acted largely as a rubber-stamp for the executive. In the new American republic, however, the principle was brought to bear on the executive – on the head of state – as well. Here, too, the influence of Freemasonry is apparent.

There is no question that Freemasonry contributed something to the structures and machinery of the new American government. Indeed, those structures are markedly diagrammatic, markedly geometrical in their design, reminiscent of the ingenious mechanical models produced by the 'Invisible College' and the Royal Society a century before. They reflect an application to politics of the 'experimental method' so dear to the 'Invisible College' and the Royal Society. They also reflect an application to politics of specifically architectonic principles. But if Freemasonry influenced the structures of American government, it was even more influential in the overall *shape* of that government. According to one commentator:

Though free, we were not yet united. The loose Articles of Confederation did not provide a strong national government, common currency or consistent judicial system. Men of vision realized that another step must be taken if the weak Confederation of American States was to become a strong, unified nation. Again Freemasonry set the pattern in ideology and form. Since the Masonic federal system of organization was the only pattern

33 English Masonic Knights Templar apron, *c*.1800.

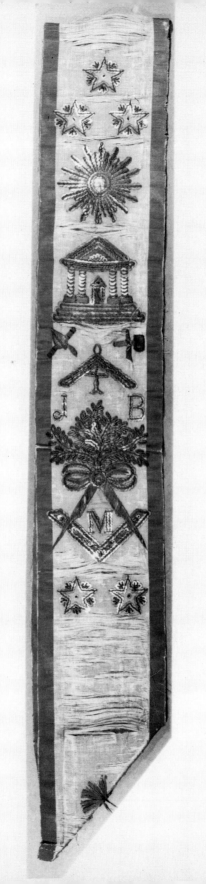

34 *opposite* Masonic sash worn by Benjamin Franklin as Master of the French Lodge, Neuf Soeurs in Paris, 1779–81.

35 *above* Masonic apron worn by George Washington and presented to him by General de Lafayette, embroidered by Madame de Lafayette in 1784.

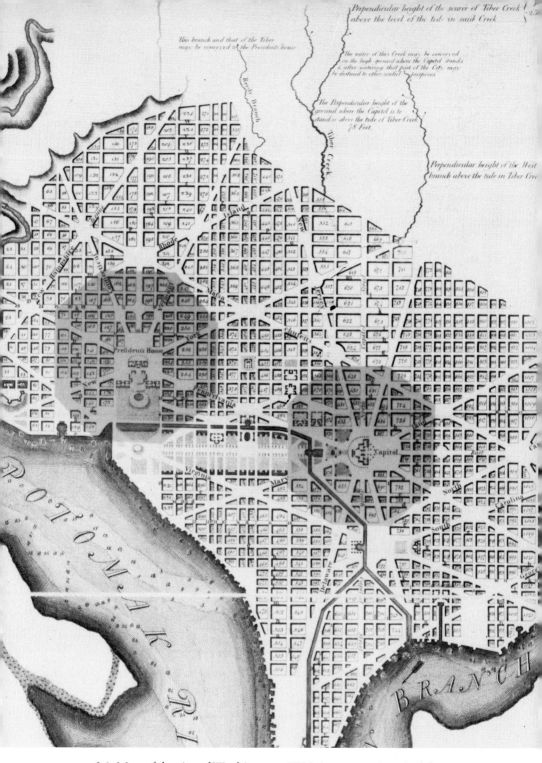

36 Map of the city of Washington, 1792, incorporating modifications
introduced by Washington and Jefferson. Indicated are the octagonal
patterns centred upon the White House and the Capitol.

for effective organization operating in each of the original Thirteen Colonies, it was natural that patriotic Brethren intent on strengthening the fledgling nation should turn to the organizational base of the Craft for a model. Regardless of the other forces that affected the formation of the Constitution during the Constitutional Convention in 1787, the fact remains that the federalism established in the civil government the Constitution created is identical to the federalism of the Grand Lodge system of Masonic government created in *Anderson's Constitutions* of 1723.[5]

This statement comes from an American Freemasonic writer, and he is both overstating and oversimplifying his case. The reality was much less clear-cut, much more complicated and emerged only gradually out of much energetic debate. And yet the general substance of the assertion remains valid. Freemasonry *did* provide a smoothly working model of an effective federal system – and, perhaps, the only such model of the time. That fact was much more apparent to the delegates at the Constitutional Convention than it is to us today, when federal systems obtain in a number of institutions and are pretty much taken for granted. In the eighteenth century, Freemasonry offered dramatic testimony to the effect that a federal system *could* work. It provided a desperately needed precedent. If such a system was demonstrably workable in Freemasonry, there was at least a prototype for its application to government.

Masonic Influence on the Constitution

As we have seen, the early events of the American War for Independence – the events from, say, the 'Boston Tea Party' to the Declaration of Independence – had a momentum of their own. Men found themselves confronted almost daily with *faits accomplis*, of which they then had to make the best and on which they had to build. This had necessitated constant improvisation, in which a number of organisations were involved – not just Freemasonry, but also such fraternities as the radical 'Sons of Liberty'. And among the individuals playing prominent roles at the time, only a percentage of them were Freemasons. Freemasonry had exerted a moderating influence; but it was not the only influence at work, and it had neither the authority nor the latitude to shape things entirely in accordance with its ideals. Except in some of its rhetoric and phraseology, the Declaration of Independence, for example, could not be called a Freemasonic document.

The Constitution of the United States, on the other hand, in a very real sense, can. By the time the Convention assembled to devise the Constitution, Freemasonic influences had prevailed and were unequivocally dominant. Other organisations, such as the 'Sons of Liberty', had, after serving their purpose, been dissolved. Even the Continental Army had been disbanded. At the time of the Constitutional Convention, Freemasonry was not just the only organisation to have 'stayed the course'. It was also the only real organisational apparatus of any kind operating across state boundaries, throughout the newly independent colonies.

In its final form, of course, the Constitution was a product of many minds and many hands, not all of them Freemasonic. The prose of the document itself was Thomas Jefferson's, and he, though sometimes claimed to have been a Freemason, was probably not. But there were ultimately five dominant and guiding spirits behind the Constitution – Washington, Franklin, Randolph, Jefferson and John Adams. Of these, the first three were not only active Freemasons, but men who took their Freemasonry extremely seriously – men who subscribed fervently to its ideals, whose entire orientation had been shaped and conditioned by it. And Adams's position, though he himself is not known to have been a Freemason, was virtually identical to theirs. When he became president, moreover, he appointed a prominent Freemason, John Marshall, as first Chief Justice of the Supreme Court.[6] It was Marshall who subsequently established the court on a footing equal to that of Congress and the Presidency.

In the debates and discussions which eventually culminated in the Constitution, Adams – though not actually present at the time – was in accord with Washington, Franklin and Randolph. Only Jefferson was 'odd man out'. And it was Jefferson who eventually gave way, falling into line with the position of the Freemasons. The new republic, when it emerged with the Constitution, conformed to their ideal image, and that image reflected the ideals of Freemasonry.

The Masonic Leadership of Washington

On 17 September 1787, the draft Constitution was accepted, approved and signed by thirty-nine of the forty-two delegates present. Between 7 December and 25 June of the following year, each of the states individually ratified it. Maryland ceded ten square miles of its territory to Congress, as specified by the Constitution, and this land – the District of Columbia – became the site of the new federal capital.

On 4 February 1789, Washington was elected first president of the United States and John Adams his vice-president. The inauguration was on 30 April. The oath was administered by Robert Livingston, Grand Master of New York's Grand Lodge and father-in-law of the dead General Richard Montgomery. The marshal of the day was another Freemason, General Jacob Morton. Yet another Freemason, General Morgan Lewis, was Washington's escort.[7] The Bible used for the oath was that of St John's Lodge No. 1 of New York. Washington himself at the time was Master of Alexandria Lodge No. 22, Virginia.[8]

Thirteen days before the inauguration, Franklin had died, half of Philadelphia turning out for his funeral. Five days after the inauguration, the French Estates-General met at Versailles and on 17 June formed a National Assembly, declaring themselves, not the king, the true representatives of the French people. On 14 July, a Parisian revolutionary mob stormed the Bastille. On 14 December, Alexander Hamilton submitted proposals for establishing a National Bank. Jefferson opposed them but Washington signed them through. On the American dollar bill was printed the 'Great Seal' of the United States. It is unmistakably Freemasonic – an all-seeing eye in a triangle above a thirteen-stepped, four-sided pyramid, beneath which a scroll proclaims the advent of a 'new secular order', one of Freemasonry's long-standing dreams.

On 18 September 1793, the cornerstone of the Capitol was officially laid. Grand Lodge of Maryland presided over the ceremony and Washington was asked to serve as Master. The affiliated lodges under Maryland's jurisdiction were in attendance, as was Washington's own lodge from Alexandria, Virginia. There was a great procession, which included a company of artillery. Then came a band, followed by Washington himself, attended by all officers and members of the lodges in full regalia.

When he reached the trench in which the south-east cornerstone was laid, Washington was presented with a silver plate commemorating the event and inscribed with the designations of the lodges in attendance. The artillery fired a volley. Washington then descended into the trench and placed the plate on the stone. Around it, he placed containers of corn, wine and oil – standard symbolic accoutrements of Freemasonic ritual. All present joined in prayer and Masonic chanting, and the artillery fired another volley.

Washington and his entourage then moved to the east of the cornerstone, where the president, standing on a traditionally

Masonic three-stepped rostrum, delivered an oration. More Masonic chanting followed, and a final volley from the artillery.[9]

The gavel, the silver trowel, the square and the level used by Washington for the ceremony are today held by Potomac Lodge No. 5 of the District of Columbia. The apron and the sash he wore are held by his own lodge, Alexandria No. 22.

Subsequently, the Capitol and the White House were each to become focal points of an elaborate geometry governing the layout of the nation's capital city. This geometry, originally devised by an architect named Pierre l'Enfant, was subsequently modified by Washington and Jefferson so as to produce specifically octagonal patterns incorporating the particular cross used as a device by Masonic Templars.

Six years and three months later, in December 1799, Washington died. He was buried at his home at Mount Vernon, with full Masonic honours, by Alexandria Lodge No. 22, whose members were his pallbearers.

Postscript

In the American War for Independence, Freemasonry was ultimately apolitical, or only incidentally political. There were Freemasons on both sides. There were Freemasons among radical and conservative factions on both sides. For the most part, Freemasonry constituted a voice of temperance and moderation, but some individual Freemasons were militantly revolutionary and others were staunchly reactionary. This kind of distribution was to continue for the duration of the eighteenth century and into the nineteenth. But in many people's minds, Freemasonry had become so closely associated with American revolution and independence that it began, increasingly, to acquire a radical image. That image, needless to say, was to be reinforced by the French Revolution.

Certainly Freemasonry played an important role in the events in France. Lafayette, by then a high-ranking and long-established Freemason, was eager to import to his own country the ideals he had seen actualised in America. Many of the leading Jacobins – Danton, for example, Sieyès and Camille Desmoulins – were active Freemasons. Throughout France, on the eve of the Revolution, Freemasonry provided militant conspirators with a valuable network for intelligence, recruitment, communication and organisation. To that extent, it was already becoming an ideal repository for paranoia.

In 1797, an ultra-conservative French prelate, the Abbé Augustin de Barruel, published a book, *Mémoires pour servir a l'histoire du jacobinisme*, which was to become a perverse landmark in the history of Western social and political thought. Barruel's book in effect ascribed the whole of the French Revolution to a Freemasonic plot directed at both established secular authority and the Church. This work was to trigger a wave of hysteria, to sire a still-growing corpus of similar literature and to become a veritable bible for

263

adherents of conspiracy theories. From Barruel's rabidly paranoid text derived the clichéd nineteenth-century image, still promulgated today, of Freemasonry as a vast international conspiracy, revolutionary and militantly anti-clerical, dedicated to the overthrow of existing institutions and the establishment of a 'new world order'. As a result of Barruel, nebulous and neurotic fears were to be projected not just on to Freemasonry, but on to secret societies in general, throughout the nineteenth century and well into the twentieth. By virtue of Barruel, the secret society became a spectre haunting the public mind and threatening to undermine the very foundations of civilised society – a bogeyman of a stature similar to that accorded, with somewhat more justification, international terrorism today.

Not surprisingly, perhaps, Barruel's work became, on occasion, a kind of self-fulfilling prophecy. Lured by the glamour and romanticism of Barruel's garish imagination, certain individuals – Charles Nodier in France, for example, and the arch-conspirator Filippo Buonarroti – made a point of inventing, then writing, talking and disseminating information about, wholly fictitious secret societies. With inquisitional fervour, the authorities would respond accordingly, and perfectly innocent people would be harried and persecuted for alleged membership of these clandestine, non-existent organisations. As a defensive measure, the hapless victims would form themselves into a real secret society which conformed to the blueprint of the fictitious one. Thus a number of covert revolutionary cadres – some of them Masonic or quasi-Masonic – were born. Thus, once again, myth engendered 'history'.

Unquestionably, Freemasonry, or offshoots of Freemasonry, did contribute to various revolutionary movements in nineteenth-century Europe. Both Mazzini and Garibaldi, for example, were active Freemasons, and Freemasonry – largely through the so-called *Carbonaria* – played an even more important role in the unification of Italy than it did in the foundations of the United States. In Russia, too, Freemasonry was deemed to be subversive, and sometimes was so. Pushkin, for instance, writes of his membership in a lodge in Kishinev, whose activities in the 1825 Decembrist Plot led to a ban on all lodges in the country. Needless to say, the ban proved unenforceable, but it drove a number of Russian radicals into exile abroad, where they became heavily involved in foreign Freemasonry. Dostoevsky chronicles this process in *The Possessed*. The 'real-life' equivalent of Dostoevsky's revolutionaries was, of course, Bakunin.

Ultimately, however, the reality of the situation was more complex and less clearly definable. If Freemasons were active in the revolutionary movements of nineteenth-century Europe, they were equally active in such régimes as Metternich's Austria, for example, or the Prussia of Friedrich Wilhelm III and IV. Here Freemasonry was as entwined with the establishment as it was in Britain, where Grand Lodge continued to exemplify the Victorian virtues of sobriety, temperance and moderation. Even in France, there were as many conservative Freemasons as there were radicals and revolutionaries.

A list of nineteenth-century European Freemasons is illuminating simply by virtue of its lack of consistency. On the one hand, it includes such figures as Mazzini, Garibaldi, Bakunin, the young Alexander Kerensky in Russia, Daniel O'Connell and Henry Grattan in Ireland. On the other hand, it also includes two nineteenth-century kings of Prussia, three French presidents (Doumer, Faure and Gambetta) and that nemesis of political unrest, Talleyrand. In Britain, the list of nineteenth-century Freemasons includes George IV, William IV, Edward, Prince of Wales (subsequently Edward VII), Canning, Lord Randolph Churchill, the Marquis of Salisbury and Cecil Rhodes. Most of Napoleon's marshals were Freemasons; but so, too, were their most prominent adversaries – Nelson, Wellington and Sir John Moore in Britain, Kutuzov in Russia, Blücher in Prussia, as well as Scharnhorst and Gneisenau, the founders of the Prussian General Staff. In the arts, English Freemasons included Sir Walter Scott, Rider Haggard, Bulwer Lytton, Conan Doyle, Trollope, Kipling and Wilde. On the Continent, Pushkin's radical Freemasonry in Russia was offset by that in Germany of the arch-conservative Johann Wolfgang von Goethe.

This list is necessarily selective and by no means definitive. It serves, however, to illustrate the impossibility of ascribing any political orientation, or even political consistency, to Freemasonry. And what applies in Europe applies elsewhere as well. In Latin America, for example, as in Spain, Italy and other Catholic countries, Freemasonry offered a focus of opposition to the stranglehold of the Church. In consequence, most of the figures associated with Latin American independence, such as Bolívar, San Martín and later Juárez, were active Freemasons. But so, too, were the Spanish viceroys, aristocrats and land-owners from whom they wrested their fledgling republics, modelled assiduously on the pattern of the United States. In Brazil, both the empire of Pedro II and the republic that supplanted it were dominated by Freemasonry.

To the north, at least a dozen American presidents, apart from Washington, are known to have been Freemasons: Monroe, Andrew Jackson, Polk, Buchanan, Andrew Johnson, Garfield, Theodore

Roosevelt, Taft, Harding, Franklin D. Roosevelt, Truman and Ford. Texas's war for independence from Mexico was effectively directed by Freemasons such as Sam Houston. Davy Crockett, Jim Bowie and the other defenders of the Alamo were all members of the same Strict Observance lodge. During the American Civil War, Freemasonry was prevalent on both sides, but played a particularly important role in the institutions, and especially the army, of the Confederacy. All of that, however, to coin a cliché, is another story. So, too, are the Masonic origins of the Ku Klux Klan – which was not, initially, the noxious organisation it later became, but a charitable institution designed to protect widows and orphans from the depredations of Northern 'carpet-baggers'.

It is in America that our story comes full circle, for it is there that the Knights Templar have received the most fulsome public homage to be paid them anywhere in the world. This homage takes the form of a youth organisation sponsored by Freemasonry, the Order of DeMolay. The Order of DeMolay was established in Kansas City, Missouri, in 1919, by one Frank S. Land, and:

> ... takes its name from Jacques DeMolay, the last Grand Master of medieval Knights Templar, who was burned at the stake on an island in the Seine River near the Cathedral of Notre Dame on March 18, 1314 for his fidelity and integrity to the members of his Order.[1]

The Order of DeMolay numbers some eighty-five chapters in all fifty of the United States, in the District of Columbia and in twelve nations abroad. From its headquarters in Kansas City, it is governed by an International Supreme Council which operates under the auspices of Grand Lodge of Florida and is composed of 250 'eminent Masons from throughout the World'. Each local Chapter must be sponsored by a Masonic body, and the governing body, or Advisory Council, of each Chapter must consist of Master Masons. Membership in the Order itself consists of boys between the ages of fourteen and twenty-one.

> DeMolay, through initiation, teaches seven virtues; they are: Filial Love (love of parents), Reverence (reverence for sacred things), Courtesy, Comradeship, Fidelity, Cleanness (cleanness of thought, word and deed), and Patriotism.[2]

One cannot but wonder what boys in the Order are taught about Jacques de Molay himself, about the Templars and about the particular transgressions of which they were accused. To our knowledge, there is no mention of any of that in the Order's literature. That literature does, however, albeit with somewhat imperfect syntax, elaborate on the Order's objectives:

> The Order of DeMolay tries to supplement the teachings of home, church and school. Thereby better fitting a young man for duties of citizenship, which is his rightful heritage. DeMolay is unalterably opposed to a church, a school and the seat of civil government being housed under one roof. It feels that these three Freedoms are the cause of our Country's greatness and must stand on their own foundations and under separate roofs.[3]

To our knowledge, there is nothing in any sense pernicious about the Order of DeMolay. On the contrary, it does laudable enough work, and probably offers a more or less sane corrective for some of the ills to which America is prone, such as militant fundamentalism. But it is all rather remote from the white-mantled warrior-mystics who sought to storm heaven with their swords seven hundred years ago. And there is perhaps a slightly García Márquezesque quality about the very existence of this organisation, issuing from the heart of 'middle America', dedicated to fostering personal and civic virtues in generations of American youth, yet named after a medieval French knight executed for blasphemy, heresy, sodomy, necromancy and assorted other forms of misconduct that would mortify even the Ewings of Dallas, the Carringtons of Denver and all the depraved denizens of Peyton Place. One is tempted to imagine the bearded old Templar Grand Master himself gazing down – or up – on the organisation which today bears his name. Would he be touched, flattered, amused, or simply mystified?

APPENDIX 1

Masonic Field Lodges in Line Regiments under Major General Amherst: America, 1758[1]

Regiment	Lodge
1st Foot	No. 11, Irish Grand Lodge
15th Foot	No. 245, Irish Grand Lodge
17th Foot	No. 136, Irish Grand Lodge
22nd Foot	*No Lodge* (later, in 1767, Lodge No. 132, Scottish Grand Lodge)
27th Foot	No. 24, Irish Grand Lodge
28th Foot	No. 35, Irish Grand Lodge (Captain Span, November 1760, Grand Master, Quebec)
35th Foot	No. 205, Irish Grand Lodge
40th Foot	No. 42, Antients Grand Lodge
42nd Foot	No. 195, Irish Grand Lodge
43rd Foot	*No Lodge* (later, in 1769, Lodge No. 156, Scottish Grand Lodge)
44th Foot	*No Lodge* (later, in 1784, Lodge No. 467, English Grand Lodge)
45th Foot	*No Lodge* (later, in 1766, Lodge No. 445, Irish Grand Lodge)
46th Foot	No. 227, Irish Grand Lodge
47th Foot	No. 192, Irish Grand Lodge (1759, Lt Guinet, Grand Master, Quebec)
48th Foot	No. 218, Irish Grand Lodge
55th Foot	1st Scottish military Lodge; no number recorded
58th Foot	*No Lodge* (later, in 1769, Lodge No. 466, Irish Grand Lodge)
60th Foot	*No Lodge* (Later, in 1764, Lodge No. 448, English Grand Lodge)
Fraser Highlanders (later 78th Foot)	Lodge, No. unknown but Colonel Fraser in July 1760 was appointed Grand Master of Quebec

---

[1]Sources: Gould, *The History of Freemasonry*, vol. vi, pp. 400–3; Milborne, 'The Lodge in the 78th Regiment', pp. 23–4; Fortescue, *A History of the British Army*, vol. ii, pp. 296, 300, 316, note 2, 323, 325, 361.

APPENDIX 2

Masonic Field Lodges in Regiments in America, 1775–7 (excluding Canada)[1]

In command was Sir William Howe who had, as a member of his staff, Brigadier-General Augustine Prevost who, from around 1761, had been the head of the Ancient & Accepted Scottish Rite for the British Army.

Regiment	Commander	Lodge
16th Dragoons	Col. John Burgoyne	*None*
17th Dragoons	Col. John Preston	No. 478, Grand Lodge of Ireland
4th Foot	Col. S. Hodgson	No. 147, Grand Lodge of Scotland
5th Foot	Col. Earl Percy	No. 86, Grand Lodge of Ireland
7th Foot	Col. R. Prescott	No. 231, Grand Lodge of Ireland
10th Foot	Col. E. Sandford	No. 299, Grand Lodge of Ireland No. 378, Grand Lodge of Ireland
15th Foot	Col. Earl of Cavan	No. 245, Grand Lodge of Ireland
16th Foot	Col. J. Gisborne	No. 293, Grand Lodge of Ireland
17th Foot	Col. R. Monckton	No. 136, Grand Lodge of Ireland
22nd Foot	Col. T. Gage	No. 251, Grand Lodge of Ireland
23rd Foot	Col. Sir W. Howe	No. 137, Grand Lodge of Scotland
26th Foot	Col. Lord Gordon	No. 309, Grand Lodge of Ireland
27th Foot	Col. E. Massey	No. 205, Grand Lodge of Ireland
28th Foot	Col. C. Grey	No. 35, Grand Lodge of Ireland

33rd Foot	Col. Earl Cornwallis	No. 90, Antients Grand Lodge
35th Foot	Col. H. F. Campbell	*None*
37th Foot	Col. Sir E. Coote	No. 52, Antients Grand Lodge
38th Foot	Col. R. Pigot	No. 441, Grand Lodge of Ireland
40th Foot	Col. R. Hamilton	No. 42, Antients Grand Lodge
42nd Foot	Col. Lord J. Murray	No. 195, Grand Lodge of Ireland
43rd Foot	Col. G. Cary	No. 156, Grand Lodge of Scotland
44th Foot	Col. J. Abercrombie	No. 14, Prov. G. Lodge of Quebec[2]
45th Foot	Col. W. Haviland	No. 445, Grand Lodge of Ireland
46th Foot	Col. J. Vaughan	No. 227, Grand Lodge of Ireland
49th Foot	Col. A. Maitland	No. 354, Grand Lodge of Ireland
52nd Foot	Col. J. Clavering	No. 370, Grand Lodge of Ireland No. 226, Grand Lodge of England
54th Foot	Col. M. Frederick	*None*
55th Foot	Col. J. Grant	No. 7, Grand Lodge of New York
57th Foot	Col. Sir J. Irwin	No. 41, Antients Grand Lodge
60th Foot (3 Batt)	Col. Dalling	*None*
60th Foot (4 Batt)	Col. A. Prevost	*None known*, but perhaps an A&A Scots Rite.[3]
63rd Foot	Col. F. Grant	No. 512, Grand Lodge of Ireland
64th Foot	Col. J. Pomeroy	No. 106, Grand Lodge of Scotland
71st Foot	Col. S. Fraser	No. 92, Grand Lodge of Scotland

---

[1] Sources: *A List of the General and Staff Officers and of the Officers in the Several Regiments Serving in North America* (New York, 1778); Gould, *The History of Freemasonry*, vol. vi, pp. 400–3; Milborne, 'British Military Lodges in the American War of Independence', in *Transactions of the American Lodge of Research*, vol. x, no. 1, pp. 22–85.

[2] 44th Foot: Lodge founded 1760 in Quebec and revived as No. 18 in 1784. Its status in 1775–7 is uncertain.

[3] 60th Foot, 1st Battalion, held Lodge No. 448, Grand Lodge of England.

Notes and References

Note

The full bibliographical details, when not cited here, are to be found in the Bibliography.

Prelude

1 Letter, 2 November 1978.
2 Stuart, *Sculptured Stones of Scotland*; Drummond, *Sculptured Monuments in Iona and the West Highlands*; Steer and Bannerman, *Late Medieval Monumental Sculpture in the West Highlands*; *The Royal Commission on the Ancient and Historical Monuments of Scotland: Argyll 1971–84* (in progress).
3 When the Temple was suppressed and its holdings conferred on the Knights of St John, the circular Templar church at Garway had been pulled down, while the Order's graves had been deliberately defaced and desecrated. (The Order of St John had similarly destroyed the circular church of the Templars at Bristol, building, as at Garway, a conventional rectangular chapel.) One slab, however, bearing the anonymous straight sword, had been torn from the ground and built into the window-frame of the structure which replaced the original church. Thus it had survived, escaping the effacement – by time, human hands or both – which was the usual fate of Templar gravestones.
4 Ronen and Olami, *Atlit Map*. The best preserved tomb of the Templar Mason is today on display in the Rockefeller Museum, Jerusalem.

1 Bruce and his Struggle for Power

1 Duncan, *Scotland: The Making of the Kingdom*, p. 111.
2 Platts, *Scottish Hazard*, pp. 139–43.
3 The inscription was recorded in Latin as: '*Ni fallat vatum Scoti hunc quocunque locatum/Invenient lapidem, regnare tenentur ibidem.*' ('Unless the prophets err, the Kingdom of the Scots will endure wherever they find this stone placed.') See Dart, *Westmonasterium*, iii, Chap. 1, p. 12.
4 Edward himself was accused by the Scots of necromancy:

> Men said he fostered on the sly
> A spirit that would give reply
> To any question that he pleased.

See Barbour, *The Bruce*, p. 113.

5 Barrow, *Robert the Bruce*, p. 184.
6 Ibid., p. 208, quoting *The Chronicle of Walter of Guisborough*, p. 367.
7 Barbour, op. cit., p. 66.

> And yet, some men there are that say
> The conflict went another way.
> But howsoever the quarrel fell
> He died thereby, I know full well.

8 Barrow, op. cit. p. 210, note 3.
9 Mackay, *Robert Bruce*, p. 93.
10 Ibid., p. 102.
11 Barrow, op. cit., p. 229.
12 14 January 1310, Berwick. See *Calendar of Documents Relating to Scotland*, vol. iii, p. 190.
13 Barrow, op. cit., p. 293.
14 Barbour, op. cit. p. 269.
15 MacDonald, *The History of Argyll*, p.141.
16 Barrow, op. cit., p. 428, quoting a copy printed in 1688.
17 Barbour, op. cit., p. 468.
18 Report by Henry Jardine in *Transactions of the Society of Antiquaries of Scotland*, vol. ii (1822), pp. 442–3.

2 Military Monks: the Knights Templar

1 It appears that they were in existence by 1114, in which year the Bishop of Chartres wrote of the 'milice du Christ', the joining of which entailed chastity, to Hugues, Comte de Champagne, prior to his departure for the Holy Land. Hugues was listed as a member of the Order in 1124, after their official foundation. See Baigent, Leigh, Lincoln, *The Holy Blood and the Holy Grail*, pp. 57–62.
2 Seward, *The Monks of War*, p. 37.
3 *The Anglo-Saxon Chronicle*, AD 1128 (p. 202).
4 See Melville, *La vie des templiers*, pp. 93–6.
5 Knowles and Hadcock, *Medieval Religious Houses: England and Wales*, pp. 292–7. This is the standard list, but it is incomplete; it does not, for example, list Bristol. The income listed is also deceptive, since it gives the value given by St John in 1338, and many properties had deteriorated greatly by that time.
6 *Close Rolls of Henry III*, vol. i, p. 368 (1230) and p. 477 (1231).
7 Knowles and Hadcock, op. cit. The Templars had at least eleven preceptories in Yorkshire, and two other manors. All these had many additional holdings. Temple Newsom, for example, also held property near four towns and held at least six churches. See also Martin, 'The Templars in Yorkshire'.

8 Gwynn and Hadcock, *Medieval Religious Houses: Ireland*, pp. 327–31. While this is the standard list of holdings, it cannot be regarded as definitive.

9 Easson, *Medieval Religious Houses: Scotland*, pp. 131–2. Again, while this is the standard list, it is not complete.

10 Ferris, 'The Financial Relations of the Knights Templars to the English Crown', pp. 15–16.

11 Ibid., p. 16, note 1, quoting Rymer, *Foedera* vol. i, p. 514. This relates to the repayment in 1274 of a loan made to Edward I in the Holy Land.

12 Ibid., p. 10.

13 Addison, *The History of the Knights Templars*, p. 112.

14 Seward, op. cit., p. 213.

3 Arrests and Torture

1 Mazières, 'La venue et le séjour de templiers du Rousillon', pp. 235, 245.

2 Hugues de Châlons, Pierre de Modies and Falco de Milly, all of whom were related. Hugues de Châlons, and probably Pierre de Modies, were nephews of the Paris Templar Treasurer, Hugues de Pairaud. See Barber, *The Trial of the Templars*, pp. 66, 266, note 8.

3 Barber, op. cit., p. 101, quoting from Finke, *Papsttum und Untergang des Templerordens*, vol. ii, p. 339. In this testimony the Templar preceptor states that Hugues de Châlons had escaped with all Hugues de Pairaud's 'treasure'.

4 Baigent, Leigh, Lincoln, *The Holy Blood and the Holy Grail*, pp. 45f.

5 Addison, *The History of the Knights Templars*, p. 206.

6 Ibid.

7 *Calendar of Close Rolls 1307–1313*, 20 December 1307, p. 14.

8 Ibid., pp. 179, 181.

9 Ibid., p. 189.

10 Ibid., p. 206.

11 Ibid., p. 295.

12 Addison, op. cit., p. 263; see also Barber, op. cit., p. 200.

13 Baigent, Leigh, Lincoln, op. cit., pp. 44–5.

14 Oursel, *Le procès des templiers*, p. 28.

15 Barber, op. cit., p. 202.

16 Ibid.

17 For example, there was a hospital for elderly and infirm Templars at the preceptory of Denney in Cambridgeshire. In 1308, ten or more such Templars were arrested there.

18 Addison, op. cit., p. 274.

19 Briefly, our argument is this: as the arrests in France, unlike those in England, were sudden, we assume that the relative proportion of Templars of the various ranks apprehended would reflect the proportion pertaining generally in the Order. Of those listed in the French reports, 11 per cent were knights, 29 per cent sergeants and 12 per cent chaplains. The proportion of three sergeants to each knight accurately reflects that of the medieval armies. In England, of course, there was plenty of time for the active Templars to escape, and so while the proportion of chaplains arrested at 11 per cent was similar to France, those of the knights and sergeants was much less. However,

it is clear that many *did* escape: there were at least seventy-four major holdings and preceptories of the Order in England, yet only fourteen preceptors were caught, just one being a knight. No preceptor was caught for the large recruitment centre of Faxfleet on the Humber, nor for Willoughton in Lincolnshire – one of the largest bases in England. Neither were any found for Wetherby, for Temple Bruer or Foulbridge, to name a few. All of these bases would have had at least two but more likely upwards of a dozen brethren in residence. Clearly our top estimate of ninety-three militarily active Templars at large after the arrests in England must be regarded as conservative.

As a guide, we can note that the Waterman *MS* lists, for 1338, at least fifty-five and possibly sixty knights and sergeants of the Order of St John in England, and we must remember that St John was smaller than the Temple. It is not credible that the Templars would have had any less, and so the estimates current in literature of some ten to twenty military Templars in England can be disregarded.

4   The Disappearance of the Templar Fleet

1   Wood, 'The Templars in Ireland', p. 348.
2   Bain, *Calendar of Documents Relating to Scotland*, p. 103.
3   Wilkins, *Concilia magnae britanniae*, vol. ii: Testimony of Walter de Clifton pp. 380–1, and of William de Middleton, p. 381.
4   Seward, *The Monks of War*, p. 50.
5   Addison, *The History of the Knights Templars*, p. 213.
6   Aitken, 'The Knights Templars in Scotland', p. 34.
7   Seward, op. cit., p. 205.
8   Haye, *The Persecution of the Knights Templars*, p. 114.
9   Bothwell-Gosse, *The Knights Templars*, p. 105.
10 The best review of von Hund and the 'Strict Observance' system is found in Le Forestier, *La franc-maçonnerie templière et occultiste*, vol. i, pp. 103–238. The 'Mull' legend is on pp. 160–1. Von Hund's list of Grand Masters of the Templars is found in Thory, *Acta latomorum*, vol. i, pp. 282–3.
11 The Story of the 'Larmenius' Charter, together with a transcription and translation, is found in Crowe, 'The "Charta Transmissionis" of Larmenius'. The so-called 1705 Statutes were printed in Brussels, 1840, as *Statuts des chevaliers de l'ordre du temple*, by the Convent-Général de Versailles.
12 Crowe, op. cit., p. 189.

5   Celtic Scotland and the Grail Legends

1   Baigent, Leigh and Lincoln, *The Holy Blood and the Holy Grail*, pp. 245–76.
2   Ibid., p. 256.
3   Oursel, *Le procès des templiers*, p. 208. The original report by the Inquisition reported that the legend referred to the 'head of one of the Eleven Thousand Virgins'. This strongly suggests that the 'm' was in fact the astrological sign for Virgo – which looks very similar.

4   Barber, *The Trial of the Templars*, p. 249.
5   See Roach in his edition of Chrétien de Troyes, *Le conte de graal*, p. 306, and Ritchie, *Chrétien de Troyes and Scotland*, p. 18.
6   Ritchie, op. cit., p. 10.
7   Ibid., p. 23.
8   Duncan, *Scotland: The Making of the Kingdom*, p. 141.
9   Platts, *Scottish Hazard*, pp. 127–77.

6   The Templar Legacy in Scotland

1   Addison, *The History of the Knights Templars*, pp. 285–6.
2   Cowan, Mackay and Macquarrie, *The Knights of St John of Jerusalem in Scotland*, pp. 47–8.
3   Larking, *The Knights Hospitallers in England*, p. 201.
4   Robertson, *An Index drawn up about the year 1629*, p. 11, no. 36.
5   Ibid., p. xxvi.
6   Ibid., p. xxx.
7   Maidment, *Abstract of the Charters and Other Papers*, lists three baronial properties previously Templar and 514 others.
    For two centuries the self-contained patrimony of 'Terrae Templariae' was maintained and administered by the Order of St John – or the combined Order of St John and the Temple. Properties were leased and a designated official acted as overseer and collected rents. This official was usually designated as the 'Temple bailie'. It appears that each region of Scotland had its own 'Temple bailie', who reported back to the Prior of St John at Torphichen. Thus, for example, one Alexander Spens is named as 'Temple bailie' for Fife in 1490. Other individuals, named as 'bailie of the Temple lands', are cited for Lennox, Angus and Gowrie, Berwick and Ayr. See Cowan, Mackay and Macquarrie, op. cit., p. lxviii.
8   See, for example, Maidment, *Templaria*, 'Charter granted by King James IV of Scotland'. The usage is '*Fratribus Hospitalis Hierosolimitani, Militibus Templi Solomonis . . .*'. Curiously, in this charter which is dated 1488, James IV *reaffirmed* all the ancient rights and privileges not only of the Order of St John but also of the Templars. This must be proof that as late as the fifteenth century the Templars had some legal existence.
9   Scottish Record Office, RH6/114 and 115. The latter is printed in Cowan, Mackay and Macquarrie, op. cit., pp. 51–3.
10 Maidment, *Abstract of the Charters*, pp. 8–9. The six baronies listed as being in the hands of the Order of St John were: Torphichen, Thankerton, Denny, Auldliston, Ballintrado (Balantrodoch) and Maryculter. The first, Torphichen, was the only preceptory the Order of St John held in Scotland prior to the suppression of the Templars, while the last three were known to have been held by the Templars. It is therefore reasonable to suppose that the remaining two were also part of the Templar patrimony in Scotland.
11 Maidment, *A Rental of all the annual rents and Temple lands*.
12 Seton, *A History of the Family of Seton*, vol. ii, p. 751.
13 Cowan, Mackay and Macquarrie, op. cit., p. liv and pp. 184–5. The relative, John James Sandilands, eventually found himself in serious trouble: by 1564,

when he had already been deprived of his habit and expelled from the Order, he and two companions stole and melted down a chalice, reliquary, crucifix and other pieces from a church. He confessed under torture and was apparently executed that same year. See ibid., p. 190.

14 Maidment, *Templaria*, 'Information for John Lord Torphichen', p. 3.

15 Ibid., p. 5.

16 Cowan, Mackay and Macquarrie, who have documented every known Scottish member of the Order of St John, do not mention David Seton. Neither is there any record of his existence in the archives of the Monastery of Ratisbon (See Dilworth, *The Scots in Franconia*). The Maltese archives published by J. Mizzi also fail to mention his name.

However, the consensus seems to be that the poem must be given the benefit of the doubt. No one has suggested that the poem is a forgery or a fantasy, and Dr Macquarrie, in correspondence to us (14 February 1988), said that he had, for some time, been intrigued by the poem and mention of David Seton. He concludes by suggesting that there might be some truth in the story but he has not been able to take it further. He welcomed further information.

17 Seton, op. cit., vol. ii, p. 751.

18 Porter, *A History of the Knights of Malta*, vol. ii, pp. 303–4.

19 Ibid.

20 *Statutes of the religious and military Order of the Temple*, p. xv. Searches made in the archives of the National Library of Scotland, Aberdeen University Library, St Andrews University Library, Edinburgh University Library and the British Library Manuscripts Department have so far failed to turn up a copy of this poem.

7 The Scots Guard

1 Forbes-Leith, *The Scots Men-at-Arms and Life-Guards in France*, vol. i, pp. 35–46.

2 Daniel, *Histoire de la milice françoise*, vol. ii, p. 170.

3 Forbes-Leith, op. cit., vol. ii, p. 156.

4 Ibid., vol. ii, p. 52. The grouping of thirteen was significant in many chivalric and religious organisations – the Garter Knights being perhaps the most well known of the former. In the Scots Guards the twenty-five men plus commander gives two groups of thirteen. The seventy-seven men of the 'garde' plus their commander forms six groups of thirteen. There was an overall Captain of the Guard, making a total for the contingent of 105. This arrangement is maintained until 1568 when small variations again begin to appear.

5 Ibid., vol. ii, p. 27. The annual cost to the French crown of the complete Guard was 25,691 *livres* – an enormous cost. See Ibid., vol. ii, p. 30.

6 Personal communication, 2 December 1987.

7 Forbes-Leith, op. cit., vol. i, pp. 101–2.

8 Laver, *Nostradamus*, pp. 45–8. See also Cimber, *Archives curieuses de l'histoire de France*, 1 sér. tom. 3, p. 295. On 5 February 1556 a dispatch arrived from Rome containing a horoscope of the king drawn up by Luca

Gaurico; it had previously appeared in his book published 1552, but it was not taken seriously until the accident.

9 In 1555 Nostradamus published the first three of his 'centuries' and a part of the fourth. The quatrain which is taken to refer to the death of Henry II is *Century* 1:35. Hutin (*Les prophéties des Nostradamus*, p. 124) cites the rare 1558 edition, which wording we have followed.

10 Baigent, Leigh, Lincoln, *The Holy Blood and the Holy Grail*, pp. 139, 417, note 6.

11 Forbes-Leith, op. cit., vol. ii, p. 189.

8 Rosslyn

1 Philo-Roskelynsis, *An Account of the Chapel of Roslin*, p. 28.

2 See Michael Bradley's recent study of this material, *Holy Grail Across the Atlantic*. Other discussions of this material are: Major, *The Voyages of the Venetian Brothers Zeno to the Northern Seas in the Fourteenth Century* and Pohl, *Prince Henry Sinclair*.

3 Sinclair's informant, a fisherman, stated that some twenty-six years earlier he had been wrecked upon an island in the 'New World'. He was, during the course of many years' captivity, taken to the south where a great civilisation existed: '. . . they grow more civilised towards the south-west, where the climate is milder, and they have cities, and temples to their idols, in which they sacrifice men and afterwards eat them. In those parts they have knowledge of gold and silver.' (Major, op. cit., p. 14.) Sinclair intended that this fisherman should accompany him on the planned Atlantic voyage. Unhappily the fisherman died just before his departure.

4 Hay, *Genealogie of the Sainteclaires of Rosslyn*, p. 27.

5 Ibid.

6 Waite, *A New Encyclopaedia of Freemasonry*, vol. ii, p. 28. See also ibid., p. v.

7 Hay, op. cit., p. 27.

8 Ibid., pp. 157–8. This charter is dated *c.* 1600–1601. See also Thory, *Acta latomorum*, vol. ii, pp. 15–17.

9 *The Manuscripts of his Grace the Duke of Portland*, vol. ii, p. 56. This letter is unsigned and undated, but Rylands, 'The Mason Word: the Earls of Roslin and Freemasonry', argues for a date of 1678.

10 Pick and Knight, *The Pocket History of Freemasonry*, pp. 178–9.

11 Ibid., p. 179. For a biography of Schaw and other Master Masons to the Crown, see MacBean, 'The Master Masons to the Crown of Scotland'. See also Stevenson, *The Origins of Freemasonry*, pp. 26–51.

12 Hay, op. cit., pp. 157–8.

13 Hay, ibid., pp. 159–63; Thory, op. cit., vol. ii, pp. 18–22.

14 Lyon, *History of the Lodge at Edinburgh*, p. 98.

15 MacRitchie, *Scottish Gypsies under the Stewarts*, p. 56.

16 Ibid., p. 63.

17 Hay, op. cit., pp. 135–6.

18 MacRitchie, op. cit., pp. 57–8.

19 Adamson, *The Muses Threnodie*, p. 32.

20 MacRitchie, op. cit., p. 57.
21 Barker Cryer, *Drama and Craft*. This was given as the 'Prestonian Lecture' in 1974 and privately printed the same year.
22 Ibid., pp. 26, 33.
23 Ibid., pp. 35–7.
24 It seems likely that the enacting of the murder of John the Baptist was a contributing factor to the eventual drama involving Hiram Abiff. See ibid., p. 32.

9 Freemasonry: Geometry of the Sacred

1 All biblical quotations come from *The Jerusalem Bible*, edited by Father Roland de Vaux. English edition edited by Alexander Jones (London, 1966).
2 *The Song of Songs* (The Song of Solomon), IV:8.
3 The rituals, passwords, grips, signs and other aspects of Masonic practice are given in at least three books, two currently (1988) in print: Carlile, *Manual of Freemasonry*; Hannah, *Darkness Visible*; Dewar, *The Unlocked Secret*. Carlile is the first, and was apparently the basic source for the two later works.
4 The 'Cooke Manuscript'. See Gould, *The History of Freemasonry*, vol. i, p. 84.
5 The 'Grand Lodge Manuscript No. 1', reproduced in Sadler, *Masonic Facts & Fictions*, pp. 199–208. In the MS the architect is said to be the son of Hiram, king of Tyre. He is given the name *Aynone*, which is considered to be a mistranslation of Hebrew *Adonai* and indicates that the reference is to Adoniram, with whom Hiram Abiff was often confused.
6 Selected extracts published in English as *Journey to the Orient*, 1972. The story of the murder of Hiram (called Adoniram by Nerval) is entitled 'Makbenash' on pp. 204–9.
7 Vitruvius, *De architectura*, IV.c.IX.
8 Ibid., I.c.I:3.
9 Ibid., III.c.I:9.
10 James, *Chartres*, p. 49.
11 Ibid., p. 111.
12 Book review, *New York Times*, April 1974.
13 Aitken, 'The Knights Templars in Scotland', p. 20. In Scotland the commercial activities of the Templars had reached such a point that they were threatening the well-being of the trade guild members. A law was passed to ensure that 'no Templar should meddle in buying or selling goods belonging to the guild unless he were a guild member'. As the Templars did not curtail their commercial activities, it follows that some must have joined the relevant guilds.
14 The best account of the events and the 'Hermetic' background to renaissance art is found in Frances Yates, *Giordano Bruno and the Hermetic Tradition*, London, 1964, and reprinted on numerous occasions. She explains, for example, that the renaissance masters were 'attempting to influence "the world" by favourable arrangements of celestial images, so as to draw down favourable influences and exclude non-favourable ones' (1978 edition,

p. 75), and that many examples of renaissance art constructed for these eminently practical reasons were 'complex talismans': '... Botticelli's "Primavera" is surely such an object, designed with such a purpose' (1978 edition, p. 77).

15 Plato, *Timaeus*, p. 179.
16 Letter dated 3 June 1546. See Hay, op. cit., p. 134.
17 Several of the works of Frances Yates deal with this period, particularly *The Occult Philosophy in the Elizabethan Age*, *The Art of Memory*, *Astraea* and *Giordano Bruno and the Hermetic Tradition*.
18 See Durkan, 'Alexander Dickson and S.T.C. 6823', and Yates, *The Art of Memory*, pp. 260–78.
19 Yates, *The Art of Memory*, p. 274. Indeed, Dickson was one of Bruno's most assiduous propagators. When Bruno visited England in 1584 he met with two of Dickson's closest friends – Fulke Greville, Lord Brooke, and Sir Philip Sidney. Dickson is almost certain to have been present.
20 Yates, *Theatre of the World*, p. xi.
21 Ibid., p. 192.
22 Ibid., p. 194.
23 Ibid., p. 196.
24 Evans, *Rudolf II and His World*, p. 84.
25 The best exploration of this period is again by Frances Yates, under this phrase as title: *The Rosicrucian Enlightenment*.
26 Ibid., p. 58.
27 Ibid., pp. 179–96.
28 Ibid., p. 224.

10 The Earliest Freemasons

1 Adamson, *The Muses Threnodie*, p. 32.
2 'Buchanan Manuscript'. See Gould, *The History of Freemasonry*, vol. i, p. 98.
3 Rothes, *A Relation of Proceedings Concerning the Affairs of the Kirk of Scotland from August 1637 to July 1638*, p. 30.
4 Eight years later, on the execution of Charles I, Charles II was proclaimed king in Scotland. He arrived in the country in 1650, *accepted the Covenant* and, in 1651, was formally crowned at Scone. His army was defeated by Cromwell, however, and he was driven back into exile in France until the Restoration in 1660.
5 Pick and Knight, *The Pocket History of Freemasonry*, p. 44.
6 General Hamilton (brother of Earl of Haddington) was initiated into Mary's Chapel Lodge, Edinburgh, on 20 May 1640. See Lyon, *History of the Lodge of Edinburgh*, p. 86.
7 See *Dictionary of National Biography*, entry under MURRAY.
8 Ibid. See also Stevenson, *The Origins of Freemasonry*, pp. 166–89.
9 Ibid.
10 Ibid., quoting Wood in *Athenae Oxon.*, ed. Bliss, vol. ii, p. 725.
11 Ibid., quoting Birch in *History of the Royal Society*, vol. i, pp. 508, 510.
12 Yates, *The Rosicrucian Enlightenment*, p. 254.

13 Ibid., p. 226.
14 Maier, *Themis Aurea: The Laws of the Fraternity of the Rosie Crosse*. This dedication is signed by N.L., T.S. and H.S.
15 Pick and Knight, op. cit., p. 45, quoting from Ashmole's diary.
16 Ibid.,
17 Yates, *The Rosicrucian Enlightenment*, p. 254. She also states her conclusion that, 'We have . . . a chain of tradition leading from the Rosicrucian movement to the antecedents of the Royal Society' (p. 224).
18 Agrippa, *De occulta philosophia libri tres*, c.XXXIX.
19 Agrippa (trans. J.F.), *Three Books of Occult Philosophy*, chap.XXXIX (p. 77).
20 Pick and Knight, op. cit., pp. 73–4.
21 Anderson, *New Book of Constitutions of the Freemasons*, p. 106. The assertion must be considered unproved. In the year that Wren died (1723) Anderson published his first *Book of Constitutions*. In it he twice mentioned Sir Christopher Wren but neither time stated that he was a Freemason. However, in the 'New' *Book of Constitutions* of 1738 Anderson affirms that Wren was Grand Master of the Fraternity. It would seem impossible to avoid the conclusion that this was not stated in 1723 because Wren's colleagues, still alive, would have challenged it. It does, though, seem possible that Wren was a member of the Fraternity. There is a handwritten note by John Aubrey (a friend of Ashmole) on the reverse of folio 72 of the manuscript of his *Natural History of Wiltshire*, stating that on the day of writing, 18 May 1691, there was to be a major gathering of Freemasons at St Paul's to initiate Wren as a member. See Hamill, *The Craft*, p. 36.
22 Hamill, op. cit., pp. 34–5.
23 Plot, *The Natural History of Staffordshire*, pp. 316–18. The legendary history of Freemasonry and King Athelstan has been fully explored by Alex Horne in his *The York Legend in the Old Charges*. He concludes that there is little historical truth in the story.

11 Viscount Dundee

1 Lenman, *The Jacobite Cause*, p. 29.
2 Terry, *John Grahame of Claverhouse*, p. 2.
3 Ibid., pp. 352–4.
4 Waite, *A New Encyclopaedia of Freemasonry*, vol. ii, p. 223.
5 Tuckett, 'Dr. Begeman and the alleged Templar Chapter at Edinburgh in 1745', p. 46, quoting Begeman.
6 Yarker, *Notes on the Scientific and Religious Mysteries of Antiquity*, p. 124.
7 *Statutes of the Religious and Military Order of the Temple*, p. xv. It has been argued that the author of this 'Historical Notice' was W. E. Aytoun, Professor of Rhetoric and Belles Lettres at Edinburgh University. See Chetwode Crawley, 'The Templar Legends in Freemasonry', p. 232. Aytoun appears in the above work as Grand Prelate of the Scottish Templar Order. He certainly had access to early records of Scottish Freemasonry and Templarism through his links with Alexander Deuchar, who reformed the Order in Scotland in the late eighteenth century. Aytoun purchased the 'Saint

Clair' charters of the early seventeenth century, which had been in the hands of Alexander Deuchar, and presented them to the Grand Lodge of Scotland, where they remain to this day.

8 Maggiolo, 'Mémoire sur la correspondance inédite de dom Calmet . . .'

9 Barrington, *Grahame of Claverhouse, Viscount Dundee*, p. 409.

10 Letter dated 14 August 1987.

11 *Memoirs of the Lord Viscount Dundee*, pp. 52–3.

12 The Development of Grand Lodge

1 Seton, *A History of the Family of Seton*, vol. i, p. 274; see also Hughan, *The Jacobite Lodge at Rome 1735–37* for fuller details of this lodge. George Seton, Earl of Winton, was elected 'Great Master' on 23 April 1736; see ibid., p. 23.

2 Trevelyan, *England under the Stuarts*, p. 471, quoting Swift.

3 McLynn, *The Jacobites*, p. 140.

4 'The Minutes of Grand Lodge', p. 5f.

5 United Grand Lodge of England, *Grand Lodge 1717–1967*, p. 50.

6 Clarke, 'The Establishment of the Premier Grand Lodge', p. 5.

7 Pick and Knight, *The Pocket History of Freemasonry*, pp. 68–9; Anderson, *New Book of Constitutions of the Freemasons*, p. 109.

8 Tuckett, 'The Origin of Additional Degrees', p. 5.

9 Ibid., p. 25.

10 In 1751 a rival Grand Lodge, formed by Freemasons primarily of Irish Grand Lodge persuasion, claimed to work under ancient rules and practices. This was called the 'Antients', and the 1717 Grand Lodge was called the 'Moderns'. Unlike the 'Moderns', the 'Antients' worked the higher degrees, in particular the Royal Arch. In 1813 the two systems were reconciled and merged forming the United Grand Lodge of England, which continues today.

11 Waples, 'An Introduction to the Harodim', p. 120.

12 Robbins, 'The Earliest Years of English Organised Freemasonry', pp. 70–1, quoting *London Journal* for 16 June 1722.

13 Wharton was publicly accused of being the leader of the Jacobites, and he certainly, upon leaving England, joined the Jacobite cause.

14 Gould, *The History of Freemasonry*, vol. iv, p. 375.

15 'The Minutes of Grand Lodge', pp. 5–6.

16 Anderson, *A Sermon Preached in Swallow-street*, p. 15. It appears likely that even before 1717 Anderson was a Freemason: an attack upon him in *No King-Sellers* mentions him as being a 'Crafts Master' (p. 10) and adds that his 'Brethren in the Ministry, as he calls them, have more than one Office of Intelligence about the Exchange where they often meet' (p. 14). The Exchange was the locality of at least two early Masonic lodges: the Crown Tavern Lodge was behind the Exchange in the 1723 list of lodges, as was the Ship Tavern Lodge.

17 Anderson, *The Constitutions of the Freemasons*, p. 50.

18 Ibid.

19 Tuckett, 'The Origin of Additional Degrees', p. 20.

20 'The Minutes of Grand Lodge', p. 235 (13 December 1733).

13 The Masonic Jacobite Cause

1 See the two articles on the curious 'Harodim' degree by Waples; see also Barker Cryer, 'A Fresh Look at the Harodim'.

2 11 July 1688; see Tuckett, 'The French-Irish Family of Walsh', p. 190.

3 Ibid.

4 Lepper and Crossle, History of the Grand Lodge of Free and Accepted Masons of Ireland, vol. i, p. 147.

5 Ibid., p. 147, note 1.

6 See Tuckett, op. cit., and Lepper, 'The Poor Common Soldier', pp. 151–3. In 1772 the military lodge working in this regiment of the French army made an application to French Grand Orient to be recognised as the 'Senior' lodge in France. Sufficient evidence was apparently produced for this claim to be accepted by a decision of Grand Orient in 1777. The claim was that the lodge had been in the regiment since 25 March 1688. See Tuckett, p. 195; Lepper, p. 152.

7 The earliest written history of the origins of Freemasonry in France is that of the astronomer Joseph Jerome Lefrançais de Lalande, who in 1773 wrote that the first lodge was founded in Paris in 1725, by the Earl of Derwentwater – meaning Charles Radclyffe, who, until the death of his young nephew, did not actually hold the title. See Gould, The History of Freemasonry, vol. v, pp. 136–7; Thory, Acta latomorum, vol. i, pp. 21–2, repeats this data. Chevallier, in Histoire de la franc-maçonnerie française, vol. i, p. 5, writing in 1974, indicates the possibility of the formation of Radclyffe's Lodge of St Thomas (apparently after Thomas à Becket) being founded 12 June 1726. He admits, though, that without additional documentation the truth cannot be known.

8 Moss, 'Freemasonry in France in 1725–1735', Part 2, p. 91.

9 'The Minutes of Grand Lodge', p. 6.

10 Tunbridge, 'The climate of European Freemasonry 1730–1750', p. 97.

11 Chevallier, op. cit., vol. i, p. 7.

12 Pick and Knight, The Pocket History of Freemasonry, p. 84. They give 1728 as the date of this foundation.

13 Chevallier, op. cit., vol. i, p. 7.

14 Henderson, Chevalier Ramsay p. 20. The Philadelphians had been founded by Dr Francis Lee in 1696 and were concerned with 'neo-Boehme specula tions'.

15 It is the regent, Philippe d'Orléans, who, it is claimed, in 1705 presided over a reconstitution of the Order of the Temple and had new Statutes of the Order drawn up, those now used by the Ancient and Sovereign Military Order of the Temple of Jerusalem. See p. 75 of The Temple and the Lodge.

16 Chevallier, op. cit., vol. i, p. 18.

17 This second version is translated in Gould, op. cit., vol. v, pp. 84–9.

18 Ibid., p. 85.

19 Ibid.

20 Ibid., p. 87.

21 Ibid., pp. 87–88.

22 Ibid., p. 88.

23 Ibid., p. 88.
24 Chevallier, op. cit. vol. i, p. 25.
25 Ibid., pp. 11–13.
26 Ibid., p. 38.
27 On 30 December 1739 there is first mention of new brothers being initiated into the 'Lodge of the King'; see Chevallier, ibid., p. 41. The members of this are unknown, but Chevallier points out that at a reception earlier the same month at the Hôtel de Bussy were Radclyffe, Maurice de Saxe, the Duc d'Antin and nine others, including two more dukes. Chevallier wonders whether these are the members of the 'Lodge of the King' and points out (pp. 42–3) that of the thirteen familiars of Louis XV who dined with him, eight were known Freemasons, one possible and another, the Comte de Noailles, was master of a lodge at Versailles by 1744. Of these familiars and dining companions, three were present at the meeting at the Hôtel de Bussy with Radclyffe.

It is clear that Louis XV could easily have come under sufficient Masonic influence to cause him to think seriously about joining the Order. It seems clear that he did not, but it seems equally clear that on occasion he expressed the desire to do so, indeed to become Grand Master of the French Freemasons. See Chevallier, ibid., pp. 43, 100–6.

14 Freemasons and Knights Templar

1 Chevallier, *Histoire de la franc-maçonnerie française*, vol. i, p. 70.
2 'A new crusade to re-establish the true monarch of Great Britain' (ibid., p. 23).
3 Ibid., p. 14. The source of these changes was said to be Charles Radclyffe.
4 Ibid., p. 15.
5 Tuckett, 'The Origin of Additional Degrees', p. 10.
6 Thory, *Acta latomorum*, vol. i, p. 52.
7 Le Forestier, *La franc-maçonnerie templière*, pp. 109, 135–6.
8 Von Hund managed to produce very few 'original' documents. One was this list, produced at the convention held at Wilhelmsbad. It is published in Thory, op. cit., vol. i, p. 282.
9 Baigent, Leigh, Lincoln, *The Holy Blood and the Holy Grail*, pp. 413–4, note 20. This list goes up to the death of Riderfort in 1190. The remainder of von Hund's list also differs markedly from those normally found, and of course his also insists upon a continuity, through Scotland, of the Order. Of the validity of these later sections we can say nothing, except that if it is based upon valid historical information, it has clearly become corrupted and mistranslated.
10 This group, Stella Templum, dates back to the late eighteenth century, when Alexander Deuchar orchestrated a Scottish Templar revival. Deuchar, though, had access to much of what remained of earlier material pertaining both to Jacobite Templarism and Scottish Freemasonry. The 'Saint Clair Charters', for example, were in his possession. It is in the hands of Deuchar's Order that the David Seton poem first surfaces, although by this time the group had been effectively taken over by Freemasonry and Deuchar himself forced out of leadership.

The aim of Stella Templum was, and still is, to gather and preserve all material relating to the undercurrents of Scottish culture and heritage. Accordingly they have assiduously gathered all writings, regalia, artefacts, letters and oral histories in the knowledge that if they did not, these 'esoteric' aspects would be subsumed by the dominant English culture.

11 Stella Templum archives.

12 Henderson, *Chevalier Ramsay*, p. 197.

15 The First American Freemasons

1 Cerza, in Cook, *Colonial Freemasonry*, p. 106.

2 Ibid., p. 107.

3 *The Boston Newsletter*, 5 January 1719; see *Transactions of the American Lodge of Research*, vol. iv (1942–7), p. 130.

4 Heaton, in Cook, op. cit., p. 153.

5 Lafontaine, 'Benjamin Franklin', p. 5.

6 Heaton, in Cook, op. cit., p. 156.

7 Cerza, 'Colonial Freemasonry in the United States of America', pp. 224–5; see also Sherman and Sanford in Cook, op. cit., pp. 72–4.

8 Sherman and Sanford in Cook, op. cit., p. 74.

9 Gould, *The History of Freemasonry*, vol. vi, p. 401. This was Lodge No. 11 on Irish Grand Lodge list, warranted on 7 November 1732 and struck off with the return of the warrant by Colonel Maunsell in April 1847; see Crossle, *Irish Masonic Records*, p. 22.

10 Lodge No. 245, Irish Register, warranted in 1754; see Gould, op. cit., vol. vi, p. 401.

11 Lodge No. 170, Antients Grand Lodge, established in the 3rd Foot in 1771; and Lodge No. 448, English Grand Lodge, established in the 60th Foot in 1764; see Gould, ibid., pp. 401–2.

12 See Lepper, 'The Earl of Middlesex and the English Lodge in Florence', p. 6.

13 The Freemasons at Frederick's court were: Robert Nugent, Comptroller of the Household, Junior Grand Warden, Grand Lodge of Ireland in 1732; Arthur St Leger, Viscount Doneraile, Grand Master Grand Lodge of Ireland in 1740; Charles Sackville, Earl of Middlesex, Founder of the Lodge at Florence in 1733, presumed Irish Grand Lodge connection; Joseph Sirr, Equerry, later, in 1773 and 1774, respectively Junior Grand Warden and Senior Grand Warden in Grand Lodge of Ireland; Henry Brydges, Marquis of Carnarvon, Gentleman of the Bed Chamber, in 1737 Grand Master of Grand Lodge of England; and Frederick's chaplain in 1727, the ubiquitous Dr John Desaguliers, who in 1719 had been Grand Master of Grand Lodge of England and subsequently held a number of high-ranking posts in the Order. It was Desaguliers who initiated Frederick himself in 1737.

14 A lodge was first warranted in the 20th Foot between November 1736 and the following February 1737. This warrant, though, appears to have been mislaid, for Lord George Sackville himself in December 1748 was granted a 'Warrant of Confirmation' for Lodge No. 63 (Irish Grand Lodge). His two

wardens were Lieutenant-Colonel Edward Cornwallis and Captain Milburne; See Rogers, 'Lancashire Military Lodges', p. 106.

15 Lepper, *History of the Grand Lodge of Free and Accepted Masons of Ireland*, pp. 182–3.

16 Fortescue, *A History of the British Army*, vol. ii, p. 323. Howe was Colonel of the 55th Foot which had, in 1743, the first military lodge warranted by Grand Lodge of Scotland; see Gould, op. cit., p. 402.

17 Thomas Desaguliers served under Wolfe at Louisbourg as colonel of the 3rd Battalion, Royal Artillery, and became a lieutenant-general in the Royal Artillery and equerry to George III. While he is known to have been an active Freemason, records of his Masonic career are lacking; see Gould, op. cit., vol. iv, p. 350, who considers that he was likely initiated into the 'Horn' Lodge. Certainly, by 1738, he is noted as a Freemason in Anderson's second edition of the *Constitutions* (p. 229).

18 See Appendix 1.

19 Gould, op. cit., vol. v, p. 51.

20 Ibid., pp. 59–60.

21 Ibid., vol. vi, p. 410. Colonel Richard Gridley was the younger brother of Jeremy Gridley, Provincial Grand Master of North America from 1755, based in Boston. Richard Gridley was raised Master Mason on 4 April 1746, in St John's Lodge, Boston. In 1769 he was Deputy Grand Master of St John's Grand Lodge. He ended his military career as a major-general of artillery in the Continental Army.

22 Rogers, op. cit., p. 108.

23 For details of the Quebec Grand Lodge, see Rogers, ibid., and Milborne, 'The Lodge in the 78th Regiment (Fraser's Highlanders)'.

24 The following were Freemasons before, during, or just after the French and Indian War, and reached rank of general in the Continental Army: General Benedict Arnold, before 1765; General Joseph Frye, before 1760; General Richard Gridley, 1746; General Hugh Mercer, 1761; General John Nixon, before 1762; General Israel Putnam, 1758; General George Washington, 1752; General Richard Montgomery, accepted 1775, presumed to have joined Lodge in 17th Foot during French and Indian War, but no records survive; General David Wooster, Master of Hiram Lodge No. 1, New Haven, 1750, but date of joining unknown. See Heaton, *Masonic Membership of the Founding Fathers* and Denslow, *10,000 Famous Freemasons*.

16 The Emergence of Masonic Leaders

1 *A letter from Cicero, the Right Hon. Lord Viscount H–E* (London, *c.* 1781), p.19.

2 Gould, *The History of Freemasonry*, vol. iv, p. 344.

3 Ibid., p. 344, note 2. The third royal brother, the Duke of Cumberland, was initiated on 9 February 1767; see ibid., p. 344, note 4.

4 See Appendix 2.

5 LaFontaine, 'Benjamin Franklin', p. 31, quoting *Gaine's Mercury*, 2 July 1781.

6 Heaton, *Masonic Membership of the Founding Fathers*, p. xvi.

7 In the papers of William Eden, Lord Auckland – who ran an espionage network for George III – is a report from an English agent, Captain Hynson, who reports: '. . . you will be surprised to hear Doctor Franklin say that whenever Great Britain would show a disposition for peace he would be the first to give up this independence. Mr. Dean he said had made the same declaration. But Doctor Franklin said he knew they had no mind for peace, he said, Mr Lee lived in a higher stile [sic] than he had ever done and had a great deal of pride, he dare say would wish to continue as he was, therefore was the only one that would be against giving up the Independence but declared it would be given up immediately on England showing a disposition for *peace . . .*' (letter, 10 December 1777, British Library. Add. Mss 34414, f. 406).

8 Heaton, op. cit., p. iv.

17 The Resistance to Britain

1 Sherman and Sanford, in Cook, *Colonial Freemasonry*, p. 76.

2 Ibid., p. 77.

3 Cameron, 'On the Origin and Progress of Chivalric Freemasonry in the British Isles', p. 157. See also Cameron, 'Notes on the Earliest References to the Masonic Knights Templars Degree', p. 79, which mentions that Lodge No. 296, Irish Grand Lodge Register, was warranted in 1758. The Knight Templar Degree is mentioned in its by-laws, which are unfortunately undated; it is possible that the degree existed as early as 1758. The Lodge was inactive by 1791.

4 A full list of members of St Andrew's Lodge from 1756 to 1906 can be found in *The One Hundred and Fiftieth Anniversary of the Lodge of St Andrew*, pp. 273–301. Paul Revere was initiated on 4 September 1760; John Hancock in Quebec before 1762.

5 Abbott, in Cook, op. cit., p. 169.

6 See Labaree, *The Boston Tea Party*, pp. 141–2, for Joseph Warren, Griswold, *The Boston Tea Party*, p. 61, for Paul Revere, and Jaynes, 'The Boston Tea Party', in Bassler, *Military Masonic Hall of Fame*, p. 222, for the 'North End Caucus'.

7 A list of the 'Loyal Nine' is given in Griswold, op. cit., p. 19. The three members of the 'Loyal Nine' who were also members of St Andrew's Lodge, Boston, were: Thomas Chase, initiated 1767; Thomas Crafts, initiated 1761; Henry Welles, initiated 1760.

8 Cerza, 'The Boston Tea Party and Freemasonry', p. 208.

9 Ibid.

10 No definitive list of participants in the Boston Tea Party exists. Upwards of 200 people were involved. Studies have been made of family documents and in 1835 seven surviving participants helped compile a list. The result was 110 names; see Griswold, op. cit., pp. 141–3. We can add to this list the names of the 'Loyal Nine' who most certainly would have participated. The source for members of St Andrew's Lodge is note 4, above. Warren, Webb and Hancock are added in Bassler, op. cit., p. 222.

Participants in the Tea Party who were also members of
St Andrew's Lodge

Stephen Bruce	Freemason since 1767
Thomas Chase	Freemason since 1767
Adam Collson	Freemason since 1762
Thomas Crafts	Freemason since 1761
John Hancock	Freemason since 1762
Samuel Peck	Freemason since 1756
Edward Proctor	Freemason since 1763
Paul Revere	Freemason since 1760
Thomas Urann	Freemason since 1760
Joseph Warren	Freemason since 1761
Joseph Webb	Freemason since 1760
Henry Wells	Freemason since 1760

Participants in the Tea Party who later joined St Andrew's Lodge

David Bradlee	joined 1777
Samuel Cooper	joined 1795
Robert Davis	joined 1777
Samuel Gore	joined 1778
Abraham Hunt	joined 1777
Daniel Ingersoll	joined 1782
Amos Lincoln	joined 1777
Eliphalet Newell	joined 1777
Henry Purkitt	joined 1795
William Russell	joined 1777
James Swan	joined 1777
Nathaniel Willis	joined 1779

11 *The One Hundred and Fiftieth Anniversary of the Lodge of St Andrew*, p. 293.
12 Guard rosters for the evening of 29 November and morning of 30 November 1773 are to be found in Griswold, op. cit., p. 144. Those who participated in the events of 16 December 1773 are indicated. One member of St Andrew's Lodge and of the militia Guard, Thomas Knox, does not appear to have been involved in the Tea Party.
13 Heaton, op. cit., p. 57.
14 *Webster's Guide to American History*, p. 56.
15 Ibid., p. 57.
16 Mansfield Hobbs, *The Contribution of Free Masonry and Free Masons to the Success of the American Revolution*, p. 17.
17 Heaton, op. cit., p. 45.
18 Ibid., p. 79.
19 Ibid., p. 44.
20 Ibid., pp. 59–60.
21 Ibid., pp. 85–6.
22 Ibid., pp. 53–4.
23 Ibid., pp. 61–2.
24 Ibid., pp. 2–3.

25 Van Gorden, *Modern Historical Characters in Freemasonry*, p. 320. Van Gorden notes that Ethan's brother was a Freemason, member of Vermont Lodge No. 1.

18 The War for Independence

1 Einstein, *Divided Loyalties*, p. 3.
2 Amiable, *Une loge maçonnique d'avant 1789, la R.L. Les Neuf Soeurs*, pp. 136, 145.
3 LaFontaine, 'Benjamin Franklin', p. 17.
4 Towers, *Dashwood: The Man and the Myth*, pp. 157–60. This refers to the Chapter Room at Dashwood's Medmenham Abbey and the rites which were conducted within.
5 *Encyclopaedia britannica* (Chicago, 1947), vol. xix, p. 940, article on John Montagu, Fourth Earl of Sandwich.
6 McCormick, *The Hell Fire Club*, p. 107.
7 Towers, *Dashwood: The Man and the Myth*, p. 220.
8 Kemp, 'Some letters of Sir Francis Dashwood', p. 219, letter dated 28 September 1769.
9 Gruber, *The Howe Brothers and the American Revolution*, p. 54.
10 *A Letter from Cicero to the Right Hon. Lord Viscount Howe* (London, 1781), p. 26.
11 Ibid., p. 5.
12 Ibid., p. 6, quoting the *Morning Post*.
13 Wilkes was in effect their representative in London. In 1775 and 1776 he was in close contact with Arthur Lee (brother of Richard Henry Lee), who was in London. Lee later joined Franklin and Deane in Paris. Wilkes was sending money to the playwright Beaumarchais, who in turn sent it to the American Colonies; see Maier, *From Resistance to Revolution*, p. 256.
14 Letter from the Reverend John Vardill to William Eden, 14 December 1777: 'Mr. Lupton and Dr. Bancroft are in London. Mr. Lupton and Mr. Petré spent yesterday evening with Mr. Wilkes, Hartley, etc.' (see British Library, *Add.Mss* 34414, f. 427.
15 Records on file at United Grand Lodge of England, London.
16 See Chapter 16, note 7, above.
17 Ibid.
18 For a résumé of Bancroft, see Einstein, op. cit., pp. 4–15.
19 Amiable, op. cit., p. 253. Apart from Franklin and Bancroft, very few other non-Frenchmen were members of this lodge at the time. The English speakers were George Forster, the naturalist who accompanied Captain Cook, a Scotsman named Campbell, who is otherwise unidentified, and the Scottish sailor fighting for the American Colonists, John Paul Jones. In addition there is one Bingley, otherwise unknown, who is presumably English or American. Other nationalities were represented by six Italians, two Spaniards, and one each from Russia, Poland, Sweden and Germany.
20 George III, writing to Lord North, says that he is convinced that Bancroft is 'entirely an American and that every word he used on the late occasion was to deceive . . .'; see *The Correspondence of King George the Third*, vol. iii,

p. 532, letter no. 2132, 31 December 1777.

21 Ibid., vol. v, p. 24, letter no. 2952, 1 March 1780, Lord Stormont to George III.

22 Deacon, *A History of the British Secret Service*, p. 112–13.

23 Heaton, *Masonic Membership of the Founding Fathers*, pp. 100–1.

24 Ibid., p. xvi.

25 Paine, *Gentleman Johnny*, p. 75.

26 Ibid., p. 85.

27 Ibid., p. 84.

28 Fitzmaurice, *Life of William, Earl of Shelburne*, vol. i, pp. 247–8.

29 Adams, *The Papers of Lord George Germain*, p. 29. On this date Howe received a copy of the orders instructing Burgoyne to move south and join with Howe at Albany. It is not known whether this dispatch also contained an explicit order to Howe to move north and meet Burgoyne. What is beyond doubt is that Howe knew that so far as Germain and Burgoyne were concerned, he was *supposed* to move north. Howe claimed that he had not received the orders. The War Office claimed they had been sent, but neither Germain nor D'Oyley could produce an office copy of them, and thus could never prove they had been sent. Either they were not, or Howe or some other interested party contrived to remove the War Office's copy prior to any investigation.

30 Paine, op. cit., p. 118.

31 Fortescue, *A History of the British Army*, vol. iii, p. 207.

32 See note 29, above.

33 Robertson, *England Under the Hanoverians*, p. 513.

34 Ibid.

35 Paine, op. cit., p. 119.

36 Adams, op. cit., p. 31.

37 Robertson, op. cit., p. 514.

Interlude

1 Milborne, 'British Military Lodges in the American War of Independence', p. 50.

2 Ibid., p. 67.

3 Pick and Knight, *The Pocket History of Freemasonry*, p. 251, and Gould, vol. vi, p. 415.

4 Gould, 'Military Masonry', pp. 47–8.

5 Milborne, 'British Military Lodges in the American War of Independence', pp. 31–2.

6 Green, in Cook, *Colonial Freemasonry*, p. 53. De Kalb is supposed to have been a member of Continental Army Lodge No. 29, which was formed in 1780; absolute proof, though, is lacking. See Heaton, *Masonic Membership of the Founding Fathers*, pp. 84–5, and Mackey, *Encyclopaedia of Freemasonry*, vol. i, pp. 514–15. Moira, at the time, was unlikely to have been a Freemason; see Hamill, 'The Earl of Moira', p. 32.

7 Lepper, '"The Poor Common Soldier"', p. 156, quoting the Minutes of the Grand Lodge of Ireland, 5 September 1793.

8 Milborne, 'British Military Lodges in the American War of Independence', p. 61, and Chetwode Crawley, 'General George Washington and Lodge No. 227 (I.C.)', p.96.
9 Milborne, op. cit., pp. 37–8.

19 The Republic

1 Heaton, *Masonic Membership of the Founding Fathers*, p.56.
2 Hume, 'Of the first Principles of Government', in Watkins, ed., *Theory of Politics*, p. 152.
3 Hume, 'Whether the British Government Inclines More to Absolute Monarchy or to a Republic', in ibid., p. 167.
4 While Anderson as late as 1738 sees no reason to have a specific rule in this case, it is clear that later that century Lodge members were able to impeach their master and remove him. In such a case the senior warden acted in his stead until the next election on the following St John's Day.
5 Clausen, *Masons Who Helped Shape our Nation*, p. 82.
6 Marshall was a member of Lodge No. 13 at Richmond, Virginia. From 28 October 1793, he was Deputy Grand Master of Virginia and served briefly as Grand Master. See Mackey, *Encyclopaedia of Freemasonry*, vol. ii, p. 627.
7 Morgan Lewis, brother in law to both Robert Livingston and General Richard Montgomery, was Grand Master of Grand Lodge of New York from 1830 to 1843. He was a Mason by 1777. See Case, *Roll of the American Union Lodge*, p.380. Jacob Morton was Master of St John's Lodge No. 1, New York, in 1788 and replaced Livingston as Grand Master of Grand Lodge of New York in 1801, retaining this position until 1805 See Denslow, *10,000 Famous Freemasons*.
8 Cerza, 'Colonial Freemasonry in the United States of America', p. 227.
9 Denslow, *Freemasonry and the Presidency*, pp. 18–20, quoting the Columbian *Mirror* and the Alexandria *Gazette*, 23 September 1793.

Postscript

1 Hollis, *Allied Masonic Groups and Rites*, p. 19.
2 Ibid., p. 20.
3 Ibid., pp. 19–20.

Bibliography

Abstract of the Charters and other papers recorded in the Chartulary of Torphichen from 1581 to 1596, ed. James Maidment (Edinburgh, 1830)

ADAMS, R. G., *The Papers of Lord George Germain* (San Marino, 1928)

ADAMSON, H., *The Muses Threnodie* (Edinburgh, 1638)

ADDISON, C. G., *The History of the Knights Templars* (London, 1842)

AGRIPPA, H. C., *Three Books of Occult Philosophy* (London, 1651)

AITKEN, R., 'The Knights Templars in Scotland', *The Scottish Review*, vol. xxxii (1898), pp. 1f.

ALLEN, C. M., *Memoir of General Montgomery* (Philadelphia, 1912)

AMIABLE, L., *Une loge maçonnique d'avant 1789: la R . . . L . . . Neuf Soeurs* (Paris, 1897)

ANDERSON, A. O., *Early Sources of Scottish History*, 2 vols (London, 1922)

ANDERSON, J. *A Sermon Preached in Swallow-street, St James, on Wednesday Jan 16, 1711/12 being the National Fast-Day.* (London, 1712)

——*The Constitutions of the Freemasons* (London, 1723)

——*Royal Genealogies* (London, 1732)

——*New Book of Constitutions of the Freemasons* (London, 1738)

The Anglo-Saxon Chronicle, trans. James Ingram (London, 1912)

BAIGENT, M., LEIGH, R. and LINCOLN, H., *The Holy Blood and the Holy Grail*, (London, 1982)

BANNERMAN, J., *Studies in the History of Dalriada* (Edinburgh, 1974)

BARBER, R., *The Knight and Chivalry*, 2nd edn (Ipswich, 1974)

BARBOUR, J., *The Bruce*, trans. and ed. Archibald A. H. Douglas (Glasgow, 1964)

BARKER CRYER, N., 'A Fresh Look at the Harodim', *Ars quatuor coronatorum*, vol. xci (1978), pp. 116f.

——*Drama and Craft* (London, 1974) (A shortened version printed in *Ars quatuor coronatorum*, vol. lxxxvii (1974), pp. 74f.

BARRINGTON, M. J., *Grahame of Claverhouse, Viscount Dundee* (London, 1911)

BARROW, G. W. S., *Robert Bruce and the Community of the Realm of Scotland*, (London, 1965)

——*Robert the Bruce and the Scottish Identity* (Edinburgh, 1984)

BASSLER, R. E., *Military Masonic Hall of Fame* (n.p.p., 1975)

BATHAM, C. N., 'A Famous French Lodge (Les Neuf Soeurs)', *Ars quatuor coronatorum*, vol. lxxxvi (1973), pp. 312f.

BEDFORD, W. K. R., and HOLBECHE, R., *The Order of the Hospital of St John of Jerusalem* (London, 1902)

BELLOT, H. H. L., *The Inner and Middle Temple* (London, 1902)

BLACKETT-ORD, M., *Hell Fire Duke* (Windsor Forest, 1982)

BOTHWELL-GOSSE, A., *The Knights Templars* (London, 1912)

BRADLEY, M., *Holy Grail Across the Atlantic* (Willowdale, 1988)

BRITTON, J., *The Architectural Antiquities of Great Britain*, 5 vols, (London, 1807)

BRYANT, A., *The Age of Chivalry* (London, 1963)

BURNES, J., *Sketch of the History of the Knights Templars* (Edinburgh, 1840)

BYRNE, F. J., *Irish Kings and High Kings* (London, 1987)

Calendar of the Close Rolls Preserved in the Public Record Office: Edward II, AD 1307–1313 (London, 1892)

Calendar of Documents Relating to Scotland, ed. Joseph Bain, 4 vols, (Edinburgh, 1881–8)

CAMERON, A. I., *The Scottish Correspondence of Mary of Lorraine* (Edinburgh, 1927)

CAMERON, C. A., 'On the Origin and Progress of Chivalric Freemasonry in the British Isles', *Ars quatuor coronatorum*, vol. xiii (1900), pp. 156f.

——'Notes on the Earliest References to the Masonic Knights Templars Degree', *Ars quatuor coronatorum*, vol. xvi (1903), pp. 79f.

CAMPBELL, M., *Mid Argyll, a Handbook of History* (Oban, 1974)

CARDINALE, H. E., *Orders of Knighthood, Awards and the Holy See*, ed. and rev. Peter Bander van Duren (Gerrards Cross, 1985)

CARLILE, R., *Manual of Freemasonry* (London, n.d.)

CARR, H., *Mother Kilwinning, Lodge No. 0* (London, 1961)

——(ed.), *The Early French Exposures (London, 1971)*

CASE, J. R., 'Roll of the American Union Lodge', *Transactions of the American Lodge of Research*, vol. vi (1952–6), pp. 356f.

——*Fifty Early American Military Freemasons* (Bethel, 1955)

CERZA, A., 'The Boston Tea Party', *Colonial Freemasonry*, ed. Lewis C. Wes. Cook (Missouri, 1973–4) (vol. 30 of *Transactions of the Missouri Lodge of Research*)

——'The Boston Tea Party and Freemasonry', *Ars quatuor coronatorum*, vol. xcviii (1985), pp. 207f.

——'The American War of Independence and Freemasonry', *Ars quatuor coronatorum*, vol. lxxxix (1976), pp. 169f.

——'Colonial Freemasonry in the United States of America', *Ars quatuor coronatorum*, vol. xc (1977), pp. 218f.,

CHANNING, E., *A History of the United States*, 6 vols (New York, 1977)

CHARPENTIER, J., *L'ordre des templiers* (Paris, 1977)

CHETWODE CRAWLEY, W. J., 'General George Washington and Lodge No. 227 (I.C.)', *Ars quatuor coronatorum*, vol. xxiii (1910), pp. 95f.

——'The Templar Legends in Freemasonry', *Ars quatuor coronatorum*, vol. xxvi (1913), pp. 45f., 146f., 221f.

——'The Sackville Medal: The Earl of Middlesex and Irish Freemasonry, 1733', *Ars quatuor coronatorum*, vol. xiii (1900), pp. 142f.

CHEVALLIER, P., *La première profanation du temple maçonnique* (Paris, 1968)

——*Les ducs sous l'acacia* (Paris, 1964)

——*Histoire de la franc-maçonnerie française*, 3 vols (Paris, 1974)

CHRÉTIEN DE TROYES, *Le conte du graal*, trans. William Roach (Paris, 1959)

——*The Story of the Grail*, trans. R. W. Linker, 2nd edn (Chapel Hill, 1952)

The Chronicle of Walter of Guisborough, ed. Harry Rothwell (London, 1957)

CLARK, G. N., *The Later Stuarts 1660–1714* (Oxford 1934)

CLARKE, J. R., 'The Establishment of the Premier Grand Lodge', *Ars quatuor coronatorum*, vol. lxxxi (1968), pp. 1f.

CLARKE, W., *Bicentenary History of the Grand Lodge of Ireland* (Dublin, 1925)

CLAUSEN, H. C., *Masons Who Helped Shape Our Nation*, (Washington, 1976)

Close Rolls of the Reign of Henry III preserved in the Public Record Office (London, 1902)

The Complete Peerage, by G.E.C., 13 vols (London, 1910–59)

COOK, L. C. W., ed. *Colonial Freemasonry* (Missouri, 1973–4)

The Correspondence of King George the Third, ed. John Fortescue, 6 vols (London, 1928)

COUNTRYMAN, E., *The American Revolution* (London, 1986)

COWAN, I. B., MACKAY, P. H. R., and MACQUARRIE, A., *The Knights of St John of Jerusalem in Scotland* (Edinburgh, 1983)

CROSSLE, P., *Irish Masonic Records* (Dublin, 1973)

CROWE, F. J. W., 'The "Charta Transmissionis" of Larmenius', *Ars quatuor coronatorum*, vol. xxiv (1911), pp. 185f.

CURTIS, E. E., *The Organization of the British Army in the American Revolution* (New Haven, 1926)

CURZON, H. DE, *La règle du temple* (Paris, 1886)

CUTTS, E. L., *The Sepulchral Slabs and Crosses of the Middle Ages* (London, 1849)

DAILLIEZ, L., *Les templiers: ces inconnus* (Paris, 1972)

DANIEL, G., *Histoire de la milice françoise*, 2 vols (Amsterdam, 1724)

DART, J., *Westmonasterium or the History and Antiquities of the Abbey Church of St Peters, Westminster*, 2 vols (London, 1723)

DEACON, R., *A History of British Secret Service* (St Albans, 1980)

DENNISTOUN, J., *Memoires of Sir Robert Strange*, 2 vols (London, 1855)

DENSLOW, R. V., *Freemasonry and the Presidency*, (n.p.p., 1952)

DENSLOW, W. R., *10,000 Famous Freemasons*, 4 vols (Missouri, 1959)

DEWAR, J., *The Unlocked Secret* (London, 1966)

Dictionary of National Biography, ed. Leslie Stephen and Sidney Lee, 63 vols (London, 1885–1900)

DILWORTH, M., *The Scots in Franconia* (Edinburgh, 1974)

DONALDSON, G., *Scotland: James V–James VII* (Edinburgh, 1987)

DORAN, J., *London in the Jacobite Times*, 2 vols (London, 1877)

DRUMMOND, J., *Sculptured Monuments in Iona and the West Highlands* (Edinburgh, 1881)

DUNCAN, A. A. AM., *Scotland: The Making of the Kingdom* (Edinburgh, 1975)

DURKAN, J., 'Alexander Dickson and S.T.C. 6823', *The Bibliotheck*, vol. iii, no. 5 (1962), pp. 183f.

EASSON, D. E., *Medieval Religious Houses: Scotland* (London, 1957)

EDGE, J. H., 'A Short Sketch of the Rise and Progress of Irish Freemasonry', *Ars quatuor coronatorum*, vol. xxvi (1913), pp. 131f.

BIBLIOGRAPHY

EDWARDS, J., 'Rent-Rolls of the Knights of St John of Jerusalem in Scotland', *Scottish Historical Review*, vol. xix, part 3 (1922), pp. 202f.

EDWARDS, L., 'Three early Grand Masters', *Ars quatuor coronatorum*, vol. lviii (1947), pp. 226f.

EINSTEIN, L., *Divided Loyalties* (London, 1933)

EVANS, R. J. W., *Rudolf II and His World* (Oxford, 1984)

FERRIS, E., 'The Financial Relations of the Knights Templars to the English Crown', *The American Historical Review*, vol. viii (1903), pp. 1f.

FINKE, H., *Papsttum und Untergang des Templerordens* 2 vols (Münster, 1907)

FITZMAURICE, LORD, *Life of William, Earl of Shelburne*, 2 vols (London, 1912)

FLEMING, A., *The Four Maries* (Glasgow, 1951)

FORBES-LEITH, W., *The Scots Men-at-Arms and Life-Guards in France* (Edinburgh, 1882)

FORREST-HAMILTON, J., *The Order of St John* (Glasgow, 1950)

FORTESCUE, J. W., *A History of the British Army*, 13 vols (London, 1899–1930)

FRAZER, J. G., *The Golden Bough*, abridged edn (London, 1976)

FULLER, R., *Hell-Fire Francis* (London, 1939)

GORDEN, J. H. van, *Modern Historical Characters in Freemasonry* (Lexington, 1985)

GOULD, R. F., 'Military Masonry', *Ars quatuor coronatorum*, vol. xiv (1901), pp. 42f.

——*The History of Freemasonry*, 6 vols (London, n.d.)

GREENHILL, F. A., *Incised Effigial Slabs in Latin Christendom*, 2 vols (London, 1976)

GREEVES, R., 'The Galloway Lands in Ulster', *Transactions of the Dumfriesshire and Galloway Natural History and Antiquarian Society*, 3rd ser., vol. xxxvi (1959), pp. 115f.

GRISWOLD, W. S., *The Boston Tea Party* (Tunbridge Wells, 1973)

GROOME, F. H., *Ordnance Gazetteer of Scotland: A Survey of Scottish Topography*, new edn, 6 vols (London, 1894–5)

GRUBER, I., *The Howe Brothers and the American Revolution* (Williamsburg, 1972)

GUYOT, [CHEVALIER], *Manual of the Knights of the Order of the Temple*, new edn (Liverpool, 1830)

GWYNN, A., and HADCOCK, R. N., *Medieval Religious Houses: Ireland* (London, 1970)

HAMILL, J., 'The Earl of Moira, Acting Grand Master 1790–1813', *Ars quatuor coronatorum*, vol. xciii (1980), pp. 31f.

——*The Craft* (Wellingborough, 1986)

HANNAH, W., *Darkness Visible* (Chulmleigh, 1984)

HARRIS, R. B., *History of the Supreme Council, 33°* (Washington, 1964)

HAY, R. A., *Genealogie of the Saintclaires of Rosslyn* (Edinburgh, 1835)

HAYE, A. O., *The Persecution of the Knights Templars* (Edinburgh, 1865)

HEATON, R. E., *Masonic Membership of the Founding Fathers* (Silver Spring, 1974)

HENDERSON, G. D., *Chevalier Ramsay* (London, 1952)

HEXTALL, W. B., 'The "Lord Harnouester" of 1736–1738', *Ars quatuor coronatorum*, vol. xxvi (1913), pp. 22f.

BIBLIOGRAPHY

HOLLIS, W. M., *Allied Masonic Groups and Rites* (n.p.p., 1966)

HORNE, A., *The York Legend in the Old Charges* (Shepperton, 1978)

HUGHAN, W. J., 'Origin of Masonic Knight Templary in the United Kingdom', *Ars quatuor coronatorum*, vol. xviii (1905), pp. 91f.

——*The Jacobite Lodge at Rome* (Torquay, 1910)

HUME, D., ed. Frederick Watkins, *Theory of Politics* (McGill University, Montreal, 1951)

HUTIN, S., *Les prophéties de Nostradamus* (Paris, 1981)

JACKSON, J., *Historical Tales of Roslin Castle* (Penicuik, 1837)

JAMES, J., *Chartres: The Masons Who Built a Legend* (London, 1985)

JAYNES, H. H., 'The Boston Tea Party – December 16 , 1773', *Military Masonic Hall of Fame*, ed. R. E. Bassler (n.p.p., 1975)

JOHNSON, M. M., *Freemasonry in America prior to 1750* (n.p.p., 1917)

JOINVILLE, J., *Life of St Louis* (Harmondsworth, 1976)

KEMP, B., 'Some Letters of Sir Francis Dashwood, Baron Le Despencer, as Joint Post-Master General, 1766–81', *Bulletin of the John Rylands Library*, vol. xxxvii, no. 1 (September 1954), pp. 204f.

——*Sir Francis Dashwood* (London, 1967)

KNOWLES, D., and HADCOCK, R. N., *Medieval Religious Houses: England and Wales* (London, 1953)

LABAREE, B. W., *The Boston Tea Party* (Oxford, 1964)

LAFONTAINE, H. T. C. DE, 'Benjamin Franklin', *Ars quatuor coronatorum*, vol. xli (1929), pp. 3f.

LARKING, L. B., *The Knights Hospitallers in England* (London, 1857)

LAVER, J., *Nostradamus* (London, 1942)

LEES, B. A., *Records of the Templars in England in the Twelfth Century* (London, 1935)

LE FORESTIER, R., *La franc-maçonnerie templière et occultiste aux XVIIIe et XIXe siècles*, 2nd edn, 2 vols (Paris, 1987)

LENMAN, B., *The Jacobite Cause* (Glasgow, 1986)

LEPPER, J. H., '"The Poor Common Soldier", A Study of Irish Ambulatory Warrants', *Ars quatuor coronatorum*, vol. xxxviii (1925), pp. 149f.

——'The Earl of Middlesex and the English Lodge in Florence', *Ars quatuor coronatorum*, vol. lviii (1947), pp. 4f.

——and CROSSLE, P., *History of the Grand Lodge of Free and Accepted Masons of Ireland*, 2 vols (Dublin, 1925)

LESLIE, N. B., *The Succession of Colonels of the British Army from 1660 to the Present Day* (London, 1974)

LEWIS, S., *Topographical Dictionary of England*, 7th edn, 4 vols (London, 1849)

——*A Topographical Dictionary of Ireland*, 2 vols (London, 1837)

A List of the General and Staff Officers and of the Officers in the several Regiments serving in North America (New York, 1778)

LYON, D. M., *History of the Lodge of Edinburgh* (Edinburgh, 1900)

The Mabinogion, trans. Jeffrey Gantz (Harmondsworth, 1976)

MACBEAN, E., 'The Master Masons to the Crown of Scotland', *Ars quatuor coronatorum*, vol. vii (1894), pp. 101f.

McCORMICK, D., *The Hell Fire Club* (London, 1958)

MACDONALD, C. M., *The History of Argyll* (Glasgow, 1951)

MACDONALD, M., *The Land of Knapdale* (Oban, 1986)
——*Loch Awe and its Environs* (Oban, 1987)
MACKAY, J. A., *Robert Bruce, King of Scots* (London, 1974)
MACKENZIE, W. M., *The Battle of Bannockburn* (Glasgow, 1913)
——*The Bannockburn Myth* (Edinburgh, 1932)
MACKEY, A. G., *Encyclopaedia of Freemasonry*, rev. edn, 2 vols (Chicago, 1929)
MACKIE, J. D., *A History of Scotland* (Harmondsworth, 1964)
McLYNN, F., *The Jacobites* (London, 1985)
MACPHERSON, D., *Rotuli Scotiae in Turri Londinensi et in Domo Capitulari Westmonasteriensi asservati*, 2 vols (London, 1814–19)
MACRITCHIE, D., *Scottish Gypsies under the Stuarts* (Edinburgh, 1894)
MAGGIOLO, M., 'Memoire sur la correspondance inédite de dom Calmet, abbé de Senones, extrait du journal de son sejour à Paris, mai 1706 a juillet 1715', *Memoires lus à la Sorbonne* (Paris, 1863), pp. 101f.
MAIDMENT, J., *A Rental of all the annual rents and Temple lands founded throughout the whole Kingdom of Scotland beginning from the Boundaries towards England and so descending through the whole Kingdom from the said Boundaries all the way to the Orkneys*, Ms, *c.* 1823, 1839 and undated, National Library of Scotland, no. acc. 8090
——*Templaria* (Edinburgh, 1828–30)
MAIER, M., *Themis Aurea: The Laws of the Fraternity of the Rosie Crosse* (London, 1656)
MAIER, P. R., *From Resistance to Revolution* (London, 1973)
MAITLAND, R., *The History of the House of Seytoun* (Glasgow, 1824)
MAJOR, R. H., *The Voyages of the Venetian brothers Zeno to the Northern Seas in the Fourteenth Century* (Boston, 1875)
The Manuscripts of his Grace the Duke of Portland: The Historical Manuscripts Commission, Thirteenth Report, Appendix, Part II (London, 1893)
MARTIN, E. J., 'The Templars in Yorkshire', *The Yorkshire Archaeological Journal*, vol. xxix (1929), pp. 366f.
MAZIÈRES, M–R., 'La venue et le séjour de templiers du Rousillon à la fin du XIIIme siècle et au début du XIVme dans la vallée du Bézu (Aude)', *Mémoires de la société des arts et des sciences de Carcasonne*, 4me série, tome iii (1957–9), pp. 229f.
MEEKREN, R. J., 'Grand Lodge', *Ars quatuor coronatorum*, vol. lxix (1957), pp. 87f.
MELVILLE, M., *La vie des templiers* (Paris, 1974)
MENZIES, G., *Who are the Scots?* (London, 1971)
MILBORNE, A. J. B., 'British Military Lodges in the American War of Independence', *Transactions of the American Lodge of Research*, vol. x. no. 1 (1966), pp. 22f.
——'The Lodge in the 78th Regiment (Fraser's Highlanders)', *Ars quatuor coronatorum*, vol. lxv (1953), pp. 19f.
'The Minutes of Grand Lodge', *Quatuor coronatorum antigrapha*, ed. W. J. Songhurst, vol. x (1913)
MIZZI, J., *Catalogue of the Records of the Order of St John of Jerusalem in the National Library of Malta* (Malta 1964 etc.)

MORISON, S. E., COMMAGER, H. S., and LEUCHTENBURG, W. E., *The Growth of the American Republic*, 2 vols (Oxford, 1980)

MORRIS, J. E., *Bannockburn* (Cambridge, 1914)

MOSS, W. E., 'Freemasonry in France in 1725–1735' *Ars quatuor coronatorum*, vol. xlvii (1938), pp. 47f.

NEILL, E. D., *The Fairfaxes of England and America* (Albany, 1868)

NERVAL, G. DE, *Journey to the Orient* (London, 1972)

NICHOLSON, R., *Scotland: The Later Middle Ages*, (Edinburgh, 1978)

No King-Sellers: Or, a brief Detection of the Vanity and Villany in a Sermon entitul'd, No King-Killers (London, 1715)

ONAHAN, W. J., 'Scotland's services to France', *The American Catholic Quarterly Review*, vol. xxi (January–October 1896), p. 321f.

The One Hundred and Fiftieth Anniversary of the Lodge of St Andrew 1756–1906, (Boston, 1907)

OURSEL, R., *Le procès des templiers* (Paris, 1959)

PAINE, L., *Gentleman Johnny: The Life of General John Burgoyne* (London, 1973)

PARKER, T. W., *The Knights Templars in England* (Tucson, 1963)

PARTNER, P., *The Murdered Magicians* (Oxford, 1982)

PERKINS, C., 'The Trial of the Knights Templars in England', *The English Historical Review*, vol. xxiv (1909), pp. 432f.

——'The Knights Templars in the British Isles', *The English Historical Review*, vol. xxv (1910), pp. 209f.

PHILO-ROSKELYNSIS, *An Account of the Chapel of Roslin* (Edinburgh, 1774)

PICK, F. L., and KNIGHT, G. N., *The Pocket History of Freemasonry*, rev. edn (London, 1983)

PIQUET, J., *Des banquiers au moyen age: les templiers* (Paris, 1939)

PLATO, *Timaeus*, trans. R. G. Bury (London, 1929)

PLATTS, B., *Scottish Hazard* (London, 1985)

PLOT, R., *The Natural History of Staffordshire* (Oxford, 1686)

POHL, F., *Prince Henry Sinclair* (London, 1974)

POLLARD R. J., *One Nation Under God* (Washington, 1972)

PORTER, W., *A History of the Knights of Malta*, 2 vols (London, 1858)

PRESTON, W., *Illustrations of Masonry* (facsimile of 1804 edn) (Wellingborough, 1986)

Proceedings of the Grand Lodge of Massachusetts 1733–1792 (Boston, 1895)

REANEY, P. H., *The Origin of English Place Names* (London, 1969)

RICHESON, C., 'The Aftermath of Revolution', *A Tug of Loyalties*, ed. Esmond Wright (London, 1975)

RITCHIE, R. L. G., *Chrétien de Troyes and Scotland* (Oxford, 1952)

ROBBINS. A. F., 'The Earliest Years of English Organised Freemasonry', *Ars quatuor coronatorum*, vol. xxii (1909), pp. 67f.

ROBERTSON, C. G., *England Under the Hanoverians* (London, 1949)

ROBERTSON, W., *An Index drawn up about the year 1629, of many records of charters granted by the different sovereigns of Scotland between the years 1309 and 1413 . . .* (Edinburgh, 1798)

ROGERS, N., 'Lancashire Military Lodges', *Ars quatuor coronatorum*, vol. lxxvi (1963), pp. 101f.

ROLLESTON, T. W., *Myths and Legends of the Celtic Race*, 2nd edn (London, 1922)

BIBLIOGRAPHY

RONEN, A., and OLAMI, Y., *Atlit Map* (Jerusalem, 1978)

ROSSLYN, Earl of, *Rosslyn* (Kirkaldy, n.d.)

ROTHES, JOHN, Earl of, *A Relation of Proceedings Concerning the Affairs of the Kirk of Scotland from August 1637 to July 1638* (Edinburgh, 1830)

ROWAN, A., *Northwest Ulster* (Harmondsworth, 1979)

The Royal Commission on the Ancient and Historical Monuments of Scotland: Argyll, 5 vols (Glasgow, 1971–84)

RUVIGNY and RAINEVAL, Marquis of, *The Jacobite Peerage* (Edinburgh, 1904)

RYLANDS, W. H., 'The Mason Word: the Earls of Roslin and Freemasonry', *Ars quatuor coronatorum*, vol. vii (1894)

SAINT CLAIR, L–A de, *Histoire généalogique de la famille de Saint Clair*, (Paris, 1905)

SANDRET, L., 'Recueil historique des chevaliers de l'ordre de Saint-Michel', *Revue historique, nobiliaire et biographique*, 3e Série, tome iv (Paris 1879), pp 193f., 344f., 466f., 505f.; vol. v (Paris, 1880), pp. 67f., 257f., 334f.

The Scots Peerage, ed. J. Balfour Paul, 9 vols (Edinburgh, 1904–11)

SCOTT, S. D., *The British Army* (London, 1880)

SETON, G., *History of the Family of Seton*, 2 vols (Edinburgh, 1896)

SEWARD, D., *The Monks of War* (St Albans, 1974)

SHELBY, L. R., 'Medieval Masons' Templates', *Journal of the Society of Architectural Historians*, vol. xxx, no. 2 (1971)

SKENE, W. F., *The Coronation Stone* (Edinburgh, 1869)

SLEZER, J., *Theatrum scotiae* (London, 1693)

Statutes des chevaliers de l'ordre du temple (Brussels, 1840)

Statutes of the religious and military Order of the Temple as established in Scotland with an historical notice of the Order (Edinburgh, 1843)

STEER, K. A., and BANNERMAN, J. W. M., *Late Medieval Monumental Sculpture in the West Highlands* (Edinburgh, 1977)

STEVENSON, D., *The Origins of Freemasonry* (Cambridge, 1988)

STOKES, J., 'Life of John Theophilus Desaguliers', *Ars quatuor coronatorum*, vol. xxxviii (1925), pp. 285f.

STUART, J., *Sculptured Stones of Scotland*, 2 vols (Aberdeen, 1856)

TAYLER, A. N., and H., *John Graham of Claverhouse* (London, 1939)

TERRY, C. S., *John Graham of Claverhouse* (London, 1905)

THORP, J. T., 'The Rev. James Anderson and the Earls of Buchan', *Ars quatuor coronatorum*, vol. xviii (1905), pp. 9f.

THORY, C. A., *Acta latomorum ou chronologie de l'histoire de la franche-maçonnerie française et étrangère*, 2 vols (Paris, 1815)

TOWERS, E., *Dashwood: The Man and the Myth* (Wellingborough, 1986)

TREVELYAN, G. M., *England under the Stuarts* (London, 1938)

TRIMEN, R., *The Regiments of the British Army* (London, 1878)

TUCKETT, J. E. S., 'The Origin of Additional Degrees', *Ars quatuor coronatorum*, vol. xxxii (1919), pp. 5f.

——'Dr. Begemann and the Alleged Templar Chapter at Edinburgh in 1745', *Ars quatuor coronatorum*, vol. xxxiii (1920), pp. 40f.

——'The French–Irish Family of Walsh and the Lodge in the French–Irish Regiment of Walsh', *Ars quatuor coronatorum*, vol. xxxviii (1925), pp. 189f.

BIBLIOGRAPHY

TUNBRIDGE, P., 'The Climate of European Freemasonry 1730 to 1750', *Ars quatuor coronatorum*, vol. lxxxi (1968), pp. 88f.

UNITED GRAND LODGE OF ENGLAND, *Grand Lodge 1717–1967* (Oxford, 1967)

VITRUVIUS, *De architectura*, trans. Frank Granger, 2 vols (London, 1970)

WAITE, A. E., *A New Encyclopaedia of Freemasonry*, rev. edn, 2 vols (New York, 1970)

WALKER, D. P., *The Ancient Theology* (London, 1972)

WALLACE, J., *Scottish Swords and Dirks*, (London, 1970)

WAPLES, W., 'An Introduction to the Harodim', *Ars quatuor coronatorum*, vol. lx (1950), p. 118f.

——'The Swalwell Lodge', *Ars quatuor coronatorum*, vol. lxii (1951), p. 80f.

WARD, E., 'Early Masters' Lodges and their Relation to Degrees', *Ars quatuor coronatorum*, vol. lxxv (1962), pp. 124f.

WARD, J. S. M., *Who was Hiram Abiff?* (Shepperton, 1978)

WATERTON, E., *Roll of the English and Irish Knights Hospitallers Copied from MS by Edmund Waterton circa 1860* (London, 1903)

Webster's Guide to American History, ed. Charles van Doren and Robert McHenry (Springfield, 1971)

WILKINS, D., *Concilia magnae britanniae et hiberniae*, 4 vols (London, 1737)

WILLIS, P., and LEA-JONES, J., 'The Legacy of the Knights Templar and the Knights Hospitaller (The Order of St John) in Bristol', *Temple Local History Group Newsletter*, vol. iii (1987), pp. 15f.

WOOD, H., 'The Templars in Ireland', *Proceedings of the Royal Irish Academy*, vol. xxvi (1906–7), pp. 327f.

YARKER, J., *Notes on the Scientific and Religious Mysteries of Antiquity* (London, 1872)

YATES, F., *The Rosicrucian Enlightenment* (St Albans, 1975)

——*Astraea* (Harmondsworth, 1977)

——*The Art of Memory* (Harmondsworth, 1978)

——*Giordano Bruno and the Hermetic Tradition* (London, 1978)

——*The Occult Philosophy in the Elizabethan Age* (London, 1979)

——*Lull and Bruno* (London, 1982)

——*Renaissance and Reform: The Italian Contribution* (London, 1983)

——*Ideas and Ideals in the North European Renaissance* (London, 1984)

——*Theatre of the World* (London, 1987)

Index

Abercorn, Earl of *see* Paisley, Lord
Abercrombie, General James, 208
Abiff, Hiram (Adoniram): murder of, 122, 124–31
Ackroyd, Peter, 129
Adams, John, 227, 239, 260, 261
Adams, Samuel, 224, 225, 226, 227
Adamson, Henry, 119, 150
Agrippa von Nettesheim, Heinrich Cornelius, 156–7
Alexander III, King of Scotland, 21–4, 189
Alfonso XI, King of Castile and León, 39
Allen, Ethan, 229, 230
American colonies: Freemasonry in, 180, 181, 188, 198, 201–11; *see also* United States
American War for Independence, 205, 212–55; and Freemasonry, 252–5
Amherst, Lord Jeffrey, 204–5, 208–10, 214, 215–16, 217, 227, 228, 229, 230, 232, 239, 242, 243, 248, 253
Ancient and Sovereign Military Order of the Temple of Jerusalem, 75
Anderson, James: *Constitutions*, 179–80, 202
Andrea, Johann Valentin, 144, 145
Andríc, Ivo, 89
Anglican Church: and Freemasonry, xiii–xiv, 161, 192
Anglo-Saxon Chronicle, The, 43, 82
Anjou, Fulk, Comte de, 43
Anne, Queen, 162, 171, 178, 179
Antin, Duc d', 190
Apprentice Pillar: in Rosslyn Chapel, 112
Arbuthnot, John, 178
architecture: and Freemasonry, 131–4, 159
Argens, Marquis d', 194
Argentein, Hugh of, 44
Argyllshire, Scotland: and the Templars, 1–13, 77
Army, British: and the American War for Independence, 212–20, 216–20, 253–5; regimental field lodges, 184, 203–5, 216–20, 222, 223, 253–5, 269–71
Arnold, Benedict, 229, 230, 250

Arthur, King, 77, 80, 82, 88
Ashmole, Elias, 155–6, 157, 158
Astarte (goddess), 126
Athelstan (Saxon king), 123–4, 129, 135
Auckland, William Eden, Lord, 236–7, 238
Aughrim, Battle of, 163
Austria: Freemasonry in, 192
Avignon Captivity, 38, 51
Aytoun, W. E., 166

Bacon, Francis, 201
Bakunin, Mikhail, 192, 264
Balcarres, David Lindsay, Lord, 153
Baliol, John, King of Scotland, 24, 26, 189
Bancroft, Edward, 237
Bannockburn, Battle of, 18, 34–7, 42, 77, 83
Banquo of Lochaber, 20
Barbour, John, 29, 35
Barruel, Abbé Augustin de, 263–4
Bassac, General Robert, 168
Baudelaire, Charles, 131
Beaton, James, 141
Becket, Thomas à, 45
Belcher, Andrew, 203, 222
Belcher, Jonathan, 202, 203
Benedict XI, Pope, 51
Bernard, Saint, 42, 43, 90
Bible, The: God as architect in, 124
Blanchefort, Bertrand de, 58
Blanke, Imbert, 66
Blenheim, Battle of, 90
Boniface VIII, Pope, 26, 27, 51
Boston, St Andrew's Lodge of, 221–5, 230, 252
Boyle, Robert, 145, 155, 158, 185
Boyne, Battle of the, 163, 164, 177
Bran the Blessed, myth of, 79–80
Brant, Joseph, 253
Bristol: and the Templars, 46
Britain: and the American War for Independence, 212–20, 233–8; *see also* Army, British; England; Scotland
Brooklyn, Battle of (Battle of Long Island), 240

Brown, John, 223
Bruce, Edward, 34, 37
Bruce, Marjorie, 28, 32, 37, 164
Bruce, Mary, 32
Bruce, Neil, 32, 98
Bruce, Robert, King of Scotland, 12, 18–19, 64, 65; alliance with France, 103; and the Battle of Bannockburn, 34–40; death, 39–40; emergence of, 24–8; Flemish ancestry, 82; and fugitive Templars, 74–5; and the Grail Romances, 77–8, 79, 80, 81; and the Knights Hospitaller, 95; and the murder of John Comyn, 28–34; and the North Esk valley, 111; opening of grave of, 39–40, 130
Bruce, Stephen, 225
Brunne, Robert of, 81
Brunswick, Ferdinand, Duke of, 218
Buchan, Isabel, Countess of, 31, 32
Buchan, John Stewart, Earl of, 104
Burgoyne, Sir John, 214, 242–9
Burke, Edmund, 242
Burnham, Joseph, 253
Byzantine Empire, refugees from: and esotericism, 137, 138

Calmet, Dom Augustin, 166, 167, 168, 169
Campbell, Marion, 9
Campbell, Sir Neil, 2, 7, 37
Carleton, Sir Guy, 239, 242, 243, 244, 246, 247, 248, 249, 252
Cathare thought, 42, 58–9, 80
Catholic Church: and Freemasonry, 149, 190–2; Holy League, 139–40
Celtic 'cult of the head', 79–80
Celtic Scotland: and the Grail romances, 77–83
Centuries, The (Nostradamus), 108
Champagne, Hughes, Count of, 43–4, 80
Charles I, King of Britain, 109, 150, 152, 153, 154, 157
Charles II, King of Britain, 152, 154, 155, 162, 164, 177, 184, 186
Charles IV, King of France, 103
Charles VII, King of France, 103, 104
Charnay, Geoffroi de, 55
chivalric orders, 92–3, 105
Christianity: and architecture, 133–4; and Freemasonry, xii–xiii, xiii–xiv; and representational art, 133–4
Christian Unions, 144, 145
Civil War, see English Civil War
Clarke, J. R., 175
Clement V, Pope, 51
Clement XII, Pope, 190
Clement XIV, Pope, 93
Clement, Joseph, 253–4
Clermont, Comte de, 190
Clifford, Lord, 194
Clinton, Sir Henry, 214, 215, 217, 218, 242, 249, 250
Cochrane, Lady Jean, 164
Columbus, Christopher, 56
'Comacine Masons', 124
Company of Jesus (Jesuits), 93

Comyn, John, 24, 27; murder of, 28–34
Conte du Graal, Le (Troyes), 80–2
Cornwallis, Lord Charles, 213, 214, 217–18, 240, 242, 249–50, 252, 254
Cornwallis, Edward, 205, 217–18
corruption: and Freemasonry, xii–xiii
Courtrai (Flemish town), 83
Covenanters, 152–3
Cromwell, Oliver: Protectorate of, 145, 151, 152, 156, 158–9
Crusaders: army, 62; and Freemasonry, 189; and the Knights Templar, 17
Cryer, Revd Neville Barker, 121, 122
Cudworth, Ralph, 158
Culloden, Battle of, 195–6
Cumberland, Duke of (brother of George III), 217
Cumberland, William, Duke of, 195, 204, 205
Cyprus: Templars in, 45, 52

Dalriada, Kingdom of, 19, 78
Danton, Georges Jacques, 192, 263
Darnley, Henry Stewart, Lord, 114
Dashwood, Sir Francis, 205, 234–6, 238
David I, King of Scotland, 19, 20, 26, 42, 43, 78, 81, 82, 83
de Bohun, Henry, 35, 77
de Burgh, Elizabeth, 28
de Clifton, Walter, 64
de Hastings, Richard, 44
de Jay, Brian, 59
de la More, William, 56–7
de Middleton, William, 47
DeMolay, Order of, 266–7; see also Molay, Jacques de
de Stapelbrugge, Stephen, 58, 59
de Stoke, John, 59
de Thoroldeby, Thomas Tocci, 59
Deane, Silas, 236, 237, 241, 249
Declaration of Arbroath, 38, 98
Dee, John, 141–2, 144, 145, 155, 157
Desaguliers, John, 158, 179, 186, 187
Desaguliers, Thomas, 209
Descartes, René, 185
Desmoulins, Camille, 263
Dickinson, John, 233
Dickson, Alexander, 140–1
Diderot, Denis, 211
Dilettanti Society, 205, 234, 235
Divine Comedy (Dante), 54
Dostoevsky, F., 264
Douglas, Sir James, 39
Douglas, William, 26
Douglas family: and the Scots Guard, 106
Drayton, Elias, 229
Du Plessis, Marie, 101
Dundee, John Grahame of Claverhouse, Viscount, 164–70

Edward I, King of England, 24–6, 28, 29, 32, 33, 48, 49, 59, 77
Edward II, King of England, 33, 34, 36, 38–9, 56, 57, 58, 59, 60, 63, 64, 66, 69
Edward III, King of England, 92

Elijah (prophet), 130
England: Grand Lodge in, 171–82, 191, 192; Templars in, 43–6, 48, 49, 56–60, 63
English Civil War, 145, 151, 152, 156, 158, 159
Erskine, John, Earl of Mar, 166–7, 168, 169
Eschenbach, see Wolfram von Eschenbach
esotericism, 135–9, 141–2, 153
Evelyn, John, 154, 158

Fabré-Palaprat, Bernard-Raymond, 75
Falkirk, Battle of, 27
Fénelon, François, 187, 188, 193
Ferdinand of Aragón, King of Spain, 135
fitz Alan, Walter, 20
Fitzgerald, Lord Edward, 238
Flamel, Nicolas, 136
Flanders: esotericism in, 138; and the Templars, 66; ties with Scotland, 82–3
Flanders, Philippe d'Alsace, Comte de, 80, 82, 83
Fleury, André Hercule de, Cardinal, 188, 189, 190
Fludd, Robert, 142, 144, 157
Fos, Roncelin de, 58–9
Fox, Charles, 242
France: and the American War for Independence, 239, 249, 250–1; Freemasonry in, 130, 192; and Jacobite Freemasonry, 184–90; neo-Templar orders, 92; persecution of Protestants in, 162; and the Scots Guard, 103–10; Templars in, 44, 46, 49, 51–5, 65–6, 67–8, 91–2
François, Emperor of Austria, 191, 192
Franklin, Benjamin, 202, 207, 219, 233–4, 235–6, 237, 238, 239, 241, 249, 252, 260; death, 261
Fraser, Simon, 32, 210
Frazer, Sir James, 128
Frederick, Prince of Wales, 158, 205, 234
Frederick the Great, King of Prussia, 191
Freemason (ship), 202
French Revolution, 182, 261, 263
French–Indian War, see Seven Years War
Frye, Joseph, 229
Fuentes, Carlos, 135

Gage, General Thomas, 225–6, 227, 230, 232
Galloway, Scotland: and the Grail Romances, 81
Galway: and the Templars, 70
Gama, Vasco da, 55
García Márquez, 135
Garter, Order of the, 92
Gates, Horatio, 228, 247, 250, 254
Gaurico, Luca, 108
Gautier, Théophile, 131
George I, King of Britain, 171, 183
George II, King of Britain, 171, 204
George III, King of Britain, 205, 215, 217, 233
Germain, Lord George, 242, 243, 244–7, 248

Germany: refugees from, and Rosicrucianism, 144, 145, 150–1; Templars in, 55
Glorious Revolution (1688), 162–4, 172, 173
Gloucester, Henry, Duke of, 217
Golden Bough, The (Frazer), 128
Gonneville, Geoffrey de, 59
Grahame of Claverhouse, John, Viscount Dundee, 164–70
Grahame, David (later Viscount Dundee), 167–8, 169
Grahame, Robert, 169–70
Grail legends: and Celtic Scotland, 23, 77–83
Grand Lodge: and the American colonies, 202–3; in England, 171–82, 191, 192; in Ireland, 183–4, 198, 202, 204, 209, 217
Grand Orient, 190
Green Man, cult of, 79, 119, 120
Greenhill, F. A., 10
Gridley, Richard, 210
guilds, medieval: and Freemasonry, 181; and miracle plays, 121–2; stonemasons, 136–7
Guinet, John, 210–11
Guise, Charles de, Duc de Mayenne, 141
Guise, François, Duc de, 107, 109
Guise, house of: and esotericism, 138–9; and the Holy League, 139–40; and the Scots Guard, 106, 107, 109, 110; and the Stuarts, 101
Guise, Marie de, Queen Regent of Scotland, 100, 101, 106, 110, 138, 139
gypsies: and Rosslyn, 118–22

Haak, Theodore, 158
Haddington, Thomas Binning, Earl of, 101
'Haly Kirk and her Theeves' (poem), 102
Hamilton, Alexander, 261
Hamilton, General Alexander, 153
Hamilton, James see Paisley, Lord
Hamilton family, 154, 168; Flemish descent, 82; and Freemasonry, 117; and the Scots Guard, 105, 106
Hancock, John, 223, 227, 239, 252
Harrison, Benjamin, 233
Hartlib, Samuel, 158
Hasolle, James, 155
Hay, Elizabeth, 101
Hell Fire Club, 177, 178, 234, 235
Helmont, Francis van, 158
Henri II, King of France, 107–9
Henri III, King of France, 109
Henri IV, King of France, 109
Henry, Patrick, 223, 226
Henry, Prince, the Navigator, 55
Henry I, King of England, 20, 43, 44
Henry II, King of England, 43, 45, 49
Henry III, King of England, 46, 48, 49
Herbert, George, 159
Hermes, 129, 134
Hesse, Prince Karl of, 218
Hill, Willis, Lord Hillsborough, 234–5
history: and myth, 87–90

History of the Kings of Britain (Monmouth), 81
Holland, Freemasonry in, 189
Holy Grail: and the Templars, 91
Holy Land: and Freemasonry, 189; and the Templars, 17, 67
Holy League, 139–40, 141
Home, Alexander, 197
Hood, Robin: legend of, 88, 118, 119–20
Howe, Lord George, 208, 209, 228, 229, 232, 242
Howe, Admiral Lord Richard, 236, 237, 249
Howe, Sir William, 209, 214, 215, 216, 217, 226, 230–3, 239, 252; and Saratoga, 240–9
Hugo, Victor, 131
Hume, David, 181, 185, 187, 211, 218, 252, 257
Hund, Baron Karl Gottlieb von, 74, 75, 76, 194–5, 196–7, 198, 221, 223
Hundred Years War, 103
Hurry, Sir John, 186

Inishail (island): Templar graves on, 11–12
Inquisition, The: persecution of the Templars, 54, 55–60
'Invisible College' of the Rosicrucians, 145, 151, 155, 159, 201, 258
Ireland: Freemasonry in, 180; and the Glorious Revolution, 163–4; Grand Lodge in, 183–4, 198, 202, 204, 209, 217; rebellions, 214, 237–8; and the Siege of Londonderry, 89–90; Templar properties in, 46–7; Templars in, 63, 63–4, 65, 67, 69–71, 74
Isabelle of Castile, Queen of Spain, 135
Islam: and Freemasonry, 124, 131–3; and the Templars, 59, 68–9
Islay, Isle of, 12, 69
Italy: esotericism in, 138; unification of, 192, 264

Jacobites: and Freemasonry, 103, 173–4, 176–7, 179–81, 183–92, 193, 198, 202–3, 204, 205; rebellion (1715), 175; rebellion (1745), 204, 210
Jaime II, King of Majorca, 68
James II, King of Scotland, 115
James V, King of Scotland, 106, 110, 114, 138, 139
James VI and I, King of Scotland and England, 115, 116, 118, 143, 144, 145, 150, 151
James VII and II, King of Scotland and England, 89, 162–3, 164, 166, 167, 171, 184, 185
Jay, John, 233
Jeanne d'Arc (Joan of Arc), 88, 103
Jefferson, Thomas, 239, 260, 261, 262
Jerusalem: Latin Kingdom of, 45, 52
Jesuits (Society of Jesus), 93
Jews and Judaism: and Freemasonry, 181, 124–34; and the Templars, 59
John, King of England, 45, 48, 49

John XXII, Pope, 38–9
Johnson, Sir William, 253
Jones, John Paul, 234
Jura, Isle of, 12, 69

Kalb, Johann de, 241, 250, 254
Keith, General James, 174
Keith, Sir William, 39
Keppel, Augustus, 242
Killiecrankie, Battle of, 164–5, 167
Kilmarnock, Earl of, 194, 196–7
Kilmartin, Templar graves at, 5–13
Kilmory chapel (Argyllshire), 13
Kilneuair church (Argyllshire), 12
Kingston, James, Lord, 184
Kirkmichael, John, 103
Knight of the Red Feather, 194, 196–8
Knight Templar Degree, 222–3
Knights Hospitaller of St John, 17, 66, 67, 94–7, 102, 104
Knights of Christ, 17, 55–6
Knights Templar, *see* Templars, Knights
Knox, John, 119
Knox, Thomas, 225
Kosciuszko, Tadeusz, 241

Lafayette, Marquis de, 241, 250, 252, 263
Lamberton, William, Bishop of St Andrews, 26, 27, 28, 30, 31, 64–5
Larmenius Charter, 75–6
La Rochelle: and the Templars, 46, 67, 68, 69, 70
Lauffield, Battle of, 109
Lawrence, D. H., 235
Lee, Arthur, 236, 237, 239, 249
Lee, George, Earl of Lichfield, 177–8, 234, 235
Lee, Richard Henry, 223, 239
l'Enfant, Pierre, 262
Leslie, George de, 197
Lewis, General Morgan, 261
Ligonier, General Sir John, 204, 205, 208
Lindsay, Alexander, 154
Lindsay, David, Lord Balcarres, 153
Lindsay, John, 3rd Earl of Balcarres, 164
Lindsay, Rodulph, 96
Lindsay, Walter, 99
Lindsay family, 82, 153, 155
Livingston, Robert, 227, 239, 261
Locke, John, 145, 185, 211, 218, 252, 257
Lodge de Bussy (France), 186, 190
London: Great Fire (1661), 159; Templar properties in, 44–5, 46
Londonderry, Siege of, 89–90, 163–4
Lorraine, Francois, Duc de, 158
Long Island, Battle of, 240
Lorraine, house of: and esotericism, 138–9; and the Holy League, 139–40; and the Scots Guard, 106, 107, 109, 110; and the Stuarts, 101; *see also* Guise
Louis XI, King of France, 92
Louis XIV, King of France, 162
Louis XV, King of France, 186, 187, 188
Louis XVI, King of France, 237, 239; execution of, 91–2

Loyola, Ignatius, 93
Lull, Raymond (Lully), 135

MacAlpin, Kenneth, King of Scotland, 19, 22, 23
Macbeth (Shakespeare), 19, 20
MacDonald, Angus Og, 37, 69, 73
McGonagall, William, 150
MacLean, Sir James Hector, 185, 186, 187
Maidment, James, 98, 101
Majorca: Templars in, 68
Malcolm III, King of Scotland, 19
Malcolm IV, King of Scotland, 82, 83
Malta, Siege of (1565), 62
Mar, Isabel of (wife of Robert the Bruce), 27–8
Mar, John Erskine, Earl of, 166–7, 168, 169
Margaret, Maid of Norway, 24
Maria Theresa, Empress of Austria, 158, 180
Marie de Guise, *see* Guise
Marshall, John, 260
Marvell, Andrew, 159
Mary II, Queen, 162, 163, 171
Mary Queen of Scots, 106–7, 109, 114, 118, 140, 141; and the Setons, 100, 101
Mason's Mark, 183
Master Mason, Degree of (Third Degree), 130
Maxwell, William, 229
Mercer, Hugh, 228
Methven, Battle of, 32, 98
Midsummer Night's Dream, A (Shakespeare), 119
military lodges, *see* Army, British
Milton, John, 151
Minden, Battle of, 205
miracle/mystery plays, 121–2
Moira, Francis Rawdon, Earl of, 254
Molay, Jacques de, 18, 53, 55, 59, 65, 75, 91, 194; and the Order of DeMolay, 266–7
monasticism: in Scotland, 21, 23
money lending: and the Templars, 48
Monmouth, Geoffrey of, 81
Montbard, André de, 43
Montcalm, Marquis de, 209
Montesquieu, Charles de, 185, 186
Montgomery, Alexander Seton, 10th Earl of Eglinton, 197–8
Montgomery, Gabriel de, 107–8
Montgomery, James de, 107
Montgomery, General Richard, 227, 239, 243, 261
Montgomery family, 153, 168; Flemish descent, 82; and Freemasonry, 117; and the Scots Guard, 105, 106, 107–8, 113; and the Setons, 197–8
Moray, Sir Robert, 153–5, 157, 158, 159
Moray of Dreghorn, Sir William, 154
More, Henry, 158
Morris, Robert, 233
Morton, General Jacob, 261
Muslims, *see* Islam
Myle, John, 118

Nerval, Gérard de, 130–1
Newton, Sir Isaac, 155, 158, 172, 185, 187
Nixon, John, 228–9
Nodier, Charles, 131
Norris, John, 238
North America, *see* American colonies; United States
Nostradamus, 108

Oglethorpe, General James, 180, 203
O'Heguerty, Dominic, 185, 186
Old Testament: human sacrifice in, 128–9; myth and history in, 87; Templar translations into vernacular, 44
'Olive Branch Petition', 233
Omedes, Juan d', 99
Order of St John, *see* Knights Hospitaller of St John
Orléans, Philippe (Égalité), 192
Orléans, Philippe d', regent of France, 187
Orléans, Siege of, 103

Paisley, Lord, 158, 179, 187, 204
Palatine, Count Friedrich (later King of Bohemia), 144, 150–1, 157, 171
Papacy: and the Templars, 43; and the Jesuits, 93; *see also* Catholic Church
Paradise Lost (Milton), 151
Parzival, 78, 79, 80, 91
Payens, Hughes de, 43, 44, 80
Perlesvaus, The, 78–9, 80, 91
Philippe IV, King of France, 18, 37, 51–5, 56, 63, 65, 68, 71
Pitt, William (later Earl of Chatham), 208, 242
Plantagenet, Geoffroy, 43
Plato, 138, 142
Plot, Robert, 160–1
Poitiers, Battle of, 135
Poor Knights of the Temple of Solomon, *see* Templars, Knights
Poor Robin's Intelligence, 159–60
Pope, Alexander, 178–9, 187
Porter, Whitworth, 102
Portugal: Templars in, 55–6, 68
Prevost, Augustine, 210
Price, Henry, 203, 221–2
Proctor, Edward, 225
Provins, Guiot de, 78, 91
Pulaski, Casimir, 241
Pushkin, A., 264
Putnam, Israel, 228
Pythagoras, 129, 132, 134

Radclyffe, Charles, Earl of Derwentwater, 174, 178, 185, 186, 187, 196, 197, 234
Radclyffe, James, Earl of Derwentwater, 174, 175, 178, 185, 186, 187
Ramsay, Andrew Michael (Chevalier), 167, 187–90, 193, 194, 197
Ramsay, Michael de, 197
Ramsay family, 168
Randolph, Edmund, 256–7, 260
Randolph, Peyton, 226, 227
Rathlin (island), 32

Revere, Paul, 223, 224, 225, 226
Richard I, King of England (Couer de Lion), 45, 51
Robert I, King of Scotland, *see* Bruce, Robert
Robert II, King of Scotland, 37, 39
Robin Hood and Little John (play), 118, 119–20, 121
Rodney, Admiral George, 242, 250
Rosicrucianism, 144–5, 150, 151, 154, 155, 156, 157, 158, 159, 201
Roslin, Battle of, 28
Rosslyn Chapel, 111–22, 129, 228
Rousseau, Jean-Jacques, 211
Royal Society, 145, 152, 154, 155, 156, 157–8, 159, 185, 187, 201, 233, 258
Russia, Freemasonry in, 264

Sackville, Charles, Earl of Middlesex, 234
Sackville, George (later Lord Germain), 205
Sackville, Lionel, 1st Duke of Dorset, 205
St Clair, Arthur, 228
Saint Clair Charter, 117
St Clair of Rosslyn, Sir William, 210; *see also* Sinclair
Saint Francis, Order of, 234, 235
St John, Order of, *see* Knights Hospitaller of St John
St Lazarus, Order of, 187
St Maur, Aymeric de, 45
St Michael, Order of, 105
St Omer, Osto de, 44
Sandilands, Sir James, 1st Baron Torphichen, 99–100, 101, 169, 170, 198
Sandilands, James, 2nd Baron Torphichen, 100–1
Sandilands, John, 170
Sandwich, Earl of, 234, 235, 237, 242
Saratoga, Battle of, 241–50
Scandinavia: and the Templars, 69
Schaw, William, 116–17
Scone, Stone of, 21, 26
Scotland: Celtic kingdom of, 20–4, 189; Freemasonry in, 180, 183, 189; and the Glorious Revolution, 163; and the Grail romances, 77–83; Grand Lodge of, 222, 223; Templar graveyards in Argyllshire, 1–13; Templars in, 47, 63, 64–5, 66, 69–70, 71–3, 74–5, 76, 87–102
Scots Guard, 92, 94, 103–10, 153, 155
Seton, Alexander, *see* Montgomery, Alexander
Seton, Alexander, Earl of Winton, 174
Seton, Alexander de, 97
Seton, Christopher, 29, 32
Seton, Sir Christopher, 98
Seton, David, 98–102, 103, 106, 169, 198
Seton, Lord George, 101, 114, 141
Seton, Lord George, Earl of Winton, 172
Seton, James, 101
Seton, John, 32
Seton, Mary, 101
Seton, Robert, 101
Seton family, 98, 101–2, 153, 155; Flemish descent, 82; and Freemasonry, 117; and

the Montgomeries, 197–8; and the Scots Guard, 105, 106, 109
Seven Years War (French–Indian War), 205, 207–11, 212, 214, 215, 218, 221, 223, 227, 228, 230, 232, 243
Shelburne, Earl of, 245
Sherman, Robert, 239
ships, Templar, 46, 61; disappearance of, 53, 63–76
Sidney, Sir Philip, 140–1
Sieyès, Emmanuel Joseph, Comte, 192, 263
Sinclair, Henry, Bishop of Ross, 114
Sinclair, Lord James, 164
Sinclair, Oliver, 114
Sinclair, Sir William, 39, 113, 113–14, 115–16, 118, 119, 129, 139, 228
Sinclair Charters, 151
Sinclair family, 168; and Rosslyn Chapel, 112–18; and the Scots Guard, 105, 106, 113
Skene, John, 201–2
skull-and-crossbones: in Freemasonry, 129–30
Smith, Adam, 218, 252, 257
Society of Jesus (Jesuits), 93
Society of United Irishmen, 238
Solomon: building of Temple of, 124–5, 126–7, 129; worship of goddess Astarte, 126
Son of the Widow, 112; in *Le Conte du Graal*, 81
Song of Solomon, 126
'Sons of Liberty', 224, 225, 226, 259, 260
Spain: and the American War for Independence, 239; 'esoteric' teaching in, 135–6; first lodge in, 186; Freemasonry in, 192; Templars in, 44, 55, 68, 69
Span, Thomas, 210
Stark, General John, 228
Stella Templum, 197
Stephen, King of England, 44
Steuben, Baron Friedrich von, 241, 250, 252
Stewart, Walter the, 20, 28, 37; *see also* Stuart
Stewart family: Flemish descent, 82
Stoke, John de, 59
Stormont, Lord, 237–8
Strict Observance Freemasonry, 74–5, 76, 195, 196, 198, 218
Stuart, Charles Edward (Bonnie Prince Charlie), 172, 185, 187, 194, 195, 234
Stuart, Elizabeth (later Queen of Bohemia), 144, 150–1, 157, 171
Stuart, James (The Old Pretender), 171–2
Stuart family: and Freemasonry, 117; and the Scots Guard, 105–6
Stuart monarchy: and Freemasonry, 150–2, 156, 157–61; and the Glorious Revolution, 162–4; and Jacobite Freemasonry, 193; *see also* Jacobites
Sweden, Freemasonry in, 189
Sween, Loch, 12, 37
Swift, Jonathan, 173, 178–9

Tebas de Ardales, Battle of, 39

Templars, Knights (Order of the Poor Knights of Christ and the Temple of Solomon), 41–50; architecture and building, 136–7; arrests and torture of, 51–62; attitudes to, 41–2, 49–50, 90–1; cross found, on Viscount Dundee, 165–70; cult of the head (Baphomet), 53, 79; escape from persecution, 60–2; escape routes of fleet, 66–73; exploitation of myth of, 90–4; financial influence of, 47–50; and Freemasonry, 193–8, 221; and the Grail Romances, 77, 78–80, 83, 91; and the Knights Hospitaller, 94–7; lands after dissolution, 94–7; legends of survival, 73–6; numbers of, 60–2, 65–6; refugees, 64–6; reputation, 49–50; rise of, 42–7; in Scotland, 47, 63, 64–5, 66, 69–70, 71–3, 74–5, 76, 87–102
Teutonic Knights, 17, 52, 55, 69, 94–5
Thirty Years War, 144, 145, 150–1
Tone, Wolfe, 238
Tory Party, 172–3, 174
Troyes, Chrétien de, 80–2
Troyes, Council of, 43

United States: constitution, 256–62; and Freemasonry, 265–7; see also American colonies; American War for Independence

Vaughan, Henry, 158–9
Vaughan, Thomas, 157, 158–9
Verneuil, Battle of, 104
Voltaire, François, Marie Arouet de, 211, 234
Voyage en Orient (Nerval), 130–1

Waite, A. E., 165–6
Wallace, William, 26–7, 28
Walsh, Anthony Vincent, 185
Walsh, Captain James, 185

War of the Austrian Succession, 204, 207, 209
War of the Spanish Succession, 172, 207, 212
Ward, Artemus, 230
Warren, Joseph, 219, 223, 224, 226–7, 230
Washington, George, 207, 208, 211, 215, 219, 227, 229, 239, 251, 252, 254; and the Constitutional Convention, 256–7; masonic leadership of, 260–2; and Saratoga, 242, 247, 249, 250
Wellesley, Sir Arthur (later Duke of Wellington), 214
West, Milborne, 210
Wharton, Duke of, 174, 177, 178, 186–7, 205, 234, 235
Wharton, Captain George (later Sir), 155
Whigs, 173, 174
Whipple, Abraham, 223
Wilkes, John, 234, 236
Wilkins, John, 155, 157, 158
William I, King of Scotland (the Lion), 83
William III, King (William of Orange), 163, 165, 171
Williamson, Robert, 101
Wishart, Bishop of Glasgow, 30, 31
Wolfe, James, 203, 205, 208–9, 210, 214, 217, 227, 228, 229, 230, 232, 239, 243
Wolfram von Eschenbach, 78, 79, 81, 90, 91, 135–6
Wooster, David, 227–8, 229
Wren, Sir Christopher, 155, 158, 159

Yarker, John, 166
Yates, Frances, 144, 154, 156
York, Edward, Duke of, 217
Young, John, 210

Zulu (film), 62

To Dad
With love from
Billy
Christmas '90